ENTER NIGHT:

A BIOGRAPHY OF METALLICA

Also by Mick Wall

Diary of a Madman – the Official Biography of Ozzy Osbourne
Guns N'Roses: the Most Dangerous Band in the World
Pearl Jam
Run to the Hills: the Authorized Biography of Iron Maiden
Paranoid: Black Days with Sabbath & Other Horror Stories
Mr Big: Ozzy, Sharon and My Life as the Godfather of Rock,
by Don Arden
XS All Areas: the Autobiography of Status Quo
John Peel – a Tribute to the Much-Loved DJ and Broadcaster
Bono – In the Name of Love
W.A.R. the Unauthorised Biography of W. Axl Rose
When Giants Walked the Earth – A Biography of Led Zeppelin
Appetite for Destruction

ENTER NIGHT:

A BIOGRAPHY OF METALLICA

MICK WALL

St. Martin's Press ❧ New York

ENTER NIGHT. Copyright © 2010 by Mick Wall. All rights reserved. Printed in
the United States of America. For information, address St. Martin's Press, 175
Fifth Avenue, New York, N.Y. 10010.

www.stmartins.com

Library of Congress Cataloging-in-Publication Data

ISBN 978-0-312-64989-0

First published in Great Britain by Orion Books, an imprint of the Orion Publishing Group Ltd, an Hachette UK Company

First U.S. Edition: May 2011

10 9 8 7 6 5 4 3 2 1

For Vanessa Lampert

CONTENTS

ACKNOWLEDGEMENTS

This book could not have been written without the invaluable aid of the following people, to all of whom I owe the utmost thanks.

First and foremost, my wife Linda Wall, who journeyed with me there and back. Also my agent and good friend Robert Kirby of United Agents and Malcolm Edwards at Orion, in whom resides the true spirit of gentleman publishing. Sincere gratitude also to Elizabeth Beier at Saint Martin's Press. Also Charlotte Knee, Ian Preece and Stephen Fall. Class acts. As, too, are Michelle Richter, Katy Hershberger, Brendan Fredericks, Gemma Finlay and Angela McMahon.

Heartfelt thanks also to two people whose researches on my behalf went beyond the call of duty: Joel McIver and Malcolm Dome. Then there are those whose input was less specific but who, again, were there for me, often just in the nick of time. They are: Diana and Colin Cartwright, Damian McGee, Bob Prior, Chris Ingham, Scott Rowley, Sian Llewellyn, Ian Fergusson, Russ Collington, Alexander Milas, Megan and Dave Lavender, and Yvonne and Kevin Shepherd. Most especially, though, Evie, Mollie, Michael, Tad and Ruby, who always helped as best they could, bless them.

And finally, of course, Lars Ulrich, James Hetfield and Kirk Hammett, for the memories and the music . . .

PROLOGUE

Just Before The Dawn

It was cold that rotten dark morning, the temperature dropping to just below freezing as the dirty-white tour bus trundled along the old single-lane highway. Still only late September but in Sweden, where in summer the sun never sleeps, the nights were now growing long again. Soon the heavy snows would come and there would be twenty-four-hour darkness, that bleak mid-winter period when the national suicide rates went up, along with the consumption of drugs and alcohol. For now, though, the road ahead lay clear. It was cold and dark out there all right, but there hadn't been rain for days, the ground beneath the spinning wheels of the vehicle dry as old bones.

Only the driver was awake – so he later said. Everyone else – the four-man band, their tour manager, three-man backline crew – were all sleeping in the thin wooden bunks bolted into the sides of the bus at the back, cardboard placed over the windows to keep out the draught. The bus, an English model with the usual right-hand drive, was not ideal for long night journeys across non-English roads where traffic drove on the right, not the left. But both it and the driver were experienced. Unlike the young band they were carrying, they had travelled these roads many times before. Nothing had ever gone wrong; nothing would go wrong now, either.

And then it did.

They argued about it afterwards. They argue about it still, a quarter of a century later. Was there ice on the road? It was certainly cold enough, and yet there had been no rain – no snow or ice particles – in any of the days leading up to it. Had the driver fallen asleep then?

Or was he drunk, perhaps, or stoned? If so, why did the police, who arrested him at the scene, later let him go, free of all charges? Could there have been something wrong with the bus? Again, forensics said no. Mechanically, when they came to examine the wreckage, everything checked out fine. All anyone knew for sure afterwards was that the bus got into trouble when the road took a slight left bend. The first the driver, seated on the right, knew about it was when he realised the bus had slipped over the hard shoulder and was headed onto the hard gravel along the side of the motorway, its right-side wheels careering over the dirt.

Fully alert now, eyes wide open, the driver swung the steering wheel hard to the left, willing the bus back onto the road. For a moment, he thought he had it. But the back end of the bus skidded to its right, the huge back wheels unable to gain purchase as they now also left the road and began bumping along in the dirt. The panicking driver fought to control the situation.

No good. People were beginning to wake at the back, falling from their bunks, crying out. The bus continued its lurching, backwards skid. Within seconds it had turned itself fully around, facing back the way it had come, its wheels finally stopping as they thumped sickeningly into the kerb on the opposite side of the road. There was the sound of breaking glass, more shouts and cries and then the most terrifying moment as it keeled over onto its side and hit the ground with a thunderous crash.

Of the nine people onboard, two lay trapped beneath the bunks, which had collapsed on top of each other, left to right, as the bus turned over. Five sustained minor injuries – a broken toe, something else – and one lay dead beneath the stricken bus, his legs poking out from under its side. The driver was lucky. He would jump free with only minor cuts and bruises.

Dawn lay just across the horizon but the hour was still dark, still freezing cold. One of the first to leap from the wreckage had been the drummer, a short skinny kid with long tea-coloured hair who now took off, sprinting down the road, not knowing where he was going, just that he was fucking gone, so freaked out he couldn't even feel the pain of his broken toe, the smart young schemer so used to seeing round corners yet never seeing this. No way.

Behind him came the guitar tech, a six-foot seven-inch giant of a man who had crawled from where he'd been thrown out of his collapsing bunk towards the front left exit, now a hatch in the ceiling through which he climbed, clothed only in his underwear, his giant's back in agony where he had thumped it against the lip of his bunk as the crash of the bus had thrown him sideways and down.

From the rear emergency exit came the singer, tall, deranged, also just in his underpants and socks, yelling and screaming, bloody of mind, followed by the guitarist, another short skinny-arsed figure, coughing and crying, his large dark eyes brimful of night sky and ashes. Everyone was shouting and screaming, no one knew what was going on, what to do, what was happening. It was still dark, freezing cold, and no one was prepared for it, for this, whatever this was. All they knew was that it was bad, fucked-up bad. Big time fucked-up bad...

By the time the second tour bus carrying the rest of the crew turned up over an hour later, the first of seven ambulances had also arrived but only the tour manager seemed to know what had actually gone down, and he was in such shock he had no idea how to convey it to the rest of them. That, as they climbed aboard the ambulances and headed for the hospital, they would be leaving behind one of their own. Not just anyone, either, but the one they all felt carried with him most of the luck. The one they all cherished above the rest, above each other, that they always looked up to, even as they made fun of him, or chose to disregard his advice, his sense of integrity and of right and wrong, always that little bit too much for the rest, just young fucks not always into what was right but what was fun right now.

The darkness lifting, grey dawn sky blurring over their heads, they climbed into the ambulances and drove off, not knowing yet that they were leaving behind not just their past but their future. The one they had all dreamed of and shared with each other, spoken and unspoken, right up to the moment the bus hit that invisible patch of ice, the fucking driver if not asleep then not awake enough to follow the bending road; the map to the treasure they all knew was theirs to share right up till the moment the devil took a hand in things and changed their lives for ever.

Right up to the moment Cliff Burton, bass player, left before them, taking with him the soul of the band with the dumbest heavy metal name ever: Metallica.

PART ONE

Born To Die

'Fuck it all and fucking no regrets!'

– James Hetfield, 'Damage, Inc.', 1986

ONE
THE PRINCE

It was such a bizarre, unexpected moment that for years afterwards I wondered if it had really happened, or whether it was some sort of trauma-induced false memory. Yet the vision of Lars hopping on crutches towards me down the steps of the Hammersmith Odeon still remains now, despite all the days and years and lifetimes that have since passed between us.

I don't remember the gig – who it was or what it was – just that moment as he lurched down the steps at speed towards me, calling my name.

'Hey, Mick, you fuck! What's happening?'

Its front doors bolted, the fans having long since left, I could only assume he had been malingering at the same after-show drinks thing I had, idling at the upstairs bar backstage into the early hours, now in search of a taxi home. Yet I had not seen him. But then the frame of mind I was in, my field of vision had been limited, tunnelled down to some wincingly sharp needlepoint within. It was my first outing since my mother had died a couple of weeks before. Younger than I am now, she had been struck down by cancer of the brain and the ending, although relatively sudden, had been preceded by extremely unkind circumstances, excruciating for her, godless to those of us in attendance.

He was down the steps in an instant, his face close to mine. 'Hey,' he said. There was a brief bit of banter in which I motioned questioningly towards the crutches. 'My toe,' he said, as though it was such ancient news it barely rated a mention. I must have looked baffled. 'I broke it.' I stared at him. 'In the crash,' he added, impatiently.

I was used to rock stars, even the ones who weren't really famous yet like Lars, expecting you to know every minute detail of their working lives and to be suitably fascinated by them. But still ... broken toe? Crash? What crash?

But that wasn't what he was interested in. What he wanted to know was: 'So were you here for us too?'

Again, I was baffled. He read it instantly. 'When we played here, you dork!' Oh ... now I got it. Metallica had also played the Hammersmith Odeon recently. As their latest champion in the British rock press, it was not unreasonable for Lars to have expected me to be there for the band's first headline appearance at a prestige venue like that. But of course I hadn't. Instead I had either been at the hospital or coming home from the hospital or getting ready to go to the hospital. Either that or I had just been in hell.

I didn't know then, though, how to put something like that into words. I barely knew how to say it to myself, let alone someone else. I was twenty-eight and my world had simultaneously shrunk and expanded in ways I was struggling to grasp. He was twenty-two and not remotely interested anyway. All that mattered was Metallica, you fuck!

'No,' I said, too exhausted even to lie about it. 'Was it good?'

'What?' he exploded. 'Was it good? You weren't there?' He looked at me, disappointment flecked with anger and shock. 'Yeah, it was fuckin' good! You really missed a great fuckin' gig! The place was sold out and the fans went crazy!'

'Oh,' I said, 'that's great. Sorry I missed it, man.'

His outraged eyes studied mine. A precocious child growing rapidly into a full-on fuck of a man, Lars may have been too in love with Metallica and what it gave him when he looked in the mirror to see past it long enough to think seriously about almost anything else, but he was not a stupid person, and in that instant he must have gotten an inkling of something else going on in my face – not what exactly, just enough of something to forgive this transgression, although not enough to forget, not for the foreseeable anyway – because he changed the subject and after a bit more inconsequential banter he hobbled off again, still unhappy with me but not quite so offended, or so I feebly hoped. Him and his broken toe ...

I watched his back disappear into the night, accompanied by his minder,
looking for their ride home or wherever they were going next.
Crash, I thought, what crash?

The first time James Hetfield met Lars Ulrich he had him pegged. 'Rich kid,' he said to himself. You know the type: got everything; an only child who didn't know the meaning of the word 'no'. And so he was. Born into a house as big as a castle, in the elegant town of Hellerup, the most fashionable part of the municipality of Gentofte, in eastern Denmark, Lars Ulrich arrived on Boxing Day, 1963. A late Christmas present for a childless couple in their mid-thirties – old, in those days, for having babies – Lars was regarded as special from the day he was born. It was a view he would quickly grow to share.

His father, Torben, was a tennis-playing veteran of over a hundred Davis Cup matches – during which time he led the team to several finals – and a fully paid-up member of the emerging post-war jet set; his mother, Lone, a bohemian 'den mother' who would spend her days keeping her perpetually moving husband's feet on the ground; or trying to. A star of the amateur tennis era who was already forty yet still winning Grand Slam matches when he belatedly turned professional in the late 1960s, Torben's interests were not confined, however, merely to sport. With the umbrella Danish sports authority in that amateur era limiting participation in tournaments abroad to just fifty-six days per year, he had time – just – to also become a skilled writer for Denmark's *Politiken* newspaper, a regular horn player in various jazz ensembles, and later artist, film-maker and practising Buddhist. A long-haired, splendidly whiskered Gandalf-like figure whose obsession with physical and mental fitness continued long after his professional sports career ended, as he recalled in a 2005 interview: 'Maybe I played tennis in the afternoons, and then I would go play music at night, and then after that I had to go up to the newspaper and write reviews, and after that maybe I would go meet some of my friends in the morning and have breakfast, and then I had to go to band practice at noon and play tennis at 3.00. All of a sudden I hadn't slept for three or four days.'

His only son would also grow up bristling with round-the-clock energy; his earliest childhood memories enmeshed with his father's ongoing obsessions and hyperactive lifestyle.

'Up until when I started school when I was seven we would travel all over,' Lars told me in 2009. 'America, Europe, we went to Australia a couple times ... We spent a winter in South Africa, I think, in '66 or '67.' His father 'would go out to the Australian Open in January every year. And this was back in the days when you didn't just jump on [a plane]. It was like a real journey to get there ... and we spent a lot of time in Paris and London and all these places.' Tennis, though, was just 'the day job, really'. At home, 'we had art all over the house': art and music. A lover of jazz at a time when Copenhagen was a hotbed for contemporary jazz musicians, Torben played both clarinet and saxophone, and as a child Lars grew up in a household that rang to the sounds of, as he recalls, 'Ben Webster, Sonny Rollins, Dexter Gordon', all of whom 'spent considerable amounts of time in Denmark. So it was a very healthy scene and [my father] wrote a lot about it.'

Lars' bedroom at home was opposite the music room where Torben kept his record collection, from which a continuous stream of music flowed. Neneh Cherry, daughter of sax legend Don and, later, a singing star in her own right, grew up in the same neighbourhood and was a childhood friend. 'There was also like tons of people hanging out and there was like a lot of like late-night activity – listening to a lot of jazz records and a lot of Hendrix and Stones and The Doors and Janis Joplin ... So there was a lot of musicians and writers and artists and stuff like that, that were circulating through the house as I was growing up.' As well as rock and jazz, said Torben, Lars would have been exposed to 'Indian music, all kinds of Asian music, Buddhist chants, classical music. His room was right next to the room where I played all this music all night long, and sometimes maybe he would have heard them even while he was sleeping, so he could have picked up a lot of this stuff even without being conscious of it.'

Torben's close ties to the nascent jazz scene in Denmark led to the late Dexter Gordon becoming Lars' godfather. Indeed, the first appearance Lars made on a professional stage was at the age of nine, bounding on and yelling into the mike during a Gordon appearance at a nightclub in Rome, where his parents had gone during a night off at the Italian Open. 'Like some dog who runs amok for a moment,' his father would later recall. The globe-trotting also gave Lars a facility for languages, able to converse from an early age in Danish, English, German and 'little bits of other stuff'. It was an itinerant lifestyle that would mean he was 'always comfortable on the road. I'd been places with my father we've never gotten to in Metallica.' It also gave the boy a supreme sense of entitlement; a super self-confidence that meant no door would remain closed to him for long, the very idea that he might not be welcome somewhere never entering his head.

Although Lars would also inherit his father's love of music and art, it was his mother, Lone, who gifted him the managerial abilities he would later bring to his career with Metallica. As well as taking good care of the two men in her life, 'My mum was definitely the organiser and kind of the business head,' he told me when last we spoke in 2009, our umpteenth interview in a relationship that now goes back more than a quarter of a century. 'I mean, my dad didn't know what time of day it was, what month it was, you know, what year it was. He didn't know what country he was in. He was one of these guys that was just beautifully lost in the moment all the time. I mean that in a very positive sense [and] my mum was sort of full-time care-taking all the practical elements of his life. So it's definitely from my mum's side that I've inherited some of my sort of anal organisational skills.'

First and foremost, in those earlier days, there was tennis. Torben's own father had also been a tennis star. For over twenty years he had been an advertising executive who participated in seventy-four Davis Cup matches before becoming president of the Danish Lawn Tennis Association. Almost inevitably, although there was no overt pressure exerted on him to do so, Lars grew up expecting to follow in what had practically become the family business. For Lars, though, tennis and a love of music would eventually dovetail in an even more significant way. In 1969, during the family's by now annual six-week stay in London – built around Wimbledon and satellite tournaments in East-bourne and at Queen's – the five-year-old Lars was taken to his first rock concert: the famous free concert by the Rolling Stones, given to over 250,000 people in Hyde Park. He still has pictures his parents took of him there. 'I think that I'd been dragged along to some jazz events, you know, at some of the local jazz clubs in Denmark up through the years,' Lars told me. Most often, he said, at a favourite haunt of the Ulrichs called Montmartre, which Torben helped run. 'But in terms of rock concerts the '69 Stones' gig was the first one, yeah.' His first genuine musical love, though, was for heavy rock stars of the early 1970s such as Uriah Heep, Status Quo and, most especially, Deep Purple, who he saw perform live for the first time when he was just nine. Torben's friend, South African tennis player Ray Moore, had been given passes for the show, which was being held in the same arena as one of his tennis tournaments. When a friend dropped out at the last minute, he offered the spare ticket to Torben's son instead. It quite literally, Lars said, 'blew my mind!' He couldn't get it out of his head 'for days, weeks!' He immediately nagged his father into buying him Purple's *Fireball* album. In this, though, Torben, for once, was not entirely supportive. 'He'd say it was square and the drummer was too white,' Lars recalled. But the son was not listening to the father. 'I have an obsessive personality,' he would later recall. 'When I was nine years old, it was all about Deep Purple.' As he got older, he would stake out the band. 'I would spend all my time sitting outside their hotel in Copenhagen, waiting for Ritchie Blackmore to come out so I could follow him down the street.' When, nearly thirty years later, I asked the now grown-up, father-of-three what his favourite album was he had no hesitation. 'My all-time favourite is still *Made in Japan*,' the double live Purple collection from 1972. The first show he ever had front-row tickets for, though, was Status Quo, at the Tivoli Koncertsal in Copenhagen, in 1975, which he later described for me as 'a bit of a mind-fuck'. He was eleven and all he could think of was how he had gotten there. 'How did I get so close? Were any of the drunks that had come over from Sweden gonna beat me up, or even worse puke on me?' So close to the stage Lars could barely see up to where the band was standing mere feet away, Quo frontman Francis Rossi 'looked like a rock god, over ten feet tall, with five feet of long hair and a Telecaster that looked like a kick-your-ass weapon'.

He began hanging out at Copenhagen's best-known album-oriented record shop, the Holy Grail, where 'the guy who worked there was my hero', introducing him to then less well-known rock artists such as Judas Priest, Thin Lizzy and UFO. He would fantasise about being in his own rock band, write down names of songs and album titles in old school exercise books, living in his own make-believe world of rock stardom. Rock music became the one thing the increasingly independent youngster didn't feel required to share with his parents. It also provided company for a solitary child growing up on the road, surrounded by kindly tennis 'uncles' and 'aunts' and accustomed at home to plenty of arty elders who let him do as he pleased. As Lars later told the writer David Fricke, 'From that point of view it was a pretty open upbringing.' It meant, though, that he was expected to fend for himself in this bohemian atmosphere. 'I always had to wake myself up in the morning and bike myself to school. I'd wake up at 7.30, go downstairs, and the front door would be open – six hundred beers in the kitchen and living room and nobody in the house. Candles would be burning. So I'd close the doors, make breakfast and go to school. I'd come home and have to wake my parents up . . .' While this made him 'very independent' it often left him quite lonely. 'As far as my parents were concerned, I could go see Black Sabbath twelve times a day. But I had to find my own means, carrying the paper or whatever, to get the money to buy the tickets. And I had to find my own way to the concert and back.' The passion for loud, heavy rock – music that more than matched his outgoing, room-filling personality – continued throughout his early teens, and although his future was still bound to the same tennis courts his father had become famous on, that dedication slowly began to ebb. This process speeded up when, aged thirteen, his grandmother bought him his first drum kit – not just any beginner's kit, either, but a Ludwig: drummer gold in rock circles.

Given his extrovert personality and, some would say, over-willingness to be the mouthpiece for Metallica, I once asked him why such an obvious frontman had ended up at the back of the stage as a drummer. 'Well, there's just one problem,' he chortled. 'I couldn't [sing]. I mean, when I tried to sing in the shower it bothered me. And so if I couldn't even capture an audience of one in the shower, you know, I realised that was not gonna happen. And I just always loved drumming. I mean, I can't remember ever having a conscious moment where I sat there and said, "Being a drummer and having my Type A personality is kind of gonna clash." It just never dawned upon me that I would not be able to be myself. That whole thing of like, oh my God, if you're a drummer you have to shut up and only speak when spoken to and hang out in the background. That never registered on my radar.'

Ironically, it wasn't until he took his most serious step as a fledgling tennis pro that his commitment finally switched for ever to becoming a drummer: enrolment, at sixteen, in Nick Bollettieri's now world-famous – then the first of its kind – tennis academy in Florida. Says Lars, 'When you grow up in [tennis] circles it's almost like you get dragged into it. I can't remember ever sitting there and making like a super-conscious decision about being a professional tennis player; it was what I knew. It wasn't until a little later, after I finished school, and we moved to America for me to actually pursue this tennis thing more full-on – out on my own, out of the shadow of my dad's wing – that I realised that not only did I not have the talent to really follow in his footsteps, but I certainly didn't have the discipline. You know, you're sixteen, you're just having a couple beers, you're having your first experience with girls and other things, and all of a sudden it's like, I gotta be out there six hours a day hitting fucking tennis balls back and forth? It just got a little . . . too disciplined for my tastes.' He laughed.

In the end, he spent less than six months in Florida studying with Bollettieri. 'I went the first year in 1979 after I finished school – to kind of see if I wanted to do that. I was still kind of infatuated with it enough. That was the first year [it opened], way before Monica Seles or [Andre] Agassi or Pete Sampras or any of the other guys [that went there].' A top-ten-ranked junior in Denmark, coming to America proved a rude awakening. Moving from Miami to Los Angeles, 'I was gonna go to this high school 'cos my dad was very close with Roy Emerson, the tennis player. And so I went to the same high school as [Roy's son] Anthony Emerson and I was gonna be on the tennis team with him. Well, guess what? I wasn't one of the seven best players at the high school. I didn't actually make the fucking tennis team at high school! That's how competitive it was. It was pretty crazy.' There were other discouragements. Torben was tall; Lars was short, just five foot six, a marked disadvantage. Yet Bollettieri himself believes now that with proper application Lars might have made it as a wealthy mid-level tennis pro. 'He could move extremely well and had a lot of ability.' And while 'We knew Lars was not going to be as tall as his father, nor did we expect for him to really bulk up', the real problem was 'he was not dedicated to the rigorous work it would require'. Or as Torben put it in a 2005 interview with Leigh Weathersby: '[Lars] was very interested in tennis at that time, but he was also very interested in music. After a year he still wanted to go out and listen to the concerts and I think at the Academy they were not so keen that he stayed out, so he was reprimanded there for keeping some late hours.' At which point, Lars told me, 'I sort of realised that maybe this tennis thing was gonna get kind of set to the side and maybe this music thing was gonna be more of a full-time thing.'

If a natural adolescent interest in girls, beer and the occasional puff on a joint were all key factors in moving Lars away from the wooden racquet and more towards the full metal racket, the young Ulrich's disaffection with tennis also coincided with a moment in rock that was about to write its own noisome chapter in musical history: the self-styled and cumbersomely named New Wave of British Heavy Metal (NWOBHM). 'It was March 1980,' Lars would later recall, 'and I walked into a record store in America, searching for the latest Triumph album or some such shit, and I was over at the import bin poking around. Now this was still before I was truly aware of what was going on in England, so when I came across an album called *Iron Maiden* I had no idea who or what they were. The front cover illustration of "Eddie" [the mummified corpse that would adorn all the formative Maiden record sleeves] could have been done by any one of a hundred bands, but the exciting live shots on the back of the sleeve really stood out. There was something so fucking heavy about the whole vibe – such aggression. Funnily enough, I never even heard the record until I returned to Denmark because I didn't have a record player with me.'

Without realising it, Lars had stumbled on one of the most important touchstones in what was fast becoming a watershed moment in rock history. By the late summer of 1979, although still unsigned to a major record label, Iron Maiden was already a band clearly on the up. Boosted by the unforeseen success of *The Soundhouse Tapes*, a self-financed EP of a three-track demo recorded for next to nothing, *Sounds* – then one of the most popular weekly music magazines in Britain – had run its first live review of the band: a show at the Music Machine, in London's Camden Town, where Iron Maiden had been sandwiched between Black Sabbath copyists Angel Witch, and the more bluesy, old-style boogie of Samson (featuring future Maiden vocalist Bruce Dickinson, then known as Bruce Bruce). *Sounds'* deputy editor Geoff Barton, who was there that night, would later write: 'I do definitely recall Maiden being the best band of the evening, infinitely preferable to the Sabs-worshipping Angel Witch and way ahead of Samson.' What really intrigued Barton, though, he would later tell me, 'is that a band like Iron Maiden or Angel Witch could even exist at a time like that', when punk and new wave had apparently killed off the hard rock and metal genre. Sensing the makings of a follow-on feature, Barton talked *Sounds* editor Alan Lewis into allowing him to put together a coverall piece not just on Iron Maiden, but on a whole new generation of rock heavies he dubbed, in deliberately eye-catching tabloid style, the New Wave of British Heavy Metal. 'To be honest, I didn't really feel that any of these bands were particularly linked in a musical way,' says Barton now, 'but it was interesting that so many of them should be then emerging at more or less the same time. It was a good thing for the genuine rock fans who had really gone to ground, hiding in their wardrobes waiting for punk to go away.' They had begun 'by doing a feature on Def Leppard, who had just released their first, independently produced four-track EP, *Getcha Rocks Off*. Then Maiden came along', followed by 'Samson and Angel Witch, then Tygers of Pan Tang and Praying Mantis, and so we did features on them, too, and it just kept going from there.'

What not even Barton had foreseen, however, was the enormous purchase that one almost comedic phrase dreamed up one rainy afternoon in the *Sounds* office would have on the music world. 'We ran the [NWOBHM] feature and the response we got from both the readers and other bands was just phenomenal. It was obvious that, whatever you called it, there was definitely something going on out there. Suddenly there were new heavy metal bands springing up everywhere, it seemed. Of course, not all of them were as [good] as bands like Iron Maiden and Def Leppard, but the fact that they were even trying was news back then and we just ran with it for about two years in the end.' Ironically, considering the short srift most of the post-punk music critics could be expected to give any band called Praying Mantis or Angel Witch, the motivation behind this resurgence came from a similar dissatisfaction as punk with what a new generation of record-buying kids saw as the self-indulgent, album-oriented monoliths that had preceded them. By 1979, bands such as Led Zeppelin, Pink Floyd, ELP and Yes (all prominent members of the ruling rock royalty of the day) were rarely seen on British stages, and when they did deign to make a fleeting appearance, they invariably spurned the idea of actual touring in favour of a more languorous (not to mention lucrative) handful of dates at a large, impersonal arena like Earls Court in London. Rock bands had become grandiose and pompous; the music they played grown old before its time. As a result, the gap between those on stage and those off had never been greater.

Punk's response was a desire to see the past wiped out; to start again from the ground up. But in its hurry to tear down the edifice, punk had overlooked the obvious – that at its foundations, hard rock and heavy metal was not so different from what the best punk rock imagined itself to be: raw, alive, unafraid to offend, unafraid to be ridiculed and spat on for the clothes it wore and the lifestyle it chose to expound; alert to the creative possibilities of existing defiantly outside the mainstream. NWOBHM bands had also absorbed the more practical lessons of punk: that you could release limited editions of your own records on small independently run labels, as a spur to later getting longer-term deals with one of the major labels. Hence Def Leppard's *Getcha Rocks Off* EP, released on their own Bludgeon Riffola label, and Iron Maiden's home-grown *The Soundhouse Tapes* EP (original copies of which both now exchange hands for several hundred pounds). Saxon and Motörhead, although neither fell strictly speaking into the NWOBHM category, found themselves lumped in anyway, almost entirely by accident of timing and the fact that their first records were also released by independent labels.

Also like punk, NWOBHM fans started their own fanzines: titles such as *Metal Fury* and *Metal Forces*, in the UK, and similar titles around the world like *Metal Mania* and *Metal Rendezvous* in the USA and *Aardshok* in Holland, had all made the leap from the back-room press onto the shelves of record stores and newsagents as the demand for articles on the new, revitalised UK rock scene rapidly grew. With *Sounds* leading the way, the rest of the large-circulation British music press also moved to get in on the act. Malcolm Dome, a life-long hard rock and heavy metal devotee then working as Deputy Editor for Dominion Press, publishers of educational scientific journals such as *Laboratory News*, had begun contributing articles on the NWOBHM scene to *Record Mirror* in 1980, and later became a leading writer for *Kerrang!*. He now describes the years between 1979 and 1981 – the apotheosis of the NWOBHM – as 'some of the most exciting for new rock music this country has ever witnessed'. Dome had been recruited to *Record Mirror* after their previous in-house rock correspondent, Steve Gett, had been poached by the more prestigious *Melody Maker*, keen not to miss out on what they rightly viewed as a coming wave of important and – more to the point – increasingly popular music. By 1981, the mainstream UK music press was even ready to give birth to the world's first dedicated rock and metal magazine, *Kerrang!* – originally begun by Geoff Barton as yet another adjunct to *Sounds'* ongoing nurturing of the no longer quite so jokey NWOBHM scene, now about to become a significant part of the media landscape not just in Britain but around the world.

As Dome recalls, 'Maiden were regarded as at the top of the pile of the NWOBHM. With the possible exception of Def Leppard, they were obviously streets ahead of everyone else. But, of course, like any scene, it completely fed upon itself.' As a result of all the media attention they were now attracting, both Maiden and Leppard would score big record contracts: the former with EMI, the latter with Phonogram. Indeed, it became a race between the two as to which would break into the national charts first. Maiden's commercial potential had been made apparent to EMI when their *Soundhouse Tapes* EP, given limited release in November 1979 on their own Rock Hard Records, sold five thousand copies. Never intended for retail, the five thousand seven-inch vinyl copies of *The Soundhouse Tapes* were made available by mail order only, priced £1.20, including postage and packing, and were distributed by a friend of the band named Keith Wilfort, who enlisted his mother to help him send them out from the family home in East Ham. Miraculously, they managed to send out over three thousand copies within the first week.

After the band then signed with EMI, they spearheaded the release of a NWOBHM compilation, titled *Metal for Muthas*, released in February 1980. The brainchild of EMI young gun Ashley Goodall, *Metal for Muthas* showcased nine avowedly NWOBHM bands, most prominent being Iron Maiden, the only band on the album to have two tracks ('Sanctuary' and 'Wrathchild'). The rest of the album was a mixture of tracks from the likes of genuine NWOBHM stalwarts such as Samson ('Tomorrow or Yesterday'), Angel Witch ('Baphomet'), Sledgehammer ('Sledgehammer'), Praying Mantis ('Captured City') and more opportunistic, old-fashioned album-fillers such as Toad the Wet Sprocket, Ethel the Frog, and even former A&M artists Nutz, a band that hardly qualified as 'new' at any stage of its unremarkable career. As Malcolm Dome, who reviewed the album for *Record Mirror*, says now, 'I found it all very exciting. It was a shame they couldn't get Def Leppard or Diamond Head as well [but] I still think it was actually a fine summation of that period.'

The *Metal for Muthas* tour which followed, was more representative and featured Maiden, Praying Mantis, Tygers of Pan Tang and Raven, all bona fide members of the NWOBHM elite. Then Maiden guitarist Dennis Stratton, who'd only just joined the band, told me he was 'shell-shocked by the response [the shows] got from their fans'. He went on: 'Musically, it was bordering on punk rock ... the audience was just fanatical. To me, it was all heavy metal music, but for some reason the fans could pick out that Maiden were different.' Fellow Maiden guitarist Dave Murray remembers it as 'people just waiting for the tour to arrive. It felt like the punk thing was kind of coming to an end and there was this gap and that everybody was just waiting for something to happen again. And it was great because rock was supposed to be dead, you know, but the reality was there was loads of kids out there who were coming to the shows or forming their own bands.'

When the self-titled debut *Iron Maiden* was released in the spring of 1980, it leapt straight into the UK charts at Number Four. As a result, import copies started flooding into the USA ahead of its official release there later that year. Out on the West Coast, Lars Ulrich was one of the first to buy one. As he told me: 'I was getting *Sounds* sent to me on a weekly basis, and I was getting care packages from [independent NWOBHM specialist label] Bullet Records.' The NWOBHM, 'just gave a new spin, a different kind of edge to traditional long-haired rock music. I mean, I was a teenage Deep Purple fan from Denmark who thought it didn't get any better than that, you know, who was then suddenly thrown into this whole NWOBHM thing, and it sounds weird, but basically it changed my life.' The only snag: 'There was no one I could talk to about this stuff. It was always awkward for me when I landed in LA.' Enrolled at Backbay high school in Newport Beach, he was the foreign kid with the funny accent and weird taste in clothes and music. 'It was literally five hundred kids in pink Lacoste shirts and one guy in a Saxon T-shirt – me. I didn't like to get beat up. I wasn't like one of those guys. I was more like a loner. I was an outsider – doing my own thing, living in my own world and sort of not really relating to anything that was around me, in school or in Newport Beach' where he now lived with his family. NWOBHM was 'heavy metal played with a punk attitude', he insisted. 'My heart and soul were in England with Iron Maiden, Def Leppard and Diamond Head, and meanwhile I'm sitting here in this barren musical wasteland of Southern California being bombarded with REO Speedwagon and Styx. I had all the merchandise sent over from England. I'd walk around school with a Saxon T-shirt on and people would look at me as if I was from another planet.' He had tried to integrate himself into the local scene, he said, going to see Y&T at the Starwood club in Hollywood just before his seventeenth birthday, but the only real friends he found he could relate to – that even knew what it meant when he walked in wearing a Motörhead or Maiden tee – were those he corresponded with via the then-emerging cassette-tape-trading scene.

Finally, Lars made contact with some new, like-minded buddies in the shape of two slightly older rock fans from Woodlands Hills named John Kornarens and Brian Slagel. 'John was a big UFO fan,' says Slagel now, 'and we had gone to see [former UFO guitarist] Michael Schenker play at the Country Club, in Reseda. This must have been in about December 1980. After the show John was in the parking lot and saw a kid wearing a Saxon European T-shirt. Now nobody, aside from me and him, knew who Saxon even was in LA, let alone had a European T-shirt. So John ran up to him and said, "Wow, where did you get that shirt?" I look down the road and there's this little guy with long hair and a wrinkled Saxon T-shirt on,' Kornarens later recalled, 'so I went over the way. Lars was all excited 'cos he thought he was the only one in LA. So we started talking about the NWOBHM and the next day or the day after I'm round at his house for like a NWOBHM marathon.' Soon their nerdy little gang was joined by fellow LA-based NWOBHM anoraks such as Bob Nalbandian, Patrick Scott and, further afield, Ron Quintana in San Francisco and K.J. Doughton in Oregon, all of whom would make small but important contributions to the early development of Metallica. 'Obviously there was a lot of innocence,' Lars smiled, when I prodded him for more memories in 2009. 'There was a lot of youthful energy, there were a bunch of kids that came from all over the place that probably shared one thing in common [which] was that they were all outcasts and were all loners and had a difficult time fitting in with the kind of American way things were supposed to be – with school and goals and dreams and all this crap, right? And that we all found music and we all got off on the same things, which was this incredible thing that the British press had kind of [invented]. And I mean that in a positive way. We all believed in what this whole thing coming out of England was. Also because ... it united us, and it was something that was taking place far away, so it made it more exciting. It wasn't immediately accessible, physically. It's very easy to kind of dream yourself into that whole state. And the New Wave of British Heavy Metal did that for many of us.'

'We just thought he was some crazy Euro-metaller,' says Ron Quintana, who first met Lars at the end of 1980. However, Ron and his 'Golden Gate Park hilltop' friends soon 'came to respect his knowledge of bands we'd only read about or more commonly only seen logos of and suspected were heavy ... [Lars] knew his shit early on and was an expert on newer bands to me'. Brian Slagel, who these days runs his own successful Metal Blade label, had discovered the NWOBHM through the tape-trading scene, which he'd first gotten into at high school, swapping home-made bootlegs with an increasingly wide range of fellow fanatics. Eventually, 'I would trade live tapes [with people] all over the world,' he says now. One of the people he regularly traded tapes with was in Sweden and it was he who sent him a live AC/DC show, which he also stuck some stuff 'by a new band called Iron Maiden' onto the end of. 'It was *The Soundhouse Tapes*, three songs stuck on the end of the AC/DC stuff. I was like, "Oh, wow! This is awesome! What *is* this?"' Brian began pumping his Swedish pen-pal for info, heard about the NWOBHM, then started buying import copies of *Sounds*, 'which you could get at one of the local record stores' to find out more. Soon he had amassed an impressive second-hand knowledge of the emerging British scene and begun to share his newfound spoils with other friends. To begin with, 'There was me, my friend John Kornarens and Lars,' he recalls. Once a week they would set off together to visit all the independently run record stores they knew that sold import copies of this decidedly non-American rock. 'There were only like three or four stores and sometimes they would be an hour away from each other [by car]. There was Zed Records [in Long Beach]. Moby Disc [in Sherman Oaks] was another one closer to where I lived. And there were a couple of others I can't remember the names of now' including 'a store in Costa Mesa, which was really far. We'd all drive in one car and we'd have to go pick up Lars, who lived in out in [Newport Beach], driving all over the place. Lars was from Europe and knew stuff that we didn't know and we had stuff that he didn't have, so the three of us just became really good friends based on our love of that whole NWOBHM scene.' Lars was sixteen; Brian and John were eighteen. But Lars was the one who appeared to have the edge. 'He was this crazy little kid with this endless amount of energy. We'd drive up to one of these record stores and he'd be out of the car and in the metal section before I could shut off the engine. When he was into something, he was into it a thousand per cent.' Lars was so far into the NWOBHM scene 'that he wanted to be a part of it'.

Patrick Scott, a year younger than Lars but – because of the Danish schooling system – in the same grade year at high school, had heard of 'this little Danish kid' long before he'd met him. 'We'd all go to this place called Music Market,' he recalls. Scott and his friend Bob Nalbandian 'would go, and we'd say "Did you get the new *Kerrang!*?" And they'd say, we got one copy but this little Danish kid already came in and bought it. We'd say, who is this guy? 'Cos he beat us to it every time. Or we'd be looking for new [UK import] singles on Neat [Records] and they'd say "The Danish guy was here and he got it." And we'd get frustrated but we wanted to meet this guy. We were just hungry to meet people that were into this stuff.' When they eventually met via the small ads of a Los Angeles free sheet music paper named

The Recycler, Patrick phoned Lars, who told him: 'Come on over.' Says Scott, 'He had an amazing record collection that I drooled over and we became friends. He would come over to my house and watch the tennis. We were like one of the first families to have cable, so he'd come over to watch it and hang out with my family and things.' Another member of the clique, Bob Nalbandian, now a writer and DJ, recalls how Lars, not merely satisfied with cruising the indie stores for new records, was also a prolific collector of mail-order imports. Once, when Lars ordered a copy of Holocaust's 'Heavy Metal Mania' twelve-inch, he offered to grab one for Bob, too. A month later, Bob got a call from Lars telling him that the records had finally arrived and to come over and pick his up. 'I go, "Great, I can't wait to hear it,"' Bob recalls, 'and he says, "Yeah, but there's a problem – your copy of 'Heavy Metal Mania' got taken out of the wrapper and left on the stove." Note he said *your* copy! So my copy got warped. So I get in the car and drive seventy miles to his house just to hear it and it's awesome. I wasn't going to argue with him about my copy being all screwed up. I'm, like, "Where am I going to get another copy of 'Heavy Metal Mania'?" There were two copies: Lars had one and I had the other one. So I got my mum's ironing board out and tried to get it back into shape.'

Lars would make his friends tapes of highly prized rarities by groups such as Crucifixion, Demolition, Hellenbach, Night Time Flyer – 'all this NWOBHM stuff,' recalls Patrick Scott. In return, Scott was able to introduce Lars to bands like Accept from Germany and a next-generation outfit from Denmark named Mercyful Fate. Lars, who had met the band but never heard one of their records, was deeply impressed with their first four-track EP, simply titled *The Mercyful Fate* EP, also sometimes known as *Nuns Have No Fun*. He begged Patrick: 'I'll trade you anything of my collection for it!' But Patrick, who was equally anal, wouldn't trade. The band Lars really fell for, though, was Diamond Head, who contained some of the edginess of classic NWOBHM bands like Iron Maiden, but incorporated it into distinctly old-school rock motifs, borrowed almost entirely from old gods Led Zeppelin, Deep Purple and Black Sabbath.

Lars had first come across them via a tape of their early single, 'Shoot Out the Lights', which he regarded as 'good but not outstanding'. When, however, he read in *Sounds* about the band's independently produced, mail-order album, *Lightning to the Nations*, he couldn't resist sending off a cheque and ordering a copy. He later gleefully recalled how 'each copy was signed by one member of the quartet and it was pot luck whose autograph you ended up getting'. Lars, who had the luck of the devil, ended up with the handwritten signature of the band's singer, Sean Harris – a rare prize indeed for the NWOBHM devotee.

However, a long delay in the album's arrival at the Ulrich household resulted in Lars striking up a correspondence with Linda Harris, Sean's mother and then co-manager of the band. 'She wrote really nice letters to me [and] sent me embroidered patches and singles – but still no album! Finally, in April 1981 the white label arrived and the riffing and freshness just amazed me.' So amazed was he, in fact, that Metallica would later play live – and, later still, record – five of the album's seven tracks, including 'Am I Evil?', 'Helpless', 'Sucking My Love' and 'The Prince'. In particular, he was enthralled by a track called 'It's Electric', which he had already heard a version of on another would-be NWOBHM compilation called *Brute Force*. 'That was fucking unbelievable!' he said. 'If you take a look at the sleeve of the record now and compare the photo of Diamond Head with all the other groups there, they had an attitude and a vibe about them that none of the others could match. There was something special about Diamond Head, no doubt about it.' Any secret thoughts Lars had of becoming a musician himself were still held in check, though. Certainly, none of his collector friends had any inkling yet of his ambitions to form his own world-beating NWOBHM-type band. 'There was no mention initially that Lars wanted to form a band,' says Brian Slagel. Then one day at Lars' parents' house Brian noticed there was a drum set 'that was not put together, just sitting in the corner [in pieces]. He was like, "I'm gonna start a band" and we're like, "Yeah, right, Lars, sure."'

But when Brian Slagel started his own fanzine, *The New Heavy*

Metal Revue, he began to feel like he should hurry up and do his own thing too. 'There were so many great bands that I just loved, I kind of thought it was an interesting thing to do something like that,' Slagel says now. 'There was nobody over here in the US that really knew anything about any of these NWOBHM bands.' The first issue was 'thrown together for fun' in early 1981. 'We just wrote some reviews and some things on Maiden and some US bands, and photo-copied a few of them and tried to get them anywhere we could get them, basically.' It was around this time that Slagel also started working at a local independent record store, Oz Records, where for the first time he came into contact with 'a lot of the import dis-tributors and stuff, so I had more of an avenue to get some dis-tribution'. With the fanzine now on sale in the same independent stores that he and Lars had first gotten to know as fans hunting down import copies of NWOBHM records, the itch Lars felt to also somehow become more involved grew unbearable. It was now that he put his drum kit back together and really began practising again. The problem with being a drummer, though, is that you can only get so far playing on your own. You need other musicians to play alongside to improve your technique. Not having any musician friends remotely interested in the type of music he wanted to play, Lars tried seeking a solution to the problem by placing an ad in the classified section of local music free-sheet *The Recycler*: 'Drummer looking for other metal musicians to jam with. Tygers of Pan Tang, Diamond Head and Iron Maiden.' 'This was like February, March of 1981,' Lars told me. 'And I was just *manic* and *obsessive* with all the stuff that was coming out of England, and getting all the singles and listening to all the bands, and doing all that stuff. And over the course of that spring, in 1981, I tried to find other musicians to kind of jam with and play full-on metal with. But that was pretty unsuccessful. And then I kind of got fed up with the whole thing and wanted to go and spend the summer in Europe.'

Disillusioned with life in balmy Newport Beach, frustrated by his apparently futile attempts to find other like-minded souls to play his drums with, and, although he wouldn't have owned up to himself about it at the time, desperately looking for something to fill the gap left in his – and his parents' – life by his failure to make a go of a tennis career, Lars sought both a quick escape and, maybe, a more realistic chance of at least meeting others who felt the same way he did about music. Talking it over with his mother and father, they were, as ever, supportive. In Denmark they had allowed him to travel around alone. 'In those days in Denmark, a child of eight or nine could take the bus to the concert hall and listen and then come back on their own,' Torben recalled. 'And then sometimes he would fall asleep on the bus and the conductor would say, "Now it's time to get up and go home."' In that context, allowing your seventeen-year-old son to catch a plane across the Atlantic on his own was hardly a stretch – as long as he promised to write home and, when possible, phone, just to let his mother know he was safe, and with the unspoken agreement that when he returned he would at least settle on some sort of plan, whether that be going on to college or finding a proper job. Lars bought himself a return ticket to London and made ready to leave – alone.

Then, just a few weeks before he left, 'I got this call from this guy named Hugh Tanner who had seen my ad [and] he came down and we had a jam, and he brought this guy James Hetfield along ...' That first meeting did not go well, though. Hugh and James went down to meet Lars together. Unsure who was auditioning for whom, the first number they tried out together was 'Hit the Lights'. Lars 'had one cymbal that kept falling over', James recalled. 'We had to stop while he fixed it.' When it was over, he said, 'It was, "What the fuck was that?"' It wasn't just Lars' rudimentary abilities on the drums. It was 'his mannerisms, his looks, his accent, his attitude'. Even, he said, 'his smell', reflecting on the difference between American shower-a-day standards of hygiene and Lars' own more 'European' habit of going days without bathing, wearing the same shirt and jeans until they became stiff with sweat. As far as James Hetfield was concerned, Lars might have stepped off a spaceship. A stranger in a strange land, there was no way he could see it working out between them.

Lars was also less than impressed. James' singing voice in those days had yet to evolve into the ferocious growl it's now famous for. Instead, he sang in an affected, high-pitched aggro-castrato, part Rob Halford, part Robert Plant, part strangled squeal. Lars was also put off by what he perceived as the frankly unfriendly vibe emanating from the singer, who hardly spoke and refused even to make eye contact. His first encounter of the man who he would later characterise as 'the king of alienation ... almost afraid of social contact', Lars went away that day utterly disillusioned. 'We had a jam and not much materialised,' he told me, 'and I got kind of pissed off with the whole thing.' Not with playing, but with the idea of ever finding anyone in America to play with. Instead, he reverted to another plan he'd been hatching: to leave America behind and return to Europe. Not to Denmark, but to Britain, 'where the action was'. When, with the same incorrigible panache he had exhibited in his days waiting in hotel lobbies for Ritchie Blackmore's autograph, he wrote to Linda Harris and asked if he might come and visit her and her son one day, and maybe come and watch the band play, Linda breezily agreed, never expecting the enquiry to go any further than that. But then she had never met anyone quite like Lars Ulrich.

'Lars would always come up with these things that he wanted to do,' says Brian Slagel. 'We'd be like, "Yeah, whatever, right, Lars, sure." So he was going to go over to England, like: "I have to go over there, I'm gonna start hanging out with the bands." So, right, whatever. We figured he was gonna go. So he went, then I remember he called us one time ... "Guess what I'm doing?" "What?" "I'm hanging out with Diamond Head!" "Yeah, right." He's like "Don't believe me?" and he puts Sean Harris on the phone. Not only has he *seen* them but he's hanging out with them. It was insane! He would kind of think up these things that he wanted to do and make happen, which you really thought never could happen, the Diamond Head thing being one of many examples. It kind of blew me away, some seventeen-year-old kid on his own just going to England. That's one thing to go over and see the scene and see the shows, but to actually be able to hang out with the band was really pretty amazing.'

Looking back at Lars Ulrich's arrival in their midst now, almost three decades later, Diamond Head guitarist Brian Tatler still laughs at his young fan's audacity. 'He started sending handwritten letters over, saying "I live in [America] and I love all this NWOBHM movement." Then he must have seen that we were touring in the summer of '81, the big tour where we were doing the Woolwich Odeon, and he must have bought a ticket and decided to fly over to England and see his favourite band Diamond Head. This was just as a fan; he wouldn't say he was a drummer or anything. It would be like, "This guy, Lars, from America, has sent another letter." Then he turned up at the Woolwich Odeon and introduced himself and we were all really impressed because no one had ever flown from [America] to see Diamond Head before. It seemed like an amazing feat. I'd never been to America and he was seventeen, pitched up backstage and introduced himself! We were chuffed. We asked where he was staying and he was like, "I don't know, I've just come straight from the airport," and I said, "Come stay with me, if you like?" So he jumped in the car with us and we just squeezed him in. After that, Lars used to go everywhere with us,' including two more Diamond Head shows: one in Leeds, one in Hereford, 'all squashed up in the back of Sean's Austin Allegro'.

Lars stayed at Brian's for a week. The guitarist still lived with his parents and Lars would crash out on Brian's thinly carpeted bedroom floor, wrapped in his brother's moth-eaten old sleeping bag. Most nights they would go to the pub for a drink. 'One night we walked home 'cos we'd missed the bus and got completely soaked,' Brian recalls. 'He told me he hadn't got a spare change of clothes. So I found a pair of me brother's old yellow flares at the bottom of the wardrobe and he put those on. I probably should have took a picture. He was just a character, you know? Full of beans, full of energy. Full of the enthusiasm for the New Wave of British Heavy Metal.' When they got home from the pub they would sit together watching a Betamax video Brian had recently procured of the 1974 California Jam – the festival at which a then-unknown vocalist named David Coverdale made his debut American appearance with Deep Purple. Lars 'loved that', says Brian; 'we used to watch that into the early hours. And he used to mime the solos and all that, 'cos he was big into Deep Purple and Blackmore was it.' Another video favourite was Lynyrd Skynyrd supporting the Stones at Knebworth, which Brian had taped off the TV, Lars rolling around on the floor doing the guitar solo to 'Freebird'.

I wondered how the teenager had managed financially while he was in England. 'He'd got loads of money!' reveals Brian. 'I think maybe his dad was well off or something. I thought: how come he's got all this money? He'd got probably a hundred and fifty quid on him or something.' A substantial figure in 1981. 'He wanted to buy all these copies of *Sounds* off me. He hadn't got 'em and they'd got loads of interesting features about maybe Angel Witch or whatever. He also went to Pinnacle Records, the distributor. I think he just found his way there. He just disappeared one day and said, "I'm going to Pinnacle," and got on the train and figured it out and came back with, like, a big armful of albums and singles. He'd bought about forty records! And then we'd sit there and play them, he'd put these records on one after the other, you know, by [groups like] Fist and Sledgehammer and Witchfynde and god knows what. We'd say, "Ooh, that's good" and "Don't like that bit there". We'd sit and dissect these albums. Anyway, after a week he went to Sean's and stayed for a whole month apparently, and slept on his couch and raided the fridge. Sean said [Lars] used to stop up all night listening to "It's Electric" on the headphones.' He chuckles. More significantly, Tatler recalls how the young Ulrich would 'watch us [when] we'd rehearse. I'd go to Sean's and be writing songs and [Lars would] be sat in the corner watching, just observing ... Sean had got a little four-track, a TEAC, and we'd be making demos as we'd go. And probably [Lars] was picking up on the vibe, and this is how you write songs and this is what you do.'

He never mentioned that he played drums, though?

'He didn't mention that at all. He never once said, "I'm a

drummer," or "I'm gonna form a band" or "Can I have a go on your drums?" Maybe he didn't think he was very good, or didn't think he was up to Duncan [Scott]'s standard, I don't know. He was just a good kid [and] he had that very strange accent. That amused us for weeks.'

According to received wisdom, Lars Ulrich ended his summer sojourn in the UK by somehow finagling his way into Jackson's Studio in Rickmansworth, where another of his favourite bands, Motörhead, were in the process of recording their *Iron Fist* album. Speaking now, though, Motörhead leader Lemmy says he has 'no recollection at all of Lars being there in the studio when we were recording the album. I'm not saying he wasn't, but it's so long ago my memory is very hazy of that period.' Before adding, benevolently, 'But if Lars says he was there, then I won't contradict him.' What Lemmy does recall, however, is a very young and fresh-faced Lars Ulrich turning up at several gigs during the West Coast leg of the band's first tour of America supporting Ozzy Osbourne, earlier that same year, just weeks before Lars left for the UK. This would tally with Brian Tatler's recollection of Lars taking him to see Motörhead during his stay that summer when the band headlined Port Vale football ground, where, in a reverse of the situation in America, Ozzy Osbourne was now the opening 'special guest' act. '[Lars] told me he knew Lemmy and would be able to blag a couple of passes,' says Tatler. So they took the train to Stoke-on-Trent where Lars did indeed see Lemmy and got both himself and Brian backstage passes for the show.

'I first met Lars in about 1981,' confirms Lemmy. 'It was definitely before Metallica were even together. That first occasion was in my hotel room in Los Angeles. He introduced himself as the guy who ran the Motörhead Fan Club in America – well, it turned out that this was an unofficial branch of the Motörheadbangers, and he was the only member. He never actually had anything to do with the official fan club, although he obviously loved the band. The meeting will always stay in my mind, because he wanted to have a drink with me, and clearly wasn't used to drinking my measures, so he threw up. It wasn't that bad, and I didn't make him clear up or anything like that, but

I did insist that he wore a bib for the rest of his time with me in the room.' He adds with a smirk: 'Oddly, he threw up the next time we met as well. He hadn't got any better at this drinking lark. Maybe I should have offered to give him lessons. Or perhaps it's a strange Danish greeting. I do recall one night – it must have been in about 1985 – when I met up with Lars at the St Moritz Club [in central London]. Anyone who knew anything about me would always know I'd be down there on the fruit machine. Lars came down, and insisted we go drink for drink – and I think he paid for most of it. So, okay we did it, and he ended up virtually passing out. Give the kid credit, though, he kept coming back for more . . .'

One other band Lars Ulrich definitely did hook up with in the summer of 1981 was Iron Maiden – though not in Britain but at a small club show in Copenhagen, where he intentionally made a stop-off in order to see them before returning home to America. 'I met [Maiden bassist and founder] Steve Harris for the first time in 1981,' he recalled. They were playing 'at a place the size of your living room'. Nevertheless, for the seventeen-year-old rich kid and aspirant megastar, at that moment 'Iron Maiden were the best rock band in the world'. He added, 'But it wasn't just the music.' There was quantity as well as quality; a factor he would later utilise to deliberate effect in Metallica. Maiden would 'put ten minutes more music on albums than any other rock band'. They had 'the best packaging, the coolest T-shirts, everything'. There was 'a depth to [their] whole organisation that was great for fans like me, and it was a big inspiration for us in Metallica. I wanted to give the same quality to kids who were into our band.' It was also the last time Maiden singer Paul Di'Anno would sing with the band: sacked for allowing his drug habits to get in the way of Maiden's rocket-like upward surge. Going backstage after the show to say hello and get their autographs, Lars noticed there was clearly only one leader of Iron Maiden: Steve Harris. It taught him an important lesson, he later told Harris: 'True democracy doesn't work in a band.'

The crazy little kid with the funny accent and the energy to burn was learning fast. Or as he later put it to me, 'That's one of the reasons

Metallica exists, because I'd sit there and learn from the Motörheads and Diamond Heads and Iron Maidens, because I was so far up their asses all the time – as a punter, absorbing and learning the vibe. That's what made me realise I wanted to do this shit myself.'

TWO
THE COWARDLY LION

Miami, or maybe Tampa, the Monsters of Rock tour, 1988, walking down the hotel corridor, Kirk and I.

'Hey,' he said, 'do I smell ... what is it? Wait ... lavender?'

'Yeah,' I smiled. 'I've just been dousing myself. Gotta headache.'

'Yeah,' he said, 'lavender is supposed to be good for that, right?'

'Yeah,' I said, 'they call it the medicine chest in a bottle.'

'Sure,' he said, 'what do you do, like, put drops on your clothes?'

'Yeah,' I said, 'or maybe rub some on the inside of your wrists or your temples. Better than taking aspirin.'

'Sure,' he said.

I liked Kirk. It was a relief talking to him. We were both vegetarian, smoked a lot of weed and liked to kick back. We stood there waiting for the elevator to come. The door slid open and there was James inside.

'Hey,' said Kirk, smiling.

'Hey,' said James, not smiling.

'Hey,' I said, but he just ignored me, barely nodded. I wasn't surprised. To James I was just another one of Lars' little friends and Lars had a lot of those. I decided to ignore him and carry on my conversation with Kirk.

'So,' I said, 'are you into essential oils then?'

Kirk looked aghast. 'What?' he spluttered. 'No! I mean ... no! I've read a little about them, I wouldn't say I was like into them.' He made to laugh it off as James looked down at us and glared fiercely.

I felt like I'd just had a bucket of water – or worse – thrown over me. Like, shut the fuck up, fool! You don't talk about gay stuff like essential oils in front of James! Jesus, what are you, fuckin' crazy?

Realising my blunder, I wanted to turn and run. There was no escape, though, as we rode the elevator in silence the rest of the way down to the lobby. As we all walked into the bar together, I noticed Kirk affecting a sort of mini-Hetfield saunter. Safety in numbers, I found myself doing the same. There was a tape of an Andrew 'Dice' Clay show blaring from the big video screen on the bar-room wall and we all sat down to watch it, ordered three bottles of Sapporo (large), and began yucking it up. The Dice was a very Hetfield sort of a guy, took no shit from homos or foreigners. Told it like it was; mouth like a machine-gun. The Dice was a very Metallica sort of guy, I realised. I just hoped the smell of lavender didn't get in the way of James' beer . . .

They say opposites attract. That was not the case when Lars Ulrich and James Alan Hetfield met for the first time, in May 1981. Born in Los Angeles, on 3 August 1963, on the surface the only thing James appeared to have in common with Lars was their age. Where Lars was small and doll-like, pretty-boy Eurotrash who ate with his mouth open and would go days without showering, James was tall and rangy, a full-blooded young American of Irish-German descent who brushed his teeth twice a day and always wore clean underwear. Where Lars never shut up, James never used two words where none would do. Where Lars came from a background of money and travel, of music and art, of multilingual, open-door hippy liberalism, James came from a plain-folks working-class family with strict fundamentalist religious beliefs, latterly an absentee father and, most recently and painfully, a tragically deceased mother. Where Lars was ready to push his way through any door and say, 'Hi', James stayed in the shadows, couldn't even bring himself to meet anyone in the eye. People sometimes mistook this reticence for shyness. But James wasn't shy, he was volcanically angry; a hair trigger waiting to go off. Years later, James would tell me his 'favourite film of all time has got to be *The Good, the Bad and the Ugly*'. Why? I asked. ''Cos there's three characters in it that are completely different and I find a little piece of me in each one of them,' he said. You knew just what he meant. Whiskery and brooding, James was a man's man, born to die, a throwback to a time not that long before when Injun-killing frontiersmen that talked and walked a lot like him had built America, all guns blazing. At least, that's how he appeared from the outside. From the inside looking out, however, for the young James Hetfield the world was often a frightening place, full of mendacity and betrayal, liars that would only let you down. This was the place he feared more than anything, and which he allowed his anger to shield him from. Once memorably described as looking like the cowardly lion from *The Wizard of Oz*, James Hetfield actually resembled the wizard himself – a timid, unsure character hiding behind a big scary screen image.

James' father Virgil had been a truck driver: a big, ambitious, outdoorsy sort of guy who eventually ended up running his own trucking company. He'd married James' mother, Cynthia, when she was at her most desperate: a no longer young divorcee with two young sons, Christopher and David. Virgil was a good guy who also taught part-time at Sunday school; a responsible sort of feller who James, his first of two children with Cynthia, looked up to even though he was strict. Once, when James and his younger sister, Deanna, ran away from home, Cynthia and Virgil found them hiding 'about four blocks away'. When they got them home, James recalled, 'They spanked the shit out of us, pretty much.' Although James and Deanna would often 'fight like cats and dogs', they would always regroup in front of their parents. As James told me in 2009, 'We'd help each other clean up the mess, and cover for each other with stories. So it was one of those things: love, hate.' His older, half-brothers were more distant, 'pretty much a generation apart and unfortunately it wasn't as bonding ... not quite old enough to tell me what to do and not young enough to understand what I wanted to hear or hang with, so it was kind of an awkward middle position there, but me and my sister were pretty tight'.

When James Hetfield was thirteen, his dad walked out of the house one day and never came back, didn't even say goodbye. In the vain hope that perhaps her husband would return, Cynthia told the youngest kids that their father had merely left for a long business trip. It was weeks before she finally gave James and his younger sister

Deanna the bad news. Even then, there was no explanation, just that daddy was gone, wasn't coming back, and let's leave it at that, okay kids? No. Not okay, actually. Not okay at all, especially for Deanna, a daddy's girl who had always been the 'rebellious one', according to James, and who now went completely off the rails. James' reaction was no less turbulent but less obvious. He held it all in, put a stern face on it, not brave exactly, just expressionless, hard, what he called 'my stay-the-fuck-away-from-me face'. The one he would wear for almost all of the next twenty years. 'It was very confusing for me, as a kid, to not know what's going on,' he would later say. Coming home from school some days to find his father's things missing – retrieved by Virgil while the kids were out of the house so as to cause as little disruption as possible – didn't soften the blow, only sharpened the pain and sense of betrayal. 'It was kind of hidden. That's a big character defect that I still carry – I think everyone's hiding something from me.'

At school, before his father had left, James told me, he had been 'a pretty average student. Pretty quiet, pretty reserved, just kind of get it done and then go home and, you know, have fun and play, do whatever.' A lover of sports, the only things that held him back, he said, were the consequences of his parents' strict adherence to the Christian Science belief system. A misnomer, in that Christian Science forbids its followers any sort of practical engagement with science, including, most distressingly, modern medicine, whether that be taking aspirin for a headache or receiving hospital treatment for fatal accidents or illnesses. One of those nouveau American religions that had sprung up in the nineteenth century, that no other people on Earth would have taken seriously, it still holds huge sway in certain sections of mainly working-class US society. James still sighs heavily when asked to talk about it. 'It didn't impact on the school,' he told me. 'It wasn't like they had their own schooling or like going to a Catholic school. It certainly did affect me, though. It affected me more than my sister and my brothers, where I ... I don't know, I think I took it a little more personally.' He paused, considered his words. 'Our parents didn't take us to the doctor. We were basically relying on the spiritual power of the religion to heal us or to shield us from being sick or injured. And so at school [because] that's what my parents requested, I wasn't allowed to sit through health class, to learn about the body, to learn about illnesses and things like that. And, say, you know, I'm trying out for the football team, you have to get a physical, to get a doctor's note ... I'd have to go and explain to the coach that, hey, our religion says this. So I felt really like an outcast ... alienated. Kids would laugh about it and I took it personally and some of the more, I think, traumatic stuff for me was [when] health class would begin, I would be standing in the hallway, which was basically a form of punishment in other aspects. Hey, you've been bad, you've got to go to the Principal's office or you stand out in front of the class. So everyone who walked by would look at me like I'd been some criminal of sorts, you know?'

It was tough but, he suggests, it also 'helped mould who I was, you know?' Not that James saw it that way at the time. 'When you're young you want to be like everyone else, you don't want to be unique. But I see the uniqueness in it now and it's helped me to, uh, you know, accept and embrace the uniqueness of me.' It was those difficult early experiences of always being the odd man out at school, James now believes, that nurtured his ability to not run with the pack, to always stand just a little bit apart from the rest of the gang. 'It helped me carve my own path, and even the spiritual part of it; when you're a kid you can't really grasp the concept of spirituality. It was a very adult type of concept and for me not going to the doctor was strange. All I saw was the people in the church that had broken bones and they were healing wrong – it didn't make any sense to me. So when I was saying these things to the [sports] coaches or teachers I was just speaking for my parents, I wasn't really speaking for myself, so it was a kind of a sell-out thing, which I really never wanted to do again. But also it helped me embrace the spiritual concept later on, and actually see the power in that, along with the knowledge of doctors these days, so it did help me with my concept of spirituality.'

It would be many years, however, precipitated by lengthy and still ongoing counselling sessions, before James Hetfield was ready to give any ground on these particular points. After his father left in 1977, 'I just said to my mom: "I'm not going to Sunday school any more. Make me." That was it.' Instead, music – one of the few forms of expression open to him as a kid that could be enjoyed alone – would become first a solace, then a guard and, eventually, an inspiration. Long before he became interested in rock, though, there was the classical piano, which Cynthia – whose hobbies included amateur operatics, painting and some graphic design – first encouraged him to study when he was nine. James told me: 'What it was, my mom had seen me over at a friend's house just kind of start bashing on the piano. I was more or less playing drums on the piano and she thought, "Oh, he's gonna be a musician, okay, we'll sign him up for piano." I did that for a couple of years and it was really a bit of a turn-off because it was learning classical pieces, stuff that I wasn't listening to on the radio, you know? I remember it was an older woman's house and the cookies at the end was the big deal, so something was cool about it. But I remember she had some music that she put out that we were gonna learn, and it was called "Joy to the World" [the Christmas carol adapted from an old English hymn]. I thought it was [starts singing] "Joy to the world!", you know [the 1971 pop hit by Three Dog Night], but it was not. I got a little excited, like, "I heard my brother play that song before!" But it was theory.' Discouraged at the time, he is now 'so glad it was somewhat forced upon me because the act of left and right hand doing different things, and also singing at the same time, it gave me some inkling of what I do now. It gave me an idea of that, that's natural to do. So singing and playing are somewhat easier than it probably could have been if I hadn't [studied] piano.'

He discovered rock via his older brothers' record collection. 'I was always looking for something different, something other people didn't always dig. When I was into Black Sabbath, all my friends would go, "Oh, my mom won't let me have that album. It's scary and I'll have nightmares." I thought that was funny, so I had to go out and get it.' Groups like The Beatles 'and shit like that', he said, 'I never dug so much'. It was around now that he also tried his hand at playing his brother David's drums, but couldn't get it going. He was fourteen, he told me, before he remembers 'picking up a guitar for the first time and going, "How do they make all these noises?"' He couldn't 'remember learning' to actually play one. 'I started off with an acoustic then started fiddling around, and then learning the chords, and it just kind of went on from there, I guess. But it seemed to go pretty quickly and I was playing in a band pretty soon, like within a year or two: playing cover songs, which is certainly the way to learn guitar.' He would also 'slow down LPs, trying to learn stuff'. Listening; copying; repeating; always alone. 'I liked being alone,' he later told writer Ben Mitchell. 'I liked being able to close off the world. And music helped with that a lot.' He would put the headphones on and just drift away, digging Kiss and Aerosmith, Ted Nugent and Alice Cooper: all-American hard rock; irony-free, kick-ass music for straight-shooting dudes that didn't dance but liked to party. 'I didn't get into other stuff until being introduced to Lars.' The first concert he went to was in July 1978, just before his sixteenth birthday: Aerosmith supported by AC/DC at the Long Beach Arena. Aerosmith's 1976 album *Rocks* 'was one of the albums I could play over and over; it was filled with good stuff'. The same summer he also bought a ticket for the two-day California World Music Festival, also featuring Aerosmith, alongside Ted Nugent and Van Halen. 'I remember following around my buddy, who was selling drugs. He tore up a part of his ticket – it had a kind of rainbow edge – and he cut it into bits and sold it as acid. I was like, "What are you doing, man?" He used the money to buy beer.' Working his way through the crowd to the front, James recalled being 'blown away' by the fact that Aerosmith singer Steven Tyler addressed the crowd 'as "motherfuckers". I was like, "Whoa – are you supposed to do that?"'

Already a well-established loner at high school, like Lars Ulrich it was music that would finally bring James Hetfield into contact with other similarly obsessed classroom loners such as Ron McGovney, who later become the first bass player in Metallica. A fellow pupil at East Middle School, McGovney recalls meeting Hetfield in music class, drawn to him as 'the only guy in the class who could play guitar'.

Like James, Ron didn't belong to any of the established school cliques. 'There was the cheerleaders, the jocks, the marching band people.' James and Ron ended up with other 'laggers' like their buddies Dave Marrs and Jim Keshil, 'hanging around without any real social group'. Ron wasn't solely into rock like James. He was 'an Elvis freak' who was 'devastated' when Presley died. Instead, he and James found common ground in the music of Led Zeppelin and ZZ Top, Foreigner and Boston. Dave and Jim were more like James; they were heavily into Kiss and Aerosmith. The odd man out, Ron eventually came round to the others' way of thinking, bonding with them over British proto-metal acts such as UFO. As a result, Ron started having lessons on the acoustic guitar. 'I knew nothing about bass,' he recalls. He just wanted to learn how to play 'Stairway to Heaven'. When, later that high school year, Hetfield started hanging out with two brothers named Ron and Rich Valoz, who played bass and drums respectively, and who then teamed up with another guitar-playing pupil named Jim Arnold, McGovney offered to roadie for them. The band called itself Obsession and like all high school bands they concentrated on cover versions of songs by their favourite artists. In this instance, that meant the easiest-to-play material by Black Sabbath ('Never Say Die'), Led Zeppelin ('Rock and Roll'), UFO ('Lights Out') and Deep Purple ('Highway Star'). All three frontline members would take turns singing, Jim Arnold on the Zeppelin stuff, Ron Valoz on 'Purple Haze'. James would be the UFO guy, tackling hard-line anthems like 'Doctor, Doctor' and 'Lights Out'.

After a prolonged period rehearsing at the Valoz brothers' parents' house in nearby Downey, the new outfit eventually did the occasional gig: backyard 'keg parties', playing for free beer and the chance to show off. Mainly, though, they played every Friday and Saturday night at the Valoz brothers' place. McGovney remembers the brothers as 'electrical geniuses' who had 'wired up lights' in the loft they built in their parents' garage: 'Dave Marrs and I would sit up there and work the control panel doing the lights, strobes and stuff.' It was 'this whole show in a tiny garage'. 'We'd do Thin Lizzy,' James told me. 'We'd do like some Robin Trower … bands of the time that were somewhat heavy.' James finally bailed out on Obsession, he said, when 'I had brought an original song to play and none of them liked it so that's when I basically kind of said goodbye to them. Because I wanted to start writing some songs and they weren't interested in that.' With James went Jim Arnold, joined by his brother Chris, to form another short-lived outfit called Syrinx. 'All they played was Rush covers,' McGovney recalled. 'That didn't last long.'

All the music came to an abrupt end, though, when James' mother died agonisingly slowly of cancer, in 1980, after refusing treatment and even painkillers until right at the very end, when it was already too late. With James and Deanna forced to move in with their stepbrother, David – ten years older than James and now married and living in his own house twenty miles away in Brea, where he worked as an accountant – to begin with James would still make the twenty-mile trek back to Downey for rehearsals with Syrinx. That soon petered out as the implications of his mother's death started to sink in and a different sort of gloom descended. James also broke up with his first semi-serious girlfriend. Nothing, it seemed, would ever go right again. Unruly as ever, Deanna was soon ejected from Dave's – preferring to track down her father and join him. James, who 'wanted nothing to do with' his father, stayed put, seeing his parents' divorce as the final spur to his mother's illness. As he told *Playboy* in 2001: 'My mom worried a lot, and that made her sick. She hid it from us. All of a sudden, she's in the hospital. Then all of a sudden, she's gone.' Typically, tight-lipped James kept the devastating news of his mother's death all to himself. 'We had no idea,' McGovney later recalled. 'He was gone for like ten days and we had thought he went on vacation. When he told us that his mom had just died, we were stunned.' According to her Christian Science beliefs, there had been no funeral for Cynthia, nor any designated grieving period. No time, as James later put it, 'where you're able to cry and get support. It was just: "Okay, the shell is dead, the spirit's gone, and move on in life."'

In Brea, James enrolled at Olinda High School, where he hooked up for a time with an aspiring drummer named Jim Mulligan and yet another guitarist, named Hugh Tanner, who he approached after seeing him carrying a Flying V into school one day. They called the nascent band Phantom Lord, although it never quite got out of the rehearsal stage, mainly due to the fact that they didn't have a bass player. In desperation, James turned to Ron McGovney. Ron had never seen himself as a bass player, didn't even own a bass. But James insisted it would be easy enough and that he'd show him the basic chords. McGovney reluctantly acquiesced, renting a bass from Downey Music Center, and the four-piece began practising together at a garage at Ron's parents' place. This was a shift in scene that also precipitated James suddenly feeling brave enough to move out of his stepbrother's house in Brea and into Ron's place back in Downey, taking a job as a janitor to pay his way – the first of a succession of menial jobs that would occupy him over the next couple of years. 'My parents had a main house with three rental houses in the back,' McGovney says now. 'The property was going to be bulldozed to build a freeway. My parents let James and me live in the middle house rent-free. We converted the garage into our rehearsal studio.' Having left high school, they both had a little money coming in now too. 'I worked at my parents' truck repair shop during the day,' recalls Ron. James, meanwhile, had now gotten a job in 'a sticker factory' called Santa Fe Springs. They used their first month's salaries to insulate the garage against noise, putting up drywall, while James painted the rafters black and the ceiling silver. Along with white walls and red carpet, Phantom Lord suddenly had a space to call their own and build from.

In the final entry in his high school yearbook, under 'plans', Hetfield wrote: 'Play music. Get rich.' As with most young bands, however, Phantom Lord splintered before it had even played a gig, signalled by the departure of Hugh Tanner, a decent guitar player but one who now had his eye on a career in music management. Undeterred, the others simply stuck an ad for a guitarist in the local music free-sheet *The Recycler*. Enter, albeit briefly, Troy James, along with a change in musical direction towards what McGovney describes now as 'a glam thing'. It was still an all-American rock sound, but now leaning more towards the kind of flashy, chorus-heavy mien soon to be popularised by Sunset Strip archetypes like Mötley Crüe and Quiet Riot, both then making names for themselves on the Hollywood club scene, and like-minded, fully made-up British outfits such as Girl (fronted by future Def Leppard guitarist Phil Collen and L.A. Guns frontman Phil Lewis), whose song 'Hollywood Tease' the new band would cover. They even had a new name to go with the new sound: Leather Charm. Hard though it is now to imagine gruff James Hetfield trying to pass himself off as a pouting glam-rock singer, he threw himself wholeheartedly into the new direction, even dropping guitar to concentrate on becoming a full-on frontman. It was also in Leather Charm that Hetfield came up with his first attempts at performing original songs, three of which, in reconfigured form, would eventually be recorded two years later for the first Metallica album: a prototype of 'Hit the Lights', which Ron McGovney later claimed Hugh Tanner came up with most of; and two Charm numbers James had more of a hand in, 'Handsome Ransom' and 'Let's Go Rock 'n' Roll', an improved and much speeded-up amalgam of which later became the Metallica epic, 'No Remorse'.

Once again, however, the new band had only managed a couple of appearances at friends' backyard parties when it fell apart. This time it was Mulligan who jumped first, preferring to take up the offer of a more challenging spot in another local outfit that specialised in Rush covers. At this point Troy James also quit, leaving James and Ron alone again in their silver and black garage. To try and help out, Hugh Tanner told them about an ad he'd seen in *The Recycler*: 'Drummer looking for other metal musicians to jam with. Tygers of Pan Tang, Diamond Head and Iron Maiden'. It was the mention of Iron Maiden that had gotten his attention. None of the Leather Charm guys knew as much about the NWOBHM as Lars Ulrich – who did? But, lately, they had taken to including a version of Maiden's 'Remember Tomorrow' in their set. James and Ron, however, were apathetic about the ad. Nothing had gone right lately, why should this? Hating to see them so down, Hugh offered to reply to the ad himself and set up a meet for them with the guy who'd placed the ad – some kid with a funny accent from Newport Beach called Lars – at a local rehearsal studio he'd booked under the pretext of recording a demo, and which James later claimed they 'stiffed' Lars on the bill for. Ron, never completely convinced about trying to make it as a bass player, was now concentrating more on a possible career as a rock photographer, so didn't even bother to turn up to that first meeting with Lars. Not that it mattered. Neither James nor Hugh had anything good to say about the encounter afterwards. The kid was 'weird' and 'smelled funny'. He couldn't even really play drums. The whole thing was really a waste of time. 'We ate McDonald's, he ate herring', was how James would summarise that first meeting twenty years later. Lars was simply 'from a different world. His father was famous. He was very well off. A rich, only child. Spoiled – that's why he's got his mouth. He knows what he wants, he goes for it and he's gotten it his whole life.'

The ill feeling, however, wasn't entirely mutual. One of the first things Lars did, in fact, after returning home from his summer jaunt to Europe was call up James and invite him round to his house. James acted aloof, like he didn't even remember who Lars was, giving him the 'stay-the-fuck-away-from-me' face. Shrewdly, though, Lars felt James might be less hostile to the notion of forming a 'jam band' with him, overlooking for the time being Lars' obvious drawbacks as a drummer, if he had a better idea of who it was exactly he was dealing with. At the very least they could kick back and play some records together. Sure enough, the first time James visited Lars' parents' house his attitude instantly changed. 'I would spend days just going through Lars' record collection. He introduced me to a lot of different music.' James, who 'could afford maybe one record a week', would be flabbergasted as Lars 'would come back from the store with twenty!' As Lars would later tell me, 'When I came back to America in October of '81 I was kind of energised from hanging out in Europe and then I called up James Hetfield because I thought there was something interesting about him and he seemed like he was pretty into the same stuff I was into.' After such a stale first meeting, though, I wondered what had prompted him to persist with trying to get to know the taciturn would-be frontman. They were obviously quite different as people. 'No shit!' he snorted. 'Absolutely.' What was it then that intrigued Lars enough to try again? Initially, he said, it was because James was the only other person he'd found who might be interested in forming a band that played NWOBHM-type music 'rather than copy Van Halen'. On a deeper level, he sensed something else, too. 'Even though I didn't spend a lot of time rebelling against a lot of things because my parents were too cool to rebel against, I spent a lot of time by myself immersed in the music world. And James spent a lot of time by himself and so on, so the one thing we share, even though we come from two different worlds, and two different cultures, is we are both loners. And in each other we found something that just connected with something deeper.' He went on: 'It was very difficult for me to find anything that I could relate to in Southern California. That's why me and James became such good friends because we both sort of had social issues,' he chuckled self-consciously. 'Of a different kind but ...' He shrugged and looked away.

For James, that connection would not be manifest until later in his relationship with his new buddy, when Metallica began to assume the mantle of 'family' for him. First and foremost, it was simply about the music, he insisted. Yet the first time he went to Lars' parents' house he was deeply impressed by more than just the collection of records. The vibe was so different from his own former family home, where outsiders were rare and then only occasionally made to feel welcome, unless they shared the same religious beliefs, which would be quickly and decisively established. 'I was searching for people that I could identify with,' said James. 'I couldn't really identify too much with my family and, basically, as a child it disintegrated right in front of my eyes. There's a part of me that craves family and another part of me that just can't stand people.' In Lars' house, all were welcome, differences celebrated, individualism prized. And in Lars' bedroom there was a whole wall of records, most by groups James had never even heard of. The next time he visited this Aladdin's cave of NWOBHM treasure, he brought his tape recorder, filling cassette after cassette with the songs of Trespass, Witchfinder General,

Silverwing, Venom, Motörhead, Saxon, Samson ... it seemed never-ending. 'I bombarded James with all this new British stuff,' Lars said, 'and soon he was sold on getting something together that would stand out in the ocean of mediocrity.'

Brian Slagel recalls hooking up with Lars not long after he'd returned from Europe. 'He had a bunch of albums and, you know, I wanted to hear the stories, hanging out with [Diamond Head] and all this other stuff. I was insanely jealous, of course, but it was fascinating that he was able to do it.' Before the trip to Europe 'we were just kind of crazy kids running around. But when [Lars] came back he definitely was a little bit different. You could tell that he was so into being with the band and seeing their lives it gave him much more motivation to try to start [his own] band. That's when he was really practising, playing drums a lot and trying to find people to play with. It really solidified for him after he came back from that trip.' James had also been giving his future a great deal of thought while Lars was away in Europe, coming to the decision that he would continue as he had in Leather Charm, principally as a singer. Now, with only a drummer to jam with, he reluctantly picked up the guitar again. All they lacked initially was a bass player: inevitably, James suggested Ron McGovney, an idea which seemed to make sense to everybody – except for Ron, who didn't fancy the new partnership's chances at all. 'When he and Lars first jammed, I thought Lars was the worst drummer I had ever heard in my life,' Ron would later tell Bob Nalbandian. 'He couldn't keep a beat, and compared to [Leather Charm drummer Jim] Mulligan, he just couldn't play. So I told James, "This guy sucks, dude."' Even after Lars started coming over regularly, Ron remained unconvinced. 'I would watch him and James jam together, and it got better and better but I still didn't feel like getting back into it.'

Still very much the new kid on the block, a high school guy hanging out with older-seeming dudes who held down regular jobs, it would have been easy for the novelty to wear off, to be worn down by the long drive each day after school from Newport Beach to where Hetfield and McGovney lived, where he knew at least one of them didn't rate him at all. But this was Lars Ulrich, and now he'd finally found someone apparently willing to try and make his half-dream come even partly true he wasn't to be thwarted. Besides, he told me, 'after coming back from Europe I was on fuckin fire!' Although he never discussed it, Lars was also determined to prove to his parents that he hadn't made a bad move in dropping the tennis. That he had this music thing all figured out. 'We weren't careerist,' he would insist, years later, but Lars Ulrich never did anything by halves. So when he claimed his 'big hard-on' at that stage merely extended to 'playing fifteen New Wave of British Heavy Metal songs in LA clubs' the fact that he and James would get together 'every day at six' where they 'went for it' like there was no tomorrow shows how determined both kids were to turn these jams into something much more solid and long term. 'Playing those songs was like headbanging taken one step further,' said Lars. An apt description for everything he would attempt to do over the subsequent four decades.

Nevertheless, Brian Slagel remembers Lars being 'pretty frustrated' during this period and that he and James eventually stopped jamming for a while. 'It was going nowhere,' says Slagel. 'It was really hard for Lars because James was the only guy he met who had any sort of understanding of the kind of music that Lars was into. James was into some of the same stuff but they couldn't really find anybody to jam with.' There had been one positive development, however: the discovery of a name for the nascent band Lars and James were putatively putting together – Metallica. This, though, was not something either James or Lars could truly lay claim to. Indeed, the name 'Metallica' had been bandied about by another Anglophile friend of Lars', met through the tape-trading scene: Ron Quintana. Ron had first gotten to know Bob Nalbandian and the crew after getting a letter published in an early issue of *Kerrang!*. Inspired both by *Kerrang!* and the smaller but in his eyes equally impressive success of Brian Slagel's *New Heavy Metal Revue* fanzine, Quintana now looked to start his own like-minded American publication.

Ron Quintana recalls the night he showed Lars a list of names he had come up with as possible titles for his long-dreamed-of 'super heavy metal magazine'. Lars had travelled up to San Francisco to stay with Ron during the lull with James and the two were 'always throwing band and 'zine names around when we would hang out or go to local record stores', Quintana says. Lars had previously shown Ron a list of prospective band names – 'the worst, most generic, Americanised, like, car names. Hot-rod names, trans-am names' – including Red Vette and Black Lightning. In return, Ron showed Lars a list he'd made of possible titles for his new mag, including *Metal Death*, *Metal Mania* and several other of a similar ilk. Also on the list Ron showed Lars was the name *Metallica*. Lars said, 'Oh, that's a cool name.' Then, quick as a flash: 'What are you gonna call your magazine, how about *Metal Mania*?' Ron fell for it. 'I thought it was funny,' Quintana says now, 'because I had started *Metal Mania* in August of '81 and hadn't talked to Lars in at least six months when he called and told me he'd named his band Metallica. I was already on issue number three and happy with the *Metal Mania* name. I didn't even think Lars could play drums at that time!' Plus, he says with a laugh, 'I liked *Metal Mania* as a moniker better than *Metallica*.' Until then Lars and James had compiled a list of over twenty possible names, including Nixon, Helldriver, Blitzer and – an early frontrunner, certainly as far as Lars was concerned – Thunderfuck. Once he'd left Ron's that night with 'Metallica', though, the conversation was closed. Crazy kid all right, funny accent, clever as fuck.

It was through another friend of Lars' that he got his next significant break. Since he'd begun working at Oz Records and running his fanzine, Brian Slagel had been seeing less of Lars, Bob, Patrick and the guys. He was also now helping to promote local metal shows at a small club called The Valley, and had even begun doing a few pieces on the local LA scene for *Sounds*. He was also now doing some work with local radio station KMET – an album-oriented rock station known to its many listeners as The Mighty Met – supplying records via the store for a weekly metal show hosted by DJ Jim Ladd (soon to be famous as the 'fictional DJ' on Roger Waters' 1987 *Radio K.A.O.S.* album and tour, among many other notable cameos he has made on disc and film over the years). The fact that Lars also 'lived so far away' meant Slagel 'didn't really see him as often' any more. All that was about to change, however, when Brian had the idea of putting out his own independently produced compilation album, tentatively titled *The New Heavy Metal Revue Presents ... Metal Massacre.* Inspired by the earlier *Metal for Muthas*, 'What really motivated me,' he says now, 'was the fact that there were actually some good bands playing in LA and nobody knew or cared that they existed.' Bands like another of his faves from those days called Exciter, featuring George Lynch on guitar, who would later find fame with the band Dokken. 'I just loved that band,' says Slagel, 'and nothing ever happened with them – because nobody cared. That really bummed me out.'

A couple of years down the line, seeing the next generation of LA club bands like Mötley Crüe and Ratt, Slagel decided to do something about it. He went to some of the importers he worked with, the guys supplying records for the shop's loyal metal clientele, and told them: 'Hey, if I put together a compilation of local LA metal bands would you guys sell it? And they all said, "Sure." All motivated by what happened with the NWOBHM scene, *Metal for Muthas* and those sorts of compilations. I thought it would be a cool thing to try and put something like that together for here in LA.' At high school Slagel had worked part-time at Sears, a commission job selling typewriters and cameras, from which he'd been able to save a little money to 'go to college at some point'. Now he put every penny of those savings into the *Metal Massacre* album, along with $800 borrowed from a kindly aunt, plus a little from his mother. John Kornarens also put in what he could, in exchange for 'assistant producer' credit. All the bands had to do was volunteer their music. Says Slagel, 'I just went to all the bands and said if you can record something I can put this compilation album out, and they all said, "Sure, why not?" It was kind of the only exposure they were gonna get, you know?' Even then, 'I was barely able to scrape enough money to press twenty-five hundred copies.' The 2,500 albums would cost him 'a little over a dollar a unit, so maybe three or four thousand dollars total'. At a time when regular albums sold for $7.99 in normal stores, *Metal Massacre* would retail for just $5.50. 'They probably cost about a dollar-fifty to make, then probably another fifty cents on top for shipping, then maybe we got three bucks, maybe $3.50 for them, then we had to pay the bands a little bit. So really it wasn't a money-making venture. I didn't really care about that. I just wanted to get exposure for all these bands in LA. I didn't even think about starting a label or anything, this was more an offshoot of the magazine.'

With all the deals done with the bands 'on a handshake deal because we had no money to pay for a lawyer or anything', nothing was put into writing until a recently graduated lawyer named William Berrolm, who happened to have an office on the floor above Oz Records, offered to help Slagel draw up contracts for a cut rate $10 an hour. 'I thought I could probably afford that, maybe. So he ended up doing some contracts and we went back to the bands to get them to sign off on something. He's still our lawyer today,' Slagel adds. (Berrolm would go on to represent artists of the stature of Stevie Ray Vaughan, Garbage, Nirvana producer Butch Vig and 'a ton of big people'.)

When Lars Ulrich got to hear what his buddy Brian Slagel was now up to '[He] just called me up one day and said, "Hey, if I put together a band can I be on your compilation album?" I said, "Sure, no problem, why not?"' The only issue, says Slagel, was that 'Metallica didn't exist, at that point'. Lars and James didn't even get together to jam very often any more 'because they couldn't find anybody else to play with'. But when Lars heard about *Metal Massacre*, he decided he didn't need a band. He just needed James to agree to help record what amounted to a demo tape. Weeks passed, though, before Brian heard any more from Lars. 'I called him up and said we're kind of coming down to the wire here on getting your song on the record, what's the story? He said, "Give me a date and a time when I have to have it and I'll make sure I get it [to you] by that time."' Everything went quiet again until the day came when Slagel and Kornarens were actually at Bijou Studios, mastering the disc. They had all but given up on Lars when suddenly, at around three that afternoon, the door burst open and there stood their crazy little pal with the funny accent – holding a cassette in his hand. Brian laughs as he recalls the scene. 'They recorded the song on this little tiny Fostex recorder, like a little cassette recorder that had like four channels. It wasn't really something you would record to put out. But that's all they could find and afford. They did it basically the night before, just him and James. They had Lloyd Grant, James' guitar teacher, do the lead.'

In order to get the recording onto the finished disc, it first had to be transferred onto a reel-to-reel tape, for which the studio charged $50. More problems. Recalls Slagel: 'Lars doesn't have fifty dollars, *I* don't have fifty dollars. Luckily my friend John had the fifty dollars so he loaned us the fifty bucks so we could get the thing bumped up and mastered and finished.' Brian says he doesn't know if John ever got his fifty back. As Kornarens later recalled: 'Lars suddenly starts to panic and he gets all frantic and he looked over at me and goes, "Dude, have you got fifty bucks?" And, you know, fifty dollars was a lot of money back then. I pull my wallet out and there was fifty-two dollars in there, which was a lot of money for me to be carrying around back in 1982, but I had it, so I gave it to Lars and he says, "You're going to be known as John '50 Bucks' Kornarens on every Metallica release in the future!" Anyway, he made it onto *Metal Massacre.*'

'Hit the Lights', the track Lars and James had recorded together for Slagel's compilation, although credited solely to Hetfield/Ulrich, may well have been, as others now suggest, an old Leather Charm number originally configured by Hugh Tanner. But what the pair did with it under their NWOBHM-influenced guise in Metallica took the song in a wholly new direction, right down to Hetfield's cringe worthy, high-pitched, Diamond Head-style lead vocal. Mostly, though, it was about speed and power, and compared to every other track on *Metal Massacre* – which featured other, ostensibly far more developed groups such as Ratt, Malice and Black 'N Blue, all of whom would later land major record deals – Metallica's 'Hit the Lights' stood out like a sore thumb. Although corny of lyric ('When we start to rock / We never want to stop ... ') and featuring a typically singsong, playground-dumb melody, 'Hit the Lights' exploded from the speakers in a blur of speed and noise, sounding like one long crescendo, making everything else on *Metal Massacre* sound horribly ponderous, irritatingly slow and immediately dated. With Ulrich on drums, Hetfield on guitar, bass and vocals, it also featured a guitar solo by the only other person to appear on the track and another significant bit-part figure in the early Metallica story: a tall, black, Jamaican-born guitarist named Lloyd Grant, who Lars and James had first auditioned for the band some months before. As Grant later recalled, 'I answered an ad in *The Recycler* that read "Heavy Metal Guitarist Wanted for music much heavier than the LA scene".' Likened later by Lars to 'a black Michael Schenker', while Lloyd 'could play leads like a mother-fucker', according to James, he didn't make the cut mainly because 'his rhythm stuff was never very tight'.

James did, however, consider Lloyd good enough to take a few guitar lessons from him. Just hours before Lars was to take in the cassette of 'Hit the Lights' to Brian Slagel, James decided the track could use a little oomph in the shape of a typically blistering Lloyd Grant guitar break. As they only had a four-track recorder – one track each for guitar, bass, drums and vocals – there was no room for overdubs. However, with the end of the song tailing off into nothing-ness, James suggested they 'punch a lead [guitar solo] in on the vocal track'. And so they stopped off at Lloyd's house on their way to Bijou Studio and 'hooked up some little fuckin' amp [through which Lloyd] just ripped through a solo. It was the first take.' As James says, 'It's a fuckin' great solo!' So much so it would survive subsequent re-recordings of the track right up to the first Metallica album a year later.

According to Grant, he already knew the song from his failed audition with the band. '"Hit the Lights" was composed by James and one of his friends. I remember the day I went over to Lars' house, he said, "Check out this song" and he played me "Hit the Lights". We were both into that heavy kind of shit.' When Lars later called Lloyd with the idea of him adding a guitar solo to the recording, Grant agreed, but told him he didn't have time to 'make it over to Ron McGovney's house to do the recording so James and Lars brought the four-track over to my apartment and I did the solo on a little Montgomery Ward amp.' Lars, he added, though 'very easy to get along with', was always 'one hundred per cent intense with the music. He had very strong ideas and opinions.' James, on the other hand, 'was very quiet'.

Although it would be some time before initial pressings of *Metal Massacre* finally became available, in June 1982, now they had a tape to play people, even if it was only of a notional band, Lars and James became re-energised in their pursuit of making Metallica a flesh-and-bones reality. As Brian Slagel says, 'The *Metal Massacre* album made them a band and gave them something to do.' Unlike now, where something like that would have first seen the light of day on a MySpace page, 'At that point, for what it was worth, being on an album meant something to people.' Still unable to persuade Ron McGovney to play the bass, for a short time they recruited 'a dude with black hair' whose name, they say, none of them can now remember, and who didn't really fit the bill but was deemed better than nothing – although only just, apparently, as they ousted him soon afterwards. At this point, James finally wore Ron down. 'My musical contribution to Metallica was very limited,' McGovney says now. Unlike Leather Charm, where Ron had 'felt more of a team vibe with James', in Metallica he simply 'played what James wanted me to play. Sometimes he would take my bass and play the song, and I would just copy what he did.' From the word go, Metallica was always, he says, 'James and Lars' band'. To begin with, he says, 'We played a lot of cover songs, so both of us were just copying others' work.' Even 'Hit the Lights' 'was a Leather Charm song' that James had 'brought with him to Metallica'. Practising in the garage he shared with James, he insists that Metallica was 'just a hobby for me just like dirt bike riding or going to watch bands in Hollywood clubs'.

Where Ron's motivations lay was his business; as far as Lars and James were concerned, as long as he turned up for rehearsals it didn't matter. With an *actual track* about to be released on an *actual album*, this was no longer a time for seeking out the perfect musical partner and far more a case of 'getting the show on the fuckin' road', as Lars put it. Indeed, even James had yet to settle on what he felt would be his long-term role in the band, vacillating between wanting to be a straightforward frontman in the Steven Tyler and Sean Harris mould, and deciding his best bet was actually off to one side, head down, playing rhythm guitar.

Meanwhile, after yet another ad was placed in the *Recycler*, they finally found someone who they decided just might be the answer to their prayers. His name was Dave Mustaine and he was about to help Metallica become a legend, although not entirely in ways any of them could have foretold. 'I answered the phone one day,' McGovney remembered, 'and this guy Dave was on the other end, and he was just spieling this baloney like I could not believe.' Lars: 'I got a call from this guy and he was just so OTT: "I got all this equipment; my own photographer, my own this, my own that." He didn't have a clue what we were talking about musically, but he had enthusiasm. He was pretty quickly turned on, which was cool because everybody else in LA had this career thing – Quiet Riot, Ratt and Mötley Crüe were big bands, and everyone else in Hollywood was doing imitations.' Dave Mustaine had no desire to imitate anybody. He was already his own biggest hero.

Born, as he would tell me, 'at the witching hour' – meaning midnight or 'two minutes after', as he put it – on 13 September 1961, in La Mesa, California, David Scott Mustaine was the classic product of a broken home. The disgruntled son of an alcoholic father, John, and mistreated mother, Emily, Mustaine had grown up messed-up and furious across several different locations in Southern California, with Emily forced to keep moving to escape the abusive attentions of her only son's estranged father. By the time Dave answered the ad in *The Recycler* he lived alone in his own dishevelled apartment in Huntington Beach, from which he routinely sold weed, pot – nothing too heavy but enough of it to keep both himself and his regular customers high. A tall, good-looking guy with a lot of reddish-blonde hair and a lot more attitude, some said he was an asshole. Actually, a lot of people said he was an asshole – and often they were right. But the hard, confrontational exterior masked a highly intelligent young man with an exceptional gift as a guitarist and songwriter. Indeed it might be argued that it was Mustaine's belligerence that supplied his artistic edge: compelling, outspoken, and in his own way, supremely honest. And consequently more than a little bit scary ... If the contrived profanities and vulgar machismo were doomed to overshadow much of the brilliant music he would make throughout his rarely dull career, Mustaine was also responsible for making some of the most innovative heavy metal recordings of his time. And what a time he was destined to have.

James Hetfield, whose own shattered background meant he could relate to any embittered boy from a broken home, felt an immediate connection with his brash new acquaintance. Dave Mustaine felt it, too: 'I think that James and I are very much the same man,' he later reflected. 'I think that we grabbed an angel, split him in half, and both of us are possessing that power.' As time would go on, however, James began to see Dave less as a brother and more as an evil twin. As well as being more adept on guitar than James, he wasn't averse to usurping him onstage, too, sensing James' insecurity and seizing on it to become the frontman, announcing the names of songs, rapping with the audience, even on occasion seemingly trying to outdo James' singing. Until he joined Metallica, Dave had been in a group of unknowns named Panic, with whom he had assembled an impressive array of guitars and amps, something which the eagle-eyed Lars was quick to note, more or less deciding to offer the new guy the gig before they'd heard him play. Equally opportunistic, Mustaine picked up on the vibe immediately and made himself right at home. 'I was [still] tuning up when all the other guys in the band went into another room. They weren't talking to me, so I went in and said, "What the fuck? Am I in the band or not?" and they said, "You've got the gig." I couldn't believe how easy it had been and suggested that we get some beer to celebrate.'

Beer, it transpired, was a must at a Dave Mustaine rehearsal. 'As a kid,' he would later tell me, 'everyone always said that I was going to end up an alcoholic like my father. You see, alcoholism is hereditary, it's in the genes. I just could not drink.' Unfortunately for his career in Metallica, he was some ten years away from discovering that fact. 'In my childhood,' he went on, 'I did martial arts, and then I started getting into dope and thought no one could fuck with me. In reality, if anyone had tried it I would have been destroyed.' Maybe. But that wasn't the impression James and Lars had back in 1982. On top of the drug-dealing and alcoholism, as well as the karate-kicking, confrontational nature of this apparently unstoppable force of ill-intentioned nature, there was also an undisguised suggestion of occult knowledge. It's true, he told me, 'I believe in the supernatural. My elder sister is a white witch. I dicked around with her stuff when I was a kid.' To do what, though? Occult rituals? Invocations? 'I found a "sex hex",' he said nonchalantly, 'and I used it on this girl I had the hots for. She was this cute little babe, looked like Tinkerbell. She didn't want to have anything to do with me. So I did my little hex and the next night she was in my bed.'

Anything else?

'One time I did one on this guy who picked on me when I was going to school. He was enormous. But without going into it too much, I did a chant, basically asking the Prince of Darkness to devastate this fella and stop him messing with me. Later, the guy broke his leg and he can't walk straight now. I stopped messing with witchcraft after that, but it made me feel good at the time. Retribution,' he cackled.

Whatever else he brought to the mix, the arrival into the nascent Metallica line-up of a guitarist of Mustaine's ability brought an immediate leg-up, in terms of the band's own musical self-image. 'Pretty quickly [after Dave joined] things began to happen,' said Lars, 'because of those three words that have worked throughout our career – word of mouth. These outcasts started turning up, people who liked music a little more extreme than that served up by the American music industry. We took the riff structures of AC/DC and Judas Priest and played them at Motörhead tempos. And then we threw in our X-factor – and we don't know what it was. We had this European sound and attitude but we were an American band, and there was no one else in America doing it.'

Interviewed in *Rolling Stone* fifteen years later, Lars would claim he could 'never remember ever thinking about the future much' when

Metallica started. That he was 'always so caught up in the present. Where I come from in Denmark, this whole American thing about goals is not a big thing. You're taught very early on in America that you have to have goals. I never bought into that. We were always real comfortable in the present, in our little world, continuing with blinders on.' Back in 1982, though, the Lars Ulrich everyone knew then that they remember best now was someone who clearly had found his one true path – and wasn't about to dawdle along the way. Diamond Head's Brian Tatler recalls Lars writing to tell him about the new band. 'I've got this classic letter that says: "My band's called Metallica and we rehearse six nights a week and it's going pretty good." I think he says, "The guitarist is pretty fast, you'd like him." He doesn't mention his name but I presume it's Dave Mustaine. This would have been in early '82. And I think he sent a cassette of "It's Electric" to Sean [Harris] because they must have done a demo of that as well [which] we were flattered by – that somebody had bothered to work one of our songs out.' Mustaine, he adds, had 'worked the solo out note-perfect and that was impressive'.

Certainly there was a new focus to the band. Ron recalls him and James coming home from work each day and meeting up with Lars, who still lived at his parents' house but had recently taken a job working behind the till at a gas station to help pay his way in the band, and Dave who had his own apartment and 'was self-employed in "sales", if you know what I mean'. With the four-man line-up now seemingly set in stone, the band ventured forth to play their first gigs, beginning with a shaky set at Radio City, in nearby Anaheim, on 14 March 1982, where the set comprised largely of their three-track demo, plus one other original and a handful of Diamond Head covers posing as originals: 'Helpless', 'Sucking My Love', 'Am I Evil?' and 'The Prince', interspersed with 'Hit the Lights' and their only other original tune 'Jump in the Fire', a new number that Mustaine had brought with him, plus the NWOBHM nuggets: 'Blitzkrieg' by Blitzkrieg, 'Let it Loose' by NWOBHM hopefuls Savage and 'Killing Time' by Irish band Sweet Savage. As Lars later confessed, 'Our trick back then was not to tell people that these songs were covers; we simply let them assume they were ours. We just didn't introduce them, so we never actually laid claim to them, but . . . well, you get the idea.'

At this stage James was still trying to make it work as a guitarless frontman. With Ron sticking mostly to the shadows as he studiously plucked away at the bass lines James had taught him, and Lars gurning furiously at the back, any early showmanship, including song introductions and audience interaction, was conducted by the comfortably voluble Mustaine. 'There were a lot of people there,' James later recalled. 'We had all my school friends and all Lars' and Ron's and Dave's buddies. I was really nervous and a little uncomfortable without a guitar and then during the first song Dave broke a string. It seemed to take him an eternity to change it and I was standing there really embarrassed.' With the exception of the prematurely 'seasoned' Mustaine, none of them had ever played a regular club show before. 'Dave was the only one who really looked comfortable,' says Bob Nalbandian, who was also there. 'You could tell he was used to being up on a stage, he had no fear. The others didn't look like they really knew what they were doing.' Lars' later diary entry for that first gig read: 'Crowd: 75. Pay: $15. Remarks: 1st gig ever. Very nervous. Only band. Dave broke a string on the first song. Played so-so! Went down pretty good.'

More memorable, and impressive, were their second and third ever performances, playing two opening sets for authentic NWOBHM royalty Saxon, at the Whisky a Go Go on Sunset Strip. The band had recorded a three-track home-made demo, featuring a newly recorded 'Hit the Lights' with the new four-man line-up, Sweet Savage's 'Killing Time' and Savage's 'Let it Loose'. When they found out that Saxon was booked to play the Whisky, Ron took a cassette of the demo over to the club, where he happened to bump into Tommy Lee and Vince Neil, drummer and singer, respectively, of then up-and-coming LA glam-metal outfit, Mötley Crüe, who he'd recently taken pictures of. McGovney recalls: 'They said: "Hey Ron, what's up?" I told them that Saxon was doing a gig at the Whisky and I wanted to try to get my band to open up for them. They said, "Yeah, we were gonna open up for them but we're getting too big to open." They offered to take Ron in and introduce him personally 'to the chick that does the booking'. She must have been impressed, either by the tape or the quality of the band's contacts, because she phoned Ron the very next day and told him, 'You guys are pretty good … you remind me of this local band called Black 'N Blue' – another band, coincidentally, on the forthcoming *Metal Massacre* compilation. Says Ron, 'Anyway, she said, "Saxon is scheduled to play two nights; we're gonna have Ratt open for them the first night and your band can open the second night." So we actually have Mötley Crüe to thank for getting us that gig, which was a major break for us back then.'

Brian Slagel, who was at the Saxon show, remembers it well. James, still without a guitar to hide behind and wearing tight leopard-print pants was 'interesting', he notes kindly. 'I mean, they played decently, which was surprising enough. But [James] was so shy and didn't have a whole lot of stage presence. He was playing guitar before that obviously but they wanted him to be like the frontman. There definitely wasn't an amazing amount of confidence. You could tell he was a little intimidated. But they pulled it off pretty well. It easily could have been a train wreck and it was not. But [James] felt so uncomfortable up there that I think that's why he immediately started to play guitar [onstage] afterwards because he felt more comfortable having something else to do, other than just trying to sing.'

In keeping with the astonishingly rapid rise the band was about to experience, they also got their first mainstream review for the Saxon shows, in no lesser an organ than the *LA Times*, where music critic Terry Atkinson nailed them when he wrote: 'Saxon could also use a fast, hot guitar player of the Eddie Van Halen ilk. Opening quartet Metallica had one [in Dave Mustaine], but little else. The local group needs considerable development to overcome a pervasive awkwardness.' In his gig diary, Lars smugly noted that the band got paid a dollar more than their first gig, adding immodestly: 'Great sound this time. Dave and me played great. Ron and James so-so. Went down pretty good. Had a good time but never met Saxon.'

'Of course,' says Brian Slagel, 'John [Kornarens] and I were probably the only two people there that knew what [songs] they were playing. Everybody else just thought they were playing originals.' Everybody, that is, with the exception of Saxon singer Biff Byford, who watched them from the side of the stage with his mouth open. 'Apparently, Biff was like, "What? *What?* Why are they doing Diamond Head songs?",' recalls Brian Tatler. It wouldn't be for long. By the time Metallica were ready for a return appearance at Radio City in early June, they had added two more original numbers to their set and recorded the first in a short series of what even then were considered groundbreaking demos, beginning in April with the four-track *Power Metal* collection: a round-up of their first four original numbers, with 'Hit the Lights' and 'Jump in the Fire' now joined by another new Mustaine-driven epic, 'The Mechanix' and Hetfield's 'Motorbreath'. Later rerecorded for the now legendary *No Life 'til Leather* demo, what's interesting now about the earlier *Power Metal* demo is the way it captures the band before it had settled into its essential musical shape. James, in particular, sounds very different from the growling bad-ass he would soon portray himself as, holding the notes on the chorus of 'Jump in the Fire', for example, very much in the style of Diamond Head's Sean Harris, though with considerably less finesse.

'He later figured that he didn't sound like Sean Harris so he decided to sing gruffer,' recalled Ron McGovney, who had inadvertently given the demo its title when he took it upon himself to have some Metallica business cards made up to send to possible gig promoters. 'The card was supposed to just have the Metallica logo and a contact number. But I thought it looked too plain and decided it should say something under the logo. I didn't want to put "hard rock" or "heavy metal", so I coined the term "power metal"; I thought it had a nice ring to it. No band had used that term before as far as I knew.' When he proudly displayed the new cards for Lars, though, the drummer was aghast. 'He said, "What did you do? What the hell is power metal? I can't believe you did such a stupid thing! We can't use these cards with the words power metal on them!"' James and Dave saw the funny side, however, and sarcastically dubbed their first recording together 'the power metal demo'. Everything, though, was still in such a touch-and-go state that no one member could afford to laugh long at any other. Hetfield, in particular, was still suffering a massive crisis of confidence over his role in the band. When they landed a gig at the Convert Factory in Costa Mesa, on 23 April, they actually appeared as a five-piece: James was still out front as singer, but now there was a second rhythm guitarist, Brad Parker (stage name: Damian C. Phillips) to help beef up the sound. But as Ron recalled: 'While [the rest of the band] are getting dressed to go on stage, we hear this guitar solo so we look over the railing of the dressing room and we see Brad on stage just blazing away on his guitar. So that was Metallica's first and last gig with Damian C. Phillips. Later I think he went on to join Odin.'

It was enough to convince both Mustaine and Hetfield that no one else should be allowed to play guitar in the band. But if James was going to concentrate on rhythm guitar, he argued, they should get a 'real' singer in. It wasn't just his voice he was insecure about. Plagued by severe acne throughout his teens and early twenties, James had grown so painfully self-conscious of his looks that he avoided mirrors, felt uncomfortable around pretty girls and, most lastingly, erected a huge barrier behind which he hid, disguising his minutely sensitive feelings in a cloak of monosyllables and withering glances. Being asked to stand in front of a group as musically confrontational as Metallica, he admitted he didn't know if he could do that. After a show at Lars' old high school on 25 May with James trying to sing and play guitar – a disastrous showing which saw them performing to a virtually empty hall – the others acquiesced. Enter yet another short-lived hopeful: Jeff Warner. Again, just for one gig: back at the Convert Factory.

There was an even more brief dalliance with a singer named Sammy Dijon, from another local outfit called Ruthless. 'Sammy was a good singer,' said Ron, 'just not Metallica-style.'

They were still deep in discussion about the best way forward for James and the group when *Metal Massacre* was finally released on 14 June 1982. Although the conversation would continue, off and on, right up to the band's second album, the idea of bringing in some new guy to front the band increasingly seemed off-point. They were now a band with a track on an actual album – and James was the singer of that song. Still unconvinced, James agreed at least to continue in the role for the time being. Dave and Ron, meanwhile, were determined to ensure they too would make their presences felt the next time the band got anywhere within earshot of a recording situation. They had the *Metal Massacre* album to swan around with and show off to people, along with their name, right there on the back cover: misspelled as 'Mettallica'. Lars was on the phone to Brian Slagel about that within thirty seconds of spotting the mistake ...

THREE
LEATHER ON YOUR LIPS

One of those nights, 1986, I'm home and I'm high, me and my girlie, when the phone rings – again. Jaded, I pick it up. Pips. Someone calling from a phone box.

'Hey, Mick! It's Lars!'

A pause while I mentally shuffle through the deck for a face to go with the name.

'. . . from Metallica!'

Oh . . . yeah, Lars. How did he get my number?

'Hey, Lars. How ya doing?'

'Yeah, great . . .'

There follows the usual lengthy exposition in which I get to hear just how great he and his band are doing. There are shows that have been 'awesome'. There are people that have been 'fucking assholes' or, more often, 'great fucking guys'. There are beers that have been drunk and furniture that's fallen over and been flung out the window, laughs every-where, the party never-ending, inescapable. In the background as he rants in his mangled Danish-American accent, the unmistakable sound of a pub in full swing.

And then he gets to the point. 'Listen, I was thinking, I don't have anywhere to stay tonight . . .'

This, I know, is a lie, or an untruth. Everybody knows that whenever Lars is in London these days he stays at his new manager's posh house. But he wants something and I can already guess what it is.

'Listen, I was thinking, maybe I could come over to your place, maybe crash on the couch?'

Shit, no. Not tonight. I've only just pulled up the drawbridge. But it's hard to get a word in edgeways . . .

'. . . we could get some beers, maybe, hang out . . . whaddayasay?'

I look over at the girlie but she mouths the word 'no'. She has made the mistake of shrugging and saying 'yes' too many times before.

'. . . or maybe we could catch a gig. What's on tonight, do you know? I could meet you in Wardour Street, at The Ship. As a matter of fact, I'm there now . . .'

Finally – finally – I spot an opening and dive in with some half-hearted bit of spiel about needing to get a story finished and maybe next week or some other time perhaps, 'cos let's face it there will always be another time for someone like Lars.

'What?' he says, not buying any of it. 'You don't want me to come over?'

'No,' I say, 'of course I want you to come over. That would be great. It's just . . .'

'Oh, man! But I don't have anywhere to stay.'

'I thought you were staying at Peter's,' I say.

'Well, yeah,' he says, 'but it's so fucking boring. I need to get out, have some beers, tear it up. Come on, whaddayasay?'

The pips start to go again and so he goes to throw some more money in. But I get there first. 'Listen,' I say, 'I really can't tonight. Good hearing from you though, man. Next time . . .'

'Okay,' *he says, utterly unconvinced. And then the line goes dead. Phew. That was close. I mean, nice kid, means well, never shuts the fuck up though. I flop back down on the couch, roll one and try to forget about it . . .*

Released in June 1982, the arrival of the first limited-edition copies of Brian Slagel's epochal *Metal Massacre* album changed everything for Lars Ulrich and James Hetfield. Before it, they were two teenagers with the bare bones of an idea for a rock group. After it, they were this entity, something to be reckoned with, something called Metallica – or, rather, 'Mettallica', as they appeared on the original album sleeve and label. Lars and James didn't know whether to laugh or cry. A dream come true, yet somehow just a little bit spoiled. Lars bit his lip and accepted Brian's apologies. James said nothing, just fumed. 'They understood,' Slagel insists now. 'They were not happy about it, for sure. [But] everything they delivered was late and the typesetter made the mistake. There was no way to check it before it went to press. I was furious! We changed it of course on all other versions [and] I apologised over and over to the band. As I said they were pretty cool about it, all things considered. I think it all worked out in the end for them,' he adds dryly.

At least the existence of *Metal Massacre* gave the nascent Metallica line-up impetus. Moreover, it demonstrated something to Lars and James they had not known before: that they were actually good. It was as if the fact that they didn't yet exist outside the fevered imaginations of Ulrich and Hetfield had enabled them somehow to be more than the meagre sum of their parts. Yet to be discouraged by poorly attended gigs or a string of rejection slips from disinterested music-biz figures, they just blast it out, as sure-footed as two guys virtually miming in front of their bedroom mirrors can be. Three weeks after the release of *Metal Massacre*, the band thought they had really cracked it when they went in to an eight-track studio in Tustin called Chateau East, where they recorded what they were convinced would actually become their first stand-alone release, following another typically brusque Lars Ulrich challenge to a more established local independent label owner. Unlike Brian Slagel, though, the owner was a punk aficionado – a genre still then diametrically opposed to heavy metal – and this time Lars' bluff appeared to backfire.

'[The guy] was a real snake in the grass,' Ron McGovney would later recall. 'He had this punk label, which was a division of an Orange County record company. He said he would put up the money to have us do an EP.' But after hearing the seven tracks they came up with – comprised, essentially, of every original tune the four-man line-up had so far bolted together – he claimed to be appalled that the band had duped him into thinking they were a punk outfit and refused to release any of it. Ever resourceful, Lars suggested the band simply take the tracks and distribute them as a 'limited edition' cassette tape entitled *No Life 'til Leather* (taken from the opening line of 'Hit the Lights', and inspired by Motörhead's live album *No Sleep 'til Hammersmith*, which had been Number One in the UK charts the summer Lars was there). Along with its own makeshift sleeve with liner notes written by Lars, plus tracklisting and band logo, you wouldn't be able to buy it in the stores, in the way you could buy *Metal Massacre*, but it would burn a hole in the tape-trading scene, Lars rightly reasoned, which is exactly what it did. In fact, the seven tracks on *No Life 'til Leather* – 'The Mechanix', 'Phantom Lord', 'Jump in the Fire' and 'Metal Militia', all of which would be credited to Hetfield, Ulrich and Mustaine, but which Mustaine would later claim he had essentially written the bulk of alone, plus 'Motorbreath', another arrangement left over from Hetfield's days working with Hugh Tanner but which would now be credited solely to James, 'Seek and Destroy', by James and Lars, and in no small measure 'inspired' by Diamond Head's 'Dead Reckoning' (a track released earlier that year), plus a new version of 'Hit the Lights', this time featuring both Mustaine and McGovney (although they cannily over-dubbed onto it the original Lloyd Grant solo, too) – did everything for the band an official EP might have done, except garner reviews in the mainstream rock press. But it made up for that by the sheer force of its word-of-mouth following, something Lars understood only too well through his own avidness for obscure, hard-to-find NWOBHM releases.

Patrick Scott was enlisted to help send out copies of *No Life*. 'I was actually really the only person mailing them out,' he says now. 'It was a little bit selfish [of Lars] but it was helping a friend, too. I had these pen-pals like Metal Mike from *Aardshok*, and Bernard Doe [at *Metal Forces*], and some other pen-pals ... I would just send them demos and T-shirts then they'd send me stuff back ... But they were just going nuts over Metallica, even in countries where we thought the cool bands were, they thought Metallica was the coolest band. Not in LA but everywhere else, from other states in the US, to Japan and Sweden and England ... it was a fun time, running to the mailbox every day. Lars just kept giving me stuff to send out. He knew what he was doing.' Lars would never claim to have masterminded any particular strategy, at least not at this stage, but he understood how getting their music out this way fitted Metallica's developing profile in all sorts of useful ways. Although they would grow with the years into a much more inclusive club, the original music and mien of Metallica was quintessentially the sound of outsiders, positioned so far beyond the borders of the mainstream that they wouldn't even bother trying to force their way in; an approach so utterly at odds with the prevailing crowd-pleasing LA attitude that it appeared to make no sense at all to most of the people they performed to at the various Hollywood clubs they were now beginning to play on a semi-frequent basis.

Soon, cassettes of *No Life 'til Leather* were circulating all over Los Angeles, San Francisco, New York, London, Birmingham and Copenhagen. Band operations still centred on Ron's parents' bungalow – with Ron more often than not personally funding those activities, as he was the only one with an active credit card – but it was the start of Lars taking over the business side of the operation in terms of band profile and promotion. As he boasted to *Rolling Stone* years later, conveniently omitting the role played by Scott and others, 'I was the one who went out and bought all the tapes. I was the one who sat down and copied them. I was the one who sent them out to people. That's where it started. Somebody had to do it.' Although they did also send tapes to various record companies, that side of it 'was never that serious', insisted Lars. 'All we wanted to do was send it out to the traders, get mentioned in some fanzines.' Typical of the reaction among the tape-trading fraternity was that of future Metallica fan club chief K.J. Doughton, who also received a tape from Scott. 'After hearing the demo, I freaked out. Metallica had a distinctly European slant to their music, at a time when most US bands were light alloy at best. There were heavy Yank bands like Y&T, Riot, and The Rods, but Metallica took on the big, biblical, slash-and-burn, good-versus-evil issues. No party music. No girl-magnet ballads. Just brutal, attack-oriented audio death.' Says Scott, 'They were what we were all looking for.' He recalls playing the tape down the phone for Ron Quintana. 'I called him one day and played him "Hit the Lights" and he was like, "Oh my god!" He was just going crazy over it.' When Quintana realised it was Lars Ulrich's new band he was listening to, he 'couldn't believe it'. Says Ron now, 'None of our friends were in popular bands so I never expected a little metal mad rocker like Lars would ever be in a big band! He talked a good game, but I never heard him play till mid-'82 on tape and LP and live till later.' When Quintana then asked Scott to write an article on Metallica for *Metal Mania*, Patrick told Lars and they sat down and wrote it together. 'This was like top secret back then,' Patrick says. 'We sat in [Lars'] bedroom and he was like, "You can't tell anybody!" We were just laughing, saying these things which seemed ridiculous, like the famous line: "potential to become US metal gods".' As a reward, Lars gave Patrick a rare copy of *1980*, the one and only album by Danish punk-metal progenitors Brats, the band guitarist Hank Shermann had before he joined Mercyful Fate. 'I didn't ask for that but [Lars] had two copies. I still have that. But I sent the article to Ron and it got into *Metal Mania*.'

Musically, Metallica's influences were obvious to anyone then acquainted with the NWOBHM scene – which most American fans weren't. Mixed in with obvious touchstones such as Diamond Head and Motörhead, though, were more obscure traces, including hardcore British and American punk. Hanging out after rehearsals, they would mix their Motörhead and Angel°Witch records with new releases from the Ramones, Discharge and the Anti-Nowhere League, 'and no one flinched', said James. 'It all belonged together. It was aggressive, it had guitars. It felt good. Discharge's guitarist Bones was pulling off some serious metal riffs.' Patrick Scott recalls introducing James and Lars to Accept's *Restless and Wild* album, in particular the track 'Fast as a Shark'. 'They were a little bummed, like, "Somebody beat us to it!" They wanted to take all this stuff they loved and bring it to another level. Mainly Lars. He knew what he liked and what he didn't like. He wanted to be like them but he wanted to take it a step further and combine Motörhead with the NWOBHM bands. Heavier, faster.' It was also Patrick who first played them Mercyful Fate. James would play 'Curse of the Pharaohs' to get his guitar tone down. They loved Mercyful Fate ... they were a big influence on Metallica, as far as an approach to be progressive with time-changes and putting just riffs in. They didn't want chord progressions, they wanted *riffs*. That was the big thing. Ten riffs in one song you could make ten songs out of.'

The common thread running through all their listening habits back then – certainly the ones that were influencing their own writing – were speed, power and aggression. The first time Lars brought in a copy of Venom's *Welcome to Hell* album – the original self-styled 'black metal' release – it had a huge impact, says Ron McGovney, although not necessarily in the same way for him. 'The other guys loved Venom. I thought they sucked.' He concedes, though, 'I guess the speed of the songs may have been an influence.' Not just the speed but their fiercely uncompromising, entirely antisocial tenor, exemplified in songs such as 'Sons of Satan', 'One Thousand Days of Sodom' and 'Angel Dust'. A trio from Newcastle formed in the late 1970s and similar to Metallica in that they had a burning desire to take the influence of Motörhead, Judas Priest and Black Sabbath and essentially speed it up, by 1982 and the release of their second album, *Black Metal*, Venom's frenzied shows were attracting a frightening mix of headbangers, bikers, punks and skinheads. Combining 'the big pyro show' of Kiss with 'the satanic lyrics' of Black Sabbath, as their bassist, vocalist and lead songwriter Conrad Lant, a.k.a. Cronos, explained in 2009, Venom's credo was bite-size simple yet shockingly effective: 'Metal is the devil's music, let's make it as aggressive as we possibly can.' The extra twist: where Sabbath-era Ozzy Osbourne was always being 'a tormented soul chased by demons ... Venom wanted to *be* the demon'. The impact of Venom was such that it would help a whole new genre of rock to evolve in the USA; one which Metallica would be credited for inventing, though, as Lars says now, the real credit lies with the melting pot he and his bandmates were beginning to stir up together. 'A band like Venom had a lot to answer for. Because there were a lot of the songs on their first record that were very fast. Then you say Venom, then okay maybe throw a little Discharge in there, then you throw a little GBH in there. All of a sudden you got a little bit of punk, a little bit of metal, a little bit of Motörhead, who sort of had one foot in each world, then you add the American X-factor – and there you have thrash!'

While the formula may have been as straightforward as Lars suggests, the long-term effect was something not even he could have predicted. As such, the arrival of Metallica, and with them this new phenomenon called 'thrash metal', was a watershed moment in rock history: the end of heavy metal as it had become, post-punk – either lugubrious rhythms dredged from a river setting the scene for jiggery-pokery lyrics about Satan and his followers, or self-conscious anthems full of whinnying guitars and blow-dried vocals – and the beginning of a whole new thing that began by offering an alternative to the staid old ways and ended up replacing them. Thrash discarded those clichéd images of heavy metal as readily as punk, but kept the muscle and musicianship. Punk was about singles; thrash about albums. After that the two had more in common than not; dressed down in street clothes, determinedly proletariat, its appeal lying far beyond the remit of the pop or rock mainstream. Compared to anyone who had gone before, Metallica were closest to Motörhead in terms of stripping back rock to its most vital components. But there was a comic aspect to Lemmy and his man-boys, a knowing wink, a glint of the gold tooth that Metallica did not share. Lars and his guys were far more earnest in their musical endeavours, dressed head to foot in black, building their songs into musical movements before they could barely play their instruments. Metallica was a more purist experience and to be a thrash fan meant taking the music to a far more serious level: closer to the deep emotional abyss of *Dark Side*-era Pink Floyd or the self-absorbed self-righteousness of the early Clash. Not quite as bleak as Joy Division, but then Joy Division didn't come from sunny southern California where the light is so bright it bleaches the shadows. So while Metallica, and with them the template for thrash, would include some of the old-school rock trappings – show-stopping drum displays, cartwheeling solos on a Flying V, even the occasional power ballad – regular rock fans instantly recognised them and it for what they were: something new, something different, something less instantly likeable but perhaps more ultimately meaningful. In time, thrash would become successfully commodified and labelled – it was something to do with skateboarders, something to do with classic *Marvel* comic books, something to do with smoking pot, with taking speed, with hellacious beer drinking, something to do with tattoos and piercings and dirty white sneakers – but originally it had nothing to do with any of those things. It was simply about the obsession of a failed teenage tennis protégé with the early 1980s new wave of British metal, and the fact that Metallica was quintessentially American. Ten years earlier Lars would have been just as happy drumming in a Deep Purple-style band. Ten years later he'd have been in his element in a Soundgarden or an Alice In Chains. It just so happened that in 1982, when he formed his first – and last – band, the music they set out to play was still so unheard of, so unlikely, he ended up inventing a whole new genre on his own. As he later told me, 'We didn't call it thrash; we'd never even heard the term till we started reading about it in British magazines like *Kerrang!*. It was like, we're thrash metal? Okay, it sounded cool ...'

The term 'thrash metal' was still some way off from entering the lingua franca of international rock just yet, though. In the meantime, Metallica continued to plough a lonely furrow. 'Played like shit!' Lars would note in his gig diary after another half-empty show at Radio City in June, 'Went down so-so.' At the Troubadour in July they went on so late 'everybody had gone home', he recalled, while a show at the Whisky in August, where they 'started at 9.15 with no one around' was commemorated with one word in block caps: 'SHIT!' Looking back on those days nearly twenty years later in an interview for *Playboy*, James would recall how he and Lars simply 'liked a kind of music that was not accepted, especially in Los Angeles. We were fast and heavy. Everything about LA was short, catchy songs: Mötley Crüe, Ratt, Van Halen. And you had to have the look. The only look we had was ugly.' In fact, photos of the band in its earliest guise show them demonstrably trying to fit in with the prevailing trends while reaching out for something of their own true identity. As the writer Xavier Russell, an early champion of the band in the UK rock press, puts it, 'It was Ratt and Mötley Crüe from the waist down, black spandex and bullet belts. Then on top they'd wear Motörhead T-shirts or Saxon.' Their very first line-up shot has James dressed in billowing white shirt and tight jeans, a Motörhead-style bullet belt around his hips; Dave and Ron in much the same get up, although Dave also sports a waistcoat over his white shirt, while Ron favours a Motörhead T-shirt; and Lars, most wince-inducing of all, in what appears to be an early Metallica T-shirt but with an overshirt tied, girly-fashion, around his ribs. They all have long, blow-dried hair. At many of their earliest shows both James and Dave wore white, striped spandex pants – a look inspired by Biff Byford of Saxon. 'We had our battles with spandex,' James grudgingly admitted in *Playboy*. 'You could show off your package. "Wear spandex, dude. It gets you chicks!"'

It wasn't until halfway through the first Metallica US tour a year later, in fact, that James finally ditched the spandex, after his one and only pair of pants caught fire while he was drying them next to a heater. 'A hole melted right in the crotch. It was like, "They're not real pants, are they? They're like pantyhose."' After that, he stuck to jeans. Even their occasional good gigs left a bitter taste. The first time they got an encore, James recalled, 'It was a Monday night at two in the morning at the Troubadour and there were about ten people there.' Then, having decided what they were going to do for their first encore – 'Let it Loose' by Savage – Lars arbitrarily struck up the beat to an entirely different number, 'Killing Time' by Sweet Savage, 'because it started with drums'. James, who had forgotten the lyrics, was so furious that when the number finally came to its calamitous conclusion he walked over and screamed, 'You fucker!' at Lars, then punched him hard in the stomach. 'People were going, "Huh?"'

Metal Massacre quickly sold all 2,500 copies of its initial pressing, mainly thanks to Slagel's work at Oz Records, where the store's main independent distributors – Gem, Important and Green World – 'bought them all right away. In fact, about a month later they wanted more.' After a short-lived manufacturing and distribution deal with a small fly-by-night operation called Metalworks, which pressed up a few thousand copies but which Slagel says he was 'never paid a dime for – it was kind of a whole nightmare', Slagel negotiated his own distribution deal with Green World, later known as Enigma. It was through Green World that his Metal Blade label would blossom into an actual record company, rereleasing the original *Metal Massacre* album – the new pressing of which would also replace the original Metallica four-track with the new, eight-track version on *No Life 'til Leather* – and putting together a follow-up release, *Metal Massacre II*. From there it was a short step to releasing stand-alone records by single artists. 'I was a one-man record company,' Slagel says now, 'involved in the recording of it, the mastering of it, I did all of the artwork, did all of the promotion ... kind of everything.' Early Metal Blade releases included albums by other original *Metal Massacre* artists, Bitch and Demon Flight, followed by EPs from newer names such as Armored Saint and Warlord, both of whom would first be heard on *Metal Massacre II*. The fledgling label really hit pay dirt, however, in 1983, with the debut album from Slayer, *Show No Mercy*. Although Slagel admits he 'didn't really see a big connection at first' between Slayer's gargantuan rhythms and Metallica's sheet-metal riffs, Slayer would go on to become one of what is now regarded as the Big Four of thrash metal, and the only really serious rivals to Metallica's crown as 'inventors' of thrash, a claim that would grow in credulity as the years passed. Unlike Metallica, who would move early to broaden their musical horizons (and audience), Slayer refused to soften their approach or seek mainstream approval; the earnest, faith-keeping Clash to Metallica's more maverick, rule-breaking Sex Pistols.

Suitably encouraged, in September 1982 Brian Slagel decided to put on a dedicated Metal Massacre show in San Francisco, at a small club called the Stone. Nearly two hundred people showed up, the largest crowd most of the bands on the bill had ever played to. Metallica, who were the big hit on the night, had only been added to the bill as an afterthought. 'The bill was going to be Bitch, Cirith Ungol and

I can't remember who the third band was going to be,' says Slagel. When Cirith Ungol was forced to pull out at the last minute, 'I called Lars and asked if Metallica would like to do it, no money but a gig.' Typically, Lars agreed – then worried later about how they would actually get to San Francisco. It was to prove a wise decision that would have far-reaching consequences. As Lars observed in his gig diary, it was Metallica's 'First real great gig. Real bangers, real fans, real encores. Had a great fuckin' weekend. Fucked up a lot onstage!' Certainly, they weren't note-perfect, says Slagel, but the band was slowly starting to hit its stride, encouraged by the very different response their music received in San Francisco. Unknown even to Lars, the *No Life 'til Leather* demo had been a hit on the underground scene in San Francisco, thanks in no small part to the proselytising in Ron Quintana's *Metal Mania* fanzine. At the show, they were amazed to hear the audience actually singing some of the lyrics to the songs. Afterwards, some even asked for autographs! 'It was a trip,' says Ron McGovney, 'we couldn't believe it.'

They were also starting to write new material that reflected their improved status as a gigging band. Added to the seven *No Life 'til Leather* tracks, all of which they performed at the Stone, was another new number recently worked up in Ron's bungalow: 'No Remorse' – a tour de force built around at least three different riffs, dating back to James' pre-Metallica days, any of which would have been catchy enough to build a whole song around, but subjugated here to a greater sonic whole, laced with Mustaine's enflamed guitar solos and propelled by Lars' stop-start drums, before suddenly taking off into yet another, entirely different section, lightning-fast, the number climaxing with a bomb-blast finale. It would become the template for what would become the trademark Metallica sound in their earliest, groundbreaking years. Not that the band was ready yet to stray far from its roots. The encores were two Diamond Head songs, 'Am I Evil?' and 'The Prince', both of which were now sounding more like trademark Metallica numbers and less like covers – a line the band was still happy to blur.

The most significant outcome of the Stone show, though, was the reaction of the crowd. 'It was our first encounter with real fans,' said James. 'It was like, these people are here for us, and they like us, and they hate the other bands – and we like that 'cos we hate them too.' Says Brian Slagel, 'In LA [Metallica] were kind of looked at like a black-sheep band because they were way too heavy compared to what the other bands were doing at this point. Even Mötley and Ratt were getting more commercial and that's kind of where the scene was going. So they didn't go down so well. But when they came up to San Francisco that night, all of a sudden they have all these kids there that went *crazy* for them. Just *loved* them and loved what they were doing. It was really amazing. I was like, holy shit! Even the band was like, wow, we never saw that coming!' Eager to keep that good feeling going, the band booked a follow-up show in San Francisco, at the Old Waldorf, for October. It was only a Monday night – the deadest night of the week – but they played it like a Saturday night. They didn't even bother with the safety net of the Diamond Head covers this time, just went out and blasted through the *No Life 'til Leather* demo plus 'No Remorse'. Again, 'the people went nuts', Ron recalled. Among them was Gary Holt, guitarist in local San Francisco outfit Exodus, who would open for Metallica at a November show at the Old Waldorf – later immortalised on another officially sanctioned live tape for the traders to play with, dubbed *Metal up Your Ass*. He recalls that 'they were great but they were really sloppy. Lars could barely play his drums and they were really drunk onstage. But they had this raw punk energy.' Such was their growing reputation in San Francisco the band even took out an ad in local music free sheet, *BAM* (Bay Area Music). It cost $600, a great deal of money to shell out for an otherwise penniless unsigned band in 1982. Fortunately, they had good old Ron to pay for it – again. 'It was probably Lars' and James' idea,' said Ron. 'They laid the ad out and showed it to me and said it will cost $600. I said, "Okay, Lars ... James, where's your money?" and they said, "We don't have any money." I was the only one that had any money, so I wrote out a cheque for $600 to *BAM*. Till this day I never got that money back.'

. The only real fly in the ointment was the increasingly hard to handle Dave Mustaine. Slagel recalls the guitarist coming up at the first Stone show and telling him, 'You're gonna hear something from somebody that's not true.' Explains Slagel, 'Apparently what had happened was they had gone through all the beer that the promoter had given them and they wanted more beer. And the promoter I guess didn't feel he should give them more beer or wasn't giving them the beer quick enough. So Dave just went behind the bar and grabbed a case of Heineken and took it backstage and they drank it. When the promoter found out about it he got upset and decided not to pay them the hundred bucks [fee] and it became this big thing. I'm like, oh boy. But it was a classic Dave Mustaine moment in the early days.' Indeed, Mustaine's overbearing personality and wayward behaviour – not helped by his daily over-consumption of weed and alcohol – had been causing the band problems almost from the start. Ron, in particular, found the grating, confrontational Mustaine distinctly at odds with his own more steady, even-keel personality. Ron was the one who rented a trailer so they could load the drum riser and all their other gear and have it towed up to San Francisco in his father's 1969 Ford Ranger. Ron, who had never been to San Francisco before and found himself driving around Chinatown trying to find the club while the other three were 'back there in the camper shell drinking and partying, and I'm just pissed [off]'.

Dave was the one who dealt pot, stole beer and did all the talking onstage, acting like he was the leader of the band, not the newbie. That also made Ron 'pissed as shit'. There had already been several flashpoints between the two before the trip to San Francisco, like the Sunday afternoon James actually fired Dave from the band – before allowing the contrite guitar player to talk his way back in. Mustaine had turned up at the bungalow Ron shared with James with 'his two pit bull puppies'. Ron, who'd been taking a shower when Dave arrived, was aghast to discover when he came out that the dogs were 'jumping all over my car' – a reconfigured 1972 Pontiac LeMans – 'scratching the shit out of it'. Ron recalls James running outside and yelling, 'Hey, Dave, get those fuckin' dogs off of Ron's car!' According to Ron, Dave yelled back: 'What the fuck did you say? Don't you talk that way about my dogs!' The two men flew at each other and a nasty brawl ensued. According to Ron, 'They started fighting and it spilled into the house. I see Dave punch James right across the mouth and he flies across the room, so I jumped on Dave's back and he flipped me over onto the coffee table.' At which point James got to his feet and told Dave, 'You're out of the fuckin' band! Get the fuck out of here!' Says Ron, 'Dave loaded all his shit up and left all pissed off. The next day he comes back crying, pleading, "Please let me back in the band,"' which, to Ron's chagrin, James and Lars, not thrilled at the prospect of having to find yet another guitar player, eventually – after more from Mustaine – agreed to do.

Speaking with writer Joel McIver, in 1999, Mustaine recalled the incident with some regret, regarding it as the first nail in the coffin of his career in Metallica. 'If I had to do it all again,' he said, 'I wouldn't have brought the dog[s]. I was dealing drugs to keep myself afloat, so I had these dogs to protect my merchandise. I took them up to rehearsal one day and [one of] the dog[s] put her paws on the bass player's car. I don't know if it scratched it or left paw prints on it, or put a fuckin' dent in the car, I don't know. Whatever happened, James kicked it, we started arguing, push led to shove and I hit him. And I regret it ...' Only Lars, who was equally outgoing, for different reasons, really enjoyed Dave's company. It might be argued, in fact, that Dave Mustaine was the missing link between Lars Ulrich's ultra-confident, says-me personality and James Hetfield's stone-faced, emotionally fragile character. In common with the latter, Mustaine was a young Los Angelino who had come from a badly broken home. But where James had erected an impenetrable, monosyllabic façade to shield him from the world, Mustaine met everything head-on, ready to out-gun all comers with his fast guitar and even faster mouth and fists. Like James, Dave had an inordinate fondness for Clint Eastwood movies, particularly *The Good, the Bad and the Ugly*. Unlike James, he had an absurdist streak that meant he also loved the Pink Panther films. Meanwhile, like Lars, Dave's musical influences were broad-shouldered enough to encompass both The Beatles and Led Zeppelin, before similarly falling for the New Wave of British Heavy Metal, although in Dave's case as much as a reactionary fuck-you to the existing LA scene as for any musical merit; his tastes veering more towards the less boxed-in, more technically able end of the spectrum where Diamond Head and Judas Priest existed than the purely heavy-legged likes of Saxon or Samson. 'Motörhead, Mercyful Fate, Budgie and AC/DC' had 'all added' to his musical education, he said. 'After that, I was pretty much done.'

Lars also appreciated that Dave could be a useful guy to have around when things got out of hand in other ways. Getting shit-faced at a party with East LA metal newbies Armored Saint, Lars' big mouth got him into trouble with Saint guitarist Phil Sandoval. When Sandoval shoved Ulrich to the floor, Mustaine, never backwards at coming forwards, launched a karate kick at Sandoval which poleaxed him and resulted in a broken ankle. Years later, after Mustaine finally straightened up he sought Sandoval out and apologised, bringing him a gift of a brand new ESP guitar, in order to bring what the newly sober Mustaine referred to in counselling-speak as 'closure' to the incident. Dave had just been watching Lars' back, he explained. Sandoval understood. All little guys need a big guy to do that for them, right? Especially when the little guy has a big guy's mouth. As Mustaine would later tell me, 'I felt like I had something on everybody else. I was a bad boy. I didn't realise I was tainting my image.' Not even when he began dealing drugs from his apartment, which made him the odd man out in the band straight away. All of Metallica drank, but none had yet really experimented beyond smoking pot. Ron didn't even like getting drunk; he hated the fact that it stopped him from driving and being in control. For Lars, dope was aptly named and slowed him down. Cocaine, when he could scrounge some, was more suited to his driven, megalomaniac personality. As for James, any form of drug was simply a no-no; even simple over-the-counter medication was viewed with suspicion. As a child, he had suffered from migraines, for which the only help his parents offered was prayer 'or reading the Bible'. It wasn't until he had lived with his elder half-brother that he first swallowed aspirin. Even then, he later told the writer Ben Mitchell, 'I was freaking out. What's it

going to make me feel like, what's it going to do?' The first time
Dave offered James a hit on a joint, he nearly ran from the room in
terror. By then he had tried smoking pot – as a grand experiment,
in the same way others would have viewed their first LSD trip – but
'it hit me so hard, I freaked out'. From that point on, James would
look down disapprovingly whenever anyone, particularly from his
own band, used drugs of any description, whether viewed as 'soft' or
'hard'. That Mustaine so clearly felt the opposite to James about
drugs would help drive a further wedge between them that would
eventually result in an irreparable fissure. Though not quite yet, not
just as things were beginning to get interesting for Metallica. In fact,
the first victim of the band's steadily rising star wasn't the hard-to-
please Mustaine but the ever-dependable Ron McGovney.

According to Brian Slagel, McGovney's difficulties in Metallica
revolved around his stunted abilities on bass. 'After Metallica had
been around a while and they were getting better as musicians, the
one thing they felt was that Ron, as great a guy as he was, wasn't
progressing as much as they were. So Lars came to me and said,
"Hey, we're thinking about looking for a bass player, is there anybody
you think that would be good for us?"' Brian immediately thought
of Joey Vera, the bassist in Armored Saint, who had been on Metal
Blade, and who were about to get signed to Chrysalis. 'Joey was a
thought,' he says now, 'but [on balance] I didn't think that was gonna
work.' Joey was too committed to his own band, who were much
further down the road with their own career anyway, at that stage.
That was when Slagel came up with another idea. 'I told Lars, "Look,
there's this band called Trauma ... "'

Brian knew Trauma from San Francisco; they had been one of
the bands he was putting onto *Metal Massacre II*, with a short but
surprisingly sweet track titled 'Such a Shame'. 'Their manager had
sent me a demo with three songs, which were awesome and recorded
really well. So we put the band on *Metal Massacre II* and they came
down to play in LA. The band was pretty good but the bass player
was *phenomenal*. Really awesome.' So when later Lars asked about
bass players Brian mentioned 'the Trauma guy', who happened to

be playing in LA again in a couple of weeks, this time at the Troubadour. 'I said, "You guys should come see him and check it out."
So him and James came down to the show and Lars came up to
me – I can't remember if it was during the set or immediately after –
and said, "*That* is going to be our bass player!" And when Lars says
those sorts of things he seems to make them happen. Sure enough,
he was able to make that happen too.'

The Trauma bass player's name was Cliff Burton – the same guy
who'd been to watch Metallica's show at the Old Waldorf in October –
and 'Such a Shame' was destined to become the only track Trauma
ever released with him on it. Cliff was 'the strangest-looking dude'
Lars had ever seen on a Hollywood stage. While the rest of Trauma
sported the same image, interchangeable with any number of West
Coast metal bands then strutting their stuff, Burton took to the stage
in bell-bottom jeans and a denim waistcoat. His hair was hippy-long
and looked like it had barely seen a comb, let alone been teased and
sprayed like his bandmates' evidently had. Most impressive of all, he
really knew how to play the bass, eschewing plectrums for finger-
picking, like all the best bass players in his book, from obvious
influences such as Black Sabbath's Geezer Butler, Rush's Geddy Lee
and Thin Lizzy's Phil Lynott, to less obvious but equally significant
teachers such as American jazz player Stanley Clark, whose use of
the electric double-headed bass Cliff was in absolute awe of, and
even Lemmy, whose rumbling bass in Motörhead Cliff was in thrall
to primarily for the guitar-like way Lemmy played, and the technique
he utilised to bring distortion into his heavy-handed riffing. One
influence Burton didn't share with the rest of Metallica, though, was
an interest in NWOBHM, not even the machine-gun bass of Iron
Maiden's Steve Harris, so highly regarded elsewhere. Instead, Cliff
was more interested in trying to emulate certain guitar players –
most especially Jimi Hendrix, although Hendrix copyist Uli Jon
Roth was held in almost equal high regard, as was UFO's Michael
Schenker 'to a degree' and Sabbath's Tony Iommi, who 'also had an
influence'. Like James, Cliff also liked Aerosmith 'a lot'. As a result,
unlike standard rock players, what Cliff did on the bass could be

characterised, as Lars says, 'as playing the bass like a guitar'. Using his wah-wah pedal to create strange 'washes' and 'drags', as future Metallica guitarist Kirk Hammett later told me, 'for someone as great as Cliff was on bass, offstage he mainly played guitar. He had that kind of approach to what he did.'

Henning Larsen, who later became Metallica's drum tech, was with Lars and James at the Troubadour that first night they saw Cliff play and recalls their pop-eyed reaction. 'I could just see them go, "Oh my God! Look at that guy!" The thing that struck them most was ... here you had a guy playing lead bass! They thought that was great.' Or as James would tell me in 2009, 'our jaws fell onto the floor, and we said we've got to get this guy. So there was respect because we had searched for him to get him.' So awestruck were they, in fact, that not even the über-confident Ulrich could summon up the courage to actually talk to Cliff that first night. Instead, he and James went away and talked about it in secret, before returning to the club the following night where Trauma were playing a second show, and approached him then. James: 'We said: "We're in this band, we're looking for a bass player, and we think you'd really fit in. Because you're a big psycho." And he knew that. It was no surprise to him. But the music made him feel like that.' Ever practical, 'after we'd swapped numbers I started going to work on him immediately', said Lars.

Patrick Scott recalls being tipped off about Trauma by K.J. Doughton, who'd recently featured them in his fanzine, *Northwest Metal*. Managed by an expat Englishman named Tony Van Litt, it was through K.J.'s connection that Patrick visited the band on-set during a video shoot in Santa Anna. When Patrick asked Lars if he wanted to come along too he was taken aback at how enthusiastic Lars was for the idea. When he insisted he brought James as well, Patrick started to suspect something was up. 'He knew of them, and I didn't know that at the time. He hadn't mentioned it to me. I think he'd already seen them play. So we went down to this studio and watched them shoot this video. The band almost looked like an LA band – all except for this bass player, who looked like he always did. You

know, bell-bottoms and headbanging out of time, that crazy look.'
On the way back in the car, Lars kept talking about the bass player,
'what a great bass player he was, and did I think he'd be good in a
band like [Metallica]?'

But while not even Ron McGovney would argue he was anything
other than at best workmanlike on the bass – as he says, 'James
would show me what to play' – musical chops were only part of the
reason why the others originally began plotting to replace him with
Cliff Burton. Behind the scenes, things had steadily been going from
bad to worse. 'It was difficult for me to have to be in the middle
between my parents, who owned the house we were living in, and
the band members,' he says. 'Of course there was drinking and girls
among other things at the house and my parents didn't like it. I had
to be the bad guy many times. We used my father's truck to haul us
and our equipment, and that was another difficulty I had to deal
with. It was like trying to be a road manager and the Metallica bass
player at the same time. Yes, I did have an attitude because I didn't
think all of that should be my sole responsibility.' Then there were
his ongoing personality clashes with Dave: 'Dave Mustaine didn't
like me at all. He started stealing things from me and even arranged
to have my bass stolen at one of our gigs. He poured a beer into the
pickups of my other bass and I got an electric shock. I became more
upset about the way things were going and the attitude showed even
more.'

It wasn't just Mustaine's antics that were starting to get Ron
down. As he revealed in an interview with Bob Nalbandian's Shockwaves website in 1996, he and Lars also 'butted heads' during this
period. 'I hate when people show up late and use you all the time
and that's just what Lars did. I would have to drive all the way down
to Newport Beach to pick him up.' In the end Ron grew so tired of
the situation he told Lars he would have to arrange his own transport.
Then there was the general attitude of the others towards him. Using
his Visa card to pay for everything while the others frittered away
what little cash they had on partying ate away at him until he could
stand it no longer and he became the misery of the band. 'They

couldn't understand why I was mad. They said, "Well, you're getting the cheque after the gig," and we were only getting paid a hundred dollars per gig at the most, which [in San Francisco] didn't even cover the hotel room. Plus we drank a couple hundred dollars' worth of alcohol. I always said to them, "If I'm a part of this band, why is it up to me to pay for everything while you guys get the free ride?"' Ron suggested they get a manager to help shoulder the financial burden, but the others just laughed at him, told him to lighten up. 'Dave, at the time, was an asshole, and Lars only cared about himself. But what really hurt me was James, because he was my friend and he was siding with them and I suddenly became the outcast in the band.' Speaking now, Ron has a cooler perspective but the hurt is clearly still there buried not so deep inside. 'I suppose they all became tired of me and they started looking elsewhere for a bass player. When they saw Cliff perform with his band Trauma, I guess they decided that he was the one. I saw the writing on the wall and I knew that my days were numbered when we played in San Francisco in November of 1982. Cliff was there hanging out with the guys while I was loading equipment. When we got back to LA, I quit. It was probably a relief to the rest of the guys as well.'

That final show with Ron on bass had been at the Mabuhay Gardens, on 30 November – a bitter-sweet occasion, as it was also one of the best shows Ron had played with the band. 'Of course, the more popular we became the more I liked playing in the band,' says Ron now. Although he admits, 'We had to get liquored up to get on stage so obviously we could have been better,' the fact is, 'People who saw us in the clubs, especially in San Francisco, probably say the line-up with Dave and me in the band was fantastic.' The setlist that night – again, built almost entirely around the seven-song *No Life 'til Leather* cassette, plus 'No Remorse' and Diamond Head's 'Am I Evil?' – also contained one of the first truly authentic new numbers the band had worked up as a four-piece: 'Whiplash' – punk-fast but with added bones stuck in the throat of the melody. Ron would later look back on the writing and performing of that particular number as among his happiest memories from Metallica, rightly describing it as 'the most ultimate headbanging song. Every time we played that song it totally kicked ass.' Loading up the gear after the show, Ron McGovney espied Cliff Burton, the man who would soon replace him, standing outside in the rain. Ron, ever the practical one, went over and introduced himself, then offered the sodden bassist a lift home. After that, the drive back to LA was hellish, the others forcing him to stop at a liquor store where, according to Ron, 'they got a whole gallon of whisky. James, Lars and Dave were completely smashed out of their minds. They would constantly bang on the window for me to pull over so they could take a piss, and all of a sudden I look over and see Lars lying in the middle of Interstate 5 on the double yellow line. It was just unbelievable! And I just said fuck this shit!'

When Ron discovered the next day that Dave had contemptuously poured beer onto the pickups of his Washburn bass, while loudly disclaiming, 'I fuckin' hate Ron,' it was the final straw. 'I confronted the band when they came over for practice and said, "Get the fuck out of my house!" I turned to James and said, "I'm sorry, James, but you have to go too." And they were gone within the next couple of days. They packed all their gear and moved to San Francisco.' Ron was 'so disgusted', he sold his equipment soon after, including his amps, guitar cases, even his beloved Les Paul guitar. 'I was just so pissed with the whole thing.' By now he had also discovered the others had been talking behind his back about getting Cliff Burton into the band to replace him. These days, he claims to be sanguine about the situation. But at the time he felt 'double-crossed'. Others from the Metallica camp also felt Ron was treated badly. Says Bob Nalbandian, 'Ron got a raw deal, no doubt. Okay, he wasn't as great a bass player as Cliff Burton but he was a really nice guy who did a lot for that band and he deserved better, for sure. I mean, you look at where they went musically with Cliff in the band and you say, well, okay, you know? But they kinda used Ron and it wasn't nice.'

Perhaps the most telling judgement, however, on how well or badly Ron McGovney was treated in Metallica lies in the fact that he never felt compelled to resume his career either by forming his own band, or joining someone else's. It could be argued he was lucky to have been in the band at all. His one and only foray back into the world of rockdom came four years later when he was momentarily persuaded to give it another go with a new outfit he had more of a say in called Phantasm – which he now describes as 'progressive punk' – with singer Katon De Pena. But despite investing in a new Fender P bass and a Marshall half-stack bass amp, it never went anywhere. 'I just kept getting bombarded with the Metallica thing and the band got sick of it,' he later told Bob Nalbandian. 'A lot of kids came to our gigs just because I had been in Metallica. When we went to play Phoenix all the guys from Flotsam and Jetsam were jumping off the stage and after the show everyone bombarded me for autographs. So it just faded away after that and I haven't been in a band since.'

That was a quarter of a century ago now. These days Ron McGovney is a single dad living in North Carolina. He still goes to Metallica shows, though, whenever they are within reach and the guys still leave him tickets and backstage passes. The last time we spoke, in October 2009, he had just been to see them play on the *Death Magnetic* tour. 'I just saw them a couple of weeks ago,' he emailed me, 'and they are so cool. The backstage is very businesslike, but very comfortable as well.' The band 'were very cool to me and my kids when we went to their shows in Atlanta and Charlotte. James even dedicated the song "Phantom Lord" to me, and Lars let my kids and me stand in the sound-mixing area next to the stage. As a cool gesture to me [current bassist] Rob [Trujillo] took off his bass on stage and was going to hand it to me to play during "Phantom Lord" and "Seek and Destroy". Now I haven't played those songs in twenty-seven years, and relearning them onstage in front of seventeen thousand people could be a little embarrassing!'

McGovney may have gone relatively quietly from Metallica, but persuading Cliff Burton to leave Trauma and throw in his lot with the band was harder than Lars had imagined it was going to be. At first, Burton proved seemingly impervious to the fraught overtures of this strangely accented newcomer. Uncomfortable in the sleazy neon ooze of LA, the simple fact that Metallica lived there was enough on its own for Cliff to shrug off their initial advances. Lars, though, as Cliff was about to discover, was not so easily dissuaded. For a while it looked like he might have met his match in the inscrutably attired bassist with the moth-eaten cardigans and bum-fluff moustache. The son of first-generation hippies, who had instilled in him many of the ideals that were to define his character, even as a wild-hearted youth, Cliff, as everyone who ever knew him, even only briefly, as I did, will tell you, was clearly not like the others.

Clifford Lee Burton was born 10 February 1962. His father Ray was from Tennessee, but now worked in the Bay Area as an Assistant Highway Engineer. His wife Jan was from northern California, and worked as a teacher for the Castro Valley school district, working with students with disabilities and special needs. Baby Clifford was their third and last child, younger brother to Scott David and a sister, Connie. Scott died of a brain aneurysm when Cliff was thirteen, expiring in the ambulance that was rushing him to hospital. A huge blow to the family, it had a profound effect on the teenage Cliff, reinforcing the idea that life was not to be squandered on trying too hard to make other people happy. Time was short and the day was long. Whatever you had in mind, it was best done today, not tomorrow, which really might not ever come.

Cliff only began taking music lessons seriously 'after his brother died', his mother Jan later recalled. He told others, 'I'm gonna be the best bassist for my brother.' Jan was 'totally amazed 'cos none of the kids in our family had any musical talent'. Cliff took lessons 'on the boulevard for about a year, and then he totally outgrew [the teacher] and went to another place for a couple of years and outgrew him, too'. His biggest tutorial influence was a school teacher named Steve Doherty, who also happened to be 'a very good jazz bassist, a very fine musician. He was the one who made Cliff take Bach and Beethoven and baroque [music], and made him learn to read music and stuff like that.' Cliff would eventually outgrow Doherty, too, but not before his interest in Bach was cemented. 'He really did sit down and study and play Bach,' said Jan. 'He loved Bach.'

In 1987, Harald Oimoen, an old friend of Cliff's known better to him as budding Bay Area metal photojournalist Harald O, spent an evening at their Castro Valley apartment interviewing Jan and Ray Burton – the only time the couple spoke openly on the record about their son. Harald has kindly allowed me to use the interview here. In it, Jan describes Cliff as 'very quiet' and 'normal' except for his insistence, even from a very early age, on being 'his own person'. Playing with kids outside was 'boring'. Cliff preferred his own company inside, reading books and playing music. 'Even when he was a tiny little kid he would listen to his music or read. He was a big, big reader and he was very bright; in the third grade they tested him and he got eleventh grade comprehension.' Ray said their only major concern was when Cliff didn't start walking until he was a few weeks shy of his second birthday. 'But the doctor said, "There's nothing wrong with him. He's just smart enough to know that mom and dad will carry him around."' He laughed.

Already musical – he had begun plonking away at his parents' piano when he was just six – Cliff was a quiet, studious youngster, good at most things, though never a show-off. There was also a typically stubborn, Aquarian side to Cliff. Even as a small boy he knew what he was prepared to stand still for and what he wasn't – and nobody was going to persuade him otherwise. Says Jan, 'He was always popular and had a lot of friends. He was a very kind, very gentle kid but always his own person.' Playing Little League baseball for the Castro Valley Auto House team, he was known as a big hitter for a boy his size. Later, at Earl Warren Junior High, and then Castro Valley High School, he worked at weekends at an equipment rental yard called Castro Valley Rentals, where the older workers took to calling him Cowboy after the cheap straw hat he always insisted on wearing (it was either that or get his precious hair cut and Cliff wasn't doing that at any price).

Cliff was just fourteen when he began jamming with his first semi-official band, EZ Street. Named after a strip joint in San Mateo, Cliff later characterised the music EZ Street made as 'pretty silly, actually ... a lot of covers, just wimpy shit', as he told Harald. It was invaluable experience for the teenager, though, the band performing often at the International Cafe in nearby Berkeley. EZ Street also featured guitarist Jim Martin – visually and personality-wise something of a cross between Cliff's outside-the-box musical scientist and James Hetfield's raw, frontiersman persona – who would later go on to become the musical lynchpin in late-Eighties rock-rap innovators Faith No More. As Martin once observed: 'Most of what you see on stage at a rock show, whether it's a thrash metal gig or some heavy hip hop club, it's all about fantasy. The thing about Cliff was he was real. He wasn't acting out the part just to be in some band, he really was that guy. He never saw himself as a star. He was always just another one of the guys.'

By the time Cliff had graduated from high school in 1980, the Burton character was already fully formed: a bell-bottomed, denim-wearing, H.P. Lovecraft-reading, piano-playing, homebody who liked his beer and Mexican food, and loved his pot and acid. A self-contained free-thinker who drove a beat-up 1972 VW station wagon – nicknamed The Grasshopper – in which he liked to mix his Lynyrd Skynyrd tapes with Bach concertos and cantatas, his favourite pastime was hanging out with his friends Jim Martin and Dave Donato, going fishing and hunting, or just sitting round smoking pot and playing Dungeons and Dragons into the small hours. 'He'd stay up all night and sleep late,' remembered Jan. Dave and Jim would often be there, too. In the middle of the night Cliff would fix them all munchies-defeating omelettes. 'He loved to cook all this stuff,' said Jan, '[but] he'd very seldom wake us up. He was exceptionally considerate and loving.' He was painfully honest, too. 'Sometimes you'd think, "Oh, Cliff, I wish you weren't quite so honest." No little white lies for him and sometimes that was kind of embarrassing,' she laughed. 'We were talking about that once, and he said, "I don't have to lie for anybody. I don't want to lie." And that's how he felt about it. God, I think he hated lying more than anything. He was big on just being yourself.'

Enrolling at Chabot College, in nearby Hayward, Cliff studied classical music and theory. He hooked up again with Jim Martin, who had also joined the college, the pair forming an instrumental trio they named Agents of Misfortune – a short-lived but useful outfit in which Cliff first tried his hand at incorporating harmonics into his bass playing – part of his college studies – and improvising with distortion – a trick learned from Motörhead's Lemmy. Jim Martin would enter into the spirit of things by using a Penderecki violin bow, although this was an aspect of his talents he'd quietly dropped by the time fame found him in Faith No More. Entering the Hayward Area Recreation Department's annual Battle of the Bands contest in 1981, their audition was videoed and can still be seen on YouTube today. It's a fascinating clip to view, not least as the onstage persona Burton was to later make famous in Metallica already appears in motion. Indeed, if you listen carefully you can already hear the bones of two pieces that would later become most associated with his work in Metallica: an early extended bass solo entitled '(Anesthesia) Pulling Teeth' and the strident intro to a number that would become a cornerstone of the band's set for many years, 'For Whom the Bell Tolls'.

In 1982, Cliff joined Trauma, well known to Bay Area scene-makers, in part for their intense musicality, although they are mostly remembered now for their determined theatricality. There is a wonderfully hammy video clip of them which can also still be seen on YouTube, with a dark-haired girl tied to a cross and another blonde girl being 'sacrificed' on an altar as the band plays amid billowing dry ice, the singer standing over his sacrificial victim, wielding a silver dagger and singing about being 'the warlock of the night'. Eventually, an upside-down cross, positioned just behind Cliff, catches afire – the sort of video that looked wincingly out-of-step even back in 1982, all save for Cliff himself, who looks marvellously out of sync with the other band members, in his downbeat clothes and completely unself-conscious headbanging, his bass full of unnecessary but impressively odd jazz timings and psychedelic overtones.

Practising on average between four and six hours a day, every day, even after he joined Metallica, Cliff's musical philosophy was explained by Jan as: 'There's somebody in their garage that hasn't been discovered that's better than you are.' It would be a habit he kept up till the day he died. It was clear he took his music more seriously than anything else. So when Cliff abandoned his classic studies in order to play full-time in Metallica, his parents stood by him. Ray admitted the music his son was now focused on 'wasn't the kind of music I would have really liked him to play [but] he wanted to play it. So I wished him all the luck in the world.' Jan, though, was less equivocal. 'I didn't care what kind of music he played as long as he was good at what he did. The fact that it was heavy metal made it kind of exciting to me, rather than some la-di-dah pop or country. It was different to our lives, so I thought it was exciting.' Ray recalled Cliff telling them, '"I'm going to make my living as a musician." And that's what he did.' They set him a goal to aim for, though. As Jan revealed, 'I [had] never seen that boy give up on anything or anybody. So I knew that when he said that, he one hundred and ten per cent was going to [do] it.' However, 'We said, "Okay, we'll give you four years. We'll pay for your rent and your food. But after that four years is over, if we don't see some slow progress or moderate progress, if you're just not going anyplace and it's obvious you're not going to make a living out of it, then you're going to have to get a job and do something else."' She added, 'He said, "Fine."'

It took almost four months for Lars Ulrich and James Hetfield to persuade Cliff Burton to at least jam with Metallica. Intrigued but far from convinced yet, Cliff began turning up whenever the band played in San Francisco, something that was now happening on a monthly basis. Cliff picked up on two things straight away: how different their approach was to the more staid, far more trad-metal ideals of the cheesy Trauma – and just how much the crowds appreciated that – and how lifeless the playing was of the incumbent bassist, the well-meaning but increasingly out-of-his-depth McGovney. The only thing that put him off was the thought of having to relocate to LA. Why would he want to slum it in a city he instinctively hated, when he still enjoyed all the comforts of home in a city more naturally suited to his sensibilities?

What finally made up his mind to make the jump was the fact that, as he told Harald O, 'eventually Trauma started to … annoy me'. Specifically, the band was 'starting to get a little commercial'. 'Commercial' was Cliff's polite word for embarrassing. What the rest of Trauma saw as their inherent theatricality, Cliff saw as trying too hard to attract a wider audience. Metallica seemed to have found a way of attracting a fanatical following in the Bay Area by simply turning up as themselves. There was, however, one condition Cliff made to the band, and it was a deal-breaker: they would have to come to him. No way was he leaving home for LA – not even for the hottest new band in the Bay. He told them: 'I like it up here. So they said, "Yeah, well, we were thinking about doing that anyway." So that worked out just right. So, they came up and we got together in this room that we're sitting in now, set up the gear and blasted it out for a couple of days. It was pretty obvious straight away that it was a good thing to do, so we did it!'

Lars, who had already seen it coming, reasoned that with Ron out of the picture now anyway, and the band left with nowhere to rehearse, it was time to say, 'Okay, fuck it. LA is pretty shitty for us anyway.' According to Jan, Cliff 'was a very loyal person' who 'didn't want to leave Trauma. But Trauma wanted him to go plunk, plunk, plunk, plunk. He wanted to play lead bass and they said, "No way." He really became so frustrated at wanting to express himself musically. Metallica kept calling every week. They'd call him from LA and he'd say, "No, no." When they finally got together he'd say, "I wanna play lead bass. I want some spot in here where I can go off." And they said, "You can play anything you want, just come with us."'

It was a bold move for both sides, but most especially for the three-man Metallica line-up who agreed to relocate from LA to San Francisco. As Brian Slagel says now, 'It was a *very* big deal.' Los Angeles and San Francisco are 'polar-opposite cities'. Regarding Lars, however, Slagel states, 'I don't think it really mattered that much, 'cos he was used to kind of moving around anyway.' For James, 'a guy that grew up in LA, and for that matter Mustaine, that's kind of a big move. But the timing of it was good, too. None of them had any really strong ties to LA. They felt much more at home in San Francisco. It really was day and night ... And Cliff was clearly the right guy. I mean, he was just an unbelievable bass player. So they felt it would definitely be a big upgrade for them to get a guy like that, even to consider it.' Unlike Ron, none of them had girlfriends at this stage either. Says Slagel: 'They didn't have those ties. I guess there was a certain family tie with Lars. But I know James didn't have a great relationship with his family and the same was true of Dave. But Lars' family was so supportive, it was like, hey, if that's what you need to do to make you happy we'll be completely supportive of that. So why not move to San Francisco?'

Certainly it was something the band felt they had to do. As Lars would tell me, in San Francisco, Metallica simply 'connected to a whole different level of energy and vibe [than in LA] and there was much more passion ... there was much more of a scene. People were passionate about music, people were curious, people were open. I think in LA we had always felt like outcasts, like we never belonged. It seemed like the music was secondary to the partying. Up in San Francisco there was just a different level of passion and people reacted differently to the music. So when we decided to not only pursue Cliff but to offer ourselves to Cliff, when I told him we would be glad to leave behind LA, and when I realised that it actually became conditional for him, that the only way he would even consider joining the band would be if we moved to San Francisco, it was a no-brainer. Of course we would relocate to the Bay Area because we felt from those shows in the fall of '82 much more of a kinship, we felt like we belonged there.'

Leaving for San Francisco, they stopped off at Patrick Scott's house. 'They came over to tell me goodbye,' he says. It was a poignant moment for the school friends. Patrick knew he 'probably wasn't going to see Lars again any time soon. They said goodbye and hung out for a while and then they left.' He remembers how, 'Lars once asked my dad for ten thousand dollars to invest in the band but who in their right mind would have done that? My dad said, "How would anybody rationalise ten thousand dollars in [an unknown] rock band?

How many of them make it, you know?"' When they drove off, Patrick realised that 'James had left his high school letterman jacket at my house. I called James and told him he left his jacket there and he said, "Just throw it away; I don't really want it any more." But I kept it, I still have it actually. It says "J. Hetfield" on the neck and in embroidery on the front it says "James". I told him about it maybe five years ago and told him he could have it back if he wanted it for like his kids or whatever and he was like, "No, but keep it. Don't sell it, just keep it." And I still have it.'

So it was in the week between Christmas and New Year 1982, that Lars Ulrich, James Hetfield and Dave Mustaine packed as much of their gear as they could onto another trailer – this time paid for with their own money and not Ron's – and drove north up the California coast road to San Francisco, where they had arranged to stay temporarily at their friend Mark Whitaker's house at 3132 Carlson Boulevard in El Cerrito, in the East Bay. Whitaker was a well-known face on the SF club scene. Having taken on the role of manager for local boys Exodus, he had also helped out recently at several Metallica gigs, now becoming their full-time live sound engineer and general dogsbody. When he agreed to let James, Lars and Dave stay for a few days over the Christmas holidays of 1982, he had no idea what he was letting himself in for. By February 1983 all three had moved in permanently and Whitaker's El Cerrito house was quickly nicknamed the Metallimansion. It would become the band's HQ for the next three years – the place where they would not only write the material that would comprise some of the greatest albums of their career, but where they began to live the rock 'n' roll life they had only previously fantasised about. Or: 'every cliché that you could muster up', as Lars put it. 'Me and James each had a bedroom. Dave Mustaine slept on the couch. Dogs running around. We had the old garage converted into a rehearsal room with egg cartons. It was the refuge, the sanctuary for everybody in the neighbourhood. People would come over and live there, hang there. It was a lot of fun – when you're nineteen.' It was also the place where they would forge the 'gang mentality' they would need to keep them strong through the testing times ahead –

'this tiny little situation. Nobody can stray outside of . . . the thing you do.'

As Ron Quintana recalls, 'The Carlson pad was a fairly normal first pad away from home for three young LA transplants, but quickly things got wilder! The three of them would have nothing to do in El Cerrito but drink vodka most days and practise those days Cliff made the hour drive north from his comfortable Castro Valley parents' pad. Most nights they would hang out and drink or go to Exodus' practice studio and party or an occasional Berkeley Keystone metal show or Metal Mondays at the Old Waldorf or shows at Mabuhay or Stone.' Weekends would be spent cadging drinks at Ruthie's Inn 'or an occasional house party' where the three would join well-known party animal and Exodus vocalist Paul Baloff and guitarist Gary Holt 'and destroy someone's living room'.

It was also at 3132 Carlson Boulevard that, on 28 December 1982, Metallica held their first all-night jam session with Cliff Burton. The impact was immediate. Cliff liked everything from Bach to Black Sabbath, from Pink Floyd to the Velvet Underground, from Lynyrd Skynyrd to R.E.M. As Lars told me in 2009, 'Cliff turned me and James onto a lot of stuff at the time. From Peter Gabriel to ZZ Top to a lot of stuff that we really didn't [know]. He flew the flag for bands like Yes. We'd never really experienced a lot of that type of stuff. Of course, at the same time, he had never heard that much Diamond Head or Saxon and Motörhead, or anything like that. So there was definitely a cool give and take there.' Or as James told me, 'Besides introducing us to more music theory, [Cliff] was the most schooled of any of us, he had gone to junior college to learn some things about music, and taught us quite a few things.'

Cliff, who 'had a really bad back because he was always bent over thrashing his head', was to become an influence in many other, entirely unexpected ways, too. James again: 'He was the kind of guy, you know, him and I aligned a lot closer as friends, as far as our activities, music styles that we liked, bands that we liked, politically, views on the world, we were pretty parallel on that wavelength. But, yeah, he had such a character to himself, and it was a very strong personality, he did creep into all of us eventually.' Says Lars: 'Cliff was very, very different from James and Dave and Ron and anybody else. I mean, Cliff lived a whole different life up in the Bay Area. He was an interesting mix of the kind of hippy, trippy, non-conformist kind of vibe that was so well known about San Francisco and kind of ... in his own headspace. And then also, a whole side that I'd never really experienced in America yet, was kind of what we call the redneck element. You know, he lived out in Castro Valley. It's a good thirty- or forty-minute drive from San Francisco [and] there was a different kind of vibe out there, a little bit in the suburbs, a little bit sort of beer-drinking, hell-raising. Listening to ZZ Top and Lynyrd Skynyrd, type of thing. A little bit of that kind of vibe. So he was a very interesting mix of many different types of personalities and so on. When me and James met him I was just infatuated with his uniqueness. I was infatuated with his lack of conformity, and his sole insistence on doing his own thing, even to the point of ridicule. I mean, even at that time. Me and Hetfield were wearing as tight pants as possible and Cliff was wearing the famous bell-bottoms. There was a lot of con-tradictions about him.' Within 'the uniqueness' there was also 'a little bit of a rebellious attitude and energy, and obviously I could really relate to [that]. Being an only child from a very bohemian upbringing in Denmark and stuff, I could really relate to ... really just doing your own trip and not kind of being caught up in what everybody else wanted from you. So we really hit it off on that level.' Cliff Burton was simply 'not your basic human being', James later laughingly recalled. 'He was really intellectual but very to the point. He taught me a lot about attitude.' Cliff, said James, was 'a wild, hippy-ish, acid-taking, bell-bottom-wearing guy. He meant business, and you couldn't fuck around with him. I wanted to get that respect that he had. We gave him shit about his bell-bottoms every day. He didn't care. "This is what I wear. Fuck you."'

The four of them saw in 1983 by sitting round in the garage at Carlson Boulevard getting wasted on beer and pot and talking up their plans for the future. That was when Burton gave them his philosophy in typically Cliff-like shorthand. As he later told Harald O, 'When

I started [playing music], I decided to devote my life to it and not get sidetracked by all the other bullshit life has to offer.' Wise words the rest of Metallica would do their utmost to try and live by – even after Cliff had left them.

FOUR
NIGHTFALL AT THE HALFWAY HOUSE

Time was getting on and we were only halfway through the show. I looked up at the big studio clock.

'Where are the guests?' I asked the floor manager.

'In the toilet,' he grimaced.

'Still?'

'Yeah. I think they're ... you know ...'

Because we recorded the show so early in the morning it didn't happen often that one of the bands actually turned up drunk or stoned. But just occasionally, you got one or two, usually from one of the younger bands, who felt the need to vanish into the loos and lock the door behind them before sauntering onto the set ready for their close-up.

Then here they came, strutting, frowning, faking. The two Daves from ... I checked my crib sheet ... Megadeth. Right. I took a guess and held my hand out to the one in front with the long curly hair and the painted-on sneer.

'Dave Mustaine,' I said, acting pleased to see him. 'Welcome to the Monsters of Rock show.'

He held out his paw and allowed me to grasp it. One of the production assistants showed him to his seat while I said hello to the other Dave – Ellefson. Dave Junior, as he was fast becoming known. Junior was the band's bassist, and although he was just as fucked-up on drugs as his leader, he came without a sneer and minus the ton of attitude. They were the yin and yang of Megadeth, good cop, bad cop.

I settled myself down and watched as they sniffed loudly and leered at *the production assistant's cleavage. They wanted us to know they were bad boys and we dutifully played along.*

Then the interview began. Cameras rolling, sound and ... the floor manager made the funny hand signals for action.

I began by mentioning Mustaine's past in Metallica but he cut me short. 'That was then,' he sneered. 'This is now and I really don't think I have much to say about it. I don't speak ill of the dead ...'

Oh, but he did. Every chance he got. As soon as we took a break for the first video he got into it. How he'd written all the songs on the first Metallica album but never received the credit. How the band had been nothing until he came along. How they were hypocrites for tossing him out when they were all drinking and getting fucked up just as much as he did. How Lars couldn't play the drums and Kirk had just ripped him off. How James was scared of him.

Dave Junior, who'd obviously heard it all before and could look forward to many years more of hearing it over again, shifted in his seat and cleared his throat and tried to change the subject. But Mustaine just ignored him. This wasn't about Dave Junior or even about Megadeth. It certainly wasn't about trying to tell me anything, whoever I was, some asshole with a cable show and an Iron Maiden T-shirt.

This was all about Dave Mustaine. Always had been, always would be. God bless his broken black heart ...

In many ways, relocating to San Francisco at the start of 1983 is the real start of the Metallica story. It certainly felt that way for Lars Ulrich and James Hetfield. Speaking to me in 2009, Lars put it like this: 'What happened were two things. Number one, we started being more comfortable with ourselves, more confident. We started feeling that we were belonging to something that was happening, and that was bigger than ourselves, that we *belonged* instead of being on the outer fringes. And number two was ... Cliff. At that time, me and James were basically self-taught. Most of what we knew we'd learned from [listening to] records and so on. But Cliff had been to college, had studied music at school; was educated in music, so there was a whole different level of expertise that came in there ... a sense of melody and a whole other scope of understanding music.' San Francisco also provided a more cultural mêlée that reminded the brash young drummer of his European roots. 'I felt the kinship there right away ... You took the train around, you took the tram ... It was a bunch of kids from the city instead of a bunch of kids from the suburbs. It was big city living and obviously with the cultural scene in San Francisco, the political openness and that whole type of thing, it was ... really the closest I've found to a European big city. That's why I choose to live there still. If I was tarred and feathered and thrown out of San Francisco and told never to return I would probably go back to Europe. Because I don't think there is any other place in the States that I would feel as comfortable in, or that I feel would be home in the way that San Francisco [does].'

As Lars suggests, things began to move much faster after Cliff Burton joined Metallica. Within days of his first show with them in San Francisco at the Stone, on 5 March 1983, there was already talk of making an album. So excited were they by the possibilities of the line-up now Burton was aboard, they arranged for his second gig with them, again at the Stone, on 19 March, to be videotaped, capturing on tape his classic windmill style of bass playing, swinging his beloved 1973 Rickenbacker like an axe, wringing angry distorted tones from it one moment, loud sensuous moans the next, all the while using all ten fingers to dig out the continually propulsive rhythm. Lars, whose drumming was still rudimentary at best, struggled to keep up. Cliff even had his own showpiece within the set, an extended bass solo that would later be immortalised on the first Metallica album, already even at this early stage a highlight of the new Metallica show. 'We do what we want,' Cliff was captured on video saying. 'We don't care what anyone else thinks.' There had also been two new tracks demoed at the Metallimansion on 16 March, the first Metallica recordings to feature Cliff Burton: 'Whiplash' and 'No Remorse'. Once again, the band was quick to ensure cassette copies were shared around the fanzine and foreign magazine guys as well as their network of regular tape-traders. They also pulled off a minor coup when they persuaded a DJ at radio station KUSF FM to play both tracks on air, on the basis that Metallica was now, technically speaking at least, a local San Francisco band.

Brian Slagel had been ready to put out a Metallica record of some description since the first time John Kornarens played him the *No Life 'til Leather* tape and asked him to guess who it was. Slagel assumed it must be some bright new European band: 'It sounded awesome.' When John told him it was Lars Ulrich's group, he couldn't believe it. 'This is *Metallica?* This thing is incredible!' The problem was Slagel's fledgling Metal Blade label simply didn't have the money for the kind of project Lars had in mind. The widespread circulation of *No Life 'til Leather* and, the latest cassette on the tape-trading scene, an audience recording – from a boom box placed in front of the speaker stacks – of Ron McGovney's last show with them at the Old Waldorf at the end of November, dubbed the *Live Metal up Your Ass* demo, had done a certain job. What Metallica needed now, Lars felt strongly, was a more accomplished studio recording; something that demonstrated there was more to them than home-made demos and live tapes. As a stopgap, Slagel suggested simply releasing the seven-track *No Life* demo as an EP. 'But good as they liked it they wanted something a little bit better, if they were actually going to put together a real recording.'

One studio in LA offered to let them come in and record an album for a flat fee of $10,000. They asked Brian for the ten grand but he told them: 'I don't have ten thousand dollars! Are you kidding me?' He offered instead to try and find someone willing to invest the ten thousand. 'But back then that was a lot of money and it just never really happened. By the time they got to San Francisco, I think they were more focused on getting Cliff into the band and integrating him in and playing some shows. We had some other loose discussions about stuff but again nobody had any money and there was just no way to make a quality recording.' Nobody Brian Slagel or Metallica knew out on the West Coast, anyway. Three thousand miles away on America's East Coast, however, somebody they didn't know yet was having other ideas. His name was Jon Zazula – Jonny Z – and though he didn't have any money either, he and his wife and business partner

Marsha Zazula more than made up for that with what Jonny now calls 'the passion'. He and Marsha 'loved music so much', he says, 'that we were willing to sacrifice anything for music and for metal. "For the metal" – that's what we used to say.' It was a phrase that Jonny and Marsha would repeat like a mantra over the coming months as they struggled to keep pace with what was already one of the toughest times they would endure, even before the four beer-hungry kids in Metallica arrived on their doorstep to disrupt and forever change their lives.

At the time he heard his first Metallica recordings – a ten-track bootleg cassette of one of Ron McGovney's last shows at the Mabuhay Gardens in November – Jonny was then running a record-and-tape stall named Rock 'n' Roll Heaven in a flea market near to his and Marsha's home in Old Bridge, New Jersey. Offered a copy of the cassette by a regular customer who insisted he play it immediately, the Mabuhay tape consisted of live versions of the seven-track *No Life* demo plus the newer 'No Remorse' and 'Whiplash' and the inevitable Diamond Head cover, 'Am I Evil?', which Jonny, another N W O B H M aficionado, instantly recognised. Jonny remembers how, 'One of our customers came back from San Francisco like he saw Jesus Christ! We would be playing Angel Witch or Iron Maiden or whatever in the shop and never played a demo ... but we sold them. And [this guy] came over with a [live] tape cassette of Metallica. It wasn't even *No Life 'til Leather* and I was blown away. Actually the song that got me was "The Mechanix". That was the one that initially just blew me out of my seat. I wanted to find out where I could find these guys. This all was happening as I'm listening to the tape the first time. Then someone hands me K.J. Doughton's name and I think I called up somebody to get K.J.'s phone number and then I called him and he called Lars and then Lars called me.'

When Lars phoned during dinner one night, Jonny wasn't even sure yet what he wanted to tell this unknown new band. 'Damned if I know. I just got caught in this passion, like there's this little Led Zeppelin hanging out in El Cerrito, you know? Just a little gem that blew my mind. They seemed like America's antidote to the

NWOBHM. America really didn't have anything, especially in the east, to compete in that world.' The only concrete proposal Jonny had for them at that point was the suggestion they might like to open up at some of the shows he and Marsha had recently begun promoting locally, featuring the sorts of artists his regular customers at Rock 'n' Roll Heaven were interested in seeing. They had begun by 'being in cahoots' with the then-hot Anvil. After that came NWOBHM outfit Raven. At the same time as they first discovered Metallica, the Zazulas were also looking at bringing in Germany's best new metal act, Accept, and taking a punt on local boys Manowar. Says Jonny, 'We had Raven tearing up the place and Anvil tearing up the place before Metallica. And they were *big* successes, Raven and Anvil. That's how we started.'

Jonny and Marsha's next venture was twelve dates they were putting together: 'The shows were to be with Venom, Twisted Sister ... We [also] had Vandenberg and The Rods.' Talking on the phone to Lars for the first time, Jonny impetuously 'offered all twelve to Metallica, if they'd come over. Marsha thought I was crazy.' Lars, who had already heard through the grapevine of something happening in the north-east, told Jonny: 'Let's go! Send me some money, I'll get everybody together, we'll come over!' Jonny acted delighted, then got off the phone and immediately started worrying. Money was so tight he and Marsha still relied occasionally on handouts from her father just to buy groceries. He'd also omitted to tell Lars one other important detail: Jonny was actually halfway through serving a six-month jail sentence for conspiracy to commit wiretap fraud, while working for a company involved in trading precious metals. Or, as he puts it now, 'For being too bright and a wise guy on Wall Street.' A situation that was especially difficult as Jonny maintains to this day that he was innocent of the charges, but that his lawyer advised him to plead guilty because he couldn't afford the cost of a long-drawn-out defence trial which he was likely to lose anyway. The result: a six-month jail sentence, which he was allowed to serve at a 'halfway house'. Or 'a jail without guards,' as Jonny puts it. 'I was left with a pity plea, a wife and a beautiful baby. I never did jail time, they wanted me to be able to work and feed my family. [But] we lost everything, Marsha and I, from our Wall Street mis-experience. I would spend the week [at the halfway house] and the weekends at home. The only phone that was available to do all this organisation of the shows was done on a payphone in a halfway house with quarters, with people who'd just got out of prison waiting for the phone to speak to their girlfriends. Waiting for me on the phone for twenty minutes, they were gonna kill me. You can imagine this? Nobody knows this story.'

The six-month sentence was eventually commuted to four and a half months. In the meantime, Marsha not only had to somehow keep Rock 'n' Roll Heaven going, she had to look after their infant daughter Rikki. Friends rallied round – from 'Old Bridge militia' pals such as Rockin' Ray and Metal Joe, to the kindly neighbours across the street who sent their son over to mow their front lawn when the grass got so high other neighbours began sticking letters in the mail, complaining. Meanwhile, Jonny's father-in-law took over the weekday running of the market stall while Marsha kept Jonny's spirits up by doing every-thing she could to keep the dream alive of moving from market stall owner to local gig promoter. Says Jonny: 'I knew nothing about the business. Marsha went and got me out of the library all these books about how to be a manager, and understanding music law, and all that. I would read them at night, during the week, so that I understood all the various points of a contract – What should a band get? What's fair? – all that stuff. I learned it out of books 'cos there was no years of experience.'

What the Zazulas lacked in music-biz expertise, however, they more than made up for with sheer strength of will and a deter-mination to succeed at any cost. Indeed, Jonny and Marsha were on their way to becoming one of the most formidable partnerships in the business – both personal and professional. As Jonny recalls, 'Marsha used to go out with my best friend and she was really a bitch to me. We started out really hating each other. Marsha was a deadly girl. When she don't like you, forget it. [But] it just changed over time. We started laughing, never knew why we were mad at each other, and it just grew into this great relationship. She and I never left each other's side since.'

Rock 'n' Roll Heaven, which he and Marsha had started in 1982 with $180 cash, was doing well enough that 'by the time Metallica came along we had about $60,000 worth of inventory just from reinvesting, reinvesting, reinvesting'. From that they were able to scrape together $1,500 to send to the band so they could hire a U-Haul truck and make the cross-country road trip from San Francisco to New Jersey. 'They bought a one-way ticket. I believe Dave and Cliff were living inside the truck all the way from San Francisco, 'cos there was no car with the U-Haul. They showed up a week later without a fuckin' dime.' Living in 'a small residential, blue collar area' what Jonny and Marsha hadn't bargained for was the 'culture shock' of a bunch of drunken teenagers suddenly arriving on their doorstep. 'They come and land right on my front lawn. Basically, me penniless, them penniless, and we're going "What the fuck, man? How we gonna do this?"' The answer was for them to stay in Jonny's basement. But the band soon outstayed their welcome and the Zazulas had to move them out. 'I had a little bar in the hallway and they poured themselves a drink. Just took the bottle and started guzzling. That was the first thing.' The first time Jonny and Marsha took them down to Rock 'n' Roll Heaven, says Jonny, 'I wondered if I'd made a mistake.' Dave Mustaine was so drunk 'he spent the entire time throwing up outside. As people were leaving, he's there with long hair and vomit all over the place; just puking up a storm. To the normal people of the flea market who are selling linens and children's clothes it was like, "Oh my god, what did he bring to this market!"' Jonny, who was getting complaints 'all the time' for playing his records so loud, 'didn't need this'.

With Jonny still finishing his time in the halfway house, though, the brunt of the band's bad behaviour was born by Marsha. 'I had an infant, a husband in a halfway house and a band that was screwing everybody in the neighbourhood in my basement.' She says she wondered if she was doing the right thing 'every day. This was very far afield from anything I had ever done before. We put our entire lives on the line for them because we lived in a little suburban community, which wasn't all that impressed with the guys. And because we poured every ounce, every penny we had into them, we had to not pay our mortgage. We had [situations] where we couldn't pay electric bills and lost our electricity.' Her father, who would buy them groceries, 'to keep us fed, and in turn was then feeding the band'. Marsha adds, 'They were young teens who had all kinds of things going on in their own lives. They drank too much. They partied a little too hearty. You kind of looked at it and said, "Oh my god! Is this what I'm investing my life in? How is this all gonna play out?" But at the core of it [was] their talent, their incredible talent made you just say I've gotta keep doing this. These guys are great, these guys are different. They have that – whatever that is – that can propel them, and so you just kept going, even when some days you weren't quite sure why.'

The only member of the band who possessed any decorum, says Marsha, was Cliff Burton. 'If I have to say who was I closest to in those days, who did I bond with the most, it was Cliff. He was a *treasure* to have in my home. He was great, he was respectful. He was warm. He would help me out with Rikki, because she was so little and I would be busy doing something. It would be time for her to go to bed and so he'd read her a story or sing her a song. He was quite the human. James and Lars were just, like, diabolically different,' she chuckles. ''Cos at night James [and Dave] would want to get drunk, party and Lars of course would be out [chasing] the women.' Lars, she adds, 'really was quite the man, in his own mind ... he was a small man in white spandex pants, so you had to kind of give him a break'. Cliff, though, 'was really a hippy in a heavy metal band, with his bell-bottoms and his whole persona, just a beautiful, beautiful human being'. She adds, 'Unfortunately, he didn't have enough of a voice in the band. In terms of the decisions that were made, Lars was the ringleader and he said it and that was it, they moved in that motion. Cliff wasn't involved in that aspect of the band. He was a musician, pure.'

Blasting out the *No Life* demo from the market stall every day, says Jonny, '*Everybody* was coming round from everywhere going "What the fuck is that?" Before you know it, the siege of Metallica started.' For the rest of the band's stay, 'we only played *No Life 'til Leather* in our store'. Jonny would sit in his living room with Mark Whitaker, who had come up with the band from San Francisco as their live sound engineer and all round 'guy Friday', making more cassette copies of *No Life* to sell at the store at a knock-down price of $4.99. 'As many as we can every day, one at a time, so they had some money to eat and live while they were here. And we sold *tons* of them. It still wasn't enough, you know, but we sold a lot compared to any other band.'

Lars would hang out at the stall every day, watching, taking it all in. Lars, says Marsha, was 'always the one. He was the master, orchestrator of his destiny. And whether that came from the fact that his dad was a tennis star and he always wanted to be looked at by his dad with high regard, or what, I don't know. But he just was always, "I'm gonna get there. I'm gonna do this and we're gonna do that." He really did, for a very young man, have a very succinct plan in his mind as to how he envisioned Metallica and how he heard the music. It was really quite interesting.' At the stall where they had 'umpteen albums', Lars would commandeer the turntable. '"Oh, listen to this, listen to that. See how they do this, see how they do that." He was always involved. It wasn't like he said, okay, well, this is my music and I'm gonna do it this way. He was very aware of his predecessors in the music business, musician-wise, and always watching what was happening.' It was that fiercely competitive aspect of Ulrich's character, says Marsha, that drove Metallica. 'He just always wanted to be at the top of the heap. They were creative, as far as how they presented themselves. They came to us with their logo and it was brilliant. Then it was, "How do we work off our logo?" [Lars] was a forerunner, he really was. I don't think they would have succeeded without that competitive side of him, and being aware of everything that was going on around him . . .'

Jonny didn't really have what he calls his 'Brian Epstein moment', though, until he saw the band play live for the first time: two shows over the weekend of 8 and 9 April; the first, opening for Swedish rock darlings Vandenberg at the Paramount Theater in Staten Island; the second, supporting US metal up-and-comers The Rods at L'Amours in Brooklyn. 'It was intense, whoosh.' However, 'Every show they played had an edge. You didn't know where the fuck-up was gonna come. They were making mistakes in those days.' For Metallica this was a baptism of fire. 'These were big shows in big venues,' says Jonny. 'Marsha and I had kind of taken over the Staten Island, New York area rock shows ... venues that held up to two thousand. They didn't come in and start in little clubs, like The Beatles. We put them in front of a lot of people.' Dee Snider, frontman for Twisted Sister – a New York band then making waves in the UK – came up to Jonny during one of the shows Metallica played and asked: 'What is *that*, Jonny?'

The only real problem that Jonny and Marsha could see was Dave Mustaine. 'You didn't know with his drinking what you were gonna get,' says Jonny. 'You were either gonna get the friendly Dave, or you were gonna get the monster Dave. He was so drunk you just didn't know how he could play those notes. Everybody [in the band] was heavy into the booze but Dave was over the top.' Privately, Lars and James had already told Jonny they, too, were sick of Mustaine's loutish behaviour, his drunken antics and his confrontational atti-tude, that they were, as Lars put it, 'just gonna hang on until someone [else] came along'. Jonny's concern was that without Mustaine the band wouldn't be nearly as good. 'I was worried because even though Mustaine was so out of control, he was a real big part of the band. Some of the best songs were written with Dave Mustaine. [To replace him] it was gonna be really weird.' According to Lars, the band had already decided to replace Mustaine before their U-Haul had even reached the East Coast. 'It all kind of spilled over [then],' he said. 'There were a few things happening that became too much.' Not least the time a drunken Mustaine insisted on taking his turn driving the truck and allegedly nearly crashed it into a jeep during a snow-storm near Wyoming. 'We could have all been killed,' said James. 'We knew it couldn't go on like that, so we started looking at other stuff.'

Mark Whitaker, who also managed fellow San Franciscan metal-lists Exodus, suggested poaching their lead guitarist, a curly-haired whiz-kid named Kirk Hammett. Unlike Dave Mustaine, who was big and brash and utterly unpredictable, twenty-year-old Kirk Hammett was short, like Lars, and nerdy. Unlike Lars, he was quiet; a cool number, though already well schooled in the Metallica way, having opened for them with Exodus at the Stone and hung out at the Metallimansion. Like Cliff, he was another easygoing San Franciscan, born into a time and place famous for the flowers it wore in its extremely long hair. The kind of stoner dude you'd see walking round the Haight with buds in his beard – once he'd started to shave, which he still looked like he hadn't at the time he met Metallica. Best of all, Hammett was technically one of the best guitar players on the scene. Behind the amiable façade was an extremely determined young gun who still took lessons and practised for hours each day, no matter how wasted on weed. Not an innovator like Mustaine, certainly not such a monster personality, but with a much broader musical palette and a much steadier emotional hand – the kind of talented kid who would do what he was told. They told Mark to keep it dark but to call Kirk, check it out.

It was 1 April and Kirk was 'sitting on the can' when Whitaker made the phone call. Hammett assumed it was an April Fool's gag, said, 'Yeah, sure', and hung up, barely giving it another thought. He only knew it was for real when Whitaker called him back the following morning and told him he was Fed-Exing a tape of Metallica songs for him to learn. 'Then I started to get more calls from Whitaker: "The band wants you to come to New York to audition with them." I thought about it for like two seconds and said, "Sure, I'll check it out."' The tape arrived just four days before Metallica's first gig – with Mustaine still in place – for Jonny Z. By the time the band was onstage at the Paramount and ready to launch into 'The Mechanix' – the song Dave Mustaine wrote for them and the number Jonny still loved best – Kirk was already saying goodbye to his bandmates in Exodus and getting ready to board a plane for New York, to start his new life in Metallica, first thing Monday morning.

Nervous about how Dave would react to the news, the others decided to tell him while he was in bed, still half asleep, having been woken first thing Monday morning by Lars, who drew the short straw and was the one who actually broke the news. Lars would later joke that Dave had asked what time his flight left, to which the band replied that they'd booked him on the first Greyhound bus out of town. 'Not only was he out of the band but he had to sit on a bus for four days and think about it!' Lars laughed. Mustaine would remember it a little differently. 'Basically, when they told me to leave I packed in about twenty seconds and I was gone. I wasn't upset at all as I wanted to start a solo project during the middle of Metallica anyway.' In fact, Mustaine was devastated, becoming more furious as each hour passed on the four-day bus ride back to San Francisco, at what he would increasingly come to see as the band's betrayal of him. Specifically, what he saw as Lars' role in his sacking. 'I like James more than Lars, I think everybody does,' Mustaine was still telling people in 2008. Interviewed by Jane's Addiction guitarist Dave Navarro for his inter-net-based *Spread TV* talk show, he added, bitchily, 'I don't really like Kirk 'cos he got my job but I nailed his girlfriend before I left.' Mustaine also claimed he and Hetfield 'had planned to fire Lars so many times'. All of this may contain different degrees of truth, yet to find Mustaine still talking about it a quarter of a century later arguably says more about his own unresolved issues.

Giving his first interview since being fired from Metallica, to Bob Nalbandian, in January 1984, Mustaine gave a slightly more balanced view. 'The truth of the matter was that things just didn't click,' he said. 'I was a different person back then. I was a brash person that was always drunk and having fun and James and Lars were withdrawn little boys. James hardly ever talked to people. [James] was singing but it was I who talked in between songs. The whole thing was that I had too much to drink. But I fuck up one time and it costs me the band and they fuck up a hundred times . . .' He paused. 'There's been times when I had to carry both James and Lars because they were so drunk.' It was true. As Brian Slagel says now, 'Everybody back then was partying. None of us were sober when things were going on.' Nor was

Dave Mustaine the only one who became angry and unpleasant when drunk. Harald Oimoen recalls a late-night visit to his apartment during which a drunken James badly lost his cool, showing his mean streak after Oimoen showed him a picture he'd taken recently of Hetfield and Ulrich in bed together, goofing around, that was then used on the cover of Ron Quintana's *Metal Mania*, along with a joke picture of Eldon Hoke, a.k.a. El Duce, the notoriously overweight drummer-vocalist of Seattle's self-styled 'rape rock' band The Mentors. 'James hadn't seen it before and I hadn't realised at the time that they wanted to keep those pictures to themselves; it was like a private fun kind of thing,' Oimoen recalled. 'So I showed the magazine to James and he had a big smile on his face, he thought it was great. And then all of a sudden he realised what the picture was of and he kicked me in the stomach, and we almost got into a brawl and he said I was never taking photos of them again after that. But once the alcohol wore off and we started talking about it, it was all cool.'

Even Hetfield's later assertion that Mustaine's drug-dealing was a factor – 'the money he had coming in was not legal', James told writer Mat Snow in 1991, 'and his buddies would come in to rehearsal and things would go missing' – sidesteps the real reasons behind his dismissal. More to the point, said Hetfield, 'He was obnoxious. That was kind of what we were into back then, but when it turned in towards us, it was inevitable he'd be out.' Says Brian Slagel, 'That was James' and Lars' band from the beginning and, you know, Dave had a pretty full personality as well. It was unfortunate and a bummer because he's a phenomenally talented guy and musician. But when I heard about it I couldn't say that I was shocked.' Looking back now, Ron Quintana characterises Mustaine as 'hardcore hard rock, but he was hard to read. As well as I got along with Lars, Dave had a totally endearing personality and was the face of 1983 Metallica. Dave had charisma galore and I honestly thought they wouldn't be as good without him. But he was kind of like 1977 Ozzy: alcoholic and occasionally dangerous to himself and others.' He adds, 'Dave drank more and faster than anyone at every party and was often dead drunk by the time the party started. He often was passed out [and] if he was awake somebody might get punched! Sober, he was the life of the scene, but he never stayed sober. I don't think he ever got in a fight until he'd had a drink.' Often it would be because 'some girl gravitated towards him then her aggravated boyfriend would always show up and get bloodied'. Other times it most definitely was Dave's fault: 'He would almost always be a centre of attention and consequently a target. James was usually an ally in some shenanigan, but always in the background and usually overshadowed.' Quintana refutes any suggestion that Mustaine was still dealing drugs in San Francisco: 'Dave drank and smoked everything but didn't know enough locals to be dealing back then.' Ultimately, Quintana says, Mustaine 'could be a train wreck' but when they set off for Jonny Z's 'it looked like a strong foursome that would stick together'.

According to Bill Hale, another friendly face from those days then taking his first tentative steps as a photographer for the *Metal Rendezvous Int.* fanzine: 'Lars always had a plan.' Hale thinks Lars probably knew he was going to replace Dave Mustaine with Kirk Hammett as early as the first show Metallica and Exodus played together at the Old Waldorf in November 1982, although, 'I don't think Kirk knew it yet.' He adds, 'Dave was funny [and] he wasn't as violent as he's [now] claimed to be – none more than anyone else in San Francisco.' He cites Paul Baloff of Exodus as 'the king of excess', compared to whom, 'Dave wasn't that bad.' He also suggests that Metallica may have misfired in their decision to dump Mustaine – musically, at least: 'With Cliff and Dave, that band was monstrous! I would have put that line-up against Black Sabbath of '72 or Deep Purple [in the same era]. They were a monster band, and everybody knew, whatever it was, Metallica had *it*.' It was deeply unfair, he says, that after Mustaine got kicked out 'everybody ganged up on Dave – Dave's an alcoholic or whatever. But we all have to remember, Dave wrote most of the first [Metallica] album plus the second album, Dave [had] the ideas.' Compared to his successor, 'Dave is a much more of an aggressive player, a cutting-edge player.' That he subsequently formed his own multi-platinum-selling band, Megadeth, speaks volumes, while Hammett remains just 'a lead guitar player in a band. So you know . . .'

Hale concedes, however, that career-wise, replacing the combustible Mustaine with the rock-steady Hammett was 'why Metallica went far. All of a sudden there's just two leaders in the band.' Had Mustaine stayed, 'I can only imagine how tumultuous the whole process would have been.'

If there was a positive aspect to Mustaine's sense of betrayal, it was that it fired him up to prove the others wrong. Within months he had moved back to LA and formed his own innovative new metal band, Megadeth, in which he would not only play lead guitar but also sing. Second-in-command in the new outfit would be bassist David Ellefson, an eighteen-year-old from Minnesota who had moved out to LA with three buddies a week after graduating high school in 1983. One morning Ellefson was in his apartment chugging away on the bass intro from Van Halen's 'Running with the Devil' when he heard a voice from the apartment above scream, 'Shut the fuck up!' followed by the crash of a flowerpot hitting his window-side air-conditioner. 'I was like, jeez, these people in California aren't friendly like they are in Minnesota.' The same day one of his roommates reported seeing 'some cool-looking guy with long blond hair' walking around outside the building, barefoot. Deciding they needed 'to meet some people', one night they went upstairs to Mustaine's apartment and knocked on his door and asked where to buy some cigarettes. 'He slammed the door in our faces.' So they knocked again and asked if he knew where to buy any beer and this time 'he opens the door and lets us in'. Ellefson goes on: 'This was early June '83. He's talking about this band Metallica that he was in and which I hadn't heard of. I knew about the New Wave of British Heavy Metal but he seemed to know all about it.' Mustaine played Ellefson the *No Life* demo. 'I thought it was awesome. It had this very haunting heaviness to it that intrigued me, almost kind of scary. It had kind of a darkness to it.' Mustaine gave Ellefson the full story. 'San Francisco, New York ... playing gigs at Staten Island, Jonny Z, and then the inevitable resentment about it because he wasn't in the band any more.' Explaining why he'd been fired, 'The main thing was: "It [was about] attitude, not ability." That was his kind of tagline.'

Mustaine's new band Megadeth, he told Ellefson, would be his revenge on Metallica. 'Sure, without a doubt. It was a vengeful, spiteful return from Dave,' says Ellefson. Mustaine's ousting from Metallica 'totally explains the pressure, the angst [and] frustration' he continues to exhibit about Metallica to this very day. 'Maybe even to some degree the broken heart that Dave had about being fired. Because, you know, Dave is kind of a gentle spirit underneath all of the ferociousness and the anger. Underneath of that is a real genuine, actually real sweet guy at times. I think for him a lot of it was, yeah, obviously their success. But I never got the feeling Dave ever played guitar for money anyway. That never fuelled him.' For Dave Mustaine, 'it was more just the broken heart of losing his friendship and his buddies'. As James Hetfield later conceded, 'It's obvious [Mustaine] had the same drive as us – he went on to do great things in Megadeth.' Had he been allowed to stay, 'There would have been myself, Lars and him all trying to drive and it would have been this triangulated mess.' For that reason, not for the drinking or drug-dealing or in-fighting, but because he represented a genuine threat to the hegemony of the band, 'Dave had to go'.

Brian Slagel had seen Kirk Hammett play in Exodus and knew he was 'a great player'. Equally important, 'he seemed like a really nice guy'. When he heard about Kirk replacing Dave in Metallica, 'I knew people in Frisco who knew Kirk and I would ask around and everybody said the same thing: the guy's an *incredible* guitar player, he's a super-nice guy and he's probably the perfect fit for that band.' From the East Bay town of El Sobrante, Kirk Lee Hammett was born 18 November 1962, to a Filipino mother (Chefela) and an Irish merchant marine father. The middle child, Kirk grew up alongside an older half-brother Richard Likong (from his mother's first marriage), and a younger sister Jennifer. 'I was a typical urban child,' Kirk would tell me. 'I grew up in the city. I went to Catholic school, a couple blocks down from my house. From the time I was six years old to the time I was about twelve I would just walk to the school alone. You can't do that these days in San Francisco. You pretty much can't do that anywhere these days. But, you know, I was a very poor Catholic schoolboy.' He 'wasn't very good at being Catholic' though, he says, his main memories of his schooldays now revolving around 'reading monster magazines and horror comic books. Occasionally I'd get caught [and] the teacher would take it away.' Although he was non-confrontational, he developed a passive-aggressive stance that would later serve him well in Metallica. When the nuns threatened to call in his parents for a serious talk about his comic-reading habits, 'I remember looking at them straight in the eye and saying, "That's fine because they know all about it."' Even as an adult, Kirk was always the guy firing up a joint and reading a comic book, or watching a horror movie. His favourite: 'a tie between the original 1931 *Frankenstein* movie and *Bride of Frankenstein*'.

When, in fifth grade, he flunked his religious education class, 'I came to a conclusion that Catholicism was just hypocritical, hyper-critical . . . it wasn't congruent with my reality.' More interested these days in Buddhist philosophy, reality for Kirk Hammett as a child was a stepbrother eleven years older plugged into a percolating music scene on his doorstep that was about to change the world: '[Richard] was full-on into the whole hippy thing. He was going to the Fillmore and seeing bands like Cream, Hendrix, Santana, the Grateful Dead, Zeppelin . . . all these monumental bands and gigs.' There were also the conversations 'about LSD and acid' he overheard between Richard and his father. 'Being a merchant marine, [my father] was exposed to all sorts of things. He was very broad-minded, very open to the whole hippy lifestyle at first.' Kirk's long hair was 'another thing that the nuns really did not like. I would regularly get reminders to cut my hair because it was touching my collar.' Punishment beatings from the nuns became a regular thing: 'Generally rulers were the weapon of choice. I got some of it, you know.'

Brother Richard also played guitar and was 'a pretty big influence' on Kirk's playing. When, in 1975, their parents decided to move out of San Francisco to the suburbs, Richard, who was now twenty-three, stayed behind in the city. Kirk, who looked up to Richard and missed having him around, bought a guitar 'partly because I wanted to play, but partly because I wanted to be like him too, I wanted to emulate him'. Richard, though, was a strummer, the kind of part-time guitarist who liked to play along to Bob Dylan records. Kirk would have 'different goals, a different plan altogether'. Simply 'to become the best I could on the instrument. I wanted to be Jimi Hendrix.' He added laughingly, 'But, you know, without all the funny clothing.' As a teenager, most of what Hammett learned on guitar came from playing along to records, beginning with Hendrix's 'Purple Haze' before working his way through albums by Deep Purple, Black Sabbath, Queen, Status Quo and similar acts. By the time he'd worked out the thirty-minute-plus version of 'Dazed and Confused' from the live Led Zeppelin album, *The Song Remains the Same*, which he calls 'a riff dictionary', he was already playing in his own high school outfits. By then he'd also become obsessed by UFO's Michael Schenker, who eschewed traditional blues-based guitar solos for playing modes – 'scales that sound almost classical'. Rhythmically, Schenker was 'out the door', said Kirk. 'To this day, UFO are my favourite band in the whole world.'

Gary Holt, who understudied to Kirk in Exodus, before taking over as main guitarist after he split for Metallica, recalls 'this skinny kid with Coke-bottle-bottom glasses'. It was meeting Kirk at sixteen and seeing him play that sparked Holt's own interest in learning guitar. 'He taught me some Rolling Stones song. I don't remember what it was. But I picked up guitar really fast.' The first time either of them met Metallica was when they opened for them at the Old Waldorf. 'We were just two separate bands of complete fuck-ups. We got really drunk and we dug each other's music and we wrecked shit and broke everything and had zero respect for anything or anybody, and I think a lot of that's that punk rock attitude that we both shared.' When Lars, James and Dave moved into Mark Whitaker's El Cerrito abode, various members of Exodus would also stay over. 'We felt like it was our house, too. We had some *insane* parties at that place. We only played with Metallica five or six times but when they moved to the Bay Area we hung out constantly. We'd just get really drunk and get really ripped. I remember one night at the Metallica house not having any mixer and drinking vodka and maple syrup. Fucking awful! But it worked, you know?' They had also begun to experiment with drugs. Recalls Holt, 'Hell, before Kirk left for Metallica, him and I spent a whole summer just taking acid two or three times a week.' He adds, 'Methamphetamine was [also] a drug of choice in Exodus, which decades later spiralled out of control. But James just drank, Lars I remember getting gacked out, doing blow [cocaine] with him more than once, and Cliff just liked to get high [on pot].' In Exodus, 'if it wasn't nailed down we'd snort or swallow it. We were *all* motorheads, you know?'

Despite the stoner mien, Kirk was serious about his music. In common with James Hetfield, it was more than just a creative outlet for the teenager; it was a shield against a home life that had now turned sour as his parents' relationship began to splinter, resulting in his father walking out when he was seventeen. 'I was abused as a child,' he revealed in a 2001 *Playboy* interview. 'My dad drank a lot. He beat the shit out of me and my mom quite a bit. I got a-hold of a guitar, and from the time I was fifteen, I rarely left my room. I remember having to pull my dad off my mom when he attacked her one time, during my sixteenth birthday – he turned on me and started slapping me around. Then my dad just left one day. My mom was struggling to support me and my sister. I've definitely channelled a lot of anger into the music.' He added that he had also been abused by a neighbour 'when I was like nine or ten', adding: 'The guy was a sick fuck. He had sex with my dog, Tippy. I can laugh about it now ...' Heavy metal, he added dolefully, had the power to bring outsiders in from the cold. 'Heavy metal seems to attract all sorts of scruffy, lost animals, strays no one wants.'

Having graduated from the inexpensive Montgomery Ward catalogue special that he'd started out on, with a four-inch speaker for an amp, to a 1978 Fender Stratocaster by the time he was gigging with Gary and Exodus, he was now wielding a customised 1974 Gibson Flying V, which he took a part-time job at Burger King to save money to buy a Marshall amp for. Having graduated in 1980 from De Anaza High School, he was also now studying English and psychiatry at college when he got the call inviting him to audition for Metallica.

Like Lars, he was taken aback by the NWOBHM. Like Cliff, he'd also studied classical music, performing Haydn and Bach in a high school trio. He was also taking regular guitar lessons from someone now regarded as one of the world's greatest living players, Joe Satriani, with whom Hammett would learn the formalities of music theory, modes, arpeggios and harmonies.

An ex-New Yorker who was so shocked by news of Hendrix's death he took up the guitar himself – 'the day I heard he died, I was playing football and I went to the coach and told him I was leaving to play guitar to be like my hero,' he says now – by 1981 Joe Satriani was working out of a guitar shop in Berkeley, giving lessons, while trying to get his own club band, The Squares, off the ground. Kirk had heard of him 'from just being in the San Francisco underground metal scene and seeing a few guitar players in the scene who had a massive amount of technique, and me coming up to them and introducing myself to them and asking, "How did you learn to play like this?" And they all said the same thing, "Oh, I'm taking lessons from this guy named Joe, in this music store in Berkeley."' Kirk, who 'had to just find this guy' got on his bike and rode it to Satriani's store. 'I walked in, like "Hi, I'm here for guitar lessons. Is there a guy named Joe in the house?", and some guy in the back said, "Yeah, I'm over here."'

'The first few times Kirk came to me for lessons I remember his mother brought him,' says Satriani now. 'It was the beginning of thrash metal in San Francisco. But Kirk was really quite different, really wanting to know the secrets behind Uli Jon Roth and Michael Schenker as well as Jimi Hendrix and Stevie Ray Vaughan. He was a connoisseur, a really good head on his shoulders. He knew what he liked and had really good taste. One day he comes in and says, "Hey man, I got this audition for this band Metallica." Then I didn't see him for a bit, then he comes back and he's like, "I'm in this band and it's great! We're recording an album!" Things were just taking off for them and it was really great to see it. Then later on as they were working on other records, sometimes he would bring in songs that they were working on and he'd say, "What do you play over this?" Because James [Hetfield] would be writing some chord progressions that people hadn't written before. Whether he knew what he was doing or not, it didn't matter; he was writing some very intense music. But Kirk, who was the soloist in the band, it put him in a new stop. If he went back and looked at Schenker's solos or Hendrix solos he'd say, well, those guys didn't get into this territory either so where's my guide, you know? And so I started to introduce him to some unusual scales. And the way I did it was quite organic. I would show him a scale, explain to him that the scale comes from the notes of the chord progression and then I'd say, "But there are no rules and you have to decide what scale you're going to play and which notes from the scale you're going to emphasise. And whatever you decide, that becomes your style." Kirk was a great example of somebody who could look at what I was doing and say, "I understand where Joe is coming from but I know he wants me to take it in my own direction." And that's what he did and that's the sound that we know and love, the sound of Metallica with Kirk riding on top.'

At the time he left to join Metallica in New Jersey, Kirk had recorded one three-track demo with Exodus and held high hopes for their future. 'I started Exodus in high school. It was me and [drummer] Tom Hunting. We basically got together to just play. One day I said, "Hey, let's find a name for ourselves," so we went to the county library [in Richmond]. I went down one aisle and I saw a book and on the spine it said: *Exodus* by Leon Uris. I pointed to that and said, "That's our name right there – Exodus!" and it stuck. From the get-go we were playing original material. Although it wasn't very good, we were still playing original material, and we played a bunch of cover songs. We did the whole house-band circuit, playing for our friends' parties and at their houses. Occasionally we would rent out town halls or city halls, and put up a stage and charge tickets for a show. In the last, like, six or eight months of me being in the band it was starting to happen – starting to play places like the Old Waldorf and the Keystone, in Berkeley. And we landed this opening slot for this unknown band called Metallica that we had only just heard of and heard the demo like maybe two weeks prior.' The first time he saw Metallica, he said, 'I'll never forget it. I thought to myself, "These guys are great but they could be so much better with me in the band." I honestly thought that.' Five months later he was flying to New York to join them. 'Mark Whitaker passed an Exodus demo on to Lars and James and they listened to it and heard it and thought, okay, let's get this guy out. And, you know, we never really looked back.'

Gary Holt now insists that the rest of Exodus took the news well. But that was only after they realised there was nothing they could do about it – and after Gary realised it would mean the band was now his, virtually. 'We had a big party for Kirk. Had a food fight at his house, we went around the Old Waldorf drinking, and cut about fifty pictures of Kirk out of the band photos and put them all over the place, little Kirkies, as Paul [Baloff] called it. I mean, obviously it worked out great for Kirk, and I was already like starting to sew my own oats as a songwriter. I had already written a number of songs that ended up on [first Exodus album] *Bonded by Blood*.' Kirk leaving, 'kind of put me in the driver's seat and so I relished the opportunity. There was no hard feelings. I thought it was my chance to mould the band into the image I wanted to. Tom and I gathered, just the two of us, and really started banging songs out from all of these riffs I had already.' The bottom line, Holt admits, was 'Metallica was in New York and on the verge of making an album – something that was still a way off for us. That was the golden carrot that [Kirk] chased.'

Taking the red-eye shuttle overnight from Frisco to New York, Kirk Hammett arrived at Jonny and Marsha's house just a few hours after they'd driven Dave Mustaine to the Greyhound bus depot. Hammett now recalls his entry into Metallica as 'pretty level at that point ... we were all still in the beginnings of our careers as musicians. And when I joined the band we all got along famously ... I literally just walked in and sat down and they said, "Okay, you're in the band, let's take it from here."' Determined, however, not to become bogged down in the same battle for leadership as the one they had just disentangled themselves from with Mustaine, Lars and James laid it out for him plain and simple – an attitude Lars later shared with the readers of *Rolling Stone* as, 'Let's not bullshit ourselves, me and James ran the show. Me and James made the records. Me and James wrote the songs.' Kirk simply smiled his stoner smile and nodded his head. 'I didn't have any problem with that. It was evident that it was Lars' and James' band.' Nevertheless, it was an autocratic rigidity that would make itself evident in the music more than was perhaps good for the band as the years rolled by and Lars' and James' grip on Metallica's musical path tightened ever more. 'We still made major decisions together,' Kirk would insist. 'But whenever I had to push for an idea, I had to assume the role of diplomat. I had to sell them the idea.' Cliff, meanwhile, knew better than to argue. It may have been Lars' and James' band but they had come to him, not the other way around. As a musician, Cliff knew he was streets ahead of his new young bandmates, but he also understood band politics better than any of them. Let them do the talking in public, let them have the lion's share of the writing credits; he was secure enough in his own talents, in his knowledge of who he really was, not to wish to compete on that level. The real tests would arrive once the first album had been completed and the band could move on, to tour, to write, to become a real band – with Cliff Burton as its very epicentre.

Jonny Z, who admits he was 'scared shitless' at the prospect of the band finding a good enough replacement for Mustaine, recalls going down to the band's first rehearsal with Kirk 'and he was just blistering. He had learned the songs, like, overnight. He just came and it was like, let's go do some more gigs.' Following a nervous debut at the Showplace in Dover, New Jersey, the new Ulrich-Hetfield-Burton-Hammett line-up of Metallica was thrown into the deep end with two back-to-back shows at the much larger Paramount Theater on Staten Island, opening for Venom. Says Jonny, 'At the Showplace, I noticed Kirk would be blazing away but he'd be looking at his guitar all the time and he would stop and then he would go on. So I said to him, "Listen, Kirk, play the first part and let it rip, but look at the audience, and when you finish the first part just put your arms up in the air." He was reluctant but he did it. At the very next show [with Venom] he put his arms up in the air and the audience goes, "Argh!" It was great!' As well as 'that little shtick', it was Jonny Z who gave them the idea for some music to walk onstage to every night: Ennio Morricone's evocative theme tune to the Clint Eastwood spaghetti western, *The Good, the Bad and the Ugly*. As Jonny says, it worked so well, 'It still introduces the band today. Marsha and I are big Morricone fans and I'd always thought that would be a great piece of music for some awesome metal band to walk onstage to. And it is!'

Through his connections with the underground metal scene, Jonny had persuaded the independent label, Neat, in the UK, to front enough money to send Venom to the USA for some shows under Jonny's stewardship, on 22 and 24 of April. Venom guitarist Mantas (real name: Jeff Dunn) recalls staying at Jonny and Marsha's house at the same time as Metallica. 'We were upstairs and they were downstairs, and it was so fuckin' hot it was difficult to get to sleep anyway.' Like Metallica, Venom proved a handful for the Zazulas. 'I remember we wrecked his kitchen one night when we were trying to cook something, and set fire to the fuckin' place!' The two bands got on well. James Hetfield collapsed drunk after the first show while clutching a vodka bottle, badly cutting his hand and necessitating a trip to the nearest Emergency Room, where he needed six stitches. Dunn recalls Venom bassist/vocalist Cronos – real name: Conrad Lant – passing out drunk after that first show in the same bed as Lars. 'Absolutely pissed out of their fuckin' heads and they just fell asleep, then woke up together in the morning and said, "What the fuck is this!" Everybody just crashed out . . . I could hear Lars going nuts downstairs, and I heard my roadie saying, "I'm gonna go down and knock that cunt out in a minute, I just really want to go to sleep." Then it was quiet all of a sudden, I guess he just passed out or something.' The following day, Venom visited Jonny and Marsha's Rock 'n' Roll Heaven stall to sign autographs. Dunn recalled: 'I've still got the original poster which says, "Meet in person: Venom at Rock 'n' Roll Heaven" and then in tiny writing at the bottom: "Metallica".'

Venom's famously over-the-top show was nearly the cause of a serious accident. Dunn recalled how at the first Paramount show, 'we had these cast-iron bomb pots, right, about the diameter of a mug and eight inches high, and there were twenty-four of these along the front of the stage. One guy went along and filled the pots with blasting powder and put the fuses in, right? Then – because communication was so crap – another guy goes, "Fuck! The bomb pots!" half an hour before the show, gets up and fills them up again, not knowing the first guy had already done it!' Dunn claimed the explosion when the pots went off 'was louder than the band. One of the bomb pots – and this is no word of a lie – was found in the balcony embedded in the wall. That fucker could have killed somebody. There was a four-foot hole blown in the wood of the stage, as well. How somebody wasn't injured . . .' Hetfield shrugged, 'There were a lot of unsafe things but we loved that surprise fear factor; it just added another dimension to the show.'

The only area Metallica still felt weak in was the issue of the lead vocals. The closer Jonny took them to actually recording their first album, the more of an issue it became for them. They decided, once again, to see if they might be able to persuade someone to come in and take over the frontman role, leaving James free to concentrate on the music. Marsha offered to line up some auditions, while Lars, as ever, had ideas of his own. Bill Hale claims Lars suggested they try and track down Jess Cox, original vocalist of NWOBHM archetypes Tygers of Pan Tang, who had left the band after their debut album, *Wild Cat*, in 1980. But while Cox had the sort of gravelly voice that might have fitted, what Lars didn't know was that the singer was already embarked on a solo career that would see him moving more squarely towards the Eighties mainstream, padded shoulders, hair-sprayed mullet and all. But while Cox may have been 'number one on their list', according to Hale, it was to someone much closer to home that they next turned: the nineteen-year-old singer of another local LA outfit, Armored Saint, called John Bush.

Lars Ulrich openly admired called Armored Saint. The two bands' paths would cross more than once in the future as Lars, briefly, became something of a champion for them. In 1983, however, he and James would happily have poached their singer – if only he would agree to throw in his lot with them. In fact, Bush turned Metallica down flat. 'They got Jonny to call him,' recalls Marsha. 'But he wasn't interested.' For good reason, or so it seemed at the time. As

Bush now points out, this was at a time when Metallica had yet to release an album, and while there was already 'a giant buzz' about them, 'it wasn't like they were that far past where Armored Saint was at, at that point. It was like, I don't wanna join that band, I'm already in this band and these are all my friends.' He admits that 'whenever I tell that story now kids look at me like, you're fuckin' crazy', but that, 'Nobody anticipated what was to come – the whole face of it could have changed, *literally*. 'Cos who knows ... I could have *ruined* it,' he laughs. 'I could have ruined metal!' In fact, Bush adds, more seriously, 'The enormous key to Metallica's success, in my opinion, was the emergence of James as the frontman. His voice [in the early Metallica] is the way it is. But he turned into an awesome rock singer. You know, the riffs were great and all the fiery music and the energy and the attitude but the key to it all was the emergence of James as a singer and frontman. That's what took it to a hundred levels higher. I remember saying, "You guys don't need anybody. James is awesome!" It wasn't like I said, "I'm not right but maybe somebody else is." James was just coming into his own.' Says Marsha Z: 'James never wanted to take that frontman position. He wanted to step back and be a guitarist. He really never had a desire, I don't think, to step into that front space. But ... he did. And as he did, James became James. I think his real person came out when he took that position permanently. It was almost like it gave him, oddly enough, another voice.'

Meantime, Jonny had moved the band out of his house. 'It was too intense.' It all came to a head when the band raided their drinks cabinet one night and uncorked some bottles of champagne the Zazulas had been given as wedding presents. Jonny and Marsha talked to Anthrax, another unsigned local metal band that had a rehearsal space at a place called the Music Building in Queens where many bands also slept in their rehearsal rooms. Recalls Jonny, 'I said, you know what, they need to rehearse, let's get all their gear and get them down there too. 'Cos I had to get 'em out of the house.' There were no spare rooms going, though, so Jonny fast-talked the building manager into allowing Metallica to share Anthrax's room to rehearse, while using the loft to sleep in. 'Imagine a gutted building,' says Jonny, 'old chairs and dirt and crap thrown around in this one big giant space. They cleared a little space in the rubble for them to lay down and sleep. It was *really* horrible. Marsha and I had no idea. We were hearing complaints, complaints, complaints … But to me I wasn't really listening because I had enough to complain about myself. My place was ripped to shreds. It was like sixty people every fuckin' night walking in and out of my place. It was crazy.' For several weeks, the band lived on 'white bread and baloney'. Kirk Hammett recalled how he 'found a piece of foam on the ground, and I used that as my mattress to put my sleeping bag on'. There was no hot water, so the band was forced to bathe in cold: 'It was brutal.' Some mornings, badly hungover, having only crashed out a few hours before, they would be woken early by the piercing sounds of an opera singer going through her rehearsal routine. Anthrax leader Scott Ian recalls, 'They had no money, they had nowhere to go, so we pretty much went out of our way to help them out in any way we could. We brought them to our houses to shower, and we gave them a refrigerator and a toaster oven so they could cook the hot dogs that they were eating cold. We just hung out as much as possible.'

Eventually another pal of Jonny's named Metal Joe agreed to let the band sleep at his place, nicknamed the Fun House. Along with his best friend Rockin' Ray, Metal Joe was one of the best customers at Rock 'n' Roll Heaven. Ray 'would spend his entire paycheque on metal albums. He would take home eleven or twelve albums at a time. Then that night everybody would go to his house – I'd say about forty people – and get stoned and crazy and put it on full blast. Metal Joe left a PA's worth of speakers in Ray's house. So we would blow everybody's mind and they really got sucked into the metal.' Another supporter from the same circle was Mark Mari, who would show up at the shows wearing a World War I army helmet with the word 'metal' written on it. 'There were different gangs of metal mongers through the north-east. I would give each posse fifty tickets and say, hey, sell the tickets for the shows. These were guys your parents would run from! Scary, scary people.' But they never let Jonny down or cheated him. They would come to his house and hand over the cash when all the tickets had been sold. As a reward, 'I would give them first row. So they would be there in pride and everybody else would be behind them, you know? We'd do shows [where] we knew everybody's name in the venue. We didn't need security. That's the world that I lived in from day one, and Ray and Joe were a real big part of it, in terms of keeping the band's minds occupied and partying and hanging out and going crazy.'

By now Jonny Z had effectively taken over the day-to-day management of Metallica from Mark Whitaker. 'I'd never managed before,' he says, 'but the adrenalin was so intense.' Within weeks he had gone as far as announcing the formation of his own company, CraZed Management, in which Marsha was his fifty/fifty partner. In time they would also take on management responsibilities for Anthrax and Raven. Initially, though, 'It was all about Metallica. Everything. Every day.' Jonny adds, 'It was like someone threw us a football and we just ran all the way down the field. And everyone was coming to get us, believe me. But we scored touchdowns.'

As acting manager, Jonny's main priority now was to get a Metallica album recorded. He had his sights set higher, though, than merely getting a piece of plastic out on something like Brian Slagel's fledgling Metal Blade imprint. But despite packing the crowds in at their gigs regularly, there were no major record labels in America in 1983 interested in a band like Metallica. The biggest-selling album that year was Michael Jackson's *Thriller*. Six months after its release in November '82, it was still selling more than a million copies a month in the USA and was only halfway through a run at Number One that would last for thirty-seven consecutive weeks. On 16 May 1983, the same week Metallica began recording their first album, NBC TV broadcast *Motown 25: Yesterday, Today, Forever*, the show on which Jackson famously unveiled his 'moonwalk' during a captivating performance before his peers of his hit single, 'Billie Jean'. The next day the whole country seemed to be talking about it. Fred Astaire telephoned the twenty-five-year-old singer personally to congratulate him. *Thriller* was now well on its way to becoming the biggest-selling album of all time – an achievement that helped transform the fortunes of the US record biz, then suffering from its second slump in three years. Before *Thriller*, US industry bible *Billboard* had reported that record shipments had declined by over fifty million units between 1980 and 1982. Before *Thriller*, US record companies had been drastically reducing staff and slashing budgets. Now, in its wake, came the era of the ultra-commercial blockbuster album. When, in 1984, Columbia – which had released *Thriller* and was one of the labels that laughed Jonny Z out of the door when he tried to bring them Metallica – released the next Bruce Springsteen album, *Born in the U.S.A.*, they did so with seven singles already prepped for release from it, all of which would arrow straight into the US Top Ten. Meanwhile, their main rivals at Warner Bros readied themselves to launch five singles from Prince's next album, *Purple Rain*, while Mercury, who had seen Def Leppard's third album, *Pyromania*, beaten to the top spot in 1983 by *Thriller*, made sure they beat the odds with their next album, *Hysteria*, by hitting US radio with no less than seven singles from it – all of them major chart successes. As a result, all these albums sold more than ten million copies each in the USA alone, becoming the most successful of each respective artist's careers.

The impact of the NWOBHM on the US mainstream had been minimal, barely registering at all outside the same pockets of hardcore underground interest that Metallica itself had sprung from. Of the handful of NWOBHM bands that actually made it across to America by 1983, only Def Leppard had enjoyed significant success, and then because Leppard were colourful and exciting – their impossibly youthful image cut from the same pop-rock cloth as contemporaries such as Duran Duran, their music sculpted in the studio by 'Mutt' Lange, the same production genius who had gifted huge chart success to AC/DC, The Cars and the Boomtown Rats; video-friendly, singles-oriented, pop-in-rock-clothing. Even Iron Maiden, the only other NWOBHM band now beginning to see success in America, had done so only after replacing their original short-haired, punk-style singer Paul Di'Anno with the more generic-sounding, trad-rock vocalist Bruce Dickinson. Maiden didn't rely on mainstream pop success like

Leppard, but they still had to tailor their sheet-metal riffs for a broader audience than the one they'd launched their career with in the UK. Indeed, the only other notable successes from the UK in the same period were Judas Priest, like Maiden from a previous generation, and, in 1987, Whitesnake, who followed Leppard's MTV first template almost to the letter.

The only home-grown rock music that still held purchase with both US radio and the Top Ten album charts came from increasingly middle-of-the-road 'melodic rock' acts such as Journey and REO Speedwagon. Huey Lewis and the News, another San Francisco band in the 'soft rock' mould that hit Number One in 1983 with their *Sports* album, only did so, Lewis later revealed, after 'a huge fight' with the chiefs of their record company Chrysalis, who actually tried to get Lewis to either change his singing style or hand over vocal duties in the band to an entirely different singer. 'They actually told me: "That kind of deep voice doesn't get played on [US] radio any more,"' he told me in 1984. Fortunately for the future of the News, Lewis, a tough New Yorker who had spent years 'schlepping around the circuit', was bloody-minded enough to ignore such 'advice'. Fortunately for Metallica, Jonny Z was cut from similar, hard-as-nails New York City cloth and also ignored what the major label chiefs were now advising him to do with Metallica: forget about it.

'We'd been to everybody,' says Jonny. 'Some of the biggest names in A&R in the United States turned down Metallica. I'm talking Columbia, I'm talking Arista, I'm talking most labels. The only place where there was any kind of communication and understanding of metal was this one fellow at Elektra named Michael Alago. We would go to Michael Alago and constantly talk to him about Metallica *and* Raven.' A young rock fan from Brooklyn who had only just landed a job as talent scout, Alago would eventually be sufficiently persuaded by what Jonny Z had to tell him about Metallica to make a move. But not before the band had felt so left out in the cold that the only way they could see a way forward was to throw all caution to the wind and record the album on their own, without any record company support – in the bold hope of using it as bait to try and attract a major deal afterwards. 'It wasn't just balls,' says Jonny. 'You had to be absolutely mad to take a chance on something like that. It was like we were on a mission. And the mission was to take this band and make it a world-wide name – not knowing how the fuck to do it.'

FIVE
LONG-HAIRED PUNKS

I was homeless, sleeping rough on people's floors and couches, carrying my whole life around in plastic carrier bags, me and the portable children's typewriter. Xavier was one of the good guys, had a place in Notting Hill. The only caveat was you had to drink lots of whisky and Bourbon – Maker's Mark, Crown Royal, Old Grandad, never Jack Daniel's, 'Too touristy,' he said – and listen to Molly Hatchet. That is, play along to Molly Hatchet, on squash rackets, which we'd hammer away at like guitars, shaking our hair, performing for the grateful millions, usually at about two in the morning. Jesus, he must have had understanding neighbours, 'cos it was louder than hell in there whenever I visited and we got up to do a gig together. He'd light some candles, refill our glasses, whack on No Guts ... No Glory, pass me a squash racket and off we would fucking well go ...

This one night, though, he deviated from the norm. ''Ere, listen to this,' he grinned, pulling out the plastic from an album cover I didn't recognise. Of course, I didn't recognise most of the album covers in his collection but you could tell this was something different, obviously new, because he couldn't wait to play it. He didn't even get the rackets out. He actually wanted me to listen to it. Tired from a week spent on the floor of some draughty old squat in King's Cross, grateful not to have to sing for my supper, I flopped down on the couch and waited for it to begin. I didn't have to wait long.

It sort of faded in on a cacophony of exploding guitars and drums, more like the climactic end of an album than the beginning. Then the band found its starting place and the thing kicked off and I burst out laughing. It was the fastest, funniest thing I'd heard since the first Damned album, *and the first Damned album had been the fastest, funniest thing I'd ever heard in my life. It was FANTASTIC! Not because it was deep or momentous, but because it was – well – just so damn fast and fun. I assumed it must be some sort of punk band but when I asked for the album cover to look at, it was obvious straight away they weren't punks at all. In fact, they looked like a bunch of Iron Maiden or Motörhead fans, out for a night at the youth club disco, revved up on Anadin and cider. Then I noticed the name – Metallica – and I laughed some more. Only X could have found a metal band named Metallica!*

The next track began. 'This is the one!' he yelled in my ear. Sure enough, out came the squash rackets and up we got. Suddenly the whole thing was even more fantastic. The guitars! My god, they sounded like machines! Cars skidding and crashing, then veering away at the last possible moment in a gigantic cloud of burning rubber. It went on and on. How long was it? Fucking long, that's how long! Then suddenly this back-arching guitar solo. Wow, so they really were metal. Then back to the riff and I didn't know what it was we were listening to. It was so fucking loud and full-on and utterly unapologetic, I thought I was tripping.

When finally he left me to the couch, the bottle of Old Granddad empty, my head was still buzzing with it. 'They're gonna be huge,' he'd told me, over and over. I didn't believe it for a second; they might be amazing, a sort of teenage Godzilla, but that didn't mean anyone besides lunatics like me and Xavier would ever buy them. Still, it had been mental while it lasted. When I awoke the next day I was really very ill . . .

Freed at last from the hellish Halfway House but still on his best behaviour, Jonny Z worked his indefatigable magic on behalf of Metallica once more and somehow found them a studio to record their first album in. Acting on a tip-off from Joey DeMaio, whose band Manowar had also just recorded there, Jonny fast-talked Paul Curcio, owner of Music America Studios, near Rochester in Upstate New York, into accepting an instalment plan with which to make payments. 'This was mortgage money I'm spending,' Jonny says now, 'not something I've got put by I'm gonna invest.' The band would have to work quickly, 'Quick enough for an eight-thousand-dollar album.' In fact, the album would end up costing nearer $15,000, pushing the Zazulas to the brink of bankruptcy.

Part of the deal was that Curcio would produce the sessions, with Jonny acting as executive producer. Meaning: 'I was in the studio for most of the time. If I didn't like it, it was changed.' Later the band would complain they'd been locked out of the control room. But Jonny wasn't fooling around. 'They may think I was a control freak; I have no idea what the band's take on me was because I was definitely a strange man. Just some fuckin' oddball. I had to be!' Recorded in under three weeks, most of the band's later disaffection was directed towards the production, such as it was. Hetfield recalled: 'Our so-called producer was sitting there checking the songs off a notepad and saying, "Well, we can go to a club tonight when we're through recording. Is the coffee ready?" So right away we had a bad reflection of what a producer was.' James would complain to Jonny: 'I didn't put in my heaviness yet.' Jonny cites the track, 'The Four Horsemen' – the band's refurbished version of Mustaine's 'The Mechanix' – as a prime example. Or rather, he sings it, his voice alternating from weedy-sounding tic-tac chords to the more full-on punch of the power chords Hetfield was eventually able to get onto the recording. Jonny says that Curcio, who'd worked back in the early 1970s with the Doobie Brothers and Santana, 'flipped out 'cos he thought Kirk Hammett was this son of Santana. So he made the entire [album] like a band doing rhythm tracks under Kirk Hammett's brilliant guitar playing.' Jonny had to sit the producer down and explain. 'Then James went in and heavied-up the tracks and Paul [Curcio] was never happy with me again after that.' As far as Jonny was concerned, 'The first thing we had to beat was the vibe on *No Life 'til Leather*. That really displayed the power and force of the band. This album couldn't come out sounding like tin. It had to sound like thunder.'

Jonny would get his wish. Although he and the band would have to wait until their next album to fully capture the thunderstorm of a full-on live performance, the first Metallica album – which they had decided would be called *Metal up Your Ass*, a title Lars had been saving since his days cruising around with Brian, Bob, Patrick and the guys looking for rare NWOBHM imports – would sound like nothing else out there when it finally appeared in the summer of 1983. All ten tracks came from their existing live set and, as such, represented a musical manifesto of sorts; self-referential, self-eulogising, utterly self-absorbed. From the opener – an up-to-date version of 'Hit the Lights', its gargantuan intro now faded in and Hetfield's vocals over-dosed with echo – to the rat-tat-tat of its flag-waving finale 'Metal Militia', replete with end-zone effects of marching soldiers, this was the sound of a young band announcing itself from the rooftops, remaking the world in its own image, and doing it with all the zit-faced arrogance and faltering, still-learning-to-shave steps only a very young and brash new band can. Production-wise, all the numbers previously gathered on cassettes such as *No Life 'til Leather* and the various live tapes appear in obviously superior versions, while the addition of Burton and Hammett clearly signals a more sophisticated melodic dimension, actually slowing one or two numbers down a fraction, adding even more weight to the hammer-swinging rhythms.

Early on, Jonny Z had identified 'The Mechanix' as the stand-out *No Life* track. Sure enough, it's also the most impressive overall moment on the album, albeit re-presented in altered, much-improved form as a track now called 'The Four Horsemen'. Ron McGovney had always considered Mustaine's original lyrics 'ridiculous'. The others had been less outspoken – until Mustaine was finally out of the picture, at which point Hetfield completely rewrote them. Gone were Dave's cringe-inducing double-entendres – 'Made my drive shaft crank ... made my pistons bulge ... made my ball bearings melt from the heat ...' – and in came some typically doom-laden Hetfield musings, mixing the metal-by-numbers imagery of lines such as 'dying since the day you were born' with yet more self-referential stuff about 'horsemen ... drawing nearer, on the leather steeds they ride ...' Musically, while its chugging main riff still owed a lot to Kiss's 'Detroit Rock City', it was also the lengthiest, most complex piece on the album, full of surprising one-off motifs and thus the compositional progenitor of the increasingly complex, determinedly progressive material that Metallica would become famous for throughout the 1980s. Pitched at a considerably slower pace than Mustaine had always driven it along at, it also allowed the band to show themselves off in their best light, Burton's swooning bass underpinning the juddering riffs with a classically framed, ascending progression that eventually gives way to a much more understated guitar solo from Hammett than the frenzied strafing Mustaine had always favoured. It's a hugely ambitious number from a band still finding its feet in the studio, as if they had bolted together, Frankenstein-like, the still living parts of several other, now dead songs; one showing off their speed metal credentials, another showcasing Burton and Hammett's abilities to introduce a much more textured approach. Similarly, the tracks 'Phantom Lord' (another of the four tracks Mustaine is given a songwriter co-credit for) and 'No Remorse' (one of the four credited just to Hetfield and Ulrich, with riff partially lifted from 'Hocus Pocus' by Focus) both demonstrated that there was even more to Metallica than Jonny Z's 'thunder'. There was crooked lightning to be had too, highs and lows, moon and stars – a whole new musical horizon coming quite suddenly into view.

The other major highlight, though, was one of the album's shortest tracks, 'Whiplash'. Inspired by the wild antics of one Ray Burch, a major Metallica fan from San Francisco, who had already distinguished himself at several of their Bay Area shows by almost knocking himself out (hence also the oblique Burch-inspired dedication on the back of the album sleeve: 'bang that head that doesn't bang'), as its title suggests, 'Whiplash' cracked along at a furious pace, sounding like a cross between prime-time 'Ace of Spades'-era Motörhead and something even faster from the first, dementedly speedy Damned album. Every track on *Metal up Your Ass* teemed with energy but 'Whiplash' really does sound like the start of something new; as snotty as the rawest British punk and as rhythmically fleet-footed as early, shotgun-tempo Van Halen. There are other blisteringly paced moments on the album, such as 'Motorbreath' – a simple, four-chord verse and stop-start chorus, credited solely to Hetfield, that would be a guaranteed crowd pleaser for years to come – but if one wishes to identify the very moment thrash metal arrived spitting and snarling into the world, 'Whiplash' is indisputably it. This not least because of its prophetic chorus: 'Adrenalin stars to flow / Thrashing all around / Acting like a maniac / Whiplash ...'

The album's only weak track was, almost inevitably, its most obviously commercial: a nauseous bit of old-fashioned heavy metal nonsense – co-credited to Hetfield, Ulrich and Mustaine but actually based on one of the first songs Mustaine had ever written as a teenager – called 'Jump in the Fire'. Replete with shout-out chorus and a tediously telegraphed attempt at a catchy riff, 'Jump in the Fire' was so wince-inducingly rote it could have come from any of the chart-fixated LA glam-metal bands Metallica professed to loathe so much. To give them credit, they later recognised it as such – Lars jokingly suggesting it was, in fact, based on Metallica's half-witted attempt to emulate Iron Maiden's 1982 UK hit 'Run to the Hills' – but not before it was released as their own first UK single, though not, tellingly, their first hit. Equally straightforward but far more successful was 'Seek and Destroy', another song which would became a cornerstone of the live Metallica show for years to come, its audience sing-along on the simple, one-line chorus of 'Searching ... seek and destroy!' providing the crowd with the opportunity to roar along, encouraged by James.

The only other places where the album would remain less than convincing came somewhat embarrassingly from the band's principal members. Burton and Hammett shine throughout – the latter, despite being asked to reproduce guitar riffs, breaks and solos entirely conceived by someone else, a fact Mustaine would crow about for many years; the former in more subtle ways, and most directly in the shape of his own instrumental track, '(Anesthesia) Pulling Teeth', an attention-grabbing, avant-rock fusion of classical triads, wah-wah pedal washes and pure distortion tethered to the ground by some fairly pedestrian drumming from Lars, and based on Cliff's live show solo, introduced perfunctorily by studio engineer Chris Bubacz. Hetfield's lead vocals, however, are still woefully undeveloped, caught somewhere between the screeching, chest-beating of a Judas Priest or Iron Maiden and the richer, more intimidating vocal burr he would grow into over subsequent releases. Lars' drums – recorded in a large ballroom on the building's second floor – are scattered comically over everything, endlessly rolling crescendos that sound like what they are: the work of an overenthusiastic amateur who doesn't know when to stop.

'The first album,' Hetfield would later tell *Rolling Stone*, was simply 'what we knew – bang your head, seek and destroy, get drunk, smash shit up.' For all its instant underground cred, while many of the earlier demos of the songs had sounded like Motörhead meets Diamond Head, the finished album seemed aimed more towards the classic finesse of an early Iron Maiden or Black Sabbath. At this stage of their story, though, the first Metallica album was never going to just be about music. Its real achievement was to simultaneously define a new sensibility – the previously thought incompatible yet strangely thrilling, now it was here, melding of punk and heavy metal into something surprisingly far-reaching called thrash – and to reclaim credibility for a genre of music, heavy rock, which had become the provenance of those cultural illiterates left behind by the ground-zero arrival of punk.

First, though, Jonny and Marsha Z had to find a way to get the album released. No longer hopeful of landing a record deal once the album was recorded, with the band still sleeping on the floor at Metal Joe's and the finished recordings in a box of tapes in the corner of their living room, Jonny and Marsha took their boldest decision yet: to effectively put out the record themselves. Says Jonny, 'I figured, if we can buy [records] from a distributor, as we did as a record store, we could certainly sell them a record to sell to all the other record stores. We didn't know that nobody from the distributors wanted to talk to you. The whole thing was we just did it.' He laughs then adds, 'Maybe I could have gone to someone like Metal Blade or Shrapnel on the West Coast, but this stuff was so new-sounding I didn't know if anyone else would get it, you know? I was like the guy who didn't know if he had a great idea or a stupid one, and I knew there was only one way to find out.'

Jonny and Marsha had decided to call the label Vigilante, then changed their minds after Cliff Burton came up with a better suggestion: Megaforce, the title of a low-rent sci-fi action adventure flick released in the USA the previous summer. Tagline: 'When the force was with them, NO ONE stood a chance!' As a mission statement, it was certainly apt. In reality, it meant taking out a second mortgage on the Zazula family home. 'Some of those days were the worst days of my life,' Jonny later recalled. 'My neck was in a noose.' But with Anthrax, Raven and now even Manowar, who'd been dropped by the EMI-backed Liberty label, all knocking on their door, promising to sign to their new notional label, Jonny and Marsha pressed on. They were encouraged by Lars, who suggested taking a leaf from Motörhead's book: Motörhead's records were ostensibly released on a small UK independent label – Bronze Records – but distributed through the auspices of Polydor Records, part of the Polygram conglomerate.

Formed in London in 1971, Bronze was started by Gerry Bron, then best known for his production work on albums for heavy rock groups of the era such as Uriah Heep, Juicy Lucy and Colosseum. When Heep's deal with Vertigo ended, Bron persuaded them to let him set up their own independent, with all manufacturing and distribution of their records going through Chris Blackwell's Island Records, then the UK's most successful independent. Later releases went through EMI and by the mid-1980s they were putting their roster – which now featured NWOBHM stalwarts (Motörhead, Girlschool), punk (The Damned) and early 1970s rock goliaths (Hawkwind, Heep) – through Polydor. Jonny took Lars' suggestion seriously enough to invite Gerry Bron over to the USA, with the idea of having Bronze put out the Metallica album in the UK and Europe, while Jonny formed his own label to work with US distributors. It might have happened, too. Says Jonny, '[They were] offering money for me to get the fuck out of the way ... After that went down, Marsha and I spoke to Lars and said, why can't we just do it?'

In the USA, Megaforce found an ally in Relativity, who agreed to distribute the Metallica album, while over in the UK the newly founded independent label Music for Nations was similarly contracted to put out the album. From that point on, says Jonny, he and Marsha 'did everything; recording, producer, plus the artwork, also designed by us'. Still intending to call the album *Metal up Your Ass*, the band had originally come up with their own idea for the album sleeve: an arm coming up through a toilet bowl, brandishing a machete. Jonny, who was up for it until the appalled sales force at Relativity intervened, then had the job of trying to explain that while he was fine with it, the distributors had told him they would consider it 'commercial suicide' to put out an album called *Metal up Your Ass*, let alone one with such an obviously offensive front cover. Recalls Jonny: 'It was very stringent then. It was before [parent advisory] labelling but they still had this moral issue. Wal-Mart or any of what they call rack-jobbers, they wouldn't touch the record.' Outraged, nevertheless, at the thought of having to compromise, to keep the record stores happy, Cliff bellowed at Jonny: 'Kill 'em all! Kill 'em all!' Jonny laughs as he recounts the incident. 'Cliff got real mad, but Lars goes, "Kill 'em all ... That's a good name." I go, "That's a great name!" The next thing you know the album was called *Kill 'Em All*.' The eventual sleeve, based on another idea from Jonny, which he says the band 'were very pleased with', was as simple and brutal as the new album title: a sledge-hammer resting in a pool of blood with the shadow of a hand reaching out. A hardly less subtle image than the original sword from the toilet bowl, perhaps, this cover design – which still surfaces on T-shirts today – was one that US retailers nevertheless felt more comfortable with. The rear sleeve picture was a simple landscape portrait of the band, all doing their best to look suitably solemn, all looking impossibly young, despite Lars' attempt at facial hair.

Officially released in America on 25 July 1983, *Kill 'Em All* was not a hit but nor was it expected to be. The fact that it got as high as Number 120 in the *Billboard* Top 200 album chart was considered cause for celebration by everyone at Megaforce. Had anyone dared suggest to Jonny Z back then that the album would eventually sell over three million copies in the USA, 'I'd have thought you were even crazier than me.' What Megaforce lacked in clout was more than made up for in the freedom it allowed Metallica to forge their own identity – musically and image-wise. As Lars would later tell me, 'Early on we had a very distant attitude to the business side of things. We firmly stood our own ground on things like what we played, how we looked, how we presented ourselves. Or how we didn't present ourselves ... Just doing what we were doing. The thing is there weren't really any decent independent labels going in America when we were starting out. You really had to be the right package to get a record deal in 1983. But we said, "Fuck that!" and just plodded away, doing our own stuff and feeling great about it. Then suddenly there is an independent label and we do have a record out and a lot of people start buying it because there was never quite anything like this [musically] in America before.' The fact they were initially shunned by the major labels worked in their favour. In 1983, he said, 'the [major] record company philosophy in America has always been, well, give the public a choice of A, B or C but the menu stops there, and we'll decide that a band like Metallica will not be on the menu because they are not saleable. So all the people got to listen to hard rock through Styx or REO Speedway or whatever. And then this band Metallica came out and they thought, "Wow, where has all this shit come from? How come we haven't heard this before?" Because the record companies never believed that anything like that could actually sell. So we start selling a shit-load of records and at the same time James' lyrics are different from all the clichéd crap that all the older metal bands spew out, and people started to take notice of that.'

Initial press reception, however, was hugely mixed. With the exception of *Kerrang!*, the mainstream music press in both America and Britain largely ignored the album. The metal fanzines that had supported the band from day one, though, went ballistic. Reviewing it in *Kerrang!*, Malcolm Dome wrote: '*Kill 'Em All* sets a new standard ... Metallica know only two speeds: fast and total blur.' The UK's leading metal fanzine, *Metal Forces*, meanwhile, voted it the album of the year, and Metallica band of the year. In America, Bob Nalbandian, first off the block as ever, summed up his review of the album in *The Headbanger* with the words: 'Metallica might just be America's answer to

Motörhead' – the highest accolade Lars Ulrich or James Hetfield could have wished for in 1983.

There was only one major dissenting voice and that belonged, with a certain sad inevitability, to Dave Mustaine. Interviewed within a few months of the album's release by Bob Nalbandian, ostensibly about his new band Megadeth, Mustaine couldn't resist using the opportunity to sound off about what he saw as the dreadful shortcomings of *Kill 'Em All*. 'I'm just wondering what Metallica are gonna do when they run out of my riffs,' he sneered, adding, 'I already smashed James in the mouth one time, and Lars is scared of his own shadow.' As for his replacement, 'Kirk is a "yes" man ... "Yes, Lars, I'll do Dave's leads." "Yes, James, I'll play this."' Adding insult to injury, he claimed that 'I wrote the most songs on that whole fuckin' album! I wrote four of them, James wrote three, and Hugh Tanner wrote two!' He insisted that 'James played all the rhythm on that album and Cliff wrote all Kirk's leads, so it shows you they're having a lot of trouble with this "new guitar god".'

It was the start of a mostly one-sided verbal war between Mustaine and Metallica that would persist, in various forms, to the present day. From his endless jibes in the press about how 'Kirk Hammett ripped off every lead break I'd played on that *No Life 'Til Leather* tape', to his snide comments to Jane's Addiction guitarist Dave Navarro in 2008: 'I don't really like him because he got my job, but I nailed his girlfriend before I left – how do I taste, Kirk?' If there was any envy between Mustaine and Hammett, though, it wasn't the new Metallica guitarist who was feeling it. As Mustaine's collaborator and closest confidant, David Ellefson, points out, any 'copying' by Kirk Hammett of Mustaine's original guitar lines on *Kill 'Em All* would have been deliberate: 'To some degree Kirk put his own stamp on [*Kill 'Em All*] but that kind of music isn't just random solo over three-chord blues riff. The solo is a part of the composition, every bit as crucial to the song as the lyric and the choruses. That's what we *like* about the music. It's the difference between when I went to see Van Halen and they were like a sloppy party band, and when I went to see Iron Maiden and they played every single solo note for note. As a fan,

I hung on every note ... I wanted to hear it *exactly* the friggin' way it is on the record.' Kirk sticking to the *No Life* template was exactly what was required. 'I always saw it like they tried to honour all of the good that Dave did bring to the band. They used his songs, they gave him credit. They paid him for it. When we would drive down the street in LA and some guy would yell out, "Metallica!" to me, that wasn't "Fuck you!" to Dave. That was, "Dude, you were in fucking Metallica!"'

Despite being largely ignored by the mainstream music press, by the end of 1983 the first Metallica album was already starting to be recognised as a watershed moment in the history of rock. It showed that, far from being dead – as the post-punk British music press had been trumpeting since the day Sex Pistols singer Johnny Rotten claimed to have fallen asleep while watching Led Zeppelin, calling them 'dinosaurs' – punk and metal had a lot more in common than previously acknowledged. You could hear the musical antecedents of the juncture where Metallica come into the conversation in the iron-clad riffs and spat-out vocals of the first Stooges and Pistols albums, and there again in the warp-speed rhythms and clattering drums of the earliest Motörhead and Ted Nugent recordings. Not that Metallica seemed particularly conscious of the radical moves they would soon be congratulated for making: 'We thought that whatever we did, there'd be people who would approach [the album] with a lot of hesitation, because it was so different back then,' said Kirk Hammett. If to the uninitiated the tracks seemed to fly by in a blur, that was just the way it was, insisted James Hetfield: 'We'd just keep practising and the songs would get faster and faster, and the energy kept building up.' Playing the songs live was 'always faster' because of all the 'booze and freaks dinking around, just the excitement'.

There was, however, far more to the new sound that Metallica, knowingly or not, were now pioneering than merely playing faster to keep the freaks that came to their shows happy. Apart from its sheer speed, the defining sound of thrash was to be found in the frenzied downstrokes of James Hetfield's rhythm guitar playing. Until then, with few exceptions – the best-known being Johnny Ramone, whose single-minded reliance on downstrokes gave the Ramones their unique, 'untutored' sound – rock guitarists tended to allow their chords to ring out and resonate. Hetfield, in his determination to make his playing not just harder, faster, but to resonate in a less flamboyant way, developed what writer and guitarist Joel McIver characterises as 'a staccato, palm-muted sound'. It was James Hetfield, he says, who really promoted this style, one that is now regarded as derigueur in metal circles. It was what McIver calls Hetfield's 'super-tight downstrokes ... cupping his hand around the bridge for a perfectly taut sound' that became the key element in the quintessential Metallica sound, ergo that of thrash metal. As McIver puts it, Hetfield pioneered a technique that made metal sound 'not brash or rude or sexy, but like the future. The apocalypse had arrived, and it came in the shape of the right hand of a spotty teenager from the wrong side of the LA tracks.'

Almost immediately a whole new generation of rock and metal bands strove to emulate both the re-energised Metallica sound and the downtrodden look of its band members, beginning in general with the increased speed and intensity of the new music they were already calling thrash, and specifically with the dry-as-sand down-strokes that Hetfield had unwittingly turned into its signature sound. Dave Mustaine, initially more famous for his frenzied solos – and his barbed anti-Metallica comments – was shrewd enough to include Hetfield's rhythmic gimmicks in his own band Megadeth, as did Kerry King of Slayer and Scott Ian of Anthrax. These three bands, along with Metallica, would soon become known as the Big Four of thrash, and the arrival of *Kill 'Em All* provided the launch pad for them all, especially once the specialist metal press – led by *Kerrang!*, but quickly followed by the same fanzines that had already been supporting Metallica – got hold of the idea. As with the NWOBHM, suddenly thrash was depicted as a thriving scene unto itself, which had seemingly sprung from nowhere overnight. Or, as Lars Ulrich laughingly puts it now, 'From the mind of Xavier Russell!'

The son of film-maker Ken Russell, Xavier was a public-school-educated English teenager who had fallen in love with heavy rock in general and Lynyrd Skynyrd in particular just as the rest of his friends were falling for The Clash and The Jam. Working as a film editor in his own right, he had began writing for *Sounds* in the late 1970s as a hobby, always in longhand, mainly reviewing heavy metal imports from Europe and America. Encouraged by the magazine's deputy editor and eventual NWOBHM inventor and original *Kerrang!* editor Geoff Barton, by the early 1980s Russell would become the first writer to give the name Metallica serious media exposure in the infamously hard-to-impress mainstream British music press. 'Xavier was the person in the *Kerrang!* office really promoting Metallica's cause,' says Barton now. 'He would be banging on about them incessantly, to the point where you'd think, oh god, just to shut him up let's give them a two-page feature. So it was a hundred per cent down to Xavier, a lot of their early coverage.'

Russell wasn't a great writer but he was a major metal enthusiast and obsessive collector, in much the same way Lars and his nerdy teenage chums in California had been. When, in 1982, he was in San Francisco on holiday and noticed that Mötley Crüe – a new LA band he'd heard about but never seen perform – were playing at the Concorde Pavilion, he went along out of curiosity. Introduced at the gig to Ron Quintana, who handed him a copy of the *No Life 'Til Leather* cassette, he thought nothing of it ('People were always sticking tapes of bands you'd never heard of in your hands at gigs') until the following morning, still hungover, he popped the cassette into his Walkman, 'expecting nothing special really'. He got a shock. 'The speakers just went whoosh!' He got as far as the second track, 'The Mechanix', before pausing the tape to phone Ron. 'I said, "Where are this fucking band playing?" He said, "They're playing Monday,"' at one of the then-regular Metal Monday night gigs at the Old Waldorf. 'I went and it was Metallica, Lääz Rockit and another band, and I was just totally blown away.' At this point, Mustaine and McGovney were still in the band but they were already 'just unbelievable. At the same time, you could see this battle between Hetfield and Mustaine. It was like they were both hogging the limelight. They looked like brothers that don't get on. Mustaine was the more powerhouse one.

At the same time you could tell he was on something.'

Introduced by Ron to Lars after the show, 'Straight away we got on quite well so we stayed in touch.' Nabbing a *Metal up Your Ass* T-shirt on the way out, Xavier had come back to Britain 'and immediately started telling everyone at *Kerrang!* all about them. I wrote a "metal up your arse" feature and told Geoff Barton, "By 1991, this band will be the biggest band in the world."' Even though Burton and Hammett had yet to join the band, it wasn't all just about speed, even then, says Russell: 'What I noticed when I first saw them was that although they were playing fast you could still feel a tune in there. It definitely sounded European but it had an American slant to it.' With the exception of Venom, it was 'the most extreme form of metal I think I'd heard up till then – only better. Nothing against Venom, I quite liked them. But they were like listening to a cement mixer by comparison. Metallica always had a bit more of a tune to them, actual songs.'

While many would doubtless agree with that view, it would be wrong to dismiss the enormous part Venom played in laying the groundwork for what quickly became thrash. By the time Metallica released *Kill 'Em All*, the Newcastle-based band had already recorded three absolutely groundbreaking albums for the independent Neat label: *Welcome to Hell* (1981), *Black Metal* (1982) and *At War with Satan* (1983). Not only did they provide some of the musical footprints for Metallica to follow, they would also inspire their own self-ascribed genre, black metal, from which would come several notable acts over the next three decades. Beginning in the 1980s with, from Scandinavia, Mercyful Fate and Bathory – and in the 1990s those like Britain's Cradle of Filth, who claimed to be actual occultists, and the ghastly Burzum, from Norway, who took the whole black metal shtick to a frighteningly literal new level with church-burning, the drinking of human blood and even murder in the case of Burzum frontman, Count Grishnackh (real name: Kristian Vikernes), who received a twenty-one-year sentence in 1993 for the murder of Øystein 'Euronymous' Aarseth of rival Norwegian black metallists Mayhem. Metallica never saw themselves as being as fixated on the rock-as-devil's-music thing as Venom, but it was Venom's utter determination to take metal music to a new, much more extreme level that allowed Metallica to see what could be done, given enough bloody-minded ambition. When Venom began, said frontman Cronos in 2009, they thought of themselves as 'long-haired punks, 'cos that's all we could associate [the music] with. But when we decided to start looking at terms like "power metal", that's when we started to call what we did the thrash metal, the speed metal, the death metal, the black metal. It was really just the black metal that stuck.' Venom, said Cronos, was about, 'going places where other bands hadn't been'. Like books and movies, 'Music should be so varied in subject too.' There were, he said, to be 'no rules to what we were writing' – words that would be echoed more than once over the coming years by Lars Ulrich and James Hetfield . . .

Although 'Whiplash' contained the lines in its chorus: 'Adrenalin starts to flow / You're thrashing all around', not even Lars Ulrich claims to know who first used the term 'thrash metal' to describe Metallica's music. 'Ask Xavier,' he laughed. So I did but even he remains unclear on this point, saying only, 'I think I did.' But if he didn't invent it, it was certainly Xavier Russell who did more than anyone else to popularise the term 'thrash metal'. 'I said [to myself], "How do you define this music?" I thought, "Well, it sounds thrashy to me." Even if I didn't say it to them, I wrote it down. Some people called it speed metal but then because they weren't always fast that wasn't quite right for what Metallica did.'

Speed metal would certainly have worked as an accurate description, however, of the band that would rival closest Metallica's place at the forefront of thrash – Slayer, formed in Huntington Beach, the same surf city suburb Metallica had found Dave Mustaine in, in the same year, 1982. Led by vocalist/bassist Tom Araya and lead guitarist Kerry King, augmented by a second lead guitarist, Jeff Hanneman, and a frighteningly talented, jazz-trained drummer named Dave Lombardo, Slayer – originally known as Dragonslayer, after the 1981 fantasy film – had started out as an Iron Maiden-style sword-and-sorcery metal band. Like Metallica, they had an abiding interest in the

NWOBHM, but it wasn't until seeing Metallica opening for Saxon at the Whisky in the summer of 1982, that they shortened their name to Slayer and refocused their music towards a more original, much faster and more powerful sound, built around the screamingly atonal twin lead guitars of King and Hanneman, Lombardo's monumental drums and Araya's – unlike Hetfield's at the same stage – already fully formed grizzly bear vocals. In common more with Venom, they would cultivate a 'satanic' image, which featured pentagrams, make-up, spikes and inverted crosses. While Hammett was perfecting his Joe Satriani-tutored technique, Hanneman likened his own guitar sound to that of a 'slaughtered pig'. Slayer's lyrical themes also took on a much darker hue than Metallica's, early hair-twirling stage favourites including titles such as 'Evil Has No Boundaries', 'The Anti-Christ' and 'Black Magic'. In 1983, at the same time as Metallica was working on *Kill 'Em All*, Slayer were invited by Brian Slagel – who had been impressed by their performance opening for Bitch at the Woodstock Club – to contribute to the *Metal Massacre III* compilation. The track, 'Aggressive Perfector', led to a fully fledged deal with Slagel's Metal Blade label.

Similarly, Anthrax, who had buddied up with them during their time with Jonny and Marsha in New Jersey, would also have Metallica to thank for the radical change in direction that positioned them right at the forefront of the coming thrash phenomenon. 'Anthrax always just wanted to be Metallica,' says Marsha Z, who went on to co-manage them with Jonny. The band had been formed in 1981 by guitarist Scott Ian (nicknamed Scott 'Not' Ian at school) and another extremely talented drummer named Charlie Benante, along with bassist Dan Lilker, lead guitarist Greg Walls and vocalist Neil Turbin. Their debut album, *Fistful of Metal*, was recorded within weeks of *Kill 'Em All* hitting the street and would even be released on the same label, Jonny and Marsha's fledgling Megaforce, in January 1984. But it was a staid affair by comparison, although it did contain one proto-thrash classic in its hilariously apoplectic cover of Alice Cooper's 'I'm Eighteen'. It wasn't until Turbin, Walls and Lilker departed (Lilker to another new group of thrash wannabes, Nuclear Assault) and were replaced by singer Joey Belladonna, former bass roadie Frank Bello and guitarist Dan Spitz, recording the impressive *Armed and Dangerous* EP, that they began to be considered in the same musical ballpark as Metallica and Slayer, developing their own quirky style, less involved with mock-horror and more indebted to the comic book and skateboard culture which also sprung up around the genre. By this point, 'We really felt that we were part of something,' said Ian. 'The energy was palpable.'

Last out of the traps but viewed with as much reverence, often more, than their peers, by dint of the fact that their creator had also been one of the originators of Metallica, came Dave Mustaine's band Megadeth. 'Truthfully, I just wanted to out-metal Metallica,' Mustaine would tell Bob Nalbandian in a 2004 interview for Bob's Shockwaves website (the twenty-first-century version of his fanzine *The Headbanger*). It was a typically flippant Mustaine remark, which nonetheless held more than a grain of truth. But if Megadeth had begun as Mustaine's revenge trip on the people who had, as he saw it, betrayed him, it soon evolved, to his credit, into something more significant. Megadeth would be Mustaine's irrefutable proof that there had always been more to him than helping furbish Metallica with a sound and musical direction; his inarguably great demonstration of his own, unique talents, not just as guitarist, of which he still saw himself as one of the best, but also as songwriter, singer, band leader, visionary, star. Or, as Dave put it to me some years later: 'Fuck democracy. Democracy doesn't work in a band. I had to have my own band and make music exactly the way I wanted to hear it, with no compromises to anybody else's ego whatsoever.'

His new songs reflected his new band's name: post-apocalyptic, wise after the fact, cynicism tinged with bitter joy. David Ellefson now describes sitting on the couch in Mustaine's apartment when they first met, watching him 'playing these amazingly solid rhythm parts. I mean, they were like slabs of rock. Dave was obviously not your average long-haired virtuoso guitar player.' Two songs Mustaine sketched out for him early on – 'Devil's Island' and 'Set the World Afire' – would later become stalwarts of the earliest Megadeth shows, although the latter would not be recorded until their third album. 'They were monsters,' says Ellefson. 'They just jumped out at you. I thought, whoa, this guy's got a whole different thing going on. This had nothing to do with what all the other "hair" bands were doing in 1983.'

The first Megadeth album, *Killing is My Business . . . and Business is Good* was not released until 1985, long after Metallica, Slayer, Anthrax and several others had already made their mark. But it made up for lost time by combining the speed and fury of thrash, as gold-stamped by Metallica and Slayer, with a technical proficiency that was like nothing those other bands – the one rooted more deeply in traditional forms of telegraphed, well-played heavy metal, the other still in thrall to the Black Sabbath/Venom idea of what (black) metal should be – had yet attempted. Some detected jazz influences in the Megadeth maelstrom; others coined the term 'technical thrash' to describe the difference. But whatever one told Dave Mustaine his band sounded like, that's what they were not, as far as he was concerned. Megadeth did not exist in a vacuum, though, and was built specifically to usurp not just Metallica but every other thrash band that had come along in the intervening years between Mustaine's dismissal, although the perceived rivalry with Metallica was always at the forefront of his warp-speed vision.

'The initial stuff we were writing was slower,' recalled Ellefson. 'Songs like "The Skull Beneath the Skin" and "Devil's Island", those were all more mid-tempo songs [but] I remember all the fans up in the Bay Area writing letters to Dave saying, "Man, I hope your stuff is faster than Metallica!"' Says Bob Nalbandian, 'That was the big thing at the time, who could play the fastest. All the thrash bands were competing for that title.' When Nalbandian's review of *Kill 'Em All* in *The Headbanger* proclaimed them as 'one of the fastest and heaviest bands in the US', he recalls how Slayer immediately started taking ads in the mag claiming to be the 'Fastest and Heaviest of All US Metal Bands!' As a result, said Ellefson, 'I remember the next day we went to rehearsal and all the [new Megadeth] songs became speed metal songs. For us it happened overnight. It's amazing how these fans writing letters to the band fuelled that whole thing and to a large degree it probably changed the course of our destiny. If the music just had stayed slow and mid-tempo, it would not have had the ferociousness and the furious nature that it eventually developed into.'

Even though thrash in its original incarnation – like punk and the NWOBHM before it – would be a relatively short-lived phenomenon, its influence would continue to be felt in the Bay Area and beyond for decades. A typically next-generation example are Machine Head, also from northern California, who didn't record their first album, *Burn My Eyes*, until 1994. Vocalist Robb Flynn was fifteen when *Kill 'Em All* was first released, living in Fremont, about fifty miles outside of San Francisco, and discovering bands such as Metallica on an obscure college station called Rampage Radio. For the teenage Flynn, thrash meant bands like 'Exodus, Metallica, Slayer. None of them were very popular at the time ... a friend used to bring tapes of it into school. Also, Discharge, Poison Idea: all this punk rock and hardcore metal. We were like, fuck, this is super-cool, man! I remember one of the first times I ever got really drunk, we had picked up *Kill 'Em All* and we were walking around with this eight-inch cassette player with one speaker and we blasted "Whiplash" from this thing ... just wasted out of our minds.'

For Robb Flynn and his pals there seemed to be no discernible link between the new thrash bands and metal bands of the past: 'It didn't have any history.' No one else outside his circle of high school buddies had even heard of it. 'When we started a band and were doing backyard parties we'd cover "A Lesson in Violence" [by Exodus] or "Fight Fire with Fire" [Metallica], and all these twenty- and twenty-one-year-olds were just fuckin' not into it at all! Like, "You guys suck, man. Play some fuckin' Zeppelin!" When Death Angel came along,' an even younger band of Bay Area thrashers than Metallica, whose early demos were produced by Kirk Hammett, 'for us that was, like, amazing. Wow, here's kids our age playing this fuckin' thrash shit and playing it killer. They were fuckin' awesome!' Everybody that came along after could be traced directly back to the Big Four, though: 'When Exodus started to get heavy we were like, wow, Exodus are starting to get like Metallica, that's cool. With Possessed, we were like, oh, they're trying to sound like Slayer, they're cool.'

With very few records out there yet to buy, the early thrash scene thrived still on tape-trading and, most important of all, live gigs. As with the music, audiences divided up pretty evenly between hardcore punks and long-haired metallers. In LA, where promoters and club owners were frankly baffled by the new scene, emerging thrashers such as Megadeth and Slayer would often get shoehorned onto punk rock bills. In the Bay Area, where the culture clash was more easily recognised, the bands themselves often insisted on playing together. The result was often chaos, with the pogoing of the punks taken to a new, more violent level by the crowd-surfing of the metallists and the birth of what later became known as the mosh pit. Recalls Robb Flynn, 'You'd come out of the pits and, like, I broke my nose, I fuckin' broke my arm, come out with a sprained jaw. Just from stage-diving and pittin'. You didn't come out going, "Ouch that hurt." You came out going, like, "Fuck! I got a war wound!" It was fuckin' brutal. There's this kind of myth about the thrash thing that it was all friendly violent fun, but it wasn't. There was such an element of danger, such an element of violence. It wasn't safe to go to.' Flynn recalls one particularly memorable occasion during an Exodus show at Ruthie's Inn. 'This dude had a cow leg bone and he's in this pit, running around, this big dude, fuckin' clubbing people with this fuckin' cow-bone. Or people would set up chairs at the back of the pit and run from the back of Ruthie's and jump off the chair and launch on stage and take out the guitar player. Take out the fuckin' singer. And this was like showing affection – like, we love you guys, you're awesome. Dudes would take a beer bottle and break it on the table, take off their shirts and open up their chests with it, fuckin' bleeding, like "Yeah!" You'd be watching this, going "Holy fuck!"'

In this respect, Metallica could not claim to lead the way. That honour, such that it was, fell to Kirk Hammett's former band Exodus. Recalls guitarist Gary Holt, 'When we played our first show together with Metallica [in 1982] it was still a lot of fist-banging audience. Once Kirk left and [vocalist] Paul Baloff came into the picture, Paul and

I started crafting Exodus in our own vision, which was just brutality and violence. The audience responded in kind. Then when the infamous Ruthie's Inn opened, the shows just got really insane. Plus we had a lot of punk rock guys who came to our shows. We definitely weren't a crossover band but one thing I think Exodus should get more credit for was we had the first really crossover audience [of punk and metal fans].' People were jumping off the top of PAs 'doing full three-hundred-and-sixty-degree flips and we definitely did our best to egg it on.' Exodus was also one of the first bands to encourage stage-diving: 'That shit got pretty crazy.'

As with all music scenes, drugs also played their part. 'Everybody was on speed, that was the thing,' says Robb Flynn. 'We called it crank. We all totally got into crank. Sit there and do crank and just go in and do the craziest things that you could think of, the craziest dives.' That was fine for the fans. For the bands the mix was much broader. To the speed and crank was added weed, psychedelics, and, when they could afford it, coke. For Dave Mustaine and David Ellefson, heroin would also be on the menu, eventually over-whelmingly so. 'We went down to hell together,' says Ellefson. For others, like James Hetfield and Anthrax's Scott Ian, drugs were to be disdained completely in favour of the arguably even more punishing regimen of alcohol. 'I know our British counterparts drank a lot,' said Lars, 'but in some way it felt like we drank more. I don't know why, maybe it was because drinking had been more a staple of European culture, so it wasn't as big of a deal, or something like that. But around all those [thrash] camps in '81, '82, '83, in America, it was all about the fucking vodka bottles, and about jumping in the vodka bottles and anything went from there, you know what I mean?' He laughed. 'Smirnoff and whoever else . . .'

Thrash audiences would also connect with the skateboard scene in LA. This was an aspect of the emerging culture which filtered across to leading lights such as Metallica, who in James Hetfield (by 1985, taking a skateboard on tour with him and riding around backstage at shows) did, after all, contain one member whose LA roots genuinely reflected that scene, and, more puzzlingly, Anthrax, from New York, whose overlapping interest in the skate scene only really came with the music and clothes, particularly the latter. Anthrax became the first thrash band in the spotlight to abandon the tight black jeans of Metallica and Slayer in favour of the baggy shorts and reversed baseball caps of lesser known but disproportionately influential bands such as Suicidal Tendencies – the first-generation punk metallists featuring future Metallica man Rob Trujillo on bass. Robb Flynn: 'The big skate band for us was Suicidal Tendencies. They were from LA so they were genuinely from that skate culture, and we knew that. Going to Suicidal shows, that's when I really started noticing the crossover thing happening. You'd see gang dudes with long-haired thrasher dudes and then punk rock dudes – and chicks – all under one roof.'

All of the so-called Big Four thrash bands recorded punk covers at some point. Anthrax would record 'God Save the Queen' for their 1985 *Armed and Dangerous* EP; Megadeth would do 'Anarchy in the UK' (with Sex Pistols guitarist Steve Jones guesting) on their 1988 album, *So Far, So Good ... So What!*; Slayer would eventually release a whole album's worth of punk covers, *Undisputed Attitude*; and Metallica would intermittently record covers of songs by The Misfits, the Anti-Nowhere League, Killing Joke and others throughout their career. 'I could relate to punk lyrics,' Hetfield shrugged. 'They were about me, rather than that "Look at me riding a horse, with a big sword in my hand" typical heavy metal fantasy crap.'

Certainly, thrash dress style, if it could be called that, would have more in common with the straight-legged, collar-turned-up, safety-pinned thrift-store look of punk than it did the studded wristband and spandex-trousered image of trad-metal. Increasingly taking their cue from Cliff Burton, whose moth-eaten cardigan and bell-bottom jeans were already a trademark, by 1983 Metallica wouldn't have stuck out in any denim-bedraggled student union bar. Says Armored Saint's John Bush, 'Metallica were the ones who said we're just coming out in the way we dress as we do backstage, which was refreshing at that time, because everything was about image and what people were wearing. I sometimes think that the worst aspect of heavy metal is the imagery. It's the one thing that keeps heavy metal from maintaining a certain level of complete integrity. It's like punk rock has always had a little bit more integrity than heavy metal because of the image. That was one thing that Metallica changed that was really important.'

Comics – another abiding Burton and Hammett obsession – became another thrash signifier. First this was as reading matter and occasional inspiration for lyrics, and then it was a pointer for turning record sleeves away from the staid sword-and-sorcery, clenched-cleavage clichés exemplified in the artwork of every metal band from the Scorpions to Whitesnake, towards the new 2000 AD comic-consciousness of the mid-1980s. Here, as with skateboarding, Anthrax quickly climbed aboard the bandwagon, or at least went out of their way to telegraph their interest, with Scott Ian claiming in interview to consume seventy-five new comic titles a week, focusing on 'old Marvel stuff, and anything by Frank Miller and Alan Moore'. Anthrax drummer Charlie Benante, meanwhile, was a talented penman who drew the inner sleeve cartoons for their 1985 album, *Spreading the Disease*, then imitated 2000 AD's original Judge Dredd artwork for their 1987 single 'I Am the Law'.

Of course, it's easy to arrange the pieces into a discernible pattern now. Speaking to me more than a quarter of a century after the fact, however, Lars Ulrich insisted there was very little design to this. Thrash was simply 'something that happened sort of magically. It wasn't something that was thought about; it wasn't something that was planned [or] contrived. I don't have the fucking answer more than anybody else, but to me, what thrash became musically was the Americanised version of what [Britain] experienced in '79, '80 and '81 with Iron Maiden and Saxon and Samson and Girlschool and then everybody in the wake of that – the Diamond Heads, the Angel Witches, the Savages and so on. And in some way Motörhead floated around the outer fringes of that, even though Motörhead of course weren't really a NWOBHM band, but there was a link to them. And then you could almost say that maybe the Judas Priests and the Scorpions were the bigger brothers or something like that.' He added, 'Nobody knew that this thing was gonna be what it became. The big bands [in 1983] were still the Scorpions and Judas Priest, Iron Maiden and AC/DC. That was a whole different level. We took our cues from all those bands. Then there was the American X-factor, whatever that was, and then it sort of became thrash.' He went on, 'I mean, if you sat down with [Anthrax, Megadeth, Slayer] and everybody else . . . It's all the same food groups and all the same places that it came from. When we first met Slayer they were playing Deep Purple covers. When I first met Dave Mustaine, the band that he was in was . . . a very different thing. The Anthrax guys – a very different thing. I mean, they were heavily into Judas Priest and that type of stuff. [But] we all sat there and shared our Diamond Head records and our Motörhead records and all of a sudden Venom showed up with *Welcome to Hell* and it was, like, fuck! And then Mercyful Fate! Do you know what I mean? Then thrash came out of all that.' The crucial common ground in the original thrash scene for Lars, he said, was 'that it was American. Thrash metal, at least initially, had a geographical element also that people don't really mention.'

Geoff Barton concurs. 'It was obvious from day one that the whole thrash thing was going to explode in the coming years. But we always saw it early on, certainly on *Kerrang!*, as being associated with that whole Bay Area, West Coast thrash thing. It wasn't until a bit later on that you had groups like Anthrax from New York, and closer to home a lot of UK thrash bands such as Onslaught or Xentrix. What we now call the Big Four, though, were all American.' Because Xavier Russell was Metallica's advocate at *Kerrang!*, Barton admits he deliberately latched onto Slayer, reviewing their second release on Metal Blade, the 1984 EP, *Haunting the Chapel*. 'Thrash was something we were really quite conscious on *Kerrang!* to try and build up. It was something we were inventing, that we were roundly supporting and getting onboard the bandwagon very early on, so to speak. So not only with Metallica and Slayer but with Anthrax and Megadeth, with Possessed and Death Angel. That whole thrash genre we found really exciting and felt we really needed to embrace it.'

As soon as *Kill 'Em All* was released in July, Jonny Z had Metallica out on their first cross-country US tour, on a double bill with Raven.

Dubbed the Kill 'Em All for One tour (the Raven album at the time was called *All for One*), the thirty-one-date trek began in New Brunswick, on 27 July, and finished up on 3 September back at their old haunt, the Stone, in San Francisco. Along the way they visited many cities they had never been to before as a band: Boston, Baltimore, Chicago, Milwaukee, moving down through Arkansas, Texas and eventually back through northern California. By the time they returned to the Stone, Metallica was a very different proposition from the band that had last played there six months before. Kirk Hammett wasn't the only beneficiary of Mustaine's departure. Says Bill Hale, who caught the show, 'Dave had the attitude. When he got canned, James had to adopt that attitude. 'Cos Dave did all the talking onstage. "Fuck you, blah, blah ... this is our next song."' With Dave gone, 'James had to step up a whole lot. James really had to improve his whole game.'

Still quietly harbouring doubts about his long-term place at the front of the band, but toughened up by ten weeks of non-stop touring, Hetfield also had the added confidence that having his first album released had given him. Taking his stay-the-fuck-away-from-me face with him onstage for the first time, he'd learned on tour how to hide behind that mask, how to manipulate an audience so that it only saw what he wanted it to. He became fierce, copying Mustaine's fearless approach by swearing at the audience, almost daring them to call his bluff: 'As a kid, intimidation was a great defence for me to not have to get close to people or communicate or express my fears and weaknesses. So, going into Metallica as the staunch statue of a frontman, that intimidation factor blossomed and was a great defensive weapon. I could keep people at bay with that, and not state what I actually needed.'

The tour had also included their first outdoor shows. Lars: 'It was basically us and [Raven], a motor home and a truck with the equipment and some mattresses. We'd take turns sleeping in the motor home and the equipment truck. When we hit Arkansas, our manager had hooked up with some bogus guy who set up six outdoor shows in these fields, in towns you'd never heard of. We were down there a good week. It was a field, a stage, us, Raven and about twenty kids. We'd never experienced that summer thing with bugs, one-hundred- and-twenty-degree weather, a camper with no AC. That was a good time ...' The first Arkansas show was at the amusingly named Bald Knob Amphitheater – in Bald Knob. James kept the poster for that one: 'That name is so funny. The amphitheatre was nothing but a giant field and a big cement block. But by six o'clock, they had everything set up: food, booze, catfish sandwiches.'

While every place they played, the kids were going thrash-crazy, the band was undergoing its own musical education. Lars told me, 'The biggest thing in America was The Police, *Synchronicity*, summer of 1983. We all loved that record. We were listening to that record every day as we were driving across America on the *Kill 'Em All* tour in our camper. We were listening to Peter Gabriel, too. So there were all these other things that ... great, I mean, Witchfinder General *Death Penalty* all the way, but now we've listened to that twice we're going to listen to something else. So very quickly on, for us, it started getting much wider in its musical scope, and obviously the things that were inspiring us were the things that we wanted to try and fuck with, to try and explore.' With Cliff Burton now in charge of the in- car entertainment most days, they would have little choice. 'When Cliff came along and Kirk came along, there was such a whole other level of musical schooling there, whole other levels of inspirations. I mean, listen, of course I knew who ZZ Top were but I'd never really *heard* ZZ Top. So Cliff is sitting there playing fucking ZZ Top, he's playing Yes. Cliff is the one that brought The Misfits to us, do you know what I mean? There was this whole other world of stuff that was not on my radar. All of a sudden it was just like, fuck, yeah, I love Angel Witch, and I'll play my Diamond Head records till the cows come home but, you know ... I remember, like, Cliff sitting there listening to that 90125 record [by Yes] and it was like, "That's really good."'

On those rare nights when the band was actually booked into a small motel, James and Lars would share one room, Cliff and Kirk the other. Thus the none-too-subtle hierarchical delineations between band members were established and maintained, even then. But this had a positive benefit: 'Cliff and I were bunkies,' Kirk Hammett would later explain to me. 'We were literally, in the first few years of the band, living in each other's back pockets. I mean, we were very close.' Late at night, after a show, 'I would get my guitar out, he would get his guitar out, 'cos he really didn't play bass that much away from the stage, he was always playing guitar. And we would just jam. We would play all sorts of stuff. We would listen to music together. We had similar interests. He was way into horror movies and H.P. Lovecraft, as I was. We were coming from the same place. He enjoyed doing hallucinogenics, and so did I. He would take acid and tell me, "Hey, man, I just took some acid, whatever you do don't tell the other guys." I would say, "Sure, man. Mum's the word." Because he knew that I didn't like to take acid in any sort of like working environment, but it never bothered him.'

Cliff would trip while he was playing with the band onstage?

'Oh, yeah, totally – and often, too. Mushrooms, acid – the whole deal. You also have to understand though, too, you know, on an emotional level, Cliff was a lot older ... Not like a *lot* older [but] older, and it was a big difference. I mean, we all tended to look up to him 'cos he was the guy with the most life experience. He was always the one who exuded the most confidence, you know, he was the guy who was the most grounded as well – the guy who had the best sense of ethics and morals. Whereas we were like slash and burn, seek and destroy, he would like take a step back first and think about things and then slash and burn, seek and destroy. This was the guy who would sit around and listen to the Eagles and the Velvet Underground. He turned us onto R.E.M., he turned us onto Creedence [Clearwater Revival]. And he also loved Lynyrd Skynyrd, too – and nowadays it's the thing. Cliff Burton was ahead of his time in more ways than one.'

There was a short break at the end of the tour – but only long enough to prepare for more coast-to-coast dates that would take them up to Christmas, this time as headliners in their own right. They didn't wait for Christmas to start the party, either. 'We would drink day in and day out and hardly come up for air,' Kirk later recalled in *Playboy*. 'People would be dropping like flies all around us, but we had the tolerance built up. Our reputation started to precede us. I can't remember the [1983] tour – we used to start drinking at three or four in the afternoon.' James: 'We smashed dressing rooms just because you were supposed to. Then you'd get the bill and go, "Whoa! I didn't know Pete Townshend paid for his lamp!" Come back off the tour and you hadn't made any money. You bought furniture for a bunch of promoters.'

They were even drawing groupies to their shows now. 'Girls were always at the shows,' demurred Hammett: 'It's just that they didn't look much different from the guys.' Lars would later tell *Playboy* how the girls were now lining up to offer blow jobs. 'People would say, "Eww, she just blew that other guy ... " So? You don't have to put your tongue down her throat.' Said James, 'Back then, we all shared stuff,' adding, 'Lars would charm them, talk his way into their pants. Kirk had a baby face that was appealing to the girls. And Cliff – he had a big dick. Word got around about that, I guess.' By the end of the tour, they had all 'had crabs a couple of times, or the occasional drip-dick'.

The final show of the eleven-date winter tour was at the Agora Ballroom in Mount Vernon, New York State, on New Year's Eve, 1983. By now, the fire sparked by the release of *Kill 'Em All* had spread across the Atlantic and 1984 would find Metallica doing their best to capitalise on that astonishing fact. What the devoted young thrash metal maniacs waiting for them there would not know was that for Metallica their music was already shifting. The soon-to-be-crowned godfathers of thrash had never been solely occupied with speed. Now, with technically much more proficient players such as Cliff Burton and Kirk Hammett onboard and someone to lead the band like Lars, whose own ambitions extended far beyond the safe cubbyhole such musical margins offered, Metallica was ready to push on with a far more ambitious agenda than any of their contemporaries. They were already performing some of the new songs they planned to record for their second album, including the title track, 'Ride the Lightning', and had, in fact, already written most of what was going to be on there. And although their hardcore, deliriously proud fans would have been aghast to be told so, very little of it had to do with thrash metal . . .

SIX
CALLING AUNT JANE

There was Peter – sharp, in your face, no shit or else. And there was Cliff – whiskery, monkish, a wise head. Not quite good cop, bad cop, but certainly happy to hover in that realm when it suited them. It wasn't hard to figure. One was a natural balls-buster, liked to see the other guy flinch; could never be wrong. The other was the calm voice of reason that was never wrong either, but didn't rub your face in it, just said the words; let you draw your own conclusion.

The one I knew best was Peter. I liked him – sometimes. He talked dollars and sense, kept both eyes open, yet always made a point of stopping and saying hello, checking it out, whatever it was I was into, which back then, as we almost always met at gigs by the various bands he and Cliff managed, usually meant too much to drink and smoke and everything else the moneyed-up Eighties rock scene had to offer a young dude who actually believed tomorrow never came. As Peter didn't smoke or take drugs, rarely even sipped a beer, this meant that little by little, he grew contemptuous, began treating me like a groupie.

'What do you think I am – a fucking groupie?' I once asked him sulkily.

'Yes,' he said, then walked off, slowly.

That had been backstage at a Def Leppard show, the final date of their 1988 US tour. Leppard were then Peter and Cliff's most successful act, which was saying something as they had several successful acts, including Metallica. I had been out on several legs of the Leppard tour, interviewing them for my Sky TV show, writing about them for the covers of various magazines in Britain, America, Japan ... helping to spread the word, as I saw it. I certainly didn't feel like a groupie. Indeed,

I had flattered myself into believing I was some sort of ... friend.

Then bumping into Peter on my way back to the dressing rooms at the end of the show, that final night, he had slapped me on the back so hard – in mock greeting – it nearly knocked me off my feet. I had gotten used to the snide remarks, the disdainful looks; the rotten all-round vibe. But so many people got treated like that by Peter, I tried to shrug it off as a sort of backhanded compliment. Like, whaddayagonnadohuh? That slap shook me up, though.

Cliff was different, as far as I could tell. The day before, we had sat beside each other on Leppard's private plane as we flew from Portland to Tacoma and I had taken the opportunity to ask him about his background. He told me how he'd gotten his start working in A&R at Mercury Records, how he'd always loved what he called 'the British rock sound'. How he'd been one of the few American music-biz people that really got Thin Lizzy, how he'd tried to help break them in America but that the band was its own worst enemy. He meant drugs. Cliff didn't dig drugs. 'I don't like the feeling of being out of control,' he said. I nodded my head sagely.

Just then the plane did something sudden and dramatic and I felt the blood rush to my head. The plane did it again and this time it felt like my head was trying to jump off of my shoulders. Things got rapidly worse. I yelled, 'Fuck's sake! What's happening?'

The captain's voice came over the tannoy. 'I thought as this was our last flight we'd treat you folks to something special.' He'd put the damn thing into a nosedive, he said, its tail spinning, the plane spiralling towards the ground. I gripped the armrests of the chair and held on, terrified. Around the luxury cabin several other faces were grinning, some whooping. I couldn't believe it was happening. We were all going to die ...

I managed to swivel my head round to look at Cliff. He looked as terrified as me, his face frozen, holding on to his composure – just – as terrified maybe of losing his cool as the plane crashing.

'Make – it – stop,' I pleaded, barely able to speak. 'Please – make – it – stop—'

'That's enough,' he said, though not loud enough for anyone else to hear. A little louder: 'I said ... that's enough.'

*I looked across at Peter. He was sitting, oblivious, frowning at a maga-
zine. Then, as though picking up the signal, he tuned into Cliff's voice,
glanced up and saw the panic.*

*'Hey – that's enough!' he barked. This in turn was picked up by the
singer Joe, who repeated Peter's order and – thank God – the plane suddenly
righted itself. There were one or two disappointed voices grumbling. Like,
what the fuck? 'Hey, there are visitors on the plane today, okay?' said Joe,
one of the good guys.*

*I breathed out, tried to regain control of myself without seeming to make
some big effort. I looked at Cliff, the only other one on the plane who seemed
to feel it. He was breathing in, out, righting his wings, pulling out of the
nosedive, the man who didn't like to feel out of control. He ignored my
look, kept his eyes focused on the straight and narrow . . .*

Despite the fires Metallica were now starting all over the country, by
the end of 1983 *Kill 'Em All* had sold barely 17,000 copies in America –
a drop in the ocean in terms of US record sales; certainly not enough
to cause more than a blip on the radar of the mainstream media. 'We
knew the next album would be the one,' says Jonny Z. 'It was just a
case of finding the money to make it.'

Jonny and Marsha were broke. They had given all they had and
more to get the first Metallica album made and then put the band out
on the road. That, plus the running costs of setting up their own label
and management company, on top of the day-to-day running of Rock
'n' Roll Heaven, meant 'the well was dry' – a phrase the band got so
used to hearing they would put it next to his name on the credits of
their next album. Jonny and Marsha had been able to spring for a
limited-edition twelve-inch EP version of 'Whiplash' (along with three
other tracks from the album) to try and help promote their end-of-
year shows but again sales barely covered costs. With Anthrax in tow
as support on those final shows of 1983, the increasingly frantic crowd
reactions they were now getting meant they felt sure it was only a
matter of time before things picked up, but it all came back to the fact
that they needed to get another album out.

Enter their knight in cockney accent, Martin Hooker, then head of his own UK-based independent record label, Music for Nations. Still in his twenties, Hooker had already enjoyed a successful career in the music business, working for EMI for six years, 'handling promotion, label managing [and] lots of different jobs', he says, for artists 'from Queen to Kate Bush and all stops in between'. The one job he most coveted, however, in A&R, scouting and signing new talent, 'was the one thing I didn't do'. EMI kept denying him the opportunity, citing a lack of experience. Frustrated, Hooker decided to leave and start his own label – Secret Records, which he describes now as 'predominantly a punk label' but which really came into its own in the aftermath of the original generation of British punk rock bands.

Typical of Secret was one of Hooker's first releases, the *Punk's Not Dead* album by The Exploited – deliberately designed to distance itself from the less musically bilious 'new wave' that had followed directly on from punk and to re-establish what the band and its followers saw as original punk's aggressive, uncompromising stance, musically and image-wise. Released in March 1981, *Punk's Not Dead* went to Number One in the UK independent charts and would eventually become the biggest-selling independently released album of the year. It was not a fluke. Hooker recalls, 'We then had nine chart albums out of nine releases – things like The Exploited, the 4-Skins, Chron Gen, Infa Riot ... all sorts of things.' Released at a time – the summer of 1981 – when the UK was undergoing an almost nightly series of anti-government inner-city riots, suddenly the 'very hardcore punk' that Secret specialised in 'was big news. Literally, everything that we put out went straight in the charts.' Looking back now, he attributes this instant success to a mixture of spotting a gap in the market and 'just really liking that stuff. It was the era and it was exciting and fun.' And in terms of running your own label, 'an absolutely fantastic learning curve'.

As a result, several of the London-based major labels invited Hooker to come and run their A&R departments: 'But by that time I had the money to not necessarily do that.' Instead, his next move was to look beyond the confines of the UK punk scene towards a form of music he felt would have more international appeal. 'I was quite keen to move into a more heavy metal area.' Unlike, punk, however, Hooker was less interested in the domestic scene: 'I was very much a rock fan but I wasn't that keen on many of the NWOBHM-type bands. I was much more into the American side – Mötley Crüe and those sorts of bands.'

Towards the end of his time at Secret, Hooker signed Twisted Sister – a US metal band whose outré image lay firmly in the glam tradition but whose music veered more towards a UK punk-metal hybrid. Disentangling the band from its New York roots and replanting them in England, where he recorded their debut album, *Under the Blade*, released on Secret to great success in September 1982, had given Hooker the taste for more. 'It was a great experience. That album went straight in the chart and Dee [Snider] was one of the best frontmen I've ever seen. We got them on the Reading Festival where they just completely stole the show. So after that, I thought, this is crazy, I'm gonna start a heavy metal label and I came up with the idea for Music for Nations. I thought it was a good name for it because [metal] was the one type of music that never came in or out of fashion.' And unlike punk, 'I could see it in every country in the world.'

Working out of a small office in Carnaby Street with initially just his girlfriend Linda there to help, Hooker got Music for Nations under way at the end of 1982 by inviting contacts in the USA to send over copies of any recent metal-orientated product he might potentially look to release in Britain and Europe. Within weeks his desk was overflowing with demos and one-off independent releases. Settling on 'a handful to get the ball rolling' the first release on MFN, on 4 February 1983 – Hooker's 30th birthday – was the self-titled debut from New York outfit Virgin Steele. Attracted by the band's unashamedly American rock stance, mingled with the musical theatricality of Rainbow, the Anglo-American vehicle of former Deep Purple guitarist Richie Blackmore, equally appealing was the fact that the album had only previously been available in the USA from the band's own vanity label, VS Records. Virgin Steele's only other minor claim to fame was the inclusion of a track, 'Children of the Storm', on the

1982 compilation, *US Metal Vol. II* – almost entirely unknown outside hardcore US metal circles but, coincidentally, much admired by a certain Lars Ulrich.

Closer to Hooker's avowed intention to seek out 'Mötley Crüe-type bands', the second release on MFN was the seven-track mini-album from LA glam-metal roisterers Ratt, entitled simply *The Ratt EP*. Originally released on the little-known Time Coast Records and featuring the track, 'Tell the World', the original recording of which had been on the same *Metal Massacre* compilation that also featured Metallica, both this and the *Virgin Steele* album became unspectacular but steady sellers for Hooker and his fledgling enterprise. Next up would be Tank, a British trio fronted by former Damned bassist Algy Ward. Modelled on the punk-metal mien of Motörhead, Tank had already had two well-received albums released on the UK independent Kamaflage Records. By the time MFN put out their third, *This Means War*, the novelty was wearing off and the album did not do as well. By that time, though, Martin was already in the process of signing another new young American metal band he would have a far greater degree of success with even than his days at Secret.

'The very first time I listened to the *No Life* demo, I thought, wow, this is just fantastic! You have to remember, in those days nobody had heard of speed or thrash metal. So it was totally, totally different to all the pompous nonsense that was going on with a lot of heavy metal bands at that time. And it was totally in keeping with my kind of punk thing. Certainly my friends at all the majors thought I was mad – completely. They just didn't see it. But I just thought they were the most exciting band I'd [heard] for a very long time. We ended up doing a deal with Jonny Z to put the [*Kill 'Em All*] album out in the UK and Europe.'

Aware of the amazing job Hooker had done with his friends Twisted Sister, when Jonny and Marsha decided to go it alone with the first Metallica album, part of the plan to help allay costs and forge a presence for the band outside the USA had been to do some sort of licensing deal with either a foreign major, or, more likely, a fellow independent – hence the brief flirtation with Bronze. Says Hooker, 'Jonny wanted somebody to come in and share the costs, I think. He'd already recorded the album and then we licensed it from him.' In fact, the deal Hooker did was for three Metallica albums. But after *Kill 'Em All*, the relationship between Megaforce and MFN 'became a lot more complex'. Initially, however, with the album already paid for and completed, 'it was a straight deal to license that in'. He adds with a smile, 'I dare say that what I paid for it more than covered the recording costs at the time.'

Hooker had never met the band, let alone seen them play live. Apart from the music, 'all I had to go on were these pictures of these four spotty herberts'. Consequently, when MFN released *Kill 'Em All* in the UK 'it was really, really hard work. The initial manufacturing quantity was fifteen-hundred and it took a long time to sell them. Then after that we were remanufacturing for quite a while in five hundred units at a time.' He already had a network of distributors in every country in Europe through his days at Secret. 'I used predominantly the same people, so they were already releasing the first batch of MFN titles. I was able to slot Metallica straight into that distribution network, which was great for them.'

The key to getting Metallica off the ground properly, Martin knew, would be to get them in front of a live audience. 'In those days touring was one of the few ways you could successfully promote the acts. Unlike now, there were no metal TV shows, hardly any chance of radio airplay and no chance of [mainstream] press.' Spending the significant amounts needed to bring an American band to Britain at a time when hardly anyone outside the hardcore metal scene was yet aware of them was a risk, though. His hand was all but forced, however, when Jonny Z made it apparent there might not be a second album – unless he could find a partner to come in and help finance the project. Says Hooker: 'Jonny had run out of money. So he did a deal with us that we'd pay to record the album. We were still only getting the UK and Europe but we were kind of helping [Megaforce] out as well.' There would be no kickback from Megaforce's US sales, 'But it kind of all worked itself out because we [eventually] sold shed-loads of records, so getting the money back wasn't a problem.'

The new deal also led to Metallica spending most of 1984 actively promoting themselves in Britain and Europe. The plan, as hatched by Martin Hooker, with the encouragement of Lars Ulrich and Jonny Z, was that the band would record their second album in Europe, while also testing the waters with some exploratory UK and European dates. As with their earliest shows on the East Coast, they would begin with a handful of reasonably high-profile support shows, opening once again for Venom on their quaintly named Seven Dates of Hell tour, which began on 3 February at the Volshaus in Zurich, and continued through Germany, France, Belgium and culminated with Metallica's first outdoor European shows at the Aardschok Festival in Holland on 11 February and the following afternoon at the Poperinge Festival in Belgium. The tour was a notable success, in terms of crowd response, with the band amazed to find their music was known to many of Venom's ardent fans. Jeff 'Mantas' Dunn recalled their first gig in Zurich as 'like *National Lampoon's Vacation*. Metallica went fuckin' nuts on the first night.' When one of the band broke a window to talk to some of the fans, 'the promoters had decided that they were gonna kill them for damaging the venue'. The band ended up hiding in Venom's dressing room, 'like little rabbits caught in the headlights'.

Certainly Venom felt they had given Metallica a significant helping hand in not only introducing them to such large crowds on their first trip to Europe, but also in legitimising them through their association at such a crucial early stage in their career – a fact that Conrad 'Cronos' Lant now feels is unfairly overlooked in the Metallica story. 'We always wanted to help other bands,' he later told Malcolm Dome. 'Had we left everything down to the suits there would never have been a Metallica support.' As the years went by, however, Metallica 'just totally forgot all about the fact that we gave them the support on the Staten Island shows in '83 and that we also gave them a full European tour. We don't want a medal for that, guys. We just want you to tell it the way it is.' According to Venom drummer Tony 'Abaddon' Bray, it wasn't just profile Metallica picked up from their association with Venom. 'I would swear that [James Hetfield] suddenly started to walk like Cronos,' he said in 1996, getting up and mimicking the trademark, loose-limbed Hetfield swagger. In the same interview, Lant claimed that Kirk Hammett had learned to play by getting Joe Satriani to teach him early Venom numbers such as 'Die Hard'. He rolled his eyes as though that explained everything.

The Venom dates were to have been followed by Metallica's first UK tour, second on the bill, sandwiched between The Rods, three albums into their career but living largely now on reputation alone, and Canada's first self-styled thrash metal act, Exciter, whose debut album, *Heavy Metal Maniac*, released on Shrapnel some months before was then only available in Britain on import. Knowing none of the three would be able to headline a UK tour in their own right, Metallica's new UK agent, Neil Warnock at The Agency, had gambled on the appeal of a package featuring all three, putting together a hugely ambitious list of dates that was to climax with a show at London's Hammersmith Odeon. Says Hooker, 'It shows you where we were with this at the time because The Rods were gonna be the headliner.' There had to be some last-minute quick-thinking, however, when the tour was scrapped due to an embarrassing lack of ticket sales. Thrash metal, as an established genre of music, may have begun to achieve recognition in *Kerrang!* but it was still very much a marginal concern everywhere else. For once, however, the fans in Europe were ahead of the curve. Instead, at Hooker's instigation, the band drove straight from their final show with Venom in Belgium, to Copenhagen, where they routined their new material at Mercyful Fate's rehearsal space. A week later they were in Copenhagen's Sweet Silence Studios, recording their new album.

Ask Marsha Z now how Metallica came to record their second album in Lars Ulrich's hometown and she chuckles and says, 'Why do you think?' But there were sound reasons, too, why Metallica should record in Copenhagen. First and foremost, cost: with the band using a disused upstairs room at the studio to sleep in, there would be no hotels to pay for. Secondly, they would have use of the skills of the studio's twenty-six-year-old co-owner Flemming Rasmussen, whose production work on Rainbow's 1981 *Difficult to Cure* album, also recorded there, had been a big favourite of Ulrich's. Determined not to find themselves in the same situation as they had on *Kill 'Em All*, fighting every day to get their opinions across, they decided they would produce the album themselves – with the 'technical assistance' of Rasmussen.

Already a married man with a four-year-old son, Rasmussen offered Metallica the best of both worlds: young enough to get where they were coming from musically, expert enough in the studio to help them achieve the effects they desired. With a broad musical background in everything from rock to jazz, folk and pop, Rasmussen was also a fast worker who spoke the band's language – literally, in the case of Lars. 'We always [spoke] Danish when we were together,' he says now. It enabled them to 'talk without people knowing what we're talking about'. But while working in Copenhagen suited Lars, says the producer, 'I don't think the other guys were too keen about it.' The first time any of the others had left America, touring Europe had been an eye-opener; odd food, weird beer, different languages, but fun, travelling from strange new place to place every day. Now, holed up in a big wooden, converted factory, as far from home as they had ever been, sleeping all day, working all night, the fun factor was hugely diminished. This was hard work. Still winter, dark and cold out there, none of them could be bothered to stay awake long enough to explore Copenhagen, beyond the occasional foray to drink Elephant beer at a nearby bar.

Work in the studio would begin at seven o'clock every evening and would carry on until four or five in the morning, with a break for a meal around midnight. Flemming admits that at first the music seemed unusual to him. 'I hadn't heard a lot of that stuff in Denmark at that time. But I really liked it. I thought it was pretty brilliant, actually.' The only immediate problem was that James was lost without his usual guitar amp, a modified Marshall that had been stolen when the band's equipment van was broken into outside a gig at the Channel Club in Boston, in January. The thieves cleaned out the whole van, leaving behind just three guitars. Recalls Rasmussen, 'Nobody knew what had been done to it. So we actually started out by getting every single Marshall amp that was in Denmark at that time and [placing it] in the studio, and James would start fucking around with it.' The producer indulged his new clients. He had no intention of attempting to reproduce what he saw as the 'pretty crappy' guitar sound on *Kill 'Em All*. When, finally, James found an amp and cabinet he liked, Rasmussen says, 'we fucked around from there'. The result was a much deeper, more powerful sound. 'We actually more or less made that [new] guitar sound from scratch.' For Flemming, this was an early source of pride, as, in his opinion, James was the best musician in the band. 'James is, like, world-class. He's probably the tightest rhythm guitar player I've ever met. I hadn't heard anybody that played [downstrokes] with that kind of precision before ever in my life. So I was really impressed.' In terms of pure musical vision, 'from an artistic point of view it would probably be Cliff', although it was always 'Lars and James that were more or less in charge'.

The only real weak spots, technically, as with *Kill 'Em All*, were in James' singing and Lars' drumming. Rasmussen recalls, 'James wasn't so keen about singing at all. But we just took it bit by bit and double-tracked him and made him sound [good]. And he got more and more confident as we progressed with the work. I tried to do what I could to boost his confidence because I thought he had a good vibe to his voice and a good character and I thought it fitted the music pretty well. The fact that he was trying, you know, I really liked that.' Lars' difficulties on the drums were more problematic. 'I thought he was absolutely useless,' Flemming says now. 'I remember the very first thing I asked when he started playing was: "Does everything start on an upbeat?" and he went, "What's an upbeat?" Holy shit! The thing is that Lars is an innovative person, so his whole drumming had been based on drum fills. That was his thing. All the ones and twos in-between, he never took notice of that. He didn't really think about what was going on between the drum fills. I still think he's a great drummer in his own right 'cos I think he does some things that are absolutely amazing. But me and the guy who was his drum roadie, another guy called Flemming [Larsen] who at that time was [also] playing drums in a Danish metal band called Artillery, we started telling him about [beats]. That they have to be an equal length of time between that hit, that hit and that hit and you have to be able to count to four before you come in again . . . [Then he could play] a really good fill that nobody else had thought of doing at that time.' He pauses then adds, 'I can't imagine what they must have been like live at that time. He was speeding up and down in tempos a lot [playing] more the way he felt the songs *should* be.'

Lars remained nonplussed. As he later told me, 'It's like, five minutes after I could play drums, Metallica were going, and the shit just roller-coastered. Suddenly we're making demos, then we're touring, making our first record after only being together a year and a half . . . all of a sudden it was like, well, we have a record out but we really can't play. So I had to take drum lessons and Kirk's doing his Joe Satriani trip.' More to the point, 'We spent a lot of years trying to prove to ourselves and to everyone out there that we can play our instruments – you know, listen to this big drum fill I'm doing, and Kirk's playing all these wild things that are really difficult . . . When we were first starting out in 1981 the two big bands in America that year were the Rolling Stones and AC/DC. I clearly remember sitting at James' house going: "The worst drummers in the world are Charlie Watts and Phil Rudd! Listen to them, they don't do any drum fills, they're not doing anything. Listen to that, it's horrible! Give me Ian Paice and Neil Peart." So for the next eight years I'm doing Ian Paice and Neil Peart things, proving to the world that I can play . . .'

After the extra time spent getting the guitar and drums right, it was a relief for Rasmussen to discover that most of the songs were already worked out. 'They had really rehearsed and arranged the demos. So they were pretty set.' The only song they hadn't finished yet was one of the album's centrepieces, 'For Whom the Bell Tolls'. 'We had one day where they kind of jammed it and finished.' The bell, in question, was actually provided by the striking of an anvil. 'We put it on a backstairs when we recorded it. That was ridiculous, it weighed a ton. But [Lars] hit it with like a metal bar and it sounded really good. That was before samplers so we had to make our own sounds.' The backstairs was also where they eventually placed Lars' drum kit, 'right on the other side of the door. There's actually an apartment there now so somebody's sitting in the living room watching the telly in the spot where Lars played the drums.' Rasmussen says he knew the album was going to be special long before they'd finished it: 'I was pretty sure at that time that they were gonna be really big. The funny thing was that everybody else in the studio came from a jazz background – they kept telling me, "But they can't play!" And I went, "Fuck that! Listen to it, it's brilliant!" I was really proud. I still am, actually.' When it was over, "I was like, fuck, yeah, I wanna do more of this shit!"'

Of the eight tracks on *Ride the Lightning* – as they had decided to call the album after another of its centrepiece tracks – almost all would survive to become cornerstones of the long-term Metallica mythology: the only exception being the one track that seemed to offer a shred of light amidst the unrelenting gloom, a Thin Lizzy-esque mini-anthem in the making called 'Escape', its comparatively upbeat message – '*Life is for my own, to live my own way*' – being the exception to the rule in the otherwise unremittingly bleak landscape of Hetfield's lyrics. The rest of the album was unified by one theme: death. By mutually assured destruction ('Fight Fire with Fire'); capital punishment (the title track); war ('For Whom the Bell Tolls'); suicide ('Fade to Black'); living death through cryogenics ('Trapped Under Ice'); biblical prophecy ('Creeping Death'); even an H.P. Lovecraft-inspired monster ('The Call of Ktulu'). It was the sort of adolescent death trip any angst-ridden, acne-bedevilled teenage boy locked in his bedroom, railing impotently against an unjust world, might be expected to come up with. What set the album apart was the music. A discernible leap forward from their inspired but occasionally awkward, cheaply produced debut nine months before, *Ride the Lightning* was the first clear indication that there was more to Metallica than teen-speed and short-fuse power. Received at the time as the epitome of the emerging new thrash metal genre, listening back to it now it's clear how much it owes not to any received notions of genre-defining but to the much more traditional values of melody, rhythm and old-school musical talent. The vocals remain one-dimensional but are no longer fey, due to Rasmussen's good practice of double-tracking, adding plenty of oomph. The drums rely too much still on rolls and needless fills but there's no mistaking the depth-charged beat, thanks again to the producer's extra coaching and more experienced close-miking technique. The rest, though, could be Iron Maiden at its most fiery, from the wail of duelling guitars on the title track to the battering rhythms of 'Creeping Death'. Most clearly, if not always directly, can be felt the influence of Cliff Burton. Uninter-ested in thrash metal, per se, his own playing stoked by jazz and classical references – his tastes ranging from the southern rock of Lynyrd Skynyrd to the mystical balladry of Kate Bush – Cliff's sheer presence makes the band comfortable enough suddenly to explore such previously considered musical heresies as an acoustic ballad; songs that travel at something less than the speed of light; even a towering, Ennio Morricone-style instrumental.

Freed from the obligation of reproducing Dave Mustaine's original work, Kirk Hammett's guitars also come into their own, a universe apart from any notions of what a 'thrash guitarist' might be and much closer in aspect to the lessons he had been absorbing from that great Jimi Hendrix disciple, Joe Satriani. These were Kirk's first attempts to break free of what he later described as the 'one-voice guitar thing' of 1980s thrash, and he recalled how 'when the other guys heard the solos on "Creeping Death" and "Ride the Lightning", it was a different aspect of soloing than they were used to. Dave Mustaine played fast all the time. I play melodically. And I play parts, different sections that make the solo as hooky as possible.' Although he admitted he had 'always been very flashy', the playing on *Ride* was full of restraint and controlled aggression. Where the excitement boils over, as on what he called 'the whammy-bar craziness' at the conclusion of 'For Whom the Bell Tolls', it does so knowingly. This is not to say they had completely abandoned their commitment to being 'the fastest and heaviest': James' clench-fisted rhythmic downstrokes are much in evidence throughout. But while there would be little room for levity on the album, from its doom-laden subject matter to the ominous front cover of an electric chair suspended amidst an electrical storm, as recording artists increasingly in control of their musical destiny Metallica were already starting to subvert that idea; to play against the grain and deliberately bend the rules. The typically windmilling opener 'Fight Fire with Fire' – one of the fastest numbers they would ever record – actually begins with a short acoustic 'overture', before fizzing like a stick of dynamite into explosive life. The album closer, 'The Call of Ktulu' (printed on some pressings, unforgivably, as 'The Cat of Ktulu'), meanwhile, is an eight-minute-plus instrumental that takes its inspiration more from Morricone than it does Motörhead. A far more substantial showcase for Cliff Burton's extravagant talents on the bass than its little brother '(Anesthesia) Pulling Teeth' on *Kill 'Em All*, it's entirely symbolic of the massive strides Metallica had made as musicians since their hurriedly wrought debut. It's also an impressively bold way of concluding what it was still hoped would be the album to bring them to a wider audience than the loyal but still limited following they had so far attracted.

The real signifier of Metallica's determination not to be boxed in by the limitations of others' expectations, though, was the inclusion of a seven-minute acoustic-based ballad: 'Fade to Black'. As James later put it, 'If we'd been told when we were recording *Kill 'Em All* that we were gonna record a ballad on the next record, I'd have said: "Fuck off."' Built upon a sequence of minor guitar chords picked as an arpeggio that James came up with while idling on an acoustic, its sombre, reflective mood a million miles from the juvenilia of anything he'd attempted as a songwriter before, the lyrics – although presented as a suicide note – were initially inspired by the theft of the band's equipment that resulted in him losing his cherished Marshall. With the addition of Kirk's tastefully applied electric crunch filling in for the lack of a chorus and Lars' drums, for once, mirroring a similar restraint, 'Fade to Black' became at once the most harrowing and beautifully subtle piece of music Metallica had yet come up with.

Mostly, however, this was Metallica laying down a mission statement. In 'For Whom the Bell Tolls' and 'Creeping Death' they had, simply, created two enduring heavy metal classics that would have sounded apposite whatever era of rock history they had sprung from. The former (misprinted on early pressings as 'For Whom the Bells Toll') might just as easily have come from early-Seventies Black Sabbath, Cliff's expertly distorted bass solo which signals its beginning a marvellous, musicianly touch; the latter – destined to become a huge crowd favourite, chanting 'Die! Die! Die' – the first touchstone Metallica classic.

Not everybody was bowled over by such 'originality'. Kirk's former Exodus bandmate Gary Holt, for one, was distressed to discover, as he says now, that not only did the riff from an early Exodus number, 'Impaler', 'become like one of the best riffs on *Ride the Lightning*, on "Trapped Under Ice"', but that the now famous line in 'Creeping Death' which begins '*Die by my hand . . .*' was taken from Holt's own composition 'Dying By His Hand'. There was no question, he admits, 'that the riffs were [Kirk's]'. Nevertheless, it caused bad blood between the two for a while. 'I remember calling Kirk up and giving him a great deal of grief,' says Holt, 'and he said, "Ah, I thought I asked you if it was okay." I'm like, "No, you didn't." So I've had the *pleasure* – and I use the term loosely – of watching sixty-thousand people chant that shit [at subsequent Metallica shows over the years] yet I've never received a penny for it. I've had many people say, "Man, you should have sued." But I'm like, yeah, whatever, you know? It is what it is. I laugh about it now. I had one conversation with Kirk about it then I let it go for ever.'

But then, as Holt also points out, while both Metallica and Exodus had become known for 'playing like real furious shit', Kirk's taste was always 'a little more leaning towards the Maiden route, you know?' And if James lifted a lyrical phrase from Kirk's Exodus-era songbook, he certainly added to it in ways nobody else would have done. Inspired by the band catching a TV showing of the movie *The Ten Commandments*, the 1956 Cecil B. DeMille epic starring Charlton Heston, the lyrics of 'Creeping Death' were based on the Bible story of the tenth plague bestowed upon the Ancient Egyptians – the Angel of Death sent by God to kill every first-born child. When Cliff, in a cloud of weed, exclaimed, 'Whoa, it's like creeping death' the rest of them laughed so much they decided they had to write a song with that title. That James so cleverly wove the convoluted lyric together said much for his rapidly improving songwriting skills. Musically, it was also a revelation; a brutal rock monolith built on incredible finesse, from its juddering riff to the mesh of vocal and guitar harmonies in its chorus, Hammett's concluding double-tapped solo a masterclass in itself. 'Creeping Death' remains an all-time rock anthem, the thrash generation's very own 'Paranoid' or 'Smoke on the Water'.

The writing credits were also more evenly shared this time. The two most important tracks ('Fade . . .' and 'Creeping . . .') were credited to all four members. Two to Hetfield, Ulrich and Burton ('Fight . . .' and 'For Whom . . . '); two to Hetfield, Ulrich, Burton and Mustaine ('Ride . . .' and ' . . . Ktulu') and the least significant two to Hetfield, Ulrich and Hammett ('Trapped . . .' and 'Escape'). *Ride the Lighting* also codified a format for Metallica in the 1980s: manic opener, monumental title track, at least one death march, one big ballad and a fistful of all-out thrash crowd-pleasers. If anything, it was progressive rock Metallica were now leaning towards, making virtues of musicianship, long solos, complicated time changes; above all, lengthy numbers, Lars sitting there, as he told me, timing the recordings, ready to 'build more stuff in' if they weren't sufficiently long enough. The question remained: what would the die-hard thrash fans make of it? According to Flemming, the band 'weren't too concerned about fans not liking "Fade to Black", they were more worried about "Trapped Under Ice", which they thought was maybe a bit too poppy. That was the only concern during the recording. They joked about it almost being a single song.'

They wouldn't have to wait long to find out. Within a week of completing recording, the band was in London rehearsing for their first UK performance, headlining what would be the first of two shows in two weeks at the Marquee club in Wardour Street. Presented as an apologia for those fans who had bought tickets for the aborted

Rods tour, Music for Nations made sure the venue was packed with media and industry faces. Hopes were high, the band nervous. Things could go either way; triumph or disaster. Fortunately, recalls Martin Hooker, 'They were just *fantastic*.' By the time of the second show on 8 April, 'It was really starting to get a buzz going.' Recalls Malcolm Dome: 'They were very, very good. You still didn't think, good grief, this band is gonna be huge. But it was clear they could really pull it off live. The line-up just looked right, felt right and sounded right.' Described in the subsequent *Kerrang!* review as 'the Ramones of heavy metal', their down-at-heel image and speeded-up sound was distinctly at odds with the prevailing mid-Eighties hair-metal trend, as exemplified by the sorts of LA bands now regularly featuring on the cover of *Kerrang!* like Ratt and Mötley Crüe. They were doing the very opposite of what was happening sales-wise, recalls Xavier Russell: 'There was a lot of hype but fortunately they were good. A lot of people were impressed that maybe hadn't totally liked the *Kill 'Em All* album. For the first time, people could see there was really something there.'

One of the highlights for Lars was meeting another of his NWOBHM heroes, former Tygers of Pan Tang vocalist Jess Cox, who supported the band at the first Marquee date. Cox recalls, 'I was touring with Heavy Pettin' who pulled out [of the Marquee] at the last moment so I was going to headline and then [my agents] ITB said "Oh, there's a new band coming over and you've got to support them." I was like, "What band's this?" and they said, "They're called Metallica." I said, "I've never heard of them." They said "Well, you will, so don't worry about it."' He was amazed to discover the drummer making such a fuss over meeting him – 'I remember signing Lars' drumsticks' – blissfully unaware that Metallica had, in fact, once entertained the idea of recruiting him as their singer: 'The guys have never said this to me personally. I only found out later.'

Music for Nations had rented a flat in Cadogan Gardens in Kensington for the band to stay in; another home from home to follow Jonny and Marsha's house in Old Bridge and Mark Whitaker's garage in El Cerrito. Recalls MFN label manager Gem Howard, who became

Metallica tour manager throughout their UK and European dates that year, 'It was just a shit-hole. Getting them a flat was much cheaper than a hotel and they could invite people back and be much freer with it. But of course they had no sort of ability to clean up. I remember walking into this flat and there was a table lying on its side with food over it, someone had left a half a pound of butter on the floor and trodden on it. Loads of empty bottles and cigarette ends and God knows what ... Made Tracey Emin's bed look neat and tidy.'

Xavier Russell became a regular drinking pal during their time in London. Lars and James came back to his Notting Hill Gate flat one night where 'we played Blue Öyster Cult till about three in the morning'. Xavier recalls handing out squash rackets and the three of them miming guitar on them to Molly Hatchet's 'Boogie No More': 'The neighbours would be banging on the ceiling. Then they would put Thin Lizzy on – anything you could play along to on the squash racket. I remember we had a [Kentucky Fried Chicken] and we chucked up in the bucket!' Another time, he went to see them rehearse in Shepherd's Bush: 'Afterwards we went out drinking and I remember James was so pissed he was standing on top of the roof of this cinema in the Tottenham Court Road going mad; it was brilliant!' he laughs. James later recalled the occasion, too: 'I got arrested for destruction of property ... kicking the lights down on people. It was just one of those things we had to do when we were drunk.'

Xavier also spent time with Cliff and Kirk, but 'that was different. Cliff was really into his own little world. He had a totally different mindset, really, and that shows in his playing. And he'd always have a Lynyrd Skynyrd T-shirt on. He liked a lot of the bands I liked so we had a lot in common. While Kirk was quite funny, he'd always talk about comics. Lars was just Lars. He was the leader, in a way. And Hetfield back then just liked boozing and having fun, really. So they were all quite different characters but they all got on quite well. You could have a chat with each of them on totally different subjects. I remember [a couple of years later] going to see *Blue Velvet* with Lars when it came out, at the Gate cinema in Notting Hill Gate. We saw it twice. He was like, "Hey, we're gonna write a song about it."'

With the UK and Europe-wide MFN release of *Ride the Lightning* scheduled for 27 June, the band were back on the road that same month: four shows opening for Twisted Sister in Holland and Germany, followed by an appearance low on the bill at the Heavy Sound Festival on 10 June, then a return performance at the Poperinge Sports fields in Belgium, opening for Motörhead. Twisted Sister frontman Dee Snider, who still recalled the bunch of kids he saw playing for Jonny in Old Bridge a year before, was fond of telling people that Metallica were a nice bunch of kids but there was no way they were ever going to make it. Most non-thrash fans agreed. The most optimistic forecast among the non-believers was that maybe, if they played their cards right, Metallica might become as big as Motörhead one day. Oblivious, the band was back at El Cerrito by the time the album was released a fortnight later. Reaction was immediate. In Britain, *Sounds* became the first heavyweight music weekly to give a Metallica album a rave review, in a glowing piece written by a seventeen-year-old Motörhead fan named Steffan Chirazi – these days better known as the editor of the official Metallica fanzine, *So What*. Reviewing it for *Kerrang!*, Xavier Russell called for readers to 'soundproof the walls, get in a six-pack of beer, sit back and listen to one of the greatest heavy metal albums of all time!'

Ride the Lightning may not have been quite that but it would certainly become one of the most influential. Not all their old fans were so in thrall to its confection of illicit charms. Ron Quintana maintains now that in San Francisco, where Metallica had hardly shown their faces since temporarily relocating first to New Jersey and then to Copenhagen and London, Exodus's debut album *Bonded by Blood* – although not released until early 1985, completed in the summer of 1984 and already receiving exposure on the underground tape-trading scene – 'was liked better than *Ride the Lightning* by most of the underground kids here, and paved the way for the metal-punk crossover that spurred thrash to its heights'. In the UK, Dave Constable, then a key figure both in the pages of Bernard Doe's *Metal Forces* fanzine and, even more influentially, serving behind the counter at London's most high-profile metal-specialist record shop, Shades, in

Soho, when asked to sum up the new, emerging thrash scene in a piece for *Kerrang!*, described *Ride the Lightning* as 'a much watered-down follow-up' to *Kill 'Em All*, designed specifically for 'cracking the conservative home market'.

Both victims of the same fanzine mentality that always feels threatened when one of its own begins to attract much broader appeal, Quintana and Constable were right about one thing: *RTL* was far less about perpetuating Metallica's image as godfathers of thrash, far more about establishing their credentials as serious rock contenders, musically and commercially. Malcolm Dome, who interviewed James and Lars for the first time after *Ride* was released, recalls how 'Lars immediately struck me as being completely different. Unlike most drummers he was articulate and it was clear he and James had a long-term vision for the band. They weren't going to be here today then serving pizza tomorrow. Lars had a vision of the band being big. James was more the musical vision. In terms of business, I think he went along with what Lars said, but James was the one already talking of their music moving on.' As Lars insists now, at root *Ride the Lightning* was about 'when we started writing with Cliff', which for Lars and Metallica represented 'a giant leap forward in terms of variety and musical ability ... it was a much bigger palate'. Kirk recalled Cliff walking around during recording, proclaiming, 'Bach is God.' He had thought he was joking. 'Then realised he wasn't.' Cliff was 'a major enthusiast, understood harmonies and melody, he knew the theory, how it all worked, the only person who was able to figure out a time signature and write it on a piece of paper'. James talked of how Cliff wrote on guitar, not bass, carrying around an acoustic tuned to C. 'We don't know how the fuck he got it or why the hell he had it, but he used to play these weird melodies on it that kinda got us into the "Ktulu" vibe. He wrote a lot of our stuff on that guitar.'

Certainly more mainstream fans were now starting to queue up for Metallica. Martin Hooker recalls how it took 'weeks and months of really pushing and slogging, and advertising and getting gigs' to start the commercial avalanche that was about to begin tumbling in

Europe. 'It was the old school of hard work. I spent over a hundred thousand dollars in tour support, which in those days was a *gargantuan* amount of money. My [business] partner Steve Mason thought I was mental. But then it started to pay off and by that time we were starting to re-press in five thousands at a time and it's all starting to look much more sensible.' He adds, 'The main thing that took it to the next level was the kids themselves, the word of mouth. Apart from the occasional play on the [Radio 1] *Friday Rock Show* they were getting no radio or TV whatsoever, a bit of press from the specialists but nothing from the mainstream. But the word of mouth was just unbelievable, absolutely unbelievable.'

Hooker's right-hand man, Gem Howard recalls: 'They were four kids who were out having a great time. Things were changing in their career. They weren't that big at home [in America] at that time. Then we started touring them across Europe, which is when you started to notice it.' Spirits were high, despite their meagre surroundings. 'The gear was either in a truck or we were sharing it with Venom or Twisted Sister or whoever we were out with.' Gem, who had previously toured with The Exploited and Madness, was struck by their in-van listening habits: 'Every other band I'd worked with tended to listen to the kind of music they played. But with Metallica, they'd be playing The Misfits and smashing the van to bits while driving along. Then they'd play Simon & Garfunkel; then it was Ennio Morricone. Cliff was always the one that put on the most bizarre stuff. Lars was like the frontman. If you wanted to know anything about the band – anything at all – he would talk about it. That's really helpful 'cos it meant that everybody that wanted an interview got an interview with substance.' James 'was less sure of himself in those days. He had very bad acne early on – an embarrassment, particularly if you're trying to put yourself across as a frontman.' He recalls Hetfield still taking about getting a full-time singer in as late as the summer of 1984: 'He was always saying that they should get in a singer. He wasn't happy ... As he got older and more successful and the skin's healed up and his skinny lanky frame took on muscle, and he got the girls, he realised that, yeah, I am a frontman. Which is quite different to the reasons that most people are frontmen; most people do it because of their ego, despite having a lack of talent.'

James also stood apart from the other three when it came to some of the more usual on-the-road pursuits. 'He didn't indulge in anything other than a drink,' says Gem, 'which set him apart a bit. I remember getting [some cocaine] in at some point and [James] was like, "Oh, we shouldn't be spending the money on this." I just said, "Look under your pillow." I'd stuck a couple of bottles of vodka there and he was happy as a pig in shit. That's early days, though, when you didn't have enough money to go out and buy bottles of spirit out of your own pocket, and he just felt that he'd been catered for, which I think is a very important part of looking after any band anyway.' Or as Cliff sagely put it, 'You don't burn out from going too fast. You burn out from going too slow and getting bored.'

They also developed some good habits on tour, says Gem: 'The other thing that made them stand out from virtually everyone else that I've ever worked with is that they always had signing sessions after a show.' Even at shows they weren't headlining, they would set up tables in the corridors backstage specifically to meet and greet the fans. 'They would finish playing, go backstage, sit down, have a drink, maybe just have a quick splash of water, and then they'd come and sit there with towels round their necks and just sign until everybody had gone. They were there for probably an hour or so, talking to the kids. They'd go, "How did you like the show?" and they'd go, "Oh, it was great. I really liked that guitar solo," or, "I think you fucked up such and such tonight." They got this *immediate* feedback on their performance. Any constructive criticism, they were open to it and that's another sign of a band that isn't in it for the money. They're in it for the art.' Bill Hale says this is a tradition started by Cliff: 'He was the first one who went out and shook hands with the fans, 'cos Cliff was a fan. I would always see him do that the most.' Lars and James, though, drew on their own experiences of being fans – both pro and con. As someone who had himself always pestered his favourite bands for autographs, Lars knew the value fans placed on personal contact, however small, and the loyalty it engendered, while James recalled

Hit the lights. Left to right: Ron McGovney, James Hetfield, Lars Ulrich, Dave Mustaine. San Francisco, 1982 (*Bill Hale*)

'Lars could barely play his drums and they were really drunk onstage. But they had this raw punk energy' – San Francisco, 1982 (*Bill Hale*)

Cliff Burton, on the eve of his first gig with Metallica at the Stone, San Francisco, March 1983 (*Bill Hale*)

James Hetfield (*WENN*)

Lars Ulrich (*WENN*)

Kirk Hammett (*WENN*)

Outtakes from the band's first *Kerrang!* cover shoot, in San Francisco, 1985. ABOVE: the Metallimansion. BELOW: showing off the neighbourhood (*both Ross Halfin*)

Cliff Burton getting ready to go onstage on the *Master Of Puppets* tour, 1986
(*Ross Halfin*)

Cliff with girlfriend, Corinne Lynn, San Francisco, 1986 (*Ross Halfin*)

The site of the bus crash in Sweden that killed Burton, September 1986

his own bitter experiences writing to Aerosmith as a fan, addressing letters personally to Steven Tyler and Joe Perry: 'I expected something back . . . because they were so personal to me. I could feel their music, they were my buddies. And I didn't get anything back. I got an order form for a *Draw the Line* T-shirt. Wow, thanks a lot.' That was when he learned 'about how I would like *not* to treat our fans'.

The release in the USA on the Megaforce label of *Ride the Lightning* did not generate as much excitement at national level as it had in the UK, but Jonny and Marsha Z still had high hopes for its long-term success. 'Martin had done a great job at Music for Nations,' says Jonny. 'They had invested a lot of money in marketing and ads.' Unable to make that same level of investment, Jonny planned to launch the album with a big show at the Roseland Ballroom in New York, with Metallica second on the bill between headliners Raven, who he was also now looking after full-time, and openers Anthrax, his other main clients.

Jonny and Marsha had also continued exploring the possibility of getting Metallica signed to a major US label, targeting Michael Alago at Elektra, who Raven were also then doing demos for with a view to sealing a deal. Describing himself as, 'a real New Yorker and a real music fan', Alago was a native of Brooklyn whose life was changed, he says now, by seeing an Alice Cooper concert in 1973: 'From the age of fifteen I ran around to all the rock clubs [and] bars like CBGBs and Max's Kansas City and the Mudd club and Danceteria.' Working at a pharmacy in the East Village to help pay his way through college, in 1980 he got his first job in the music business working at the Ritz nightclub, where he began tipping off some of the record company talent scouts who regularly came down about the best of the new bands that had played there. When Jonny first met Michael in 1983 he'd just begun working at Elektra in the A&R department as a talent scout in his own right. At the time, Mötley Crüe were Elektra's flavour of the month, their first album for the label, *Shout at the Devil*, penetrating the Top Twenty and on its way to selling four million copies. Ratt had also made a chart breakthrough that summer, their first major label release on Elektra's sister label, Atlantic, the *Out of the Cellar* album, going Top Ten; while Van Halen, on the other Elektra affiliate in the WEA triumvirate, had just had their biggest album yet, the ten-million-selling *1984*, including their first Number One single, 'Jump'. Hard rock was getting bigger than big again in the US market. Nevertheless, Metallica was still viewed as an entirely different proposition, even for Elektra. For any major label to sign Metallica would still have seemed a remarkably left-field thing to do. But, says Alago, 'I was never interested in the hair bands. I liked my music fuckin' dirty and snotty.'

Having seen Metallica at the Stone in San Francisco at the end of 1983, he'd been 'blown away by the energy and charisma radiating from the stage'. When he heard *Kill 'Em All*, 'I lost my mind.' He had 'never heard a record that alive-sounding and I loved the songs and the energy'. He admits, however, he 'didn't know what to tell the company about them. I gave Lars a call or two to express my interest but at the time they had a deal with Megaforce Records.' They returned to his thoughts in the summer of 1984 with news that they were coming back to New York for a show with Anthrax and Raven. 'I was doing demos with Raven at the time because the Zazulas managed them and wanted a US deal', so he was already going to the show. The fact that Metallica would also be on the bill simply meant he would be coming early, he decided.

Jonny, who had put the whole show together as a showcase for CraZed Management talent, was delighted, inviting Alago and a slew of industry people, including record company execs, agents and – most importantly, from the Megaforce label's point of view – key distributors. Following a stonking warm-up at the Mabuhay Gardens on 20 July – their first hometown show for over nine months, supposedly secret, and billed as a performance by the Four Horsemen – Metallica was buzzing and ready to go. Alago brought Elektra chairman Bob Krasnow with him to the Roseland show, along with 'some promotion folks' – not to see Raven, but to check out Metallica. Says Alago, 'That night there was so much excitement and energy in the air I just knew it was gonna be a special evening. Metallica blew the roof off the stage. I ran backstage after the gig and basically hogged the entire evening and had them up at my office the next morning. We had a great meeting, got some beer and Chinese food and now had to figure out how to sign them away from Megaforce. Jonny was furious at me but in the end money talks and Megaforce got a financial override and the rest, my friend, is fuckin' history!'

There was a further twist to the tale, though – one that Jonny had not seen coming but which would be the real reason he was furious: the arrival on the scene of a rapidly up-and-coming New York management company named Q Prime. Fronted by Peter Mensch – a thirty-one-year-old former tour accountant for Aerosmith who had graduated in the late 1970s to day-to-day management with Contemporary Communications Corporation (CCC), known in the biz simply as Leber-Krebs, after Steve Leber and David Krebs, who formed the company in 1972 – Q Prime was fast becoming in the Eighties what Leber-Krebs had been in the Seventies: the most successful company in American rock management. Leber-Krebs' clients had included Aerosmith, AC/DC, Ted Nugent and the Scorpions; the perfect schooling for a player like Mensch who would go on to manage multi-platinum US stars such as Def Leppard, Dokken, Queensrÿche and, biggest of all eventually, Metallica. Along with his business partner Cliff Burnstein – a former Mercury Records A&R executive also schooled in the Leber-Krebs way – Q Prime was then riding the crest of a wave with the third Def Leppard album, *Pyromania*, the second-biggest-selling album in America in 1983 after Michael Jackson's *Thriller*. Now they were in expansionist mood and Metallica, having recently appeared on their radar, looked like prime candidates to be assimilated into the rapidly evolving Q Prime universe. Indeed, Mensch – overseeing the 'international' side of the company's business from his London home while Burnstein ran the New York office from his Hoboken apartment – already had a proven track record in pouncing on rising rock artists whose management support system was considerably weaker and less experienced than his own. Back in 1979, he had been instrumental in persuading AC/DC to leave Michael Browning, who had taken the band from the pubs and clubs of Australia to the brink of worldwide success, and sign with Leber-Krebs. Eighteen months later he managed to do something similar with Def Leppard, then one of the leading lights of the NWOBHM, on the verge of cementing a major deal in London with Phonogram. Neither act had cause to regret their decisions. In both instances, Mensch had overseen complete overhauls of their careers: the next two AC/DC albums would be both the best and, more importantly, biggest-selling of their careers to that point, *Highway to Hell* (1979) and *Back in Black* (1980); while Leppard were now on their way to becoming the biggest-selling British rock band in the world. When Mensch and Burnstein decided in 1982 to form their own management company, Def Leppard went with them.

Now, in 1984, Q Prime was on the hunt for new blood. Mensch had been a keen observer of the NWOBHM scene, had circled Diamond Head in their earliest, still exciting days, but had been shooed away suspiciously by Sean Harris's well-meaning but desperately inexperienced manager-mother, Linda. 'Mensch offered us the chance to open for AC/DC at two shows in Newcastle and Southampton early in 1980,' Brian Tatler recalls. 'Afterwards we had a little meeting with Mensch in the dressing room while he told us things about how the music business worked. We were very impressed, avidly listening, and it occurred to me, wouldn't it be great if Peter managed us. But Sean's mum and [her partner] Reg probably tried to keep us away, 'cos if [Mensch] had got involved he'd steal us away from them.' Mensch had also been in discussion with a young Marillion, then on the verge of major success with EMI, but again was rejected not because of any perceived lack of knowledge or experience, but rather the opposite. 'Peter Mensch was very urbane, very American, very obviously big time,' recalls former Marillion singer Fish, 'and I think, still being so sort of parochial in our tastes in those days we were offended by all that.' As with Diamond Head, Mensch's can-do demeanour proved too much for the more homespun British five-piece who signed with a manager less high-powered but more on their level personally. In both cases, it might be suggested, the bands would live to regret their decisions as their careers never quite reached the heights achieved by so many others who did have the courage to sign with Mensch and Q Prime.

One American metal band that went through a very similar experience with Q Prime in the mid-1980s and never regretted it is Queensrÿche. Like Metallica, Queensrÿche's first, eponymously titled EP had been released on their own independent 206 label in 1983, while the band was managed by record store owners from their hometown of Seattle. The band was picked up for a major deal by EMI America but two albums into its career, despite rave reviews in America and the UK, career-wise felt it was essentially treading water. Enter Q Prime, who Queensrÿche singer Geoff Tate now describes as 'extremely valuable' in getting the band to the next level. Says Tate, 'They had such clout and muscle as far as being able to demand what they felt was best for the artist. In regard to the record companies, the production, going on the road and doing deals with promoters, you know, clout with MTV. They were very well respected and they had success under their belts and so people listened to them. They didn't have a lot of opposition to their plans, and so, yeah, it was a big plus to have that kind of muscle.'

Of the four albums Queensrÿche would release over the ten years they were managed by Q Prime, the first three went platinum in America – not through putting the pressure on the band to make any commercial adjustments to their sound, Tate hastens to point out. Quite the opposite, he says: 'Q Prime had a very simple philosophy, and that is: follow your muse. Follow what it is that you want to do artistically and that will always be your calling card. At the end of the day whether you sell records or not you still have the fact that you followed your artistic calling.' The key lesson Mensch and Burnstein preached, he says, was '"Never *ever* listen to anybody. You didn't listen to anybody in the beginning and look where you are. So follow what it is that you want to do." And I liked that immediately. Upon meeting them that was the thing that really struck me, that they weren't gonna sit there and tell us what kind of clothes to wear or what kind of notes to play. They didn't have any interest in that at all. They just wanted to manage bands that had something to say. Bands that had a destiny,

I guess, you'd say.' As for the individuals, 'Peter and Cliff are true gentlemen. I have the utmost respect for both of them. They both have strengths in different areas and they were wise enough to recognise what each of them did well and allow each other to pursue those interests. Peter was always much more in control of the touring aspect and road life. Cliff was more into diplomacy and talking. Any issues within the band, he would be the one that would come and talk to everybody and kind of reason things out. Peter was kind of like the big stick; he would come in and bash people over the head.'

Be that as it may, Michael Alago insists now that he was already speaking to Jonny Z about signing Metallica 'long before Q Prime's involvement', denying that Mensch and Burnstein had any direct influence on his decision. 'At the time they were being handled by the Zazulas and not Q Prime. For me it was all about the band and their dedication to the music.' It just so happened that 'Q Prime were scouting them out the same time I signed them'. But as Jonny Z points out, it was Q Prime who 'closed the deal'. Consequently, Jonny now believes that while he was involved in preliminary discussions with Alago, Mensch and Burnstein had probably been talking to Alago's superior, Tom Zutaut. 'The deal was, basically, in conversation. Then [Q Prime] came in and closed it. They may have closed it from the top while we were working from the bottom up.' However it worked, the fact remains that by the time Metallica were ready to put pen to paper on an eight-album deal with Elektra in New York, they were no longer being managed by CraZed Management. Jonny says Marsha already had an inkling something was up, suspicious over the number of phone calls Lars would suddenly have to take from 'Aunt Jane'. Jonny chuckles ruefully, 'Marsha was telling me they kept calling Aunt Jane. Aunt Jane I think was Peter or Cliff. "I have to call Aunt Jane." We think that. But who knows?'

For Lars Ulrich, though, it wasn't about ditching Jonny and Marsha. They had 'always been good people'. But 'if we were to go next-level' they would have to take drastic steps, as they had previously with Ron and with Dave, and as they would again in the future when it came to others in their rapidly expanding organisation. For Lars, meeting Peter Mensch was like finding the final piece of the jigsaw, or being introduced to the bigger, smarter, older brother he never knew he had. Despite their outward differences – Lars the garrulous young hell-raiser to Mensch's scowling party-pooper – beneath their seemingly uncomplementary façades lay two strikingly similar egos. Both men were hugely driven, insanely ambitious overachievers, always on the clock, never able to switch off, never wanting to. Almost immediately after they started working together, Lars looked up to Peter, trusted his instincts completely, knew he was the right man for the job. By the same token, Mensch was savvy enough to see past the beers and the laughs, to grasp instantly that here was someone as determined as he to get to the top, and that it would be a good fit: Lars the smiling frontman, charming the pants off everyone he met; Mensch the enforcer standing at his side, making sure everyone paid attention and took this shit seriously.

'Interesting' is the tactful way Martin Hooker now describes his dealings with Mensch, subsequent to his takeover of Metallica: 'He was hard work, I have to say.' Gem Howard is less guarded. Working with Metallica's new American managers 'was weird. Peter Mensch seems to have not really much respect for anybody and the only time I met Cliff Burnstein, when we had a meeting with him ... they actually treated us with contempt, really. The only thing Burnstein was interested in was trying to find a Metallica sweatshirt that fitted him. That's all I remember of him.' Others share similar feelings. 'It was always difficult with Mensch really,' recalls then *Kerrang!* editor Geoff Barton, who describes his relationship with the manager as 'abrasive'. He goes on, 'Being an American, he didn't really under-stand the power of the British music press. The press in the States didn't have that same kind of influence.' So while Mensch regarded journalists like Barton as 'an ant willing to be crushed under his feet', the reality was that he exerted far less control over the then-all-powerful British music press than he would have wished.

That said, there are many who worked closely with Q Prime – former employees and record company executives – who have nothing but good to say about them. When one of the record company people who worked with Def Leppard in the 1980s became seriously ill, she awoke one morning to find her hospital room filled with flowers – courtesy of Peter Mensch. Another former employee at Q Prime's New York office from that time who left under difficult personal circumstances in the 1990s still insists they would go back to work there 'in a second', and that, despite the unhappy way they left, it was still 'the best job I ever had', pointing out the enormous pressure Mensch and Burnstein were always under. 'Faxes and phone calls at three in the morning, I don't know how someone deals with that kind of pressure.' Certainly there was no mistaking Mensch and Burnstein's abilities as managers. They didn't win every time – Armored Saint might arguably have had a bigger career had they ignored Q Prime's advice and gotten themselves over to Britain and Europe to capitalise on their early popularity there, just as Metallica had in the days before they had come under Q Prime's raven-like wing; Warrior Soul and Dan Reed Network were other Q Prime acts that arrived with a bang, media-wise, in the Eighties and left with a whimper, comparatively speaking, sales-wise. But those that did flourish under their tutelage did so spectacularly and by the end of the decade Q Prime would boast multi-platinum acts such as Def Leppard, Metallica, Queensrÿche, Dokken, Tesla and Cameo. In 1989 they were hired to oversee the Rolling Stones' *Steel Wheels* comeback world tour.

It had actually been Xavier Russell who effected introductions between Q Prime and Metallica. 'Mensch phoned asking me for their number,' he recalls now. 'This was pre-mobile phone days and they were pretty hard to track down. I remember I had to phone Kirk's mother in San Francisco. I said, "I need to track down Lars urgently." She said, "Well, we can get him to a pay phone," because they weren't on the phone at the El Cerrito house. This is how archaic it was. I then remember Lars phoning me up from a phone box in America, reversing the charges. I said, "Look, Mensch needs to talk to you. He's serious about wanting to sign you."' The next thing Xavier heard, the deal was done. He points out that Mensch and Burnstein could hardly have been the only ones sniffing around Metallica at that time. He believes Iron Maiden manager Rod Smallwood may also have been interested: 'Lars always worshipped the way Maiden was managed – their artwork, the sleeves, the tours. He always wanted to be represented by somebody like Smallwood. But I don't think Smallwood was really into that sort of music. Mensch knew something was gonna happen.'

Says Jonny, 'I got to tell you something; it shattered me to lose them, for years. Because I thought we would have proved to everybody that we could have taken it all the way. It would have happened with us as well. It was on fire when we gave up the band! Absolutely blazing! It was in the middle of everything going on.' The deal eventually struck with Elektra allowed Megaforce to continue with the US release of *Ride the Lightning* up to the first 75,000 sales. But then, says Jonny, 'The first seventy-five for any band that's brand new is [the main part of the job]. After that it's just taking orders.' He claims Howard Thompson, then a main player at Elektra, later 'came up to me and said that Marsha and I did a million-dollar job to really break this band. It would have cost Elektra millions to get the band to the level that they were handed Metallica. That's one of the best compliments I took.'

Ultimately, though, the separation was 'not very fun'. Indeed, three years later, as a guest at Jonny and Marsha's home, I would sit and listen to him semi-jokingly describe Q Prime as 'Thieves! Fuckin' thieves!' When I remind him of it now, he sighs and says: 'Can I tell you something, they probably are. What they did was probably thieveish. But the band probably came to them complaining and moaning and asking for a saviour, to get to the next level. Lars, you remember, always, *always* wanted to be in the same league as Def Leppard. He felt that if he had Def Leppard's manager, it's possible. And again, I was not proven in the arena level, in those days. Marsha and I had not done any giant venues – and they wanted to be where that knowledge was guaranteed to exist.' He is not allowed to 'discuss the terms' because of the confidentiality clause in his eventual written agreement with Metallica. 'But I'll see if I can put it to you in a mild way. We were asked, legally ... to negotiate a separation.' Another deep sigh.

'You know, if it ain't right, you can't manage a band. You don't want to be hated. I want to be loved! So it would have been punishment for us also to have gone on. It was a surprise but I can't say anything [except] I felt the history would have been the same or maybe even better with me and Marsha.'

We would never know.

SEVEN
MASTERPIECE

I sat on the corner of the bed in my hotel room, watching Gem go at it. He'd taken a picture from the wall, laid it flat on the coffee table and was chopping out lines of coke on it.

'There are two things I'd rather you didn't bring up to the band,' he said.

'Yeah, what's that?'

'One is this whole thrash thing. They're really sensitive suddenly about being called thrash. They feel like they've gone beyond all that now and that this new album is something different.'

'Okay,' I said. No biggie. It had been the same during the punk thing. I'd lost count of the amount of bands I'd interviewed in my early days on Sounds that no longer wished to be labelled simply as 'punk'. 'New wave' was the desirable new sobriquet for the would-be pop intelligentsia and so that's what you wrote – if you wanted to stay in with them. It was the same with all the old NWOBHM bands. By the time I'd started writing about Iron Maiden and Def Leppard for Kerrang! it would never have occurred to me to describe them as NWOBHM. That stuff was good for getting known in the early days but turned into a pain in the arse once it came to second or third album time. The novelty had worn off and everybody was desperate to distance themselves from it. No one still described Pink Floyd as psychedelic, did they? Or The Beatles as Merseybeat or mop-tops, God forbid.

'What's the second thing?' I asked, eyeing the coke impatiently.

'Er, this,' he said, handing me a rolled-up pound note.

I snaffled up a couple of fat ones then sat back, fighting the welling nausea as the stuff trickled down my throat.

'Why . . . They don't like coke?'

'Oh, they like it all right. A bit too fucking much! No, if they find out I've got this they'll do it all and there'll be none left for us.'

'Fuck that,' I said.

'Too right . . .'

We sat there a couple more hours, doing our thing, getting ready to go to the studio and see the band. I liked Gem. He was old-school, knew how to get the party started. The band was lucky to have him. And now they would have me, too. Not a thrash writer but a proper mainstream music critic here to bestow his blessings – or something. That was certainly the spiel I'd been on the receiving end of when I'd been invited to fly to Copenhagen to check out their new album, Master of Puppets. *'It's different this time,' I kept being told. 'This is the one that's going to break them into the mainstream.'*

I nodded dutifully then waited for the plane tickets to arrive. I didn't give a toss about who was breaking into the mainstream. I just liked Lars, who'd I'd met at Donington back in the summer. A right laugh. I'd watched his band struggling to drape their dark musical backdrop across the unfeasibly sunlit stage, while doing their best to avoid the bottles and catcalls, the usual drunken Donington crowd detritus. Then later that night, back at the hotel, wasted in the bar, Lars had pointed to the unconscious figure of Venom singer Cronos, slumped at a nearby table, face down in a sea of pint glasses, and suggested we get our pictures taken with him. We stood there sniggering while the magazine photographer aimed his lens, waggling our willies in Cronos' slumbering ears.

Now this, waiting to go to the studio to hear what Metallica had been up to in the studio all these months later. It hadn't really dawned on me yet that they might be a band to take very seriously. They were thrash metal; the musical equivalent of silly drunken boys sticking willies in your ear and I had been there many times before. Surely by now we must have seen it all, I thought . . .

Suddenly, in the autumn of 1984, everything changed for Metallica. Under their agreement with Elektra, Megaforce would hand over US rights to *Ride the Lightning* after 75,000 sales. The way the album was already flying out the door, Elektra prepared to rerelease it in November, by which time it would already have sold twice as many copies as *Kill 'Em All*. Although Jonny and Marsha were 'heartbroken' to say goodbye to the band, the Elektra deal did help Megaforce stay afloat at a time when they were still struggling with near-crippling debt. As Jonny says now, 'Our prize for breaking Metallica was losing them. But by the end people were swarming to see them.' The Elektra money he 'put into Anthrax and Raven'.

In the UK, Martin Hooker of Music for Nations was also disappointed to see the band go, but in his case the new deal worked more heavily in his favour. '[Megaforce] sold the band to Elektra for America. So Elektra were getting the rights to that album [*Ride the Lightning*] that we'd paid for. In return they very kindly gave us [the next Metallica album] *Master of Puppets* for free. We still had to pay the band a very handsome advance but we didn't have to pay any of the recording costs; which was fair because we'd paid for the previous album.' It also meant 'somebody else had the hassle of the studio side, overseeing it'. In the meantime, MFN could continue marketing Metallica records with impunity – something that they took spectacular advantage of during the latter months of 1984 when they released a twelve-inch EP of 'Creeping Death'. The B-side comprised newly minted versions of two NWOBHM classics – Diamond Head's 'Am I Evil?' and Blitzkrieg's 'Blitzkrieg' – from their days in Ron McGovney's garage. Hence the informal title they gave the single's cover versions, 'Garage Days Revisited'.

Gem Howard recalls that sales in the UK and Europe 'were just *phenomenal* on that. I think in the end we sold something like a quarter of a million copies, all told.' It wasn't just the content that sold the single – Diamond Head singer Sean Harris later recalled being nonplussed when Peter Mensch called for copyright permission to use 'Am I Evil?': 'I was like, "Well, I can't see the point, but yes you're welcome to!"' – it was the ingenious way MFN marketed the record. Tapping into his previous experience at Secret of selling multi-format 'limited edition' singles and EPs to the hardcore collector punk audience, Hooker shrewdly released 'Creeping Death' in a special coloured-vinyl edition. In America, where Elektra had elected not to release a single, MFN sold more than 40,000 copies of the 'Creeping Death' twelve-inch just on import. When orders began to outstrip their ability to manufacture more, MFN simply improvised and released it in a different colour. Recalls Gem, 'We pressed ["Creeping Death"] on every colour vinyl we could find. We'd get a phone call from an importer in New York saying could [they] have another three thousand coloured-vinyl after we'd decided to put it out in blue or something. I went, "Yeah, okay." Then I'd phone up the pressing plant and they'd say, "We haven't got any blue vinyl left." And I'd go, "Well, what have you got?" and they'd go, "We've got some yellow ... " So I'd phone back New York and say, "Can't do blue, can do yellow and you can have them in seven days, any good?" They'd say, "Okay, done." And it literally was like that. I know that we did blue, red, green, yellow, *brown*. "They've only got brown." "Okay ... " I don't actually know how many colours we did in the end. I think we did it in clear as well. And gold, of course ...'

Many Metallica fans would buy the record again and again just to collect the set. Sales began to rocket so high in Britain and Europe they began to sell more copies of the 'Creeping Death' twelve-inch than they did of *Ride the Lightning*. Boggle-eyed, the rest of the biz took note and within two years singles in multiple formats became the industry standard in the UK, with releases being staggered so that new formats appeared every week for up to eight weeks in the knowledge that many fans were simply buying repeats. (This practice was later restricted under new legislation.)

All of this was done with the blessing of the band – or certainly Lars. 'Lars was *always* the spokesperson,' points out Hooker. 'Any business you had to do, everything went through Lars.' But then Lars wasn't like other drummers. He knew there was no music to be made without the business side being taken care of too, and vice versa. As Hooker says, 'It's always helpful if you've got one guy in the band who has his business head screwed on. So many bands haven't a clue. Metallica always kind of knew where they wanted to go. They had one guy who was great doing the interviews and the business. It left the others time to take care of the music.' He adds, 'But that's also something that American bands have that English bands *never* have. Like Twisted Sister were unbelievably professional; so together and business-minded, but without selling-out on the music front. Metallica were very much that way.'

Delighted though they were over this newfound excitement abroad, now they had a major deal Metallica were in a hurry to get back on the road in America. But Burnstein and Mensch brought their experience to bear and persuaded them that their best move now would actually be to return to Europe where their profile remained highest, and begin touring as headliners. With Elektra not prepared to put their full marketing machine behind *Ride the Lightning* until it was rereleased in the States in November, a US tour in the New Year was a more sensible option, allowing momentum to build. 'Which is exactly what happened,' says Hooker. With fellow MFN act Tank in to provide support, Metallica kicked off their twenty-five-date Bang the Head That Doesn't Bang tour on 16 November with a show at the Exosept club, in Rouen, France, before moving on to Poperinge, Belgium, then heading south for shows in Paris, Lyon, Marseilles, Toulouse, Bordeaux, Montpellier and Nice. Concerts in Milan, Venice and Zurich followed before the tour arrived for seven shows in West Germany, interrupted only by a quick drive across the border for a smoke-ringed sell-out date at the notorious Paradiso club in Amsterdam. After that the highlight was a gut-busting hometown show for Lars at the Saga club in Copenhagen, which a 'very proud' Flemming Rasmussen attended, the tour concluding with more sold-out club shows in Sweden and Finland.

The final night of the tour was an ambitious one-off UK date at London's Lyceum Ballroom on 20 December. Part of a larger strategy to push Metallica's profile in Britain further towards the same level it now enjoyed in Europe, the band also appeared on the front cover of *Kerrang!* for the first time. Featured on the cover of the Christmas 1984 issue of the mag was a sole picture of a sunglasses-wearing Lars Ulrich, head thrown back in drunken exultation, and – bizarrely – spray-painted silvery pink, holding a similarly spray-painted, nuts-and-bolts-encrusted Christmas cake. It seemed an incongruous image for a band then building a stiff reputation for itself as a non-glam, walk-it-like-you-talk-it street metal outfit unprepared to bow to commercial pressures. But to the rest of the industry the subtext was clear: the pictures for the cover and inside story were taken by Ross Halfin, *Kerrang!*'s number one photographer, the story written by the magazine's deputy editor, Dante Bonutto – both close personal contacts of Peter Mensch, flown to San Francisco to hang out with the band at El Cerrito. 'I thought: how have they managed that? 'Cos Diamond Head never made the front cover of *Kerrang!*,' says Brian Tatler, laughter tinged with envy. 'The only reason he's got that, I thought to meself, is 'cos he's said, "Yeah, you can spray me, I'll do whatever you like to get on that front cover." Whereas Diamond Head would probably have been a little more, "We're not doing that! I'm not gonna be made to look silly."'

Far from being silly, as far as the band's new set-up was concerned, it was another giant leap forward. 'Getting your band on the cover of *Kerrang!* meant you immediately sold more records,' shrugs Gem Howard. Everyone who had ever shown support for Metallica in Britain was invited along to the Lyceum – also billed as a special Christmas show – headed by Bonutto, Xavier Russell and the rest of the *Kerrang!* team. Writer Malcolm Dome recalls being invited to listen through a headset to what Cliff Burton was playing onstage. 'It was surreal. I mean, he was doing what he needed to do to keep the beat and so forth, but the rest of his playing didn't seem to fit what the others were doing at all, as though he was in a world of his own. It was absolutely extraordinary.' Questioned later by Harald O about his more spontaneous approach to playing live, Cliff shrugged it off with a smile. 'Yeah, well, you get so you know the song like the back of your hand and you can just flip off and do different stuff. It's funner that way, it keeps me entertained. You know; something to do.' Sure, Cliff.

After a break back home in San Francisco – Lars resisting the urge to spend the holidays at home with his family, as Cliff and Kirk would do, in order to keep James company at El Cerrito – the first three months of 1985 found Metallica on their first extended run of US dates for over a year. Second on a three-band bill headlined by W.A.S.P., and opened by old buddies – and now fellow Q Prime clients – Armored Saint, the tour officially got under way on 11 January with a packed show at the Skyway club in Scotia, New York. It was the start of the band's longest tour yet: forty-eight shows in sixty-eight days that would establish them as the hottest new street-level band in the USA. Closest rivals Grim Reaper – the last of the NWOBHM-generation bands to get a foothold in America – had sold over 150,000 copies of their debut album, *See You in Hell* (released in the USA at the same time as *RTL* on the independent Ebony Records label, distributed by RCA). But that would be their peak. Slayer's debut *Show No Mercy* had notched up 40,000 US sales in 1984, enough to become Brian Slagel and Metal Blade's biggest hit yet but not enough to touch what Metallica was now achieving. (Anthrax and Megadeth would not release their first significant albums until much later in 1985). By the time Metallica's US tour had climaxed with a headline show at the Palladium in Hollywood on 10 March, Elektra had added another 100,000 sales to the 75,000 Megaforce had already done in the USA, the album reaching Number 100 on the *Billboard* chart. In the UK, meanwhile, the album had gone silver for over 60,000 sales; double then treble that figure across Europe. They were also now making inroads into the lucrative Japanese market, where Q Prime had set up a deal with CBS (soon to become Sony). It had cost a great deal of money to get to this position – on tour support, on advertising and promotion, on recording costs and simply keeping them fed and out of trouble – and they certainly weren't in the position yet where they could look forward to significant royalties. Indeed, when they were home Cliff was still living with his parents while James, Kirk and Lars clung to their garage couches at the Metallimansion in El Cerrito. But they were certainly on their way. You could feel it in the air at every show they did that year. When the tour finally came to a noisy, drunken halt with one last show, at the Starry Night club in Portland, Metallica dragged on the members of Armored Saint for the encores, concluding with a rowdy version of 'The Money Will Roll

Right In' by San Franciscan punk rockers Fang. A self-referential bit of theatre among the beer-laden laughter, but deep down inside Metallica were no longer even half-joking.

The band was becoming road-hardened. Even James was starting to lighten up – onstage and off. He boasted to Xavier Russell, who joined the tour for a few days, about some of the adventures he was now having. Having spent 'hours and hours in the bar' they had decided to really 'booze it up' in Armored Saint bassist Joey Vera's room. 'We were all getting really ripped and started throwing bottles out the window. They were smashing and it sounded really neat. But that soon got boring, so I threw Joey's black-and-red leather jacket out and it landed in the pool, which luckily had its cover on. We went down to get it and on the way back up to the tenth floor I decided to open the elevator doors between floors ... we then got stuck for half an hour and everyone is like freaking out and I started shouting, "Get us the fuck out of here!" We finally get up to the tenth floor and by now I'm pretty [mad] so I see this fire extinguisher hanging on the wall. So I kinda took it down and started squirting people with it – all this CO_2 or some kinda shit was comin' out of it.'

Not coincidentally, it was around this time the band picked up the nickname, first gleefully reported in *Kerrang!*, of Alcoholica. James was going through his schnapps phase. That and beer and vodka, 'embracing alcohol at a different level from the rest of us', as Lars later put it. Lars had 'more of the binge mentality. I'd go every night for three days. Then I wouldn't touch a drop for the next four.' For James it was different. Drinking was becoming another mask he could hide behind. 'I think drinking made me forget a lot of stuff at home,' he later reflected. 'Then it became fun.' It was a fan who'd come up with the name Alcoholica, designing a T-shirt based on the *Kill 'Em All* album cover, the title recast as *Drank 'Em All* and the Metallica logo supplanted by that of Alcoholica, the ghoulish hammer and blood pool replaced by an overturned vodka bottle, its contents spilling out. 'We thought it was pretty cool,' said James. 'We had shirts like that made up for ourselves.'

The booze provided a lift in other, more tangible ways too. Most significantly, Hetfield was now finding his voice – real and imagined – as the frontman. Megadeth bassist David Ellefson recalls being 'totally blown away' when he caught the Metallica/Armored Saint show at the Hollywood Palladium in March. 'I'd seen them play on *Kill 'Em All* at the Country Club [in Reseda, in August, 1983] and it was good [but] they hadn't quite settled into the pocket yet, as all bands do once you've been on the road for a few years. But when I walked in [at the Palladium in '85] I remember James coming out with his shirt off and it was just *ferocious*. Like, holy smokes, man! This band has arrived! There's nobody like this doing this.' Recalls Joey Vera, who watched Metallica from the side of the stage most nights of that tour: 'It was a fire that was beginning to burn. That's where I first saw it on a daily basis, in every small town. It's one thing to see something in a magazine, or one show in a big city, but when we were on tour together we played every shithole across the US and that's where you got to see, like, wow, this is having the same effect in front of two hundred people or in front of six hundred people.'

Hanging out on tour, they would take turns sharing buses between cities, recalls Vera: 'They were just ... very crazy. A lot of partying. They had already been to Europe. So we were always in awe of them because they had done that, begging for stories. How ugly the chicks were, how bad the food was, how many times they woke up in the gutter, so on and so forth.' As the bassist, Joey was especially drawn to Cliff: 'We had a kinship, Cliff and I, because we also listened to some jazz fusion. We'd have some conversations about Stanley Clarke and about all these other bass players that we liked when we were growing up. So he was someone who had another foot somewhere else in the music and was an excellent player and a pretty strong musical front in that band. I think that's one of the reasons the band always looked to him for approval. He also had this really strong punk aesthetic ... of doing it against the grain, going against the norm, someone who is basically an artist. That's how I always perceived Cliff, as someone who was very strongly opinionated and very much not willing to do anything which would go against what he believed in. It was pretty evident back then that that mattered to the rest of the guys too.'

Mainstream rock was so conservative in the mid-Eighties, to see this guy with the flared trousers, the denim jacket, the long, straight hair and the weird, scruffy little moustache, it was an inspiration, says Vera. He talks about how Cliff, 'almost had his own language. Just the way he would phrase things. He wasn't one of these people that would come and say hello how are you today, the weather's really nice. One time we played a show in El Paso, and we're all waiting to go onstage. He opens our dressing room door and pops his head in and says: "Weakness is emanating from the crowd." And he shuts the door. We've never forgot that. That's like one of the classic Cliff quotes.' He chuckles softly. 'We took that as, okay, well, now we've got to go out and really fucking wake these people up. The Grand Master has come in and let us know where he stands . . .'

Machine Head vocalist Robb Flynn was a sixteen-year-old Metallica fan when he caught the tour at the Kabuki Theater in San Francisco. 'That was crazy, a really intense show. The first time I'd seen a circle pit, first time I'd seen people headbanging. I went right down the front. I was like, "Holy shit, this is awesome!" I had never felt such a rush of energy. I was completely exhilarated. I didn't even drink, I got dropped off by my dad so I was sober and I remember every moment of it. After that I was just like, we gotta start going to shows and drinking and buying drugs. That just seemed like what you were supposed to do.' James Hetfield was now 'the guy who everybody related to. I loved the other guys, too, but Hetfield was extremely . . . he was just so pissed [off] it was awesome. He was just so mad about everything it was like, fuck, yeah!'

As well as top-drawer management and a major US record deal, Metallica's operation was expanding in other ways too. They now had major agency representation in both the USA – where they were now signed to ICM, personally handled by rising industry star Marsha Vlasic – and the UK, where Fair Warning co-founder John Jackson would become their booking agent. Their touring staff was also upgraded. Mark Whitaker, his time now taken up with full-time management of Exodus – making waves of their own with the *Bonded by Blood* album – was replaced by an English sound technician, 'Big' Mick Hughes, an apprentice electrician from West Bromwich who'd started out humping gear in his spare time for Judas Priest then graduated to live sound engineer with another upcoming Q Prime act, the Armoury Show. When the latter folded, Peter Mensch invited Hughes to work with Metallica, his immediate innovation to add a high-to-mid 'click' to Lars' live bass drum sound, as a way of lifting the drums out of the bottom-heavy sound he'd previously been labouring under, adding more bounce and feel. Paul Owen, another English Midlander who had previously worked for Diamond Head, was also hired as monitor engineer.

Another significant new face backstage was that of soon-to-be-tour-manager Bobby Schneider, who had been working as the drum tech on David Bowie's Serious Moonlight tour prior to receiving the invitation to join up with this, for Bobby, unknown new band. 'I had never heard of Metallica,' explains Schneider now, 'nor had I ever worked for any metal bands at all. So this was a complete new world for me.' He had been working locally in Boston when he got a call from the band's temporary new tour manager, regular Rush man, Howard Ungerleider, who Bobby had previously worked for on a Rush tour as a lighting engineer. Recalls Bobby: 'Lars' drum tech had destroyed a hotel the day before so they'd fired him. So they were looking for someone right away and pretty much offered me the job [over the phone] and I flew out [to the W.A.S.P. tour]. I remember sitting in a room with Lars when he was trying to explain to me [what he needed]. He used to switch sticks in the middle of the set, a different stick in his right hand and a couple other things. In typical Lars fashion – and I don't know the guy yet – he's explained this same thing to me fifteen times. And I look at him and go, "I *got* it." He goes, "Wow, you're pretty confident, aren't you?"'

When Ungerleider had to leave to return to Rush, he recommended that Schneider take over as tour manager. Bobby had already been tour-managing for smaller bands and handling production but this was something new: 'Howard said to Mensch, "You know they love

Bobby – you should just make him the tour manager." So that's where we started. I finished out that tour and they brought me back for a couple more. In the end, we had a six-year relationship. I definitely saw some changes in that time. I saw them grow up.'

Schneider characterises the W.A.S.P. tour now as 'a breakthrough moment' – for both himself and Metallica. 'They were blowing everybody away. I wasn't really into the metal world. I hadn't lived in that world. The W.A.S.P. guys, all being six foot six tall, were very intimidating, and they were the ones who had most equipment. But the kids weren't coming to see them. They were doing their best to be the headliner. But there was no question that Metallica [had] the vibe.' Going from working for Bowie's supremely accomplished drummer Tony Thompson to working for Lars Ulrich was also something of a leap of faith. 'James used to spit on him all the time, when Lars would really get out of time, which was *often*. He'd be so off sometimes James would just turn around and glare at him.' The spitting 'was James' way of telling him, "Dude, you're really fucking bad tonight."' Searching for the positive, Bobby likens Lars' drumming back then to being 'almost like a guitarist. You know, he's playing all kinds of triplets and fills … It never seemed that Lars fucked up the intricate parts. It was sort of the ongoing feel for it' that so enraged James it caused him to spit. And while Lars may have been the business leader of the group, as far as Schneider could tell it was Cliff Burton the band relied on for the right words in their private moments, as human beings. 'Cliff was the backbone. Cliff was the guy that everybody looked to. If there was a big decision to be made it was [done] in the inner workings. But it seemed to me, if there was something Cliff wasn't gonna like, it wasn't gonna happen. Cliff was the Keith Richards of the band. No one fucked with Cliff.'

The early weeks of the summer of 1985 found Metallica back in San Francisco, off the road but getting ready to go back into the studio and record their next album. The Metallica fire, as Joey Vera says, may have begun to burn more fiercely, but the biggest-selling album that year was the newly muscled and suddenly clean-cut Bruce Springsteen's flag-waving *Born in the U.S.A.* (no matter the counter-intuitive message of the title track being largely misconstrued by a significant number of the fifteen million Americans who eventually bought the album). Looming on the horizon was the global feel-good event of the decade, Live Aid. What place then in this larger, strictly white-hat scheme of bigger and better things for the angry bombast of a bunch of heavy-metal-worshipping young heads from the tripped-out West Coast? Somewhere far off in the shadows, perhaps, certainly nowhere near the centre. But that was okay. Metallica needed the down-time to sit and write their future. Their next album – their first recorded directly for a major American label – would be their most important yet and they all felt the pressure of that even as they kidded around and acted like it was all just a game. It would also be the first Metallica album for which there were no hold-overs from the past to fall back on; no old Mustaine or Exodus riffs to repurpose and remould into their own, more interesting new image (although Dave would later claim, erroneously, that he'd had a hand in at least one of the new tracks). Just at that moment when they needed to demonstrate they had what it took to climb out of the musical ghetto thrash metal was already beginning to resemble, they would need to start again from scratch.

As would become their habit from here on in, Lars and James initially retreated to the garage at El Cerrito alone, roughing out early demos before inviting Cliff and Kirk down to jam along with some ideas of their own. As a result, while the Hetfield and Ulrich monikers would adorn all eight of the tracks that would make up the next album, already titled *Master of Puppets* after the best of the new numbers James and Lars had begun bashing into shape, only two would bear the names of all four members (the title track and album closer, 'Damage, Inc.'); three with the addition of Hammett ('The Thing That Should Not Be', 'Welcome Home (Sanitarium)' and 'Disposable Heroes'), just one the additional Burton imprimatur (the by-now-obligatory Cliff instrumental, 'Orion'), and two simply bearing the Hetfield-Ulrich stamp ('Battery' and 'Leper Messiah'). Nevertheless, insists Hammett, 'Ninety-nine per cent of it was conceived by the four of us. There wasn't anything left over from the *Ride the Lightning* stuff, the *Kill 'Em All* stuff was already written [when I joined]. It was pretty much the definitive musical statement from that line-up, and it felt like it. We had really gotten to know each other's musical capabilities and temperaments over that three-year period. And I could tell that it was really blossoming into something that was to be reckoned with. It was very consistent. Every song we came up with was just like the greatest thing. Every time we'd write another it was like, "Oh my god! It's just another great conception," you know?'

All but two of the new songs – 'Orion' and 'The Thing That Should Not Be' – were fully completed at El Cerrito that summer. Speaking with me more than twenty years later, Hammett laughed off Mustaine's suggestion that he should have received a co-credit for 'Leper Messiah': 'Even though Dave might claim that he wrote "Leper Messiah", he didn't. There's maybe a chord progression that was in that song, like maybe ten seconds that came from him – that, ironically, is just before the guitar solo. But he did not write "Leper Messiah" at all. In fact, I remember being in the room when Lars came up with the main musical motif.' Kirk still has tapes 'recorded on a boom box in the middle of the room' of the El Cerrito sessions, including works-in-progress such as 'Welcome Home (Sanitarium)', 'Disposable Heroes', 'Master of Puppets', 'Battery' and the middle section of 'Orion': 'Cliff wrote that whole middle part complete, with bass lines, two- and three-part harmonies, all completely arranged. It was pretty amazing. We were all really, really blown away.'

Although Burton only received co-writing credits on three of the eight tracks, Hammett felt strongly that 'people don't talk enough about Cliff's contribution to that album'. Not just things like the evocative 'volume swells' on the bass intro to 'Damage, Inc.', which had evolved from the improvised bass solo he performed each night on tour, but to the overall sound and direction the band now took: 'I remember him playing the intro to "Damage, Inc." on the *Ride the Lightning* tour. It has all those bass swells and harmonies on it. What was really amazing, I remember him saying, "Yeah, it's based on a Bach piece." I asked him which one and I'm not sure if I've got the title right but I'm pretty sure he said it was "Come Sweetly Death", or something like that.' The piece Kirk's referring to is 'Come, Sweet Death', from the *69 Sacred Songs and Arias* that Johann Sebastian Bach contributed to Georg Christian Schemelli's *Musical Songbook*, which contained nearly a thousand song texts for voice and accompaniment but written down as a figured bass – musical notation indicating intervals, chords and non-chord tones, in relation to a bass note, providing harmonic structure. A very Burton-like musical preoccupation.

Continued Kirk, 'I remember when I first heard the riff to "Damage, Inc.", I thought, wow, how simple but how effective. And I have to say, that one line – "Honesty is my only excuse" – that's a great line, but it's influenced by Thin Lizzy and a track from *Shades of a Blue Orphanage*.' Again, however, Kirk has got it slightly wrong, the track he referred to, 'Honesty is No Excuse', is not from *Orphanage* but the eponymously titled debut album from Thin Lizzy, in which singer Phil Lynott ends verses with the line, 'Honesty is my only excuse'. Kirk was absolutely spot-on, though, when he said that *Master of Puppets* was characterised by 'all sorts of strange influences like that', including a short guitar passage at the end of the verse on 'Disposable Heroes' that was the guitarist's attempt at a military march. 'Like bagpipes or something. I watched a lot of war movies, trying to find something that was like a call to arms. Like something a bagpipe player would play as they were going into battle. I didn't really find anything but that's what I came up with.' He laughed. Some influences were more familiar, as with the acoustic intro to the track that would open the album, 'Battery' – another deliberate attempt at 'an Ennio Morricone thing', while still retaining some of the actual chords from the subsequent track.

With the songs all but complete, the band set about finding a studio to record them in. With Flemming Rasmussen back onboard as co-producer, Lars would have been happy to return to Sweet Silence in Copenhagen but none of the others wanted that. Enough of the cold and snow already, protested the Californian boys, let's make the album somewhere warm and sunny, even if it meant doing it in much-loathed LA. So Flemming flew into LA and he and Lars spent two weeks in July being chauffeured around in a Lincoln town car, paid for by Elektra, checking out studios. 'It's what the record company rented,' a red-faced Lars protested when one journalist bumped into him and asked jokingly if he was now a rock star. 'We didn't order it!' But rock stars are what Lars Ulrich and Metallica were fast becoming – much to their drummer's secret delight.

The problem, as Rasmussen recalls, was trying to find a studio in LA that provided a comparable set-up for the drums. 'We had like a huge storage room in the back of [Sweet Silence] with a really big, wooden room with a lot of ambience in it. That's where we ended up putting the drums [on *RTL*]. We needed a [similarly] huge live room to record the drums for [*Master of Puppets*] so we drove around checking out studios.' Unable to find what they were looking for, Lars went back to the rest of the band and again put the case to them for returning to Sweet Silence. What ultimately swung it, recalled Kirk, was that the dollar rate was such that it made recording the album in Denmark much cheaper than it would have been in America, allowing them for the first time to really take their time in the studio. 'We'd also had great results in the past with *Ride the Lightning* and knew the studio and all the people there. The familiarity of it all made sense to us. And we really wanted to be somewhere where there wasn't a whole bunch of distractions. At least, for the three of us – Lars was out all the time!'

With sessions not due to begin in Copenhagen until September, Q Prime took the opportunity to squeeze the band onto the bills of three of the biggest rock festivals that summer: England's increasingly famous annual Monsters of Rock show at Castle Donington on 17 August; the even more prestigious Day on the Green festival at Oakland Coliseum on 31 August; plus an appearance at the Loreley Metal Hammer festival in Rhein – the West German equivalent of Donington – on 14 September. Worldwide sales for *Ride the Lightning* were now approaching half a million but the band was still viewed very much as underdogs, curiosities at best, next to more established names like ZZ Top, Marillion and Bon Jovi (all of whom followed Metallica onto the stage at Donington) and Scorpions, Ratt and Y&T,

all above Metallica at Bill Graham's Day on the Green festival a fortnight later. Only the crowds seemed to really know who Metallica were, especially in Europe, where they had sold most records and were now increasingly seen as the next big thing. At the Rhein festival, at which 'Disposable Heroes' was given its first public performance, Venom was also on the bill, in the slot above Metallica. Standing backstage, listening to them pounding through 'Seek and Destroy', Jeff Dunn was astonished to hear 'the whole audience singing it. Then James shouting, "What the fuck was that?" and then the whole place going mad. James had that rapport with the audience; they were his that night. It was at that point I can honestly say that Metallica were starting to overtake us – the European gig where they definitely made their mark.'

In the hotel bar the night before the Donington show, Lars had told me they were 'in the mood to kill'. When later I asked if he thought Metallica had succeeded he nodded his head enthusiastically. Of course they had. 'When we walked onstage at Donington, I thought we were showing both the other bands and the kids in the audience that we have a different way of presenting ourselves, way, way apart from people's preconceived ideas of what a band like Metallica is all about. I think a lot of people are slowly starting to understand and appreciate that what we do, and the way we do it, is *real*. What you see is what you get, no faking. What you see of us like onstage is what we're like all the time, we don't start pretending or hamming it up.'

Certainly there was no faking the non-stop rain of objects that were hurled at the stage from the 70,000-strong Donington crowd that day, including plastic bottles full of urine. Not just for Metallica, but throughout the entire event, as if ritualistically. Marillion singer Fish, then at the height of his fame, was brave enough to tell the crowd: 'Those of you who are throwing bottles, people down the front are getting hurt, so fuck off.' This did bring a temporary halt to the disgusting deluge. But those bands lower on the bill not popular enough yet to get away with something like that were forced to grin and bear it. James Hetfield, though, had other concerns when Metallica took to the stage in the middle of a swelteringly hot afternoon.

Squeezed between Ratt and Bon Jovi, the sort of poodle-haired pop-rockers Metallica professed to despise, James announced to the crowd, 'If you came here to see spandex, eye make-up, and the words "Oh baby" in every fuckin' song, this ain't the fuckin' band!' Cue another hail of beer cans and bottles. As usual, Cliff Burton had his own way of dealing with things. Ducking beneath a flying pear, which ended up embedded in his bass bin, he coolly sauntered over to his stack, plucked out the pear, took a couple of ironic bites out of it then slung it back into the crowd, to general all-round cheers. As he later ruefully recalled, 'Donington was a day of targets and projectiles. [Stuff] was piling high on the stage all throughout the day, and freaks were flipping.' Then added with a straight face: 'I think they liked us, though.'

At the Day on the Green festival two weeks later, this time Metallica were bigger creators of mayhem than any of the 90,000 in the crowd. The show itself had been a memorable occasion. Recalls Malcolm Dome, who was there covering the event for *Kerrang!*, 'It was the first time I'd seen Metallica so high up the bill at such an important show. The headliners were the Scorpions, second on the bill were Ratt, and Metallica were just below them, with Y&T, Yngwie Malmsteen and Victory below them. I know it was a hometown show for them but this was a stadium and yet it was clear they belonged on the bigger stages. One thing about Metallica, they always grew into whatever new context they found themselves in. And yet they were still a people's band, you could tell by the audience reaction. They knew how to relate to the fans, as in we're still of the same mentality as you lot, we understand you. We are on this big stage here only because we have the music to carry it forward and entertain you but we haven't changed at all.'

As if to prove it, after the show Hetfield ran amok in a Jägermeister fit and, egged on by one of his East Bay pals, smashed up the band's dressing room. Wrecking rooms had become a regular sport on their own tours, but as James later confessed, the Day on the Green rampage was 'the worst'. Having got it into his head that, as he put it, 'the deli tray and the fruit had to go through a little vent', when the vent proved too small he simply decided to 'make a hole'. As a result, the backstage trailer the band was using to change in was all but destroyed. Promoter Bill Graham, whose long career had seen him work with prolific room-breakers such as Led Zeppelin's John Bonham, summoned the singer to his office like the headmaster summoning a recalcitrant pupil for a flogging. Graham told him sternly: 'This attitude you have, I've had the same conversation with Sid Vicious and Keith Moon.' Informed in no uncertain terms that no further destruction of property would be tolerated and that he would be sent the bill for the damage he'd already done, as James later ruefully observed, 'I realised at that point there was more to being in a band than pissing people off and smashing shit up.'

Once again, it was left to Cliff to bring things back to a more manageable state of affairs. Malcolm Dome recalls the bassist giving his bandmates a severe dressing down after the show. 'I remember him looking at Lars, like, "One more word from you and I'm gonna fucking punch you!"' That quietened things down – for a while, anyway. Kirk Hammett: 'Cliff was the most mature out of all of us. He had a quiet strength [and] was very, very confident. A lot of times the rest of us would defer to him in times of insecurities. He just had so much confidence, he had confidence to spare. He just seemed so much wiser and much more responsible than the rest of us. He was the guy when I would do something stupid, or Lars or James would do something stupid, he was the guy who would say, "What the hell were you thinking?" Or: "That was a really stupid thing to do!" He was always the guy to reprimand us.'

The day after the show, a badly hungover James, Lars and Kirk met up at San Francisco International airport to catch the flight to Copenhagen. For the first time they would be setting aside proper time to make an album, as opposed to simply tacking on some studio time at the end of a tour and aiming, essentially, just to record their live set. Everyone was buzzing, except for Cliff, who never showed up. 'I remember James, Lars and I waiting at the gate and paging him and he never showed up,' smiled Kirk. 'So we had to get on the plane without him. Cliff was good at missing things because he moved on his own time. He smoked a lot.' They tried calling him from a pay-phone but only got the outgoing message on his new answer-machine. But they understood where he was at; that big brother Cliff was probably kicking back at home in a fog of bud-smoke and beer fumes, maxed out. It didn't take much figuring. Cliff also knew the first few days at Sweet Silence were likely to involve sitting around while Lars got his drums together and James lingered endlessly over the guitar sound. He'd join them later, he decided. After the excitement of Day on the Green, he needed a change of pace anyway.

Recording at Sweet Silence started on Tuesday, 3 September 1985. The band was still jet-lagged and missing its bass player but in every other respect they were in the best shape of their lives. The hectic two and a half years the Ulrich-Hetfield-Burton-Hammett line-up of Metallica had been together had seen it coalesce over more than 140 gigs and two albums into a fist-tight proposition. In the eighteen months since they'd completed *Ride the Lightning* they had leapt forward as songwriters, as the new material they were now coming up with proved to them. They also had the ironclad confidence only nearly a million albums and singles sold worldwide can bring. 'There was a sense of [expectation],' said Kirk. 'It did feel like we had a huge amount of momentum behind us, people supporting us and pushing us all during the creation of that album . . . that this album was another big step forward.' Just to make sure, Lars had recently taken it upon himself to book drum lessons. He had been embarrassed by his amateurish approach in the studio the first time he'd worked with Rasmussen; he was going to show the producer how different things were now. Kirk, too, although always a conscientious pupil, had been away from home a long time and the summer of 1985 was his first prolonged spell back working with Joe Satriani – himself now about to embark on a recording career – since before he'd joined Metallica.

No more sleeping in the spare room, either. With Elektra now paying the bills the band could afford to book into the luxury Scandinavia Hotel, where Lars and James shared a junior suite and Kirk and Cliff shared another. 'It just made the stay a lot easier for [the other three],' said Lars. 'We thought we were just on top of the world!'

laughed Kirk. Even Cliff, who arrived at the start of the second week there, began to settle down and enjoy the surroundings. As winter arrived and the nights got longer and colder, away from the studio, with their guitars and a plentiful supply of strong black hash, Cliff and Kirk ignored the snow on the ground outside and turned their room at the Scandinavia into a home from home. 'For a bass player he played a lot of guitar,' Kirk recalled. 'In fact, he would drive me crazy with it. We'd come back to the hotel after a night of gallivanting, like totally wasted at three in the morning or whatever. But instead of crashing out he would immediately want to set up the electric guitars and start playing for a couple of hours. I'd be exhausted but then I'd totally get sucked into it and start playing along with him. He would talk me into figuring out certain guitar parts of certain songs so that I could show them to him. Eventually that led to figuring out guitar solos so that he could play them on guitar. He was obsessed with Ed King, one of the guitar players in Lynyrd Skynyrd. He said that Ed King was his favourite guitar player, which was pretty weird.'

When they weren't playing guitars together, they were playing poker. 'We'd go out and play poker for eight hours straight after being up for twenty-four hours,' said Kirk. 'We'd find a seafood restaurant that was open, eat raw oysters and drink beer, scream at the natives while we were drunk.' They were, he said, 'some of my best memories' from that time. James and Lars were also hanging out more again. As on their previous visits to Denmark, when they weren't working the two liked to get stuck into the Elephant beer. Recalled Lars, 'In late November, early December, they have something called Christmas beers, which is just an excuse for everyone to drink their Christmas sorrows away. It's twice as strong as regular beer. Every time we went out and drank these Christmas beers, James would start trying to talk Danish – completely pissed out of his face!'

Once they were inside Sweet Silence every night, however, it was all business. Far from merely carrying on where they'd left off with *RTL*, the new album would be something else again, they decided – beginning with the sound quality. I put it to Rasmussen that, listening back now, it's as though they had made some giant breakthrough with *Ride the Lightning* and were now intent on taking it somewhere new with *Master of Puppets*. 'Yeah, that's exactly how it was,' he replies. 'We were pretty pleased with *Ride*. But when we were gonna do *Master* we really tried to [raise] the bar and just make everything actually better than we were capable of. We knew we had a bunch of really good songs so we put the bar up really high, really worked a lot on that.'

Luck played its part, too. The band had recently received a new Mesa/Boogie amp endorsement, 'But the new amps sounded really crappy.' So one of Flemming's first jobs, in a weird echo of his initial task on the *Ride* sessions – trying to find a new guitar amp to emulate the sound of James' stolen amp – was to 'fiddle around' until he 'actually created that guitar sound' we now hear on the album; something distinct to Metallica that, as he says, 'has more or less followed them for the rest of their career. We could all feel it.' Flemming also recalls trying to get Lars to work to a click-track for the first time, in an effort to improve his wayward timing: 'It was either that or James and Lars playing it till the drum track was cool.' To boost his confidence, Q Prime flew over Def Leppard drummer Rick Allen's favourite Ludwig snare drum – a late Seventies replica of the hand-engraved black nickel-plated brass shell-drum originally manu-factured by Ludwig in the 1920s called a Black Beauty. 'We set it up and it was just brilliant,' Lars glowed.

These were mere details, though. What Rasmussen noticed most was the vast improvement in their overall technique. 'Musician-wise they were all like a million times better because they'd been on the road for a year and a half. James was *brilliant* at that time. It was unbelievable. Some of the rhythm guitars, he'd more or less do them in the first take then we'd start doubling up and that would more or less be the first take too.' Laying down identical rhythm tracks – one on each side of the stereo mix – Hetfield now got into the habit of adding a third layer on top, jokingly nicknamed 'the thickener'. Because of that: 'We could get *really* picky about it,' says Rasmussen, 'and make sure they were all right where they were supposed to be because James was so good at it that it was just a matter of taking the time that we needed.' Cliff and Kirk also exerted more influence this time around: 'All of them contributed more. If people had an opinion they said it. I definitely know Cliff did that a couple more times.' Although he was only co-credited with three tracks, it was Cliff's influence that gave so many of the album's tracks a neo-classical feel, by turns complex, magnificent, ominous, grandiloquent; turning them into musical pyramids of multiple movements, determinedly in opposition with the verse/chorus formula of most rock bands at that time. Where in earlier days Lars was fond of pushing each new number to such inordinate lengths they often threatened to collapse under their own weight, none of the multiple-part tracks they were recording now sounded anything other than totally spot-on.

Lyrically, the new material was several moves on from what had come before too. James may later have downplayed much of the thrusting new content as simply 'about playing live', but that was like his hero Clint Eastwood's man with no name in *The Good, the Bad and the Ugly* suggesting there might be a spot of bother further down the road. It would be another five years before Hetfield was ready to completely bare his soul and start writing brutally frank songs about his real-life emotional state, but there were no schoolboy 'Metal Militia's on *MOP*; no more glory-of-rock 'Phantom Lord's. In their place were songs about addiction (the title track, all light-and-shade dynamics, the Zeppelin of thrash); American TV evangelists ('Leper Messiah', title lifted from David Bowie's 'Ziggy Stardust'); madness ('Welcome Home (Sanitarium)', about an unjustly incarcerated patient at a mental hospital, hence the misspelled 'sanitarium' of the bracketed title, prefaced by the lonely chime of a treated guitar note); and of course their old friends war ('Disposable Heroes') and death ('Damage, Inc.') – both instant thrash classics, performed at psychotic speed, the fastest, all-out headbangers on an album that, ironically, signalled the band's fond farewell to thrash. With its woozy intro utilising a range of harmonies, volume swells and effects, 'Damage, Inc.' was also Metallica's metaphorical adieu, perhaps, to their early innocence, as they eagerly awaited the rewards and trappings of major stardom, which – although they still didn't talk about in places where they might be overheard – they were all now anticipating with varying degrees of feverish delight. Hetfield spelling it out in the lyrics: '*We chew and spit you out / We laugh, you scream and shout . . .*'

Seen as a whole, *Master of Puppets* was in many ways merely a new, vastly improved version of *Ride the Lightning*. Certainly the track sequencing followed the template almost to the letter, beginning with the atmospheric acoustic guitar intro before segueing into the super-fast, ultra-heavy opening track, 'Battery' – in reference to their days playing the Old Waldorf club on San Francisco's Battery Street; a nasty collision between punk and metal that made no apologies to either rigidly defined culture. There followed the monumentally epic title track; swaggering death march – 'The Thing That Should Not Be' (like 'The Call of Ktulu', inspired by H.P. Lovecraft, its lyric '*Not dead which eternal lie / Stranger eons death may lie*' the same paraphrased quote that also appeared on the cover of Iron Maiden's *Live After Death*, bought by Lars during their stay in Copenhagen). Then there was the spooky demi-ballad, 'Welcome Home . . .' and so on up to and including the by-now-obligatory eight-minute-plus, bass-led Burton instrumental, 'Orion'; the small white dot in the ocean of black the band veils the rest of the album in, yin to its yang, Cliff's solo seeping in so seamlessly it's unclear where the guitar fades out and the bass takes over. Nevertheless, the total track-for-track effect of *Master* was a quantum leap on from anything Metallica had achieved on *Ride*, and while these days both albums tend to be mentioned in the same breath, historically, where the former was Metallica's first excep-tionally accomplished recording, the latter would swiftly become recognised as their first stone-cold masterpiece; their *Led Zeppelin II*; their *Ziggy Stardust*; their legacy. There would never be a Metallica album quite like it again.

'It was like we'd got it right this time,' Kirk told me. 'The cohe-siveness from song to song, track to track, made perfect sense to us. It was almost as if it was self-creating. Ideas were just flowing and coming out of nowhere. From the beginning, when we first started writing, all the way to the end, it just seemed as though there was a non-stop flow of really, really great ideas. It was almost magical because it seemed like everything we played went right, every note we played was in exactly the right spot, and it couldn't ever have gone any better. It was a very, very, very special time. I remember holding the album in my hands and thinking, "Wow, this is a fucking great album, even if it doesn't sell anything. It doesn't matter because this is such a great musical statement that we've just created." I really felt that it would pass the test of time. Which it has . . .'

Certainly there was a sense of occasion to proceedings when I visited the band at Sweet Silence a week before Christmas 1985. Still fretting over the final mixes, the only track they would play me with all the vocals was 'Master of Puppets' itself; an astonishing experience I was completely unprepared for. I had been expecting first-rate heavy metal. Instead I got Sturm und Drang, the giant studio speakers veritably shaking as the maelstrom of drums and guitars came roaring volcanically from their cones. Cliff was standing next to me on one side, Lars on the other, nodding along; Cliff's eyes closed in deep concentration, Lars the opposite, his eyes almost popping out of his head, sneaking sideways glances at me, seeing how all this was going down. I asked to sit down as they then blasted out unfinished, part-vocal mixes of 'Leper Messiah', 'Battery', 'Welcome Home (Sanitarium)', just called 'Sanitarium' at that stage, and 'The Thing That Should Not Be', James and Kirk wandering in and out the door, the TV in the corner mutely showing Kirk Douglas raging away in *Spartacus*.

Afterwards, back at the Scandinavia Hotel, I sat with Lars in the bar talking, drinking Elephant beer as we taped an interview. At one point I asked why so many of their more towering numbers seemed to change course so often, going from hoodlum-fast to zombie-slow, often just as things were really starting to get going. He asked for an example and I pointed to one of the songs they had just played me: 'Master of Puppets'. 'What a riff!' I told him. 'Sabbath would have killed for that in their heyday. Then, just as things really started to take off, this big downward curve; like taking the record off and putting something else on.' Why did they have to do that? He looked at me, stunned. 'I don't know that I've ever thought about that,' he frowned. 'It may be that we try hard to stay as unpredictable as possible.' He sat there chewing it over. I hadn't meant to confuse him, it just seemed ... well, an obvious question. 'We don't like the idea of playing it safe at all,' he eventually decided. 'We always like to try and do things that work out a bit different from what even we imagined them to be.' He concluded, 'I think the key to any success we might have as a band lies in the fact that we follow our own instincts, and not what we think people want to hear.'

Five years later, once it no longer mattered, he was able to be more honest with me, and would ruminate on how 'in the past we'd do a rough version of a song and I'd go home and time it and go, "It's only seven and a half minutes!" I'd think, "Fuck, we've got to put another couple of riffs in there."' In 1985, however, right there as they were finishing up what was to become one of the most important albums of their career, he immediately went on the defensive at any suggestion that the songs might be overlong or unnecessarily convoluted: 'There have been times when we've been working on a new number that has started life as maybe a four- or five-minute piece. But we've ended up extending it just because our ideas haven't ended there.' He added tetchily, 'If we can make the number a bit longer, a bit more interesting, and still make it work, then why not?'

When I teased him and asked if they had ever tried – just once – to write a commercial hit song, he relaxed again and admitted, 'One time and one time only,' citing 'Escape', in so many words, their Thin Lizzy-esque romp from *Ride*. The fact that neither Music for Nations nor Elektra had eventually chosen it as a single – the former preferring the more à la mode 'Creeping Death', the latter not bothering to release a single at all – only reinforced their conviction, he said, that they should never 'depend on adapting to whatever mode popular music is in at any given moment. We're into sticking to what we wanna do, sticking to all the things we, as a band, believe in. And if we can stick to what we are, sooner or later people will have to change their ideas about us and not the other way around.'

I had been asked not to throw the 'thrash' word around willy-nilly, but of course I couldn't resist. What about it? I asked. Caught between the inevitable accusations of sell-out from the hardcore thrash crowd that would surely come their way once their fans had heard the new album, and the blind prejudices of mainstream critics who had never even listened to their music, merely knew the name as synonymous with thrash metal, might they be in danger of pleasing no one but themselves? Lars shrugged, admitted the whole subject irritated him 'a lot', insisting they would receive the recognition they needed from the people who mattered most – Metallica fans. Fuck the critics. 'If you take the extremes on our new album, which to my mind would be "Damage, Inc." and "Orion" – the amount of ground we cover is so big, so vast, it really pisses me off that anybody would want to stick us with one label. Yes, we do a few thrash songs but that's not all we like to do. That's by no means the only thing we're capable of doing and doing fucking well. We're not afraid to play a little slower some-times, we're not afraid to throw in melody or harmony, we're not afraid to prove to people that we are a lot more musically competent than they might expect.' Neither he nor the others, he claimed, had ever seen Metallica as epitomising the thrash movement anyway: 'I accept that we had a lot to do with the way that whole scene took off. We were the first band to sound like that. But we never thought of ourselves as a "thrash band". We were always an American band with British and European metal influences.'

Afterwards we all went out to dinner, the band, Music for Nations' Gem Howard and me. There were no stars in the room, just soldiers. Least starry of all was James, a tall yet hunched presence who eyed me suspiciously, only finally coming out of his shell after several beers and vodka chasers. The only even vague concessions to image were their choices of T-shirts. James, a serial message-bearer, was wearing the same Pushead-designed T-shirt for the then totally unknown punk rockers The Misfits that he would later be pictured in on the back sleeve of *Master of Puppets* – right next to the picture of Cliff aiming his huge middle finger straight at the camera, not a trace of mirth on his poker face. It was the same at dinner. While Lars laughed so loud the people at the next table got up and moved to another one further away, James scowled and a clearly stoned Kirk seemed immersed in his own far-off world, Cliff kept his eyes on me when he knew I was looking and only spoke when I didn't expect him to. Looking like he'd been born into a pair of faded Levi flares, Cliff was clearly a cool number, asked few questions, told no lies. But not remotely cold, just warming up nicely, thank you. I recall he had immaculate hair, long, past his shoulders but positively gleaming with cleanliness and good health. He may have liked to portray himself as a kind of neo-hippy throwback to an earlier, Woodstock-encrusted age, but Cliff Burton was clearly a meticulous person and no stranger to the mirror on the wall. When Gem and I finally escaped in a taxi, all four of them ran after us and tried to yank open the cab doors to stop us. For Gem and I, who had left our beds at six that morning in order to get to the airport in London in time to spend the day with the band in Copenhagen, the night was almost over. For Metallica, it was clear the party was only just getting started.

Flemming and Metallica never did manage to complete those mixes to their mutual satisfaction. Instead, they left Sweet Silence behind for the last time on 27 December and the master tapes were handed over in January 1985 to veteran LA-based studio fixer Michael Wagener, whose recent credits had included production work with Mötley Crüe, Dokken and Accept. Wagener may not have known much about thrash or even Metallica, at that stage, but he sure knew how to add a wonderful sheen to the mighty building blocks Metallica had painstakingly constructed at Sweet Silence with Flemming. With James and Lars looking over his shoulder, barking orders, Wagener set to work at Amigo studios on giving the latest Metallica opus a high shine.

Delighted with the results, Michael Alago gave the go-ahead for Elektra to schedule *Master of Puppets* for an early March 1986 release. He did enquire, at one point, about the possibility of a single being lifted from the album, maybe even a video to go with it – these were still the days when MTV was comfortable rotating rock videos on their daytime shows, although they had yet to actively promote any act as self-evidently uncommercial, at least in their corporate eyes, as the 'kings of thrash' Metallica. Elektra certainly had the budget to try and twist various influential MTV arms, however, if the band was amenable. The band was not. Indeed, over the coming years they would make a virtue out of their apparent refusal to make, as Lars put it, 'suck-ass fucking videos like all the other lame rock bands'. Yet this was an attitude born not of rebellious fortitude but the shrewd micro-calculations for which Ulrich would become far more famous in the American music industry than his drumming. As Lars later told me, back in the 1980s, when MTV was a solitary cable channel, as opposed to the multi-strand, globe-straddling goliath it is today, lording it over dozens of lookalike satellite music TV channels, he and Peter and Cliff at Q Prime had weighed up the various pros and cons of making a video. Star pupil that he was, Lars already had the answer. 'We figured, they're not gonna show a fucking Metallica video anyway. Why waste money making one then? We knew we'd get more publicity out of not making a video than making one.'

And so it proved. An interesting stance to take for a band whose new album would be loosely themed around the subjects of manipulation and control; the puppet master and his expertise at twanging the right strings; making the right moves. The album sleeve reflected this idea almost too perfectly: a field of white crosses – inspired subconsciously perhaps by the penultimate scene from Hetfield's beloved *The Good, the Bad and the Ugly*, where Tuco Ramirez frenziedly scavenges for gold among a field of white gravestones – under a glowering hell-red sky from which hovers the Metallica logo, above which can be seen the puppet master's hands, tugging at the strings attached to the crosses below. In fact, the image could be looked at in a number of ways, not least as a more direct reflection of the title song's pointed reference to drug addiction (*'chopping your breakfast on a mirror'*), the puppet strings those of the dealer's, the white crosses those of his doomed clientele, the already brain-dead.

But it's that more overpowering and deeply cynical image of the semi-visible forces of manipulation and control that really unsettles and eventually takes lasting root. Especially from this distance, a quarter of a century later, knowing what came next . . .

PART TWO

The Art Of Darkness

'How could he know this new dawn's light would change
his life forever? Set sail to sea, but pulled off course
by the light of golden treasure . . .'

– James Hetfield, 'The Unforgiven III', 2008

PART TWO

EIGHT
COME, SWEET DEATH

*I*t must have been ten years later. So far into the future the past was another planet. I was walking the dog around the park one day in the wind and the rain. I was in my usual dog-walking gear: old jeans I didn't mind getting torn or muddy, steel-toe-capped walking boots, several layers of T-shirts and sweaters, and the old leather Metallica jacket. Working on Kerrang! in the Eighties you'd get given a lot of stuff like that: band T-shirts, bomber jackets, baseball caps. All with the name of whatever band it was emblazoned across the front and the tour dates scrawled down the back. Hideous things you wouldn't be seen dead in, most of them. There were exceptions, though. The occasional shirt that didn't draw disdainful looks from passing females, or start fights in pubs full of beered-up lads.

The Metallica jacket was one of those. A heavy-duty, black leather replica of the classic American biker jacket; no tour dates to disfigure it; no gaudy pictures of muscle-bound monster-men brandishing swords, or scantily clad babes delightedly straddling dragons. The sort of jacket you could wear without embarrassing yourself. Except this was ten years later maybe and it was so worn and battered and encrusted with dirt and dog saliva that you could only just about make out the word 'Metallica' in miniature on the left breast pocket, and beneath that three more: 'Master of Puppets'. The only other signifier of the jacket's origins was the small hand-stitched cartoon skull that adorned the wrist of the left sleeve, now so caked in dried mud and threadbare you'd never have noticed it, unless you knew what you were looking for.

London parks are never empty, not even when it's pouring with rain, but this day the place was bare, save for me and my German Shepherd

Dog, a huge brute whose mouth was always full of squirrels and cats and other dogs. We were in among the trees, trudging along, my mind utterly gone, when I bumped into him – a Jesus-like figure with long wet hair and straggly beard, beatific smile on his young-old face, standing there before me suddenly, the rain dripping from his nose.

I looked at him fearfully. The only time strangers without dogs themselves approached you in the park it was never good news. I waited to hear what the problem was but he just carried on moving towards me, smiling.

'Hey,' he said, 'cool band.'

'What?'

'Where'd you get it?'

'What?'

He nodded at the jacket. The penny dropped.

'Oh,' I said. 'Oh . . . someone gave it to me.'

'Wow,' he said. 'Someone must love you very much.'

I didn't know where this was going, thought he might be cool, might be psycho.

'Wanna sell it?' he said.

'What?'

'I'll give you a thousand pounds.'

I looked at him. Was he serious? A thousand pounds . . .

He laughed. 'Only kidding,' he said. 'Had you going for a minute, though, eh?'

'Yeah,' I said, feeling foolish.

'Like you'd ever sell something like that,' he said.

'Yeah . . .'

'Not even for a thousand pounds, eh?'

'Oh . . . no . . .'

He walked off one way, still smiling. I walked off the other, the rain following me and the dog all the way home again.

The morning *Master of Puppets* was released in Britain, Martin Hooker walked from the MFN office in Carnaby Street across towards Wardour Street and into St Anne's Court, where Shades was situated. He was shocked by what he found. 'The kids were queueing outside all the way through the streets of Soho. They'd already got all of the albums in bags with a receipt piled up next to the till, floor to ceiling. It was something that will live with me for ever because it was like, "Holy crap!"'

The release of *Master of Puppets* in March 1986 brought both Metallica and thrash fully into the mainstream for the first time. Although it would quickly come to represent the end of Metallica's association with the genre for those fans already in thrall to its snake-belly charms, the success of the album gave thrash a name and a face the rest of the previously disinterested rock audience could at last identify with. As with David Bowie and glam, the Sex Pistols and punk, or Iron Maiden and the NWOBHM, for the vast majority of music buyers uninterested in the sordid details, at least they knew what thrash was now, what it looked like, even what it sounded like. Thrash was Metallica. And, just as with Bowie and glam and Rotten and punk, however much Metallica moved over the coming years to disassociate themselves from their perceived roots, to push their music into newer, more interesting shapes, their calling card would always remain as the 'godfathers of thrash'. Inventors of a musical legacy that now had more to do with the bands that came after them, it was the tag that both legitimised and ghettoised Metallica – a fact they would spend the rest of their career both railing against and, when it suited them, using as proof of their enduring grass-roots credibility.

On every level, though, *Master of Puppets* was a game-changer. One of the two best albums they would make, it remains, a quarter of a century later, the symbol of everything that continues to make Metallica interesting and exciting, the fact that they later moved so far away from its look and sound that they might have become another band entirely only further enhancing its occult appeal down through the generations, a momentous release seen now, justifiably so, as an utterly unrepeatable chapter in both their own story and that of rock itself.

In *Sounds*, under the heading 'Thrash on Delivery', the new album was hailed as 'a synthesis of everything good and truly Metallica ...

the slow, the fast, the melodic, topped with that exquisite Metallica guitar sound, all treble and grit'. Lars, though, was again doing his best to waylay the inevitable thrash backlash – and catch the eye of those less partisan rock buyers he felt sure would get Metallica if they only gave it a try. 'No one can simply write off Metallica as being thrash,' he said. 'The first album was, we know that, but this album is a totally different proposition.' Added James, 'We'd never try to forget what Metallica formed for, no way. It's just that maturity in style breeds better material all round. Metallica now is variety with spice.'

Once *MOP* had sold more than a million copies worldwide and grazed the UK Top Forty, even the *NME*, then the bastion of anti-metal prejudice and cultural snobbery, felt obliged to put Metallica on its cover, under the guise of a better-late-than-never 'investigation', in which they also took sidelong glances at Slayer, Megadeth and Anthrax, under the heading: 'Breaking the Thrash Barrier'. Inevitably, given the reactionary aspect of the paper's culture, begun in the 1970s as a commendable desire to disoblige various rock emperors of their new clothes, now curdled in the post-punk 1980s into an unseemly no-right-of-reply one-upmanship, Metallica became accused of purveying music 'as a manifest form of gay pop'; an approach which Lars combated with an unusually straight face. When questioned on his views of Paris – the city the interview took place in – and that of the broader music scene in general, he commented: 'I appreciate and understand a lot of the things you're talking about ... but for me and this band my interest is just music. The history of cities and what rappers get up to really takes a fifth fiddle to what we do.' It was a face-off with no clear winner. Referring to James throughout the article as 'Jim', and Cliff as 'Chris', hardly endeared the clearly dis-interested writer to the even-less-interested band, either.

As ever, *Kerrang!* led the way for both Metallica and thrash. The album received prime billing and a five-star review, concluding that while Metallica were rightly recognised as thrash metal's most prom-inent icons, the new album proved they were now 'something more, something far greater'. Just weeks before, the magazine had also

launched a bi-monthly offshoot, *Mega Metal Kerrang!*, aimed specifically at the now-flourishing thrash metal market. On the cover of
issue one: Metallica. Says editor Geoff Barton, 'People just tend to
think about what they call the Big Four these days – Metallica, Slayer,
Megadeth and Anthrax. But by [1986] there were tons and tons and
tons of bands all vying for a little piece of the thrash metal pie and we
couldn't really cover them all, to any great extent, within the pages of
Kerrang! because there was a bunch of other stuff we needed to do as
well. So *Mega Metal* was launched a hundred per cent as a thrash
metal magazine. To cover the big names but also to bring in the
relative minnows. Just do a heavier mag than *Kerrang!*, basically.'

The timing was spot-on. Metallica may have seen the fork in the
road and taken it, but those who came after had no such qualms. They
just wanted in. Not least Dave Mustaine's new post-Metallica outfit,
Megadeth, whose debut album, *Killing is My Business ... and Business
is Good,* had been selling steadily since its initial release on the independent Combat label in September 1985. Containing Dave's original,
much speeded-up version of Metallica's renamed 'The Four Horsemen' – here given back its original title of 'The Mechanix' – Mustaine
made plain his intention to 'straighten Metallica up' and prove that
Megadeth, not the band that kicked him out, were the ones to lead
the thrash generation. As Mustaine boasted at the time to Bob Nalbandian, 'I thought I'd have a hell of lot harder time coming up with
something better [than Metallica], but this is three times faster, more
advanced and a hell of a lot heavier.' It was certainly a technical
masterclass in terms of sheer musicianship, now seen as the probable
beginning point for what would later become known as techno-thrash
or progressive metal. The songs themselves all reflected Mustaine's
angry, vengeful mindset, missing the twisted humour that would
become a much-valued trademark later in the band's career. Metallica
were already in Sweet Silence recording *Master* when it was released,
but the day it reached the shops in Copenhagen Lars took the time to
go in and ask to listen to it on headphones. He got through the first
couple of tracks, put the phones down and walked out, saying, 'It was
how I expected it to be.'

It wasn't just Megadeth that now felt comfortable having a pop at Metallica in the music press. Kerry King of Slayer taunted *Kerrang!*, calling it 'the Metallica mag', before adding pointedly, 'Too many bands have started to sound commercial who started out heavy,' specifically citing 'Mercyful Fate [and] Metallica'. Slayer offered the most powerful rejoinder to Metallica's stated intention of moving 'beyond' thrash, and the most profound confirmation of the genre's strength when just six months after *Master* was released their own *Reign in Blood* arrived in a blaze of glory. Mirroring *Master of Puppets* in that it was the band's third album yet first release for a major US label – Def Jam, distributed through Geffen – *Reign* was viewed as its evil twin; an album that was everything, in fact, that *Master* was not: devoutly uncommercial, unswervingly confrontational, bringing new meaning to the idea of extreme heavy metal. Produced by Rick Rubin, whose die-hard rock and metal roots had only been hinted at in previous successful signings such as Run-DMC and the Beastie Boys – and who, tellingly, would do so much to restore Metallica's musical reputation more than a quarter of a century later – *Reign* shoved Slayer to the forefront of the thrash metal scene, ousting Metallica along the way. Indeed, Rubin went out of his way in the studio to encourage Slayer to make their already ultra-heavy sound even more aggressive and elemental. The other crucial difference was the emphasis on speed, resulting in the album's ten tracks, each a classic in its own right, being deliciously contorted into just twenty-eight minutes. Even on tracks such as 'Criminally Insane' – released as a red-vinyl seven-inch single in the UK, in a twelve-inch cardboard German cross sleeve, replete with chain for hanging round the neck – where the actual rhythm is funereal, the drums and guitars are machine-gun fast. The album's most infamous track, though, was its opener, 'Angel of Death', which listed in excruciating detail the atrocities of Nazi death-camp spectre Dr Josef Mengele, resulting in Slayer being pilloried as Nazi sympathisers, although Mengele's sickening practices are clearly meant to appal, not inspire. Ultimately, the impact of the album came from the elephantine power and needlepoint precision of moments like the demi-title track, 'Raining Blood'. As metal musicologist Joel McIver comments: '*Reign in Blood* is where the entire extreme metal pantheon starts and finishes.'

Lars Ulrich agreed, commending Slayer for being 'the most extreme' of Metallica's nearest contemporaries, going on to describe *Reign in Blood* as 'one of the best albums of '86'. He would insist on playing it for the last few minutes before Metallica went onstage: 'It really gives me a kick [and] makes me want to go out there and beat the hell out of the drum kit.' The only question, he said, was how much further Slayer would be able to take their music. 'I think they're maybe the most interesting because they're so extreme,' he conceded. 'They don't give a fuck about anything, which is cool. Maybe they don't wanna take it any further.'

The only other 'Big Four' thrash act more intent even than Metallica on breaking out of the mould were old pals Anthrax. While their 1985 album *Spreading the Disease* stuck close to the thrash template as established by Metallica, who they clearly idolised, it already exhibited signs of the band developing their own identity, from the surprisingly clean guitar sound – destined to become almost as copied as Metallica's relentlessly thrusting downstrokes – to their songwriting – such as 'Gung Ho', an almost camp take on macho soldiering, replete with martial effects – and skateboard-inspired image: shin-length shorts, gaudy, comic-book hero T-shirts, backwards-flipped baseball caps. It was a look and a sound – a whole new, much more East Coast-centric attitude – that would fully come to fruition on their next album, *Among the Living*, and attendant UK hit single, the Judge Dredd-inspired 'I Am the Law' (despite being banned by BBC radio, who blanched at the line: '*I am the law / You won't fuck around no more*'). To their everlasting credit, Anthrax would also become the first thrash-generation metal band to embrace the rapidly rising hip hop scene, taking the breakthrough moves made by Aerosmith and Run DMC on 'Walk This Way' one step further with their own seminal rap-metal classic 'I'm the Man'. 'Just because we like metal it don't mean our eyes are closed,' Scott Ian told me. By then Jonny and Marsha Z, who unlike Metallica, the band had kept as managers, had signed them to Island Records, Jonny flattering Island chief Chris Blackwell: 'You didn't get Metallica, but this thing is tremendous, and it's too heavy for any [other] label. Only a rebel like you ...'

Although they continued to be lumped in together in the media, from here on in, thrash's Big Four would take their own very different paths, while still attracting an overlapping audience. The hardcore thrashers would stay with Slayer. 'We heard *Master of Puppets* and me and my friends didn't really like it, to be frank,' recalls Machine Head frontman Robb Flynn. 'We were wanting thrash songs, and we got a couple. But there was also acoustics and lots of harmonies, and we were like, "Whoa, what's this? I'm not cool with this," and [we] kind of abandoned Metallica. I can't even tell you how many times I've gone back to that record in my life since but at the time we were sixteen. I was worshipping *Reign in Blood*, and other bands had come along that were faster and heavier and maybe scarier.' Malcolm Dome concurs: 'People were now starting to look at Metallica as *significant*, rather than just really good. Their career was going places. They'd outgrown thrash and there was very much a sense that [*Master*] was an important record. It was a leap forward for Metallica and one of the most crucial records of the era for metal. Metallica were now discussed in the same context as, say, Iron Maiden, much more mainstream, and Slayer had become the kings of thrash.' Even Xavier Russell, who had done so much to spread the Metallica message early on, now switched his critical allegiance to Slayer, describing *Reign in Blood* as 'such a defining moment' for the development of thrash, 'mainly because of the production. Metallica's [early] albums had always suffered slightly on the production. But when I heard *Reign in Blood*, I said, "Sorry Lars, but this is the dog's bollocks, mate."'

James Hetfield did not agree, putting up a spirited defence of Metallica's attitude in a typically thrash-curious article in the otherwise utterly indifferent *i-D* magazine. 'When people first started copying us it was a real compliment, but now we have to get away from the speed metal tag, 'cos all these bands have jumped on the bandwagon. The NWOBHM bands each had their own sound and feeling, but you can't tell the difference between most of the new thrash bands. It's fucked. So you're the fastest band in the world ... so what? Your songs suck.' Speaking to me around the same time, Lars went further, insisting the very reason *Master of Puppets* got so much attention was entirely based on the fact that it wasn't a thrash album. 'We wanted to make an album that left all that scene behind; something we took time over and gave our best shot. Not something with a label.' Interestingly, Gary Holt of Exodus, one of the bands Metallica was now being unfavourably compared to by hardcore thrash fans, says he agreed. It wasn't to do with who was the baddest thrash outfit, he says, it was simply down to the songs: 'Metallica made, in my opinion, probably the greatest metal album of all time in *Master of Puppets*. I don't even want to call it a thrash album, even though it's got plenty of that. It's just a great, great record. They had a jump-start and they ran, you know, they worked really hard on their craft and they succeeded, and all credit due to them, you know?'

'What it all came down to,' said Lars, when we spoke in 2009, 'was the element of variety. It was like, after you've written "Fight Fire with Fire" [and] "Battery" . . . what else are you gonna do? By repeating it you run the risk of watering it down, because they'll never be as good as what you've already done. Or you have to go somewhere else and try something else. And for us, we had to go somewhere else and try something else, because there was too much other stuff that turned us on.' As he pointed out, 'I've heard in interviews that Kerry King has a very musical broad taste, and Scott Ian and all these guys. But we . . . just . . . went for it. And I'm not saying that in a self-congratulatory way but we sort of had a little of the devil-may-care attitude. Because I think we pretty early on said listen, we're Metallica, we do what we do, and off we go now, we're gonna try all these different things and have fun on all these different levels.' Determined not to be 'boxed in by the one-dimensionality of the thrash label' they had braced themselves for 'a fucking uproar in the thrash community about the sell-outs and the acoustic guitars and all that. But we had to go on that path because that was the truth; that was our truth. The sell-out would have been not to do it because then we would have bullshitted ourselves and bullshitted our fans, and that wouldn't be right.'

Master of Puppets would also, symbolically, become the album that defined Metallica's philosophy from now on. Already so far ahead of the game in terms of whatever Slayer or Megadeth and Anthrax might be doing, far from competing for the thrash crown, Metallica had its sights set on the same mainstream rock audience that would make Iron Maiden's *Somewhere in Time*, also released in 1986, and Ozzy Osbourne's *The Ultimate Sin*, released the same month as *Master of Puppets*, the highest American-charting albums to date of both respective artists' careers. Far from being the year of thrash, the biggest-selling rock record of 1986 was Bon Jovi's *Slippery When Wet*, an album that epitomised the safe-as-milk, art-for-art's-sake, hits-for-fuck's-sake Reaganomic rock of the era more perfectly than any other. While Metallica weren't looking to sell their music to exactly the same audience, in Lars Ulrich they had at least one member who recognised they were in exactly the same business and on that level at least – making chart albums, selling out tours, building up as broad a fan base as possible – Metallica certainly did want to compete.

In America the spread of coverage for *Master of Puppets* in the print media stretched as far as generally good regional newspaper reviews and the to-be-expected smattering of raves in the metal-specific rock magazines such as *Faces* and *Hit Parader*. But the heavyweight mainstream magazines like *Rolling Stone* still kept their distance, except in the context of a general overview of the rapidly ripening thrash culture. Most gallingly, Metallica found it all but impossible to gain a foothold even in the most specialist areas of FM rock radio. With no cool video to help spread the word via MTV either, the band would have to rely on promoting their album the old-fashioned way: by simply getting out there and touring. Or as Kirk put it, 'just go on the road and tour until we dropped, which is what we literally did'. Here they did get an important leg-up, though, thanks again to the impeccable connections of Q Prime, who were able to buy them onto Ozzy Osbourne's mammoth summer tour.

'That was a real break for us,' Lars admitted. 'At the time, Ozzy was perceived as one of the most controversial metal stars in the US – he drew a really extreme type of crowd – which suited us down to the ground, because here we were as this even more extreme up-and-coming metal band that Ozzy was giving his kind of seal of approval to by taking out on tour with him.' Ozzy later told me he'd never even heard of Metallica when his wife and manager Sharon first informed him who his new tour mates would be. 'I used to walk by their trailer backstage and think they were taking the piss,' he said, ''cos all you could hear was Black Sabbath blasting out of the windows. That and all the dope smoke.' Far from trying to get a rise out of the star of the show, the band – especially Lars and Cliff, both long-term Ozzy-era Sabbath fans – simply could not believe their luck. 'We were definitely in awe of him,' said Lars. 'Ozzy was a fucking legend … but by the end of it we'd had some good times with him.' And so they had. Despite a recent much-publicised spell drying out at the Betty Ford Clinic, these were still very much Ozzy's wild years and the Metallica trailer became a more frequent stopover for him as the tour progressed and he realised it was often a good place to get a drink and a smoke – and anything else he fancied – away from the disapproving gaze of Sharon.

Ozzy's audience also quickly took to the band. 'That was really the tell-tale,' says Bobby Schneider. 'I mean, I saw it, I guess, when I was in Europe. I saw the fanatic reaction and they were selling tickets but they were still two-thousand-seaters. But when they opened for Ozzy, that's when the writing really was on the wall.' He says that at some shows Metallica were now starting to sell almost as much merchandising as Ozzy – an indication of rising success in the American music business often more significant than record sales. As Sharon Osbourne once told me, 'You can have a hit record in America and it won't mean shit when you go out on the road, especially in the rock market. The crowd that buys tickets for the show won't like you unless you really deliver, and a really good sign of that is how many of them want to buy or wear your T-shirt.' According to Schneider, by tour's end there were almost as many people in the crowd wearing Metallica shirts as Ozzy shirts. Crowd reaction 'was just phenomenal. Yet it was still a little bit underground. I don't even think they realised. And that was part of the beauty of it, actually. They were just kids out there banging it. I think they'd have been happy playing a club in front of five hundred people as they were in an arena playing in front of fifteen thousand people. Heads had not grown at all, whatsoever. There were very few demands, no rock stars. Everybody was close.'

Along with the success of the tour came increased album sales. By tour's end in August – more than fifty shows opening for Ozzy, discovering what it meant to perform to tens of thousands of people in hockey arenas, convention centres, outdoor 'sheds' and coliseums, interspersed with a dozen or so smaller theatre and fairground shows headlining in their own right – *Master of Puppets* had sold over 500,000 copies, giving the band their first gold record, and taking Metallica into the US Top Thirty for the first time, peaking at Number Twenty-Nine. It would eventually spend seventy-two weeks on the chart. A quarter of a century later, it has now sold almost seven million copies in America, and almost as many more around the rest of the world. The Ozzy/Metallica tour had been the second-biggest ticket-selling draw on the US circuit that summer (only the Aerosmith/Ted Nugent tour out-grossed them). Once again, although it may not have been so obvious to the thrash fans, Metallica were leaving behind a trail for others to follow, helping to establish a new pecking order in mainstream American rock; a sea change that would result, over the next couple of years, in Slayer opening for Judas Priest, Anthrax supporting Kiss, and Megadeth doing the honours for Iron Maiden. All of them were hoping for the same knock-on effect on their careers the Ozzy slot had given Metallica.

'I never expected it to be the success it turned out to be,' said Kirk. Compared to what else was going on in the American album charts, *Master* 'was a huge orange among the bunch of apples'. He said he was 'stunned' when it went gold. Until then he had thought: 'Maybe people just don't understand us. Maybe we're just doing something that's going over people's heads. But as we went on that Ozzy tour we converted a lot of people, night by night. And it gave us a lot of hope just to carry on. Suddenly we were selling albums and a lot of it had to do with just going out there and playing our asses off, putting on a great show, just bringing the music to the people in that way. Because radio just wasn't having us.' Kirk recalled a meeting on the back of the tour bus when Cliff Burnstein informed them they were about to have their first gold album. 'He said something really profound. He said, "You guys will be able to put down payments on houses and I'm just really proud of you." And the first thing that Cliff said was, "I wanna house where I can shoot my gun that shoots knives!" That was like a typical Cliff Burton thing to say ...'

Not everybody was impressed, of course. A *Newsweek* reporter covering the tour described Metallica, variously, as, 'ugly', 'smelly' and 'obnoxious', concluding, 'I hate them. But you can't deny their success.' Perhaps he was just thinking of Lars, who had taken to announcing proudly to anyone that would listen: 'I haven't had a shower for three days, man.' His theory for this: 'I think it's got something to do with success; the *more* successful you are the *less* you feel like washing.' Only James was able to remind Lars he had always been like that. But then those days suddenly seemed very far off indeed, with Lars now complaining in the UK press of the 'four thousand [fans] surrounding the tour bus' each night on tour. 'The demand on your time increases enormously,' he observed earnestly. It was everything he had dreamed of since he was a nine-year-old kid listening to *Fireball* by Deep Purple. Metallica also now felt the need to check into hotels under pseudonyms. As Lars pointed out, 'If the fans have access to you all the time then you'll be constantly disturbed at any hour by people.' He certainly hoped so anyway.

Fortunately, Cliff was there to stop Lars – and everyone else – from going too far up their own arses, constantly asking: 'What's real to you?' Kirk recalled how 'Cliff had a lot of integrity, and his way of expressing that integrity was in one stock sentence which I still use to this day, and it was: "I don't give a fuck." He really just cared about the music and the integrity behind the music. He was just very, very real. I don't know if he knew somehow that his time was limited but he really lived it like it was his last day, because he just wouldn't settle for anything other than what he believed in. And that taught me a lot. To this day there are things ... situations that I'm going through ... I can just picture Cliff saying, "What's real to you? What's real to us in this situation? What really matters?" And he would go through a bunch of points that didn't really matter. He would name them off and at the end of each one he'd say: "I don't give a fuck!" He was a very, very strong guy. Stubborn at times, and because of that he and I would clash sometimes. But we really were just bros and he was a big influence on all of us.'

The only real blot on the horizon occurred when James badly broke his left wrist in a skateboarding accident, backstage before a show in Adamsville on 26 June. The show had to be cancelled and for the rest of the tour James was forced to perform without a guitar, his arm in a sling. Fortunately, Kirk's guitar roadie for the tour was John Marshall of Seattle band Metal Church, who agreed to stand in on rhythm guitar until Hetfield's wrist healed enough for him to play again. Nevertheless, when they arrived back in London during the first week of September, to get ready for the start of what would be their first full-scale British tour, they did so in incredibly high spirits. James' wrist was still in plaster when the tour began on 10 September at St David's Hall in Cardiff but the band knew this was their time. *Master of Puppets* had sold as many copies for MFN in Europe as it had in the USA, reaching Number Forty-One in the UK charts, and not even an inspired performance from Anthrax – thrilled to be there as support on what would also be their UK touring debut – could put a dent in their confidence as the band put on a stunning two-hour show. 'This was still basically the set they would have done in a club,' recalls Malcolm Dome. 'No big stage shows like there would be in years to come. They had a huge backdrop of the *Master of Puppets* album sleeve, but other than that they just came out and blasted away. Just brilliant, street-level rock.'

It was the same story the following night at St George's Hall in Bradford, and the Playhouse in Edinburgh on 12 September. Interviewed backstage before the show for *Sounds* magazine, the whole band was clearly on a roll. Even Cliff – who usually did everything he could to avoid taking part in interviews, leaving it to Lars, who revelled in it – sat down and joined in. 'The difference between the rest of the metal field and Metallica,' Cliff announced, 'is the difference between punching your fist in the air rather than at a specific target.' He was disdainful of any suggestion, however, that the band had anything deeper to impart than whatever one might read into their music. 'Being in a band puts you in a position to make a statement,' he mused, 'but we're not some kind of fucking message band.' Pressed on his appreciation of classical music, a baffling subject to his inter-locutor, Cliff explained patiently how 'we all go through periods of listening to classical music', which was news to James and Lars. 'I was consumed by it,' Cliff went on, 'taking lessons, getting into theory or whatever. It leaves quite an influence. A lot of music will go in one ear and out the other, but you listen to that shit for a month and it stamps you. It leaves its mark.'

The rest of the ten-show tour continued in high spirits. Jonny and Marsha, as managers of Anthrax, were also there – the first time they had seen Metallica play for nearly two years. 'They were killing,' says Marsha now. 'Just great, and it was really nice to see them again, especially Cliff, who was very sweet and asked all about the family.' Anthrax were also enjoying themselves, treated as well as Metallica had been by Ozzy. 'We really felt that we were part of something,' recalled Scott Ian. 'The crowds were crazy and we really felt as if there was something happening.' The feel-good factor extended to Lars calling Brian Tatler when the tour reached the Birmingham Odeon, inviting him up to jam on 'Am I Evil?', which now formed part of their encores. 'I caught the bus up into Birmingham,' Brian recalls. 'They took me backstage and Lars introduced me to James. I'd never met any of them before . . . everybody seemed great, it was nice. Come show-time, Lars said go out front and watch the set then come back at a certain point and come on and do "Am I Evil?" with us. So I thought, ooh, okay. I hadn't seen that coming.' Not having his guitar with him he used one of James'. 'I didn't really know what was going to happen then James introduced me as "The guy who wrote this song . . . " Then I went on and it was great.'

Also backstage that night was a young music journalist named Garry Sharpe-Young. He was there ostensibly to interview Lars but ended up also talking to Cliff while waiting for Lars to show up.

'We talked about bands back in the US, mainly because I was trying to save my real questions for Lars,' Sharpe-Young later recalled. 'Cliff found it funny that every backstage area in the British venues was painted in prison colours.' The conversation also wandered onto the morbid topic of what Metallica would do if one of its band members died or was killed. 'We were actually talking about Led Zeppelin and John Bonham,' the latter's death five years before having been the final nail in the coffin for the already ailing band. 'What we were actually discussing was the hypothesis of Lars meeting his maker,' Sharpe-Young continued. 'Cliff said they would have a big drunken party in his honour, and then get in a new drummer. Fast ...'

The following night, a Sunday, was the last date of the UK leg of the tour: their first headline appearance at London's Hammersmith Odeon. As with the Lyceum two years before, all the metal press showed up, their ranks now swelled by various members of the main-stream music press; even some radio and TV people. This, however, as Gem Howard says, 'was still very much a word-of-mouth thing. If you knew who Metallica and Anthrax were it was probably the biggest gig anywhere in the country that month. But there were still plenty of people that had never heard of them.' He adds with a smile, 'Of course, that would change quite soon.' He also remarks on 'how far the band had obviously come since they'd last played here. I always say one gig is worth ten rehearsals, and by then they really had it all going on. Touring with Ozzy that summer had turned them into a really slick live machine.'

Before the show, James and Lars actually went next door to the Duke of Cornwall pub for a couple of beers. Among the surprised throng of faces joining them was *Kerrang!* designer and DJ Steve 'Krusher' Joule. 'For some reason Lars thought I was Bon Scott,' laughs Krusher now. 'Or at least the ghost of Bon Scott, though I can't say anyone else has ever mistaken me for him. The place was full of Metallica fans of course but everybody was being fairly cool about it. James was pretty quiet but Lars was larging it, never stopped talking the whole time. Then I remember walking back into the gig with them. No security in those days, they were just in a world of their own.'

Outside the venue, Gem recalls giving his last pair of press tickets away: 'Whenever you had a sell-out show like the Hammersmith Odeon I would stay out front, handing out the press tickets to the various journalists and other guests. By the time the band came on, though, that was it, finished. But of course there's always a couple of people that don't turn up, and I hated being left with tickets in my hand that were going to waste. So after the band came on I saw these girls outside absolutely sobbing. They were about fourteen and when I asked what was wrong they said they didn't have tickets and couldn't afford to buy any off the touts because they were asking their usual silly prices. So I said, never mind, there you go, and gave them my last two tickets. At which point I remember getting knocked to the ground as they smothered me in kisses! Then they ran off into the hall. It was a lovely moment.'

After the show, the band spent over an hour sitting at trestle tables set up in a backstage corridor signing autographs and talking to the fans. Then Lars took it upon himself to invite the band's various guests back to Peter Mensch's house in Warwick Avenue, where he was spending the night. Says Krusher Joule, 'I remember being thrown into a car with Lars and possibly James, and being driven to this very plush place somewhere near Holland Park, I think, which was Mensch's house, where I met his wife Sue, who was absolutely stunning. It was quite an amazing place, gold records all over the walls and in one of those streets where there are policemen posted at each end of the street.' Malcolm Dome, who was also there, recalls the party at Mensch's 'only going on for a couple of hours', then James, Kirk and Cliff went back to the Columbia Hotel, where the last few stragglers joined them and the partying went on till nearly dawn.

Fortunately, they had the next couple of days off – enough time to recover from their hangovers, had they actually stopped drinking long enough to get hangovers. These were party times, though, and apart from Cliff – who preferred weed to wine – James and Lars, in particular, were intent on enjoying themselves. They had barely slept when the band boarded the tour bus on Tuesday morning, for the drive, via cross-Channel ferry, to Sweden, ready to begin the European leg of the tour. *Master of Puppets* had sold more than 45,000 copies in Sweden alone – huge numbers for such a modest record-buying territory – and their first date, on 24 September, was to be at the prestigious Olympus arena in Lund. James was hoping to be able to strap on his white Gibson Explorer again but his wrist, now out of plaster but still hurting, felt weak. Nevertheless, he tried it out at the second date of the tour in Oslo and felt encouraged enough to tell John Marshall he wouldn't be needed onstage to play any more. The following night at the Solnahallen in Stockholm, James wore his guitar from the start, playing superbly, the band back to their classic four-man shape for the first time since the accident three months before. Surging with renewed confidence, the band outdid itself, Cliff in particular hitting new heights as he added a typically bizarre yet weirdly affecting version of 'The Star Spangled Banner' to his usual bass solo showcase, both the crowd and the rest of the band agape as he headbanged around the stage, his right arm windmilling. Previously he had been complaining again of back pain, brought on by his uninhibited playing style, but you'd never have known it from his performance.

There was no hotel that night. The next show was in Copenhagen, another home from home for Metallica, especially Lars, and they looked forward to some off-time after the show there. Instead, they all piled onto the tour bus straight after signing autographs at the Solnahallen, still sweating, white towels around their necks to keep them warm. It was no longer summer in Scandinavia and although the days were still light the nights were already getting cold and dark. It would be a long journey and the drivers were in a hurry to get the little convoy going: two tour buses, the lead bus housing the band, Bobby the tour manager, and the backline crew; the second bus the crew; the third the equipment truck. The trip involved several minor roads through hilly countryside. The band bus was the first to leave, most of its occupants electing to watch a video, drinking and smoking until the buzz from the gig finally wore off. There was a half-hour break at a roadside truck stop in Odeshog but by 2 a.m. most of the band was asleep in their bunks.

The bus was cramped, uncomfortable, a conventional English coach owned by Len Wright Travel, converted into a sleeper, its back seats removed and replaced with eight plywood bunks upon which were placed thin black foam mattresses. 'We had a really bad bus,' Kirk later recalled. Some bunks were more comfortable than others. John Marshall, in particular, had trouble fitting his tired six-foot seven-inch frame into one of them. Kirk and Cliff cut cards to see who got a more comfortable window-side bunk, Cliff winning by drawing the ace of spades. He and James were the last to hit the sack, though, James knocking back the vodka, Cliff smoking spliff. Their bunks were at the back, next to each other. They had both nodded off, the whole bus silent, when it first began to leave the road.

What happened next has long been shrouded in a degree of uncertainty and, it must be admitted, some of it remains so, not least the identity of the bus driver. Nobody I spoke to who was on the bus, including tour manager Bobby Schneider, seems to recall the driver's name – or if they do they are not telling for reasons it is difficult to ascertain. Nearly a quarter of a century on, nobody from the Swedish police or local press seem to have a record – or at least one they are prepared to divulge – of the driver's name, either. What *is* known, though, is that travelling south between junctions 82 and 83 of the E4 highway, they were about two miles north of Ljungby when it happened; the startled driver desperately trying to pull the bus back onto the two-lane highway, its tyres already chattering as the bus began to skid. The bus then toppled over onto its side.

The first James Hetfield knew of it was being wakened by hot coffee pouring over him from the upturned coffee machine. It was the yells and screams that snapped Kirk Hammett out of his sleep; the sharp pain in his back as his large huddled body was bundled out of his cramped bunk that alerted John Marshall. Lars Ulrich's body reacted before his mind did, sheer adrenalin propelling him through the nearest opening, the pain of a broken toe not even registering until he had stopped running down the road and begun limping back.

John Marshall was next to scramble free from the overturned bus, sitting on the grass verge, shivering in his underwear. On the bus he'd heard a noise that sounded like running water and was terrified it had fallen into a creek: 'But the noise was only that of the motor still running.' The driver was already out there, too, running around in the road, yelling and shouting, hysterically. He was the first person James saw as he jumped free from the rear escape hatch, 'freaking . . . frantic'. The second person he saw was Cliff; his skinny white legs poking out from under the bus. James couldn't take in what he was seeing, the full horror of the scene yet to unfold in his mind. In the crash, Cliff had been thrown against the window, which shattered, leaving him half in, half out of the bus as it collapsed onto its side, coming to rest on his head and upper body. James ran over, tried pulling Cliff free. No use. Cliff wasn't moving. That's when it began to sink in. Talking about in *Rolling Stone* seven years later the shock was still palpable: 'I saw him dead. It was really, really terrible.' When the bus driver then tried yanking out the blanket still tangled round Cliff's body, to give to one of the others shivering by the frozen roadside, James went insane, screaming, 'Don't fucking do that!' He 'already wanted to kill the guy', he said. Kirk, one eye blackened, sobbing, also began yelling at the driver. 'What did you do? What did you do?' Suddenly everybody was talking and yelling at once. James recalls the driver saying the bus had hit black ice, then 'walking for miles' in his underwear and socks, searching for the black ice. The sun wasn't up yet but it was no longer dark and visibility was good. But there was no black ice. At which point, 'I wanted to kill this guy. I was gonna end him, there.' Meanwhile, his guitar roadie Aidan Mullen and Lars' drum tech Flemming Larsen were still trapped on the overturned bus, buried beneath the rubble of the flimsy broken bunks, with Bobby Schneider, who'd broken his collar bone but didn't know it yet, frantically trying to free them. 'Aidan had a blanket over his face and was in shock, and was freaking out,' says Bobby. 'And I remember calming him down and pulling the blanket off and he finally made his way out.' Flemming was less fortunate. It would take the rescue crew nearly three hours to free him.

When the Swedish police eventually arrived on the scene, they arrested the driver as a matter of course – normal procedure in cases like this. By now the scene had quietened down as the first of seven ambulances arrived and the walking wounded were able to receive treatment. Mostly, it was cuts and bruises. The real wounds were all underneath, out of sight, for now anyway. Everyone was sitting around, freezing, in their underwear. John Marshall was given a pair of Lars' trousers, 'but of course they only came halfway down my legs'.

The second bus carrying the rest of the crew arrived on the scene just as the crane arrived to haul the bus back onto its wheels. Mick Hughes watched with horror as the crane 'put a big chain around the bus' and began slowly hoisting it upright again. 'I don't know if Cliff was dead at this point or not because the bus actually slipped back. They lifted it to pull him out and it slipped back and landed again on the floor.' If Cliff hadn't been dead before, he was now. His body was eventually disentangled from beneath the bus and stretchered to a waiting ambulance, at which point a thorough forensic examination of the scene began, searching for any evidence that might explain what had happened. James later claimed he'd smelled alcohol on the driver's breath; an accusation that was never proved. Others wondered, not unreasonably, if, as John Marshall tactfully puts it, 'maybe the driver was tired'? There were other mitigating factors. It was a British bus built for left-side driving, i.e. with a right-hand steering wheel. Denmark and Sweden were both right-side driving, which would make a left-hand bend at night hard to see, especially in the absolute darkness of the countryside, or if not paying adequate attention, exactly the kind of thing that falling asleep at the wheel – or even momentarily losing concentration – would make especially dangerous. Drifting off for a few seconds while going in a straight line might be survivable, but it would be fatal on a sudden bend. The driver, who was also British but who has never been named, had been driving for around six hours at that point.

Apart from the police and emergency services, the only other people to arrive on the scene that morning were – miraculously – a doctor, who happened to be passing in her car and stopped to administer first aid, and a forty-one-year-old photographer named Lennart Wennberg, then working for the Swedish newspaper *Expressen*. The bus had already been hoisted back up by the time Wennberg arrived. 'I was at the scene of the accident for maybe half an hour,' he told Joel McIver. 'I took about twenty pictures. I can't recall speaking to anyone. The police didn't mind me taking pictures, but there was someone in the band's entourage who felt I should stop taking pictures.'

Had he noticed any ice on the road?

'It was said that this may have been a cause of the accident. Personally, I consider that out of the question. The road was dry. I believe the temperature had probably been around zero degrees Celsius during the night, but slippery? No.' At the police station in central Ljungby, the driver, who Wennberg describes as 'around fifty, well built, normal height', was grilled for several hours by police investigators but later released without charge. Wennberg also took pictures of the band when they arrived by police car from the hospital and entered the Hotel Terraza in Ljungby. He recalled: 'The manager came down to me and the *Expressen* reporter in the hotel lounge to do an interview. But after a few minutes he got a phone call and never came back.'

Bobby Schneider had already given the reporter his version of events at the hospital. 'I just can't believe it,' he kept repeating. 'We were asleep when the crash happened ... when I managed to get out of the bus I saw Cliff lying there in the grass. He must have died immediately, because he went right through the window. It all went so quickly that he couldn't have felt anything, and that's a kind of comfort.' He added, 'None of the guys in the band is able to play now. We just want to get back home as quickly as possible and make sure that Cliff gets a decent funeral.' John Marshall, lying in a bed next to Bobby in the Emergency Room, was equally dazed, still trying to come to terms with what had happened. 'I remember Bobby lying next to me as they were taking blood pressure and stuff, and saying, "Cliff's gone, you know?" All of a sudden, the reality of everything hit me. Right then, I looked above, at the ceiling, and thanked whoever was up there that nobody else had been seriously hurt, and that it hadn't turned out even worse than it was.' James Hetfield wasn't about to say thank you for anything. When Bobby began rounding everybody up after they'd been patched up by the doctors, saying: 'Okay, let's get the band together and take them back to the hotel,' all James could think was: 'The band? No way! There ain't no band. The band is not "the band" right now. It's just three guys.' For once, Lars had nothing to say. He just couldn't take in what was happening. 'I remember being at the hospital and a doctor coming into the room that I was staying in, telling us that [Cliff] had died. We couldn't grasp it; it was too hard, too unreal . . .'

By now both Peter Mensch and the Danish promoter for the Copenhagen show, Erik Thomsen, had also arrived at Hotel Terraza. Bobby Schneider was arranging for the whole party to travel to Copenhagen the next day, the nearest major city with an international airport, while he stayed on an extra day. 'Something about staying and dealing with the body or something like that,' he says now, sifting through the confusing memories of that day. 'And I also remember I stayed on in Copenhagen another day to make sure that that happened.' Meanwhile, Metallica had their first Saturday night without Cliff to get through.

James and Lars shared a room, as usual. Kirk, who would normally have shared with Cliff, stayed in a room with John Marshall. John recalls they were both so shaken they slept with the light on that night. That is, when they could manage to get to sleep. Most of the band and crew had gotten drunk in an effort to combat the shock and dull the rising pain. Bobby recalls getting back to the hotel late that night and 'there being some damage issues and some other stuff. The guys drinking and just, you know, picking it out and trying to make sense of it.' No matter how much they drank, though, none could find sleep. Far from numbing his feelings, James simply fell to pieces, grief-stricken one moment, full of inconsolable rage the next. At four in the morning, the others could hear James drunk in the street outside, screaming: 'Cliff! Cliff! Where are you?' Kirk couldn't bear it any more and began crying again.

The local Ljungby newspaper, *Smalanningen*, reported the crash in its Monday edition, saying: 'The driver thought that an ice spot was the reason why the bus slid off the road. But there were no ice spots on the road. "For that reason the investigation continues," said detective inspector Arne Pettersson in Ljungby.' The report went on: 'The driver has denied that he fell asleep while driving. "The accident's course of events and the tracks at the accident location are exactly like the pattern of asleep-at-the-wheel accidents," said the police.' However, 'The driver said under oath that he had slept during the day and was thoroughly rested. This was confirmed by the driver of the other bus.'

The next day, *Smalanningen* ran a follow-up story, reporting that 'the driver of the tour bus is now free from arrest. He is forbidden to travel and must contact the police once a week until the investigation is over.' It added that the driver was 'suspected of being careless in traffic and causing another person's death. He said that the bus drove off the way because there was ice on the road. But the technical investigation from the police said that the road was totally free from ice at the time of the accident. The driver is suspected of having fallen asleep at the steering wheel ...' A further report the following day said the driver was now staying at a local hotel while a technical investigation of the bus took place. The following Monday, 6 October, the paper announced that, 'There were no technical faults on the bus of the American rock group Metallica. This was established by the National Road Safety Office in a quick investigation.' A week later it reported that the public prosecutor had lifted the travel restrictions on the bus driver, who would now be allowed to return home. Initially there had been talk of charging him with manslaughter. In fact, within months he was rumoured to be back working, driving bands all over Europe, in buses just like the one Metallica had crashed in. Others said he had changed his name. Whatever the truth, the police investigation into Cliff Burton's death, although technically still not closed, was effectively over. To this day there has never been an official explanation of why the bus left the road just before dawn that Saturday morning.

Speaking now, Bobby Schneider refuses to lay the blame specifically at anyone's door: 'Well . . . look, you know, if there's anyone to blame, I guess . . . it was the driver who was driving the bus. But . . . people get in accidents. Unfortunately, many of the laws have changed now as to how they build buses . . . unfortunately it was the perfect storm . . . what happens when the bus spins like that is that it creates centrifugal force. So it just happened that just where Cliff was sleeping was just at the apex of that. And there was a window right next to him. There was nothing between him and the window of that bus and he went out the window.' Bobby says that 'we were told that he was dead before he hit the ground'. But adds: 'I'm not proposing that that was the case. I think that had it been a purpose-built bus like they are now that he would have been in the accident like everybody else. But that was the way things were done. It was fairly standard. They don't do that any more and they haven't done that since then.' These days there would be some form of protective barrier over the windows, he says.

Bobby adds that he never saw any black ice, and notes that it hadn't been snowing. So was it down to the driver then? He pauses. 'The driver could have been going too fast. I don't really recall . . . Like I said, there's accidents that happen. We didn't have any problems with the driver up until then. It's not like he was reprimanded for driving incorrectly, or he was drinking, or we had any issues to speak of. If I remember right we had only been on the bus a couple of runs. We left London and we drove to Sweden . . . did a show in Sweden, and we were on our way to Copenhagen . . .' The rest of the band, though, will never be wholly convinced it wasn't because the driver lost control, for whatever reason. He was the only one supposedly awake at the time. The wheel was his. The responsibility was his. And so it remains. As James said, 'I don't know if he was drunk or if he hit some ice. All I knew was, he was driving and Cliff wasn't alive any more.'

With the remainder of the tour cancelled, forty-eight hours after the crash the band and crew were on their way home. Lars briefly joined Mensch at his house in London. The American members of the team were met at JFK Airport in New York by Cliff Burnstein, with James and Kirk taking a connecting flight on to San Francisco. Cliff's body remained behind in Sweden, where an autopsy would have to be carried out first before the body could be shipped back to America. It took several days, in fact, for all the correct paperwork to go through, which only added to the agony. The official medical examiner, Dr Anders Ottoson, eventually gave the cause of death as 'compression thoracis cum contusio pulm': fatal chest compression with lung damage. Cliff's passport, number, E 159240, was also cancelled and mailed to his stricken parents. It wasn't until everyone got home that the full force of the tragedy began to really kick in. Big Mick summed up a lot of the band and crew's feelings when he later observed: 'You always feel protected on tour; nothing bad can happen like this, it's not allowed, you know what I mean? This is rock 'n' roll, man, nobody dies. But they do, and it had happened, and it was hard to grasp.'

Anthrax were already in Copenhagen getting ready for that night's show when they received word of what had happened. 'From the first day that I met him to the last one we spent together in Stockholm, Cliff Burton never changed,' said Scott Ian, speaking less than twenty-four hours later. 'Even with Metallica's growing success he remained the same really nice guy I first got to know and like. His mode of dress and his manner never altered and we're all gonna miss him terribly.' Also looking forward to the show in Copenhagen that night had been Flemming Rasmussen. 'I was so proud of the success of *Master of Puppets* and this would have been the first time I'd seen them play since we'd recorded it,' he recalls. 'I was woken up at six in the morning by my mum who said that the bus had crashed. She'd heard it on the radio. I couldn't believe it! That it happened also on the way to Copenhagen, it was so weird.'

The news travelled fast. But not quite fast enough in those pre-cell phone and email days for Cliff's girlfriend back in San Francisco, Corinne Lynn. As she told Joel McIver: 'On the Friday night R.E.M. was playing in Berkeley. Cliff loved that band. He always listened to them and he was jealous that I got to go. So he said, "Call me after the show so I know what it's like." I was so excited to see them. They were playing at the Greek Theater, but there was all this lightning and rain and Michael Stipe came out onstage and said, "I'm sorry but they're not gonna let us play because they're afraid we might die tonight." I remembered that quote later.' Instead, Corinne went for drinks with a friend. Then at 'about midnight or one in the morning' tried calling the hotel in Copenhagen where Cliff should have been staying. 'The lady kept saying no, they hadn't checked in yet. I was like, "That's weird."' She thought maybe Cliff had checked in under the pseudonym he now used occasionally, Samuel Burns, but again no dice. 'Bobby Schneider always checked in under his own name, and he wasn't there either. I thought, this is so weird – and then I couldn't sleep. I would call every hour: "No, they haven't checked in." I was thinking, "What the fuck?" But I eventually went to bed.'

Eight hours ahead, it wasn't until the following morning that news of Cliff's death reached California. Still Corinne heard nothing. She had spent the morning at a friend's house and with no cell to find her it wasn't until that evening she finally got the message when her housemate, Martin Clemson, also returned home. 'Martin says, "I need to talk to you." I go, "What? What is it?" and he says, "Cliff's dead." I said, "No, he's not! What are you talking about?" He said, "There's been an accident ... "' Corinne immediately phoned Cliff's parents, who confirmed the news. 'I went up first thing the next morning. I don't think I left for maybe two weeks, except to maybe go home and get more clothes.'

Gary Holt says he was 'moving a twenty-five-gallon fish tank' when he heard Cliff had died. He was in the process of moving it out of his parents' house and into his own apartment. 'It was pretty shocking news, to say the least. You don't think about that shit happening on tour. Usually when you hear about a musician dying, it's at his own hand – you know, drugs overdose, chokes on his vomit, shit that would have been old hat to hear. But dying in a bus crash? That was the first I'd ever heard of that, you know?' Joey Vera was also at home when he received the phone call. 'I was just completely stunned and devastated, shocked and saddened. Just complete disbelief, 'cos we had just done some shows with them on the *Master of Puppets* tour. You get that sense of "This can't be right, I just saw Cliff six or eight weeks ago . . . " You just don't get those calls when you're younger and that's part of the shock. One minute he's there and one minute he's not and you can't put two and two together. It must have been just god-awful for the band. I can't imagine what they all went through. I just can't imagine seeing that, going through it.'

One of Cliff's closest friends, Jim Martin, then touring in rising stars Faith No More, recalled Cliff's mother Jan phoning him with the news: 'I was home at the time, in between tours. My heart sank.' Cliff, he said, 'was part of the think-tank'. Jim was due back on the road the next day but 'travelled home in between tour dates to attend his funeral. It was a pretty rough time, especially for his folks.' Another old friend, Dave Mustaine – estranged by circumstances, but recently reacquainted when Cliff had attended a Megadeth show in San Francisco, just before leaving for Europe – was devastated first by the news, then by the fact that none of the band had thought to let him know personally. It had been Maria Ferraro, then working for Jonny Z's Megaforce label, who had called him with the news: 'No one else from Metallica or their management did. I went straight to the dope man, got some shit and started singing and crying and writing this song. Although the lyrics have nothing to do with [Cliff], his untimely passing gave me this melody that lives in the hearts of metal-heads around the world.' The song was 'In My Darkest Hour'. It would form the centrepiece, and longest track, on the next Megadeth album, *So Far, So Good . . . So What!*

As chance would have it, Jonny and Marsha Z were in San Francisco when they heard the news. They were there to check out a new thrash metal band called the New Order, soon to change their name to Testament, whose first Metallica-influenced album, *The Legacy*, would be released on Megaforce the following year. 'We were in our hotel, pretty excited about finding this new band,' Jonny says now. 'It was about three in the morning when the phone rang. It was Anthrax's tour manager Tony Ingenere. I was like, "What's wrong? Why are you calling us in the middle of the night?" He was like, "Cliff Burton is dead. There's been a terrible accident."' Unable to get back to sleep, Jonny and Marsha went for a long walk down towards the Bay, consoling each other.

Looking back now, Marsha says she is grateful she had the chance to spend a bit of time with Cliff in England just before he died: 'Not knowing that would be our goodbye, it was such a lovely afternoon we spent together that I felt somehow comforted by it when he did go.' That had been in London, the day after the Hammersmith Odeon show with Anthrax. 'It was a day off and so we all had gone out to Carnaby Street. He had a [skull] ring that he had being made at [the specialist jewellery store] The Great Frog. So we went over there and he picked up his ring and we just went out and had lunch and sat and just caught up. He was always respectful, I think, of what Jonny and I had taken from our lives to give them that time. We just sat and reminisced about the old days when they lived in the house and the things that had been done and then of course we parted ways and Jon and I got on a plane and came back to the States.' The memory of receiving the dreadful early-hours phone call from Tony Ingenere still makes her shudder: 'That was just devastating beyond our wildest dreams that [Cliff] of all of them – that warm, settled soul – should be the one who lost his life in that episode.'

There was a special Cliff Burton Tribute section in the following week's issue of *Kerrang!*, in which several condolence messages were also placed, including one from Music for Nations, a single white page with Cliff's name and date of birth and death inscribed on it and, most strikingly, a black double-page spread from Jonny and Marsha that read simply: 'The Ultimate Musician, The Ultimate Headbanger, The Ultimate Loss, A Friend Forever'. There were also some touchingly light-hearted contributions, notably one from Anthrax: 'Bell-Bottoms Rule!! Laugh it up, We Miss You'.

Gem Howard remembers: 'I had a late holiday that year. I'd been gearing up for the UK dates then when they were over I left the following Saturday for a few days in Cornwall, thinking: they're off to Europe now; they won't need me again this tour. Then on the

Wednesday morning I bought a copy of *Sounds* and it was on the front page. I got a hell of a shock. Then I called the office and that's when I heard what had happened. It was the first Metallica European tour I hadn't been the tour manager on and, yes, I could have been on that bus with them. But I don't do any of that "if only I'd been there it might have been different" stuff, because I don't believe in it. It was an accident, accidents happen. It was just one of those things. I do remember going straight to the pub, though, and drowning my sorrows. Cliff was such a huge part of who Metallica were as a band, it seemed inconceivable he had gone. It wasn't just about his bass-playing. I sat there thinking of the times Cliff would be in the front seat of the van while I was driving, he'd be pounding away on the dashboard one moment listening to The Misfits, the next minute he'd be playing "Homeward Bound" by Simon & Garfunkel, the whole band singing along.'

There was a memorial service back in San Francisco during the first week of October, at which 'Orion' was played. His funeral was held on Tuesday 7 October, at Chapel of the Valley in Castro Valley, where he had lived with his folks most of his life. As well as Cliff's immediate family, his girlfriend Corinne and best pals Jim Martin and David Di Donato were there, along with the rest of Metallica, plus Bobby Schneider and key members of the American crew, and Peter Mensch, who had flown in especially. Other mourners included all of Exodus, Trauma, Faith No More drummer Mike Bordin, and others who knew Cliff well. After Cliff's coffin had been cremated his ashes were taken and spread at the Maxwell Ranch, a place that had held many fond memories for Cliff and his friends. As Di Donato later recalled, 'We stood in a large circle with Cliff's ashes in the centre. Each of us walked into the centre and took a handful of him and said what we had to say. Then he was cast onto the Earth, in a place he loved very much.' Recalls Gary Holt: 'It was a sombre affair, to say the least. But then you gather up at someone's house after and you get drunk and share a laugh, you know?'

Although he was cremated, there was a commemorative head-stone, engraved on it the words: IN LOVING MEMORY. Then below that a head-and-shoulders picture of Cliff taken not long before he died. Underneath: CANNOT THE KINGDOM OF SALVATION TAKE ME HOME, then at the bottom, finally:

CLIFF BURTON

THANK YOU FOR YOUR

BEAUTIFUL MUSIC

FEBRUARY 10, 1962

SEPTEMBER 27, 1986

Although they didn't know it then, the aftershocks of Cliff Burton's death would continue to reverberate around Lars Ulrich, James Hetfield and Kirk Hammett for the rest of their own lives. As Kirk Hammett told me in 2009, 'When I first joined the band there was a huge infusion of new energy and up until Cliff died we were just so psyched about everything and life in general, but that kind of ended when Cliff left.' He paused, then added, 'I still think about him every day. Something he said, something he did, just . . . something.' It was one of those things that could never be put right, said Kirk – a sentiment Lars also expressed just a few weeks after Cliff's funeral when he said, 'I wasn't too angry in the beginning. I was obviously grieving, but the anger started setting in when I realised that it's not new that people in rock 'n' roll die, but usually it's self-inflicted in terms of excessive drink or drug abuse. He had nothing to do with it. It's so useless. Completely useless . . .'

The question was where did Metallica go from here? Says Joey Vera, echoing the thoughts of many back then: 'I thought it would be the end of the band. Then you think, well, what will they do?' Lars and James already knew, and had instructed Peter Mensch accordingly, who called a meeting with Bobby Schneider and other key crew members within hours of the funeral. As Cliff had told Harald O just a few days before Metallica set out on their first arena tour with Ozzy Osbourne, six months before, when asked what advice he might have to pass on to any aspiring young musicians, Cliff had shrugged and said, 'When I first started, I decided that I would devote my life to it.' Devotion, he said, was the key, although he was sensitive enough to add the following caveat: 'I imagine there's a lot of people that devote their lives to it and don't achieve the success they want. I mean, there's many factors involved here, but that would be the main one: to absolutely devote yourself to that, to virtually marry yourself to that – what you're going to do – and not get sidetracked by all the other bullshit that life has to offer.'

The search for Cliff's replacement would begin the very next day.

NINE
BLACKENED

I t was hot, late. Too much to drink; too much to smoke ... We'd been at
it since they'd finished playing some time in the afternoon. Now here we
were back in Lars' hotel room, some outpost by the airport in Tampa. It
was a Sunday night. That is, a Monday morning, and in a few hours he
would be leaving to go back to the studio to carry on mixing the new album.
We were both having trouble keeping it together. Nevertheless, he was
insistent.

'No, no,' he said, every time I suggested we call it a night, 'one more ...'

He reached over and wound the tape forward, stopped, played a bit,
stopped, then wound it back, stopped, played a bit, stopped, wound it
forward ... eventually he found what he was looking for.

'Listen,' he said, 'to this ...'

It tiptoed out of the speakers of his ghetto-blaster, got all angry and busy,
building quickly like a funeral pyre. Then it was off and running ...

I had no idea what to tell him. I mean, on one level it sounded good –
fast, heavy, the usual Metallica thing – but on another level it was unlike
anything I had heard from them before. For a start, the drums were weird:
flat-sounding, tinny, no bounce whatsoever. I rather liked the effect but
wasn't sure if I was getting it right. Had they intended the drums to sound
so ... off?

'I like the drums,' I said loudly over the top of it. 'No echo ...'

'Reverb,' he yelled. 'No reverb. None of that shit ...'

I took another gulp of beer and sat there trying to take it in. On and on
it went.

'What's this one called?' I shouted.

No reply. I looked around, he wasn't there. I waited for him to come back. He didn't come back. I got up to look for him and found him sitting on the crapper, his black jeans around his ankles, the door to the bathroom wide open.

'Oh,' I said, 'sorry.'

'What's up?' he said, as though it were the most natural thing in the world, taking a shit with the door open, me standing there talking to him.

'Um, this one,' I said, retreating, 'what's it called?'

'"And Justice for All"!' he yelled as I found my way back into the noise of the other room.

'"And" what?' I yelled back.

'"Justice . . . for All . . . "'

Hmmm. Sounded . . . black. As in deep-down-at-the-bottom-of-the-well black. They definitely seemed to be going for something, though. A kind of anti-rock, I thought, idly.

I kept waiting for it to end, for him to finish doing his business, close the door and come back in. But it just wouldn't.

'Is it deliberate?' I yelled again.

'What?'

'Like . . . anti-rock!'

He nodded, coming through the door, doing up his belt, but I knew he hadn't heard me.

It finally finished. 'Kind of like sort of avant-garde . . . jazz . . . thrash . . . '

He looked at me. 'You're stoned.'

'No. Yeah. But it does sound . . . sort of . . . doesn't it?'

'I guess,' he said. But I had the feeling he knew what I was on about. 'It's deliberate,' he said.

Deliberate? I knew it!

'I like it,' I said. 'I really like it. You've really gone for something . . . different.'

'Thanks,' he said.

He wound it forward-backward to another track. Click, click went the drums, drone, drone went the guitars. Bottom-of-the-well shit, you know? I liked it. I really, really liked it. I really did.

I just couldn't keep my eyes open any more . . .

Although it would be years before they were able to acknowledge the fact, the hasty, seemingly perfunctory way in which Lars Ulrich and James Hetfield dealt with the death of Cliff Burton would have lasting ramifications that would go far beyond the story of Metallica. The decision to simply bring in a new bass player and continue on with their plans as quickly as possible may have looked like the right one on paper, but the role Burton played in Metallica was only partly to do with playing the bass. Even with that taken care of, Cliff's violent wrenching from the group had fatally holed the ship below the water-line. The remaining three hadn't just lost a member. They had lost their mentor, their older soul-brother; they had lost Metallica's best friend. The one who would never lie to them; never let them down, the only one who could save them from themselves.

As Malcolm Dome says, 'Cliff was a great character. Had he lived he may have taken Metallica into some very interesting directions because he was the one with the open mind and he was the one the others looked up to, because he was slightly older, and more mature and commanding. In his own way, he was the leader of the band. Even though it was James and Lars' band, it was clear they looked up to Cliff as being someone they could go to for advice. He would be the guy saying, "I don't think we should be doing this, we should do that." He didn't look like he belonged in a thrash band and that was the key – he didn't feel he had to conform.'

Instead, Lars and James – so vocal always about doing things their own way, according to their own personal feelings – now found themselves scurrying to do the right thing professionally to save their careers. In this they had the always-reliable advice of Peter Mensch and Cliff Burnstein at Q Prime, who counselled a swift regrouping, a smoothing over of the cracks, a united public face and the resumption of Metallica's medium-term plans as speedily as possible. This, after all, was an absolutely crucial juncture in the band's career, for which James and Lars had worked so hard the previous five years to get to: the very moment when they were poised to become a big-time act in their own right. Not just 'inventors' of thrash, more than just potent second-stringers to bigger, more commercially adept rock outfits, but an actual mainstream headliner themselves. At any other point in Metallica's career trajectory they might have been able to afford to take the time they needed to come to terms mentally, emotionally and spiritually with the huge loss they had just suffered. But not right now. Burnstein and Mensch had been here before enough times to know just how important – and fleeting – such moments in a rock band's career can be; how one false move could destroy the work of a lifetime. Burnstein had been one of the leading lights at Mercury Records in the late 1970s, forced to stand by impotently and watch as Thin Lizzy's career in America fizzled out in the wake of serial tour cancellations when various members left abruptly. No one had died – too many early-morning drugs and late-night fights had been Lizzy's downfall – although it could be argued that the slow, painful demise of singer Phil Lynott, dead barely five years after Lizzy's last, ill-starred US tour, could be traced back to his band's inability to make the most of their luck while it was still riding high. Mensch, meanwhile, had been key in overseeing the impossibly swift resurrection of AC/DC when their singer Bon Scott had died in 1980. Like Metallica, AC/DC had just had their first breakthrough album in America, with *Highway to Hell*. Any delay in its follow-up could have been fatal to their chances of long-term success there. Under Mensch's tutelage, however, they achieved the seemingly impossible and almost immediately found a replacement for Scott, their first album with new singer Brian Johnson, *Back in Black*, being released within months of his arrival and subsequently becoming the biggest, multi-million-selling success of AC/DC's career.

Sitting with Peter the night before Cliff's funeral, James and Lars had already made up their minds about wanting to continue with Metallica. They just needed their brilliant, all-seeing manager to spell out the reasons for them, to make it all better. Mensch put it to them succinctly. It wasn't just a case of not throwing in the towel; it was absolutely essential they understood they had not a second to spare. The cancelled European tour could be rescheduled for the new year. Mensch had already looked into that, he told them. But the Japanese tour in November – their first visit to the country, the third largest record-buying territory in the world and another important milestone on the route map to success – should not be delayed. Could they meet that deadline? Lars and James decided they could.

Professionally, it was absolutely the right thing to do, they all agreed. The human cost of this hurriedly made decision, however, would be immense, not just for the three remaining members of Metallica, but also for the poor unfortunate whose job it would be to attempt the impossible and somehow replace Cliff Burton.

'I don't understand how anyone who knows what Metallica is about could honestly think that we'd give up,' Lars would tell *Sounds* journalist Paul Elliot three months later. 'The question was not, "Are we gonna pack it in or not?" It was, "How fast can we get the whole thing back on its feet again?"' He added, 'We have to do it for Cliff . . . If he knew we were sitting around in San Francisco feeling sorry for ourselves, he'd come round and kick us in the ass and tell us to get back out on the road and continue where we left off.' This was to become the prevailing theme, repeated like a mantra, whenever the question of how they came to the decision to carry on without Cliff Burton came up. It was, as Kirk later told me, 'Because that's what Cliff would have wanted.' Uh huh . . .

The Japanese tour, just five weeks away, would give them a deadline to work to. Rejecting the suggestion of getting in a veteran simply to help them through the tour, they decided to go for broke and find a full-time replacement. 'We wanted someone young, hungry, someone new and a bit unknown,' said Lars at the time. 'Not someone that people would associate with another band.' Bobby Schneider recalls, 'Everybody got completely trashed at Cliff's funeral. And I can remember Mensch looking at me and saying, "I told you guys not to get fucked up" because we had to have this meeting afterwards. Not me and the band but Mensch and me, and I think one other.' The plan, as outlined by Peter, says Bobby, was, '"Okay, the guys want to keep going, you're gonna move to San Francisco, you're gonna set up this rehearsal, we're gonna start auditioning bass players. You're gonna run the whole thing, you're gonna look after the guys here." So I moved out.' Rich enough to no longer have to put up with the garage at El Cerrito, Lars and James had planned to buy their own properties at the end of tour. Now, back in San Francisco suddenly, they didn't have anywhere to live. 'We all got apartments down by Fisherman's Wharf and they started the process,' says Bobby.

They didn't have to search hard. Every young bass player in America seemed to be dreaming suddenly of replacing the irreplaceable. The same night they'd heard about Cliff's death, Jonny and Marsha Z had wandered down to Testament's rehearsal space. 'It was like every band in the Bay Area was there,' Jonny recalls. 'Every rehearsal space in the building was filled with bass players trying to play "Pulling Teeth". It was kinda nuts.'

Among the personal effects returned to his family after his body had been shipped back to the USA were the two skull rings that Cliff always wore, one of which the family now gave to James. Although they had only really become close in the last year of his life, of everybody in the band, James had looked up to Cliff the most. Says Schneider, 'I think of everybody, James was [most affected]. Because if you're in with James and you're part of James' family, you're part of James' family for the rest of your life. James is as true blue and loyal a person as they come and I think he was very freaked out.' He and Cliff had 'identified with each other', said James – not just through their shared love of southern rock and bands like Lynyrd Skynyrd, but also the whole outdoorsman lifestyle both were drawn to, 'hiking, camping, shooting guns, drinking beers . . .' More importantly, James looked upon Cliff as a big brother figure, very much the wise older head. Onstage, where James had always felt most insecure as frontman, yet been forced to grow into the role in the aftermath of the sacking of Dave Mustaine, Cliff's almost supernaturally confident demeanour had been a huge inspiration to him. Look now at some of the early live footage of their first shows and you'll see James habitually glancing to his right, to the space on the stage dominated by Cliff's huge presence. Seeking approval; needing validation; and getting it. It may have been Lars and James who formed Metallica, may still have been James and Lars who wrote together, but by 1986 in James' mind Metallica had become far more about how he and Cliff saw things. They had even reached a point where they had apparently begun discussing seriously the prospect of replacing Lars as drummer.

How serious this suggestion should be taken remains a hot topic for debate among Metallica aficionados. As the years have gone by there are few left who will talk openly about it – except, of course, for Dave Mustaine, who was still talking about it 2008 when he told viewers of Jane's Addiction guitarist Dave Navarro's *Spread TV* show, 'James and I had planned on firing Lars so many times. And [Lars] won't ever cop to this but he was getting canned when the guys were coming back from the European tour, before Cliff died. They planned on getting rid of him.' It was a claim he repeated during an interview with *Rolling Stone* the following year. 'That's what Scott [Ian of Anthrax] told me. He said that when Metallica got home, that James, Cliff and Kirk were going to fire Lars.' A posting on Anthrax's Twitter feed immediately issued a denial, saying, 'Story's not true. Little does anyone know but Lars actually owns the name, good luck ever kicking him out.'

It's tempting then to dismiss this as a typically provocative Mustaine aside. However, Marsha Z remains tellingly reticent to comment on the subject when I ask now how much she knew of this. She certainly doesn't deny the story is true. Malcolm Dome is less inhibited on the subject and claims he heard about it at the time from both Ian and drummer Charlie Benante. 'I remember after the crash Scott and Charlie were in London and we went out for drink at the pub near the *Kerrang!* office and Scott actually said, in so many words, [Cliff's death] may have actually saved Lars' job 'cos they were ready to fire him. He said it, absolutely said it. I think he'd been told by James or Cliff that they'd had enough of Lars. He was holding them back. I don't think now Metallica could actually work with a really good drummer because they've adapted to what he doesn't do. But at that point, with the *Master of Puppets* era when they were really starting to move forward and change and look at different ways to present music, they could have replaced him.'

Dome goes on to suggest that Slayer drummer Dave Lombardo

was being lined up. 'Dave Lombardo was definitely mentioned at one point as the guy they wanted in,' says Dome. 'I don't actually recall any other names but Dave was definitely on that list and with good reason.' An astonishingly innovative drummer, technically light years ahead of a player of Ulrich's limited scope, it's easy to see how Burton and Hetfield – already masters of their own instruments – would have been excited at the prospect of working with someone like Lombardo. Indeed, his work on *Reign in Blood*, released that year, had thrilled both men. Intriguingly, Lombardo was also about to walk out of Slayer, citing financial reasons. 'I wasn't making any money,' he said, 'I figured if we were gonna be doing this professionally, on a major label, I wanted my rent and utilities paid.' Within weeks, however, the broke drummer had been talked into returning by his wife, Teresa. Had Metallica approached him then it seems highly likely he would have jumped at the chance. Might his defection from Slayer even have been influenced by some whisper of what was allegedly going on behind the scenes in Metallica? Certainly there appears to be little doubt James and Cliff did discuss the notion of getting in a better drummer, just as James and Lars had once discussed getting in a better bass player. As the rhythm engine of the band, Burton and Hetfield would also have been the ones who most acutely felt the drag Ulrich's lack of wide-ranging drum skills imposed upon them. How seriously they entertained the idea of actually replacing Lars, however, is something only James Hetfield knows. It might have just been one of those drunk and stoned late-night rambles lots of band members have, bitching about each other behind their backs. Or perhaps they really were serious. It seems unlikely that Lars would already have patented the name 'Metallica' at that stage, and even if he had it's not beyond the realms of possibility that both James and Cliff were still young and idealistic enough to play around with the notion of starting again with a newly named outfit – maybe one that included Dave Lombardo and possibly even Kirk Hammett, Cliff's other close friend in Metallica.

Any such notions died with Cliff, though. Getting over the loss of Cliff was going to be hard enough, starting again with a new drummer as well would be simply unthinkable. Indeed, now that he was gone the relationship between James and Lars began to reassert itself. 'After Cliff died, James and Lars got really close again,' says Schneider. It had always been their band, their songs, but now they really did take control seriously for the first time since the days when there was just the two of them rehearsing in Ron McGovney's garage. Malcolm Dome recalls going out with Lars in London one night not long after when the drummer became very emotional over a few drinks and began earnestly extolling the talents of his singer. 'Lars got very drunk and went into this huge defence of how brilliant James was,' says Malcolm. 'How he never gets the credit for how great a guitarist he is. It sounded like they really had bonded through the grief of losing Cliff. And I think that bond overturned any thoughts in James' mind about, well, maybe we should actually replace Lars as well and get a new rhythm section altogether.'

That wasn't all. Cliff's death threw all the remaining members' hopes for the future into sharp relief. It didn't just draw Lars and James closer together, it focused their minds like never before on what it was they really wanted out of Metallica. Cliff's very presence had always meant the lines between musical integrity and career ambition were fuzzily drawn, hazy and disguised in wreaths of weed smoke. It was easy to see how ambitious Lars was; it was always assumed Cliff had nobler aims, which he ostensibly did, in terms of not bowing to fashion or commercial pressure. Cliff was just as keen on making the band a significant success, though. Lars had always been the brains, James the brawn. But they were young and innocent enough still to incorporate Cliff's longer-term views into the cause, or at least pay lip-service to them. They were all comfortable with the idea of selling millions of records, yes, but only on *their* terms. Certainly they never saw themselves as competing on the same terms as the likes of Bon Jovi and Whitesnake, groups that released four or five singles per album and spent hundreds of thousands of dollars on state-of-the-art videos. Metallica's blood was purer, truer; they belonged to a proud tradition that stretched back through Iron Maiden and Motörhead, to ZZ Top (before the cutesy videos) and Lynyrd

Skynyrd; all the way back to Zeppelin and Sabbath; groups that didn't kiss ass or kowtow to the Man.

Now, with Cliff gone, those values would become steadily eroded. They still talked of not selling out and only doing things their way, but the reality was that their way, without Cliff, quickly narrowed down to the laws of the jungle and the rule of tooth and claw, where only the strongest and fittest survived. Where the only voices that count are the ones the business itself takes seriously. In that respect, Metallica with Cliff had started with a disadvantage. There were always caveats about what they would and would not do; always special pleading to be judged not as others were but on their own singular terms. Now, without Cliff's sardonic voice to offer an alternative view, Lars and James were able to get down to the real nitty-gritty. In many ways it would be the making of them – a bold new pragmatism that ensured Metallica would not just survive but continue to prosper with ever-increasing abundance, no matter what.

Auditions for Cliff's replacement began straight after his funeral, in special rooms set up at Hayward, their usual rehearsal space. 'They really tried to do it so it wasn't awkward for anybody,' says Bobby Schneider. 'Guys would come in, wait in a room then come into the main rehearsal room and play.' Among the cattle call of nearly sixty people who showed up – including one kid who brought a pal just to stand by the door taping it; another who didn't even get to plug in, shown the door by James as soon as he saw the Quiet Riot autograph on his bass – were some notable applicants, such as Les Claypool of Primus, Lääz Rockit's Willy Lange, Watchtower bassist Doug Keyser, Troy Gregory of Prong . . .

One bassist who actually turned them down was Joey Vera of Armored Saint: 'I got a call from Lars asking me to come up and jam with them, because they were becoming very disillusioned. They wanted to play with some people that they knew and were familiar with. I was very honoured that he called me [but] I had to say, "Well, let me think about this overnight." And I had to come to this conclusion that . . . if I go up there and play with them, I have to go up with the intention that I'm gonna be that person [and] I'm gonna quit my band.' In the end, Joey simply decided that, 'I wasn't ready to bail on Armored Saint, who were still signed to Chrysalis. As a matter of fact we were in the middle of recording our third record with them. So it wasn't a situation I was ready to take as an opportunity for me to move on.'

Lars took it well, he says. 'He was very cool with it. I think he respected my decision at the time. He probably thought I was crazy later. But at the time, he just wanted to reach out to people he knew personally to come up and jam and take the load off of this cattle call. It must have been *horrible*, I can't imagine it ... I knew that him and I also had a kinship with a lot of other things. And it's like, I wanted to help my friend out ... I almost wanted to go up just to give them a fuckin' hug. But I had to say, it was a time in my life where I wasn't ready for that change.' He adds with a sigh, 'Of course, I get asked this question now by people that are much younger, and they have this look in their eyes, like "Are you fuckin' crazy?" The question is always: do you regret it? And my answer is always: no, because I've had a wonderful life since then.'

Then, on the afternoon of Tuesday, 28 October – exactly three weeks to the day since Cliff's funeral – Metallica found what they thought they were looking for when a twenty-three-year-old former farm boy from Michigan named Jason Newsted walked through the door at Hayward and plugged in his bass. 'Jason had the spirit,' says Bobby Schneider. 'Jason could eat, shit and sleep Metallica. It was Jason's dream.' Bobby recalls picking up the wide-eyed hopeful from the airport and Jason realising halfway through the drive that he'd left his bass amp at the luggage collection. Going back to pick it up made Jason late for his audition, which made him only more nervous. 'The kid must have had balls of steel, though,' says Bobby, because as soon as he started playing, 'I think they knew he was the one.'

It had been Brian Slagel – the very same guy who had first turned them onto Cliff – who first mentioned Jason to Lars. Just as with Trauma, the first release from Jason's current band, Flotsam and Jetsam, had been a track on one of Slagel's ongoing *Metal Massacre* compilations (*MM VII* in 1984). They had followed that with an album for Metal Blade, *Doomsday for the Deceiver*, released in July 1986, which *Kerrang!* had over-excitedly awarded six out of a maximum five stars to. 'Lars said, "Okay, cool, send me some stuff,"' Slagel recalls. He also spoke to Jason: 'I don't want to get you too excited [but] what would you think about possibly auditioning for the Metallica gig?' Jason immediately began freaking out. 'Are you kidding me? They're like my favourite band of all time!' A perfectionist by nature, Newsted had spent every waking moment since Slagel's call learning the entire Metallica back catalogue. Friends clubbed together to help him pay for the $140 plane ticket to San Francisco. When James asked him which song he'd like to play, he answered: 'Any one you like, I know them all.'

At that point there were three names on the mental shortlist: Mike Dean of Corrosion of Conformity, Willy Lange of Lääz Rockit and Kirk's boyhood friend Les Claypool of Primus. Within minutes of Jason playing, his name was also added. Said Lars at the time, 'We wanted to spend a whole day with each of the four because, for us, it's about more than whether he can play a song well. The whole vibe and attitude of the person, how we would get on with him, the friendship, was just as important.' Jason was second of the four. 'We played all day and then went out for a meal. And then we went for the big test, which was obviously the drink test.' For this, the band took Jason to one of their favourite local bars, Tommy's Joint. 'Somehow,' said Lars, 'and I swear it wasn't planned, me and Kirk and James ended up in the toilet together, pissing. So we're standing there at three in the morning, out of our faces, all of us in a line and not saying anything, and I just said without looking at anybody, "That's him, right?" And the other guys said, "Yeah, that's him."' The only one not completely drunk was Newsted himself, whose nerves were keeping him sober. He later recalled, 'They all came back and sat down and Lars said, "So, do you want a job?" And I go, "No!" at the top of my voice. People were looking at us and thinking, "What the fuck?"'

Jason Curtis Newsted was born on 4 March 1963, in Battle Creek, Michigan. Growing up on the family's horse farm, his parents bought him his first bass guitar for his fourteenth birthday. Like practically every other American boy of his generation, Jason grew up as a Kiss fan, basing his first school band, Diamond, on their songs. His second band, Gangster, had barely begun practising when the Newsted family moved from Michigan to Phoenix, Arizona. Flotsam and Jetsam, which he joined in 1982, were heavily influenced by Metallica and were the first self-styled thrash metal band in Phoenix, down to encoring with a version of Metallica's 'Whiplash' – which Jason would sing. But then he was always more than just the bass player in the group. He was the organiser, the leader, the one who wrote the lyrics and took care of the day-to-day business; the one with the energy and ambition; the Lars and James of the group all rolled into one.

The only time Newsted had seen Metallica play before he joined them had been in Phoenix on the W.A.S.P. tour two and a half years before, standing there in his Metallica T-shirt, eyes fixed the whole night on Cliff. When a friend had phoned him at six in the morning to tell him that Metallica's bassist had died in an accident, Jason couldn't believe it. It was only after he'd read it in the paper that it really hit him. 'I remember tears hitting the paper and watching them soak into the print,' he later famously recalled. As a mark of respect, all of Flotsam wore black armbands at their next gig.

Jason Newsted never had the pleasure of actually meeting Cliff Burton. When it became known he'd got the job in Metallica, Cliff's family made a point of wishing him luck. 'They were the first ones to embrace me. His parents, especially. They came down to meet me the very day I joined Metallica. His mother held on to me for a while and didn't let go. She said in my ear, "You must be the one because these guys know what they're doing," and wished me luck. Very warm, wonderful people.'

Understandably perhaps, his former bandmates in Flotsam did not share in his joy. 'There was a lot of animosity. But as time went by, they accepted it. Who wouldn't have tried out for Metallica? My heroes became my peers.' He did, however, agree to go back and play one final show with them, on Halloween. Ironically, he said, 'It was probably the best show I ever had with them because I didn't have the pressure of the business shit going on. This time I just got up there and did it and it felt good. I had plenty on my mind.' Not least when he sang 'Whiplash' . . .

Jason Newsted's first show with Metallica was on 8 November at the Country Club in Reseda, an unannounced Saturday night opening slot for Metal Church before a couple of hundred in-the-know fanatics and genuine Church fans. Essentially an extension to the solitary week of rehearsals he'd had, they performed a full-on thirteen-song set that included material from all three albums and an extended solo spot from Kirk. A second show the following night at Jezebel's in Anaheim was shorter but provided the band with a final tightening of the screw before the official start of Jason Newsted's career in Metallica. Flemming Rasmussen was at the Country Club show. 'That place was *packed*. They tried to keep it a secret but word had gone out.' Not seeing Cliff there, 'It was pretty terrible.' Seeing the new guy, 'It was strange but I was happy that they were going on, that they weren't stopping, because I thought they had much more in them.'

The five-date Japanese tour took place, as scheduled, between 15 and 20 November: three shows in Tokyo, plus one each in Nagoya and Osaka. The set now included a decent enough bass solo immediately after 'Ride the Lightning' but in every other respect Jason was seriously struggling. 'We'd all pick on him,' tour photographer Ross Halfin later told Joel McIver. 'We'd all get a cab and make him get a cab on his own. It started off as a joke and then it got really beyond a joke.' Bobby Schneider agrees: 'Jason fit [musically] but the razzing of Jason was terrible. They never really gave him a chance.' He explains, 'All of us, me included, started really making it hard for Jason. First as a joke but it started to get . . . they were sort of childish jokes in my mind, you're just razzing the new guy. But as it started coming from them as well, then a lot of people on the crew . . . because you know what that's like. Once it becomes okay to bully somebody then most people unfortunately, the shitty human nature that we have, without really realising it, you jump on.'

What Jason later characterised as 'hazing and a lot of emotional tests' included such stunts as telling everyone they introduced him to that he was gay; signing meals and drinks to his room; and invading his hotel room at four in the morning. 'Get up, fucker! It's time to drink, pussy!' Pounding on his door until it almost came off the hinges. 'You should have answered the door, bitch!' Grabbing hold of his mattress and yanking it off the bed with Jason still lying on it, then piling everything in the room – TV, chairs, desk – on top of him. Fifteen years later, Newsted still recoiled at the memory as he told *Playboy*, 'They threw my clothes, my cassette tapes, my shoes out the window. Shaving cream all over the mirrors, toothpaste everywhere. Just devastation. They go running out the door, "Welcome to the band, dude!"' The only reason he put up with it, he said, 'Because it was Metallica, it was my dream come true, man. I was definitely frustrated, fed up and kind of feeling unliked.' More recently, he said: 'I didn't sleep properly for three months after I joined Metallica. They'd charged thousands of dollars to my table at a restaurant. I had no idea about it. I was a hired musician at that point, earning $500 a week. Before I joined, I was still rubbing nickels together.' As if to add insult to injury, Lars recalled how in Tokyo, 'all these kids gave us gifts. Jason didn't get any, though – they thought he was part of the road crew. So he had a temper tantrum. Poor guy. Maybe we should have got him a T-shirt with the statement: "I'm Jason, dammit, gimme a gift!"'

Clearly there was something more going on here than the normal high jinks associated with a touring rock band. The problem was twofold. First there was Newsted's generally diffident personality; on the one hand so awed by his plunge into the deep end – not just joining his dream band but trying to replace its most important figurehead – that he tried to cover up his nervousness and lack of experience by putting on a front that more than one observer mistook as arrogance; on the other, having to find a way to come to terms with his newfound role, no longer as leader of the band but as the newbie, do-what-I-say-not-what-I-do hired hand – an incredibly precarious balancing act that almost inevitably left him flat on his face.

Then there were the more subtle tensions, which he simply could not be expected to appreciate. Jason arrived in Metallica determined to do the right thing, to not blow it, to do things to the max. This was the earnest young guy, after all, who once tacked a set of 'band rules' to the wall of Flotsam's rehearsal room. The others, however, especially Lars and James, were not only entering that new stage success brings, where the shine has worn off enough to let you mess around with things and make up your own rules, but were also still so fucked-up over Cliff's death that they were easily irritated by Jason's out-of-synch mewling. It was like Ron McGovney all over again. Jason, though good enough on bass, was never going to be as good as Cliff. Jason was a Metallica and thrash metal fan. Cliff was Cliff, into Kate Bush and Lynyrd Skynyrd, The Misfits and Lou Reed. Lars was especially outraged when Jason hinted he could use the extra practice, too. What the fuck? Jason was trying to do the 'right' thing at a time when the right thing no longer existed, had been left crushed under the bus with Cliff.

Above all, there was simply the enormous anger and resentment still growing inside all of them, James in particular. 'There was a lot of grief that turned into spite towards Jason,' admitted James in 2005. 'That is ... pretty human, I would say.' Or as Lars put it, speaking with me in 2009, 'It was difficult. I think certainly one could argue that maybe we didn't give [Jason] a fair shot. But we also weren't capable because we were twenty-two years old and we didn't know how to deal with this type of stuff. We didn't know how to get through those types of situations other than jump to the bottom of a vodka bottle and stay there for years ... we weren't particularly embrasive [sic] and welcoming, you know.' He gave a small self-deprecating chuckle. 'So I think, certainly, you know, most of the fault lies with us.'

Lars, in fact, grew to dislike Jason so much during that Japanese tour that he went to Mensch and insisted they fire him, and that the whole thing was a big mistake. 'I know for a fact,' said Halfin, 'Lars wanted to fire him. He wanted to replace him. But Peter Mensch said to him, "You've made your choice, now live with it."' He added, 'He just didn't get on with him as a person. It wasn't because of Jason's playing skills; it was purely because he didn't get on with his personality.' This was a view corroborated by Bobby Schneider: 'I remember

Mensch sitting down with them in some bar in Japan and saying, "You guys gotta fucking stop this. He's *in* your band. You've made him a band member. So just get on with it. He's the right choice."'

The trouble was Metallica hadn't just hired a bassist, they'd hired a fan. Where they had schemed and plotted to persuade Cliff to join their band, Jason had given up everything to be with them. They had replaced the one guy they all looked up to with the one guy they all looked down on – Jason Newkid, as they tauntingly nicknamed him. No wonder they felt so uncomfortable having him around all the time. He wasn't one of them and never would be. They resented him – anyone – parachuting into their story. Fuck his bass. Turn it down.

Speaking just a couple of years after Jason had been hired, Lars was still staunchly repeating the party line although he was already starting to sound like he was trying more to convince himself. 'Look, when Cliff died, we could have taken our time before deciding what to do,' he conceded. 'But we didn't, and that felt like the right thing to do.' Just a few nights after the funeral, 'I sat and drank some beer and listened to the *Master of Puppets* album – all of it. And then it hit me. The next couple of weeks would have been shit but we started setting up auditions, spending hours on the phone, and then we got Jason Newsted and started jamming, and then we initiated Jason with some club gigs ... It was good for us, the right thing for us to do. No time to dwell. From the accident to doing a gig was five weeks. The reason I talk about this is that what was right for us might not have been right for other bands ...' When the writer Ben Mitchell asked James in 2009 whether he thought they had toured again too quickly after Cliff died, the singer replied: 'I think we did everything too quickly after that. Getting a bass player, touring. We went straight back out. That was management's way of dealing with the grief: "Just play it out through your music." Now it feels like there wasn't enough grieving or enough respect paid, and enough of just dealing with each other and helping each other through. We went out on the road and took a lot of it out on Jason once he joined. It was more like: "Yeah, we have a bass player but he's not Cliff."'

There was no time for looking back in 1986, though; the Japanese dates were immediately followed by a short US and Canadian tour at the end of November, before finally returning to Europe – the scene of the crime – at the start of 1987 to finish up the dates they'd been forced to cancel when their tour bus skidded off the road and took at least one glorious possible future with it. 'I did another tour before we went back there,' says Schneider. 'Me and Flemming Larsen, actually, went out on tour with Slayer and neither one of us could sleep on the bus. I mean, I had to pass out to go to sleep. For years and years and years I had to sleep on a certain bunk or on the front couch.' To help Metallica over any residual feelings of insecurity, in fact, Q Prime hired an American bus driver to travel with them. 'He came with us and watched the other driver drive; that's what his job was … to keep an eye on things.'

When, in April 1987, they released their first long-form video, a tribute to their man down, titled *Cliff 'Em All*, it seemed from the outside like an act of closure. Basking in a renewed round of rave reviews, within weeks of its release, *Cliff 'Em All* was certified both gold and platinum in the US music video charts. All surely was now well again in Metallica's world. In fact, the deep and unsightly wounds inflicted by Burton's death would remain open, continuing to fester for at least another twenty years, by which time a despairing Newsted would finally have had enough and thrown in the towel, leaving the band to try and do what they should have done in 1986. Not tour, not record, not paper over the ever-widening cracks, hoping it would be all right when they came to again in the morning. That day was coming whether they liked it or not. Meanwhile, things would just get worse – the pain, the bitterness, the recriminations and resentments, the awful guilt – stalking their rapidly growing success like an ever-lengthening shadow, night waiting to fall.

Compiled from bootleg footage recorded by fans, personal film clips belonging to the band and photos sourced from various locations, both official and unofficial, *Cliff 'Em All* was a groundbreaking release. More than a decade before such concepts as 'reality TV', the unscripted, unplanned, apparently random nature of the material came as a delightful surprise, whether one was a dyed-in-the-wool

Metallica fan or merely a random viewer. By turns amusing, sad and surprisingly insightful, it's the kind of thing we take for granted in these YouTube-inflected times but which seemed utterly revelatory back then: Cliff chilling out smoking 'the greatest pot to hit these shores'; the band walking en masse into a liquor store and stealing enough beer and bites to see them through the evening; all this amidst a flood of Beavis and Butthead-style sniggering. Most of all, some glorious footage of the band in its earliest days, from Cliff's second gig at the Stone in April 1983, via the Day on the Green in '85 and several fan-shot bootleg clips from the summer '86 Ozzy tour, where it became clear just how powerful a presence Burton was onstage and off – and how young and unconfident James in particular often was, not least when Dave Mustaine was still ruling the roost from the opposite side of the stage. Imagine that: caught in the spotlight between Cliff Burton on one side and Dave Mustaine on the other, behind you that little lunatic Lars. No wonder James felt he had a fight on his hands just keeping up.

After the tour the plan had been to begin writing for the next album, a process broken up with a smattering of lucrative festival dates scheduled for the summer. However, things changed when Hetfield broke his arm again in yet another skateboarding accident, this time in an empty swimming pool in Oakland Hills with Kirk and their pals Fred Cotton and Pushead. James had been wearing all the protective gear this time, he had been 'just a little too vertical,' recalled Cotton. 'As soon as he came down into the bottom of the pool you could hear the snap.' Forced to cancel what should have been a career-boosting appearance on NBC-TV's highly influential *Saturday Night Live*, Cotton claims Q Prime subsequently 'made James sign something that promised he wasn't go to skateboard any more'. Instead, the focus now switched to something even more important: recording their first release under their new deal with a major British record company: Phonogram.

Master of Puppets had marked the end of Metallica's licensing deal with Music for Nations. Unlike Jonny Z in his struggle to retain control against the encroaching interests of the much larger and more powerful Q Prime, Martin Hooker was not only keen to renew the band's contract but he also had the financial means to do so. Peter Mensch, however, had bigger fish to fry. He wanted Metallica on a British and European label commensurate in size to Elektra in the USA and CBS in Japan. Specifically, he wanted them on Phonogram, where he already had Def Leppard. 'We did offer them a considerably bigger deal than Phonogram,' says Martin Hooker, 'worth well over £1 million, which at that time was the biggest deal we'd ever offered anyone.' He adds, 'Unfortunately, Q Prime weren't even prepared to discuss it as it suited their purposes to have the band at Phonogram.' In fact, says Hooker, Q Prime, who were 'amazed at our offer', had already agreed the deal with Phonogram without even speaking to MFN. 'When we found out, we then offered them a very generous new deal just to hold onto the catalogue that we already had. I explained that this would be very beneficial to the band as an extra income source that wouldn't be recouped against tour support or recording costs et cetera on the new album [as it would at Phonogram]. I thought this made a lot of financial sense for the band. Needless to say I was incredulous to find out that Q Prime had already agreed to throw the existing catalogue into the Phonogram deal.'

Says Hooker: 'My back catalogue was still selling truck-loads. So they [must have] really, really wanted those three records, to help them recoup their balance ... they obviously pressured him and eventually, I think like a year later, when the second term expired, they took the back catalogue off me, which was totally within their rights to do so, of course.' Hooker would have one last laugh, though. When Metallica left for Phonogram, MFN rereleased *MOP* as a 'limited edition' double album, claiming that the extra-wide grooves on the vinyl gave the music a more crystal-clear sound. 'I wouldn't say that it was any *better*,' concedes Gem Howard now, 'but it was *louder*. Because you can cut it much louder when you're doing it at forty-five rpm on a twelve-inch, because there's more room in the grooves, which makes it sound better ...' He goes on: 'It seems laughable now but in those days we were getting kids writing to us saying how wonderful the sound quality was and we sold tens of thousands of it – incredible.' Gem says the final figure for combined British and European sales of all three Metallica albums on MFN is now in excess of 1.5 million, or 'about 500,000 each'. *MOP* remains the single biggest-selling album Music for Nations ever released.

Dave Thorne, then senior product manager in the International Department at Phonogram in London, wouldn't normally have been involved in the Metallica campaign. Having recently worked with Bon Jovi, Rush, Cinderella, and several other rock-related Phonogram artists, however, he found himself in a central role in the Metallica deal, he says now, 'because of my connections and understanding of heavy metal'. Thorne explains how the 'key link' in the deal had been Peter Mensch's existing relationship with the label's director of business affairs, John Watson: then Phonogram's senior lawyer. The first time Thorne got wind of the deal was when he was called into the office of managing director David Simone, who was there with Watson. They told Dave they had the chance to sign Metallica and asked what he thought their long-term commercial prospects were.

'I kind of got excited and said they are *the* band at the moment in the extreme metal scene', characterising them as 'the Rush of extreme metal'. When he added that Metallica had already sold 100,000 albums in the UK alone, Simone asked, 'Yes, but is it gonna get bigger?' To which Thorne replied, 'With us as a company behind them, why wouldn't it?' Actually there were several reasons why Phonogram might not have been the right label for a band such as Metallica. As Thorne admits, all he got from the A&R department initially was 'blank faces'. He adds, 'They couldn't have told you which way you held a guitar, never mind what sort of band Metallica was. They were signing bands like Soft Cell and Swing Out Sister – all these pop-driven, indie-type things.'

He recalls Mensch coming to London for a summit meeting with Simone, Watson, Thorne, and all the various heads of department, including marketing director John Waller and his boss Tony Powell. The thrust of Mensch's presentation was: 'This is not an A&R opportunity, the A&R on this band takes care of itself. This is a marketing opportunity ...' Says Thorne, 'Mensch said, "Guys, don't get your-selves excited. We're not looking for you to be creatively involved in this. None of you except maybe that bloke" – pointing at me – "knows anything about this band. We want your sales, distribution and marketing."'

Mensch won them over but, as he'd already conceded, very little of this had to do with the music. Says Thorne, 'I suspect some of the powers that be thought, hey, this could be the new Def Leppard. I don't think there was any real analysis of whether that was feasible. What we were talking about was building a stronger bridge with a big management company who we already had a relationship with.' MFN had 'great ears, great attitude; great tenacity in delivering what they'd done [but] were literally at the limit of their capability'. To get Metallica where they needed to go next, career-wise, it would take 'serious old-fashioned marketing clout, delivering big campaigns, big discount deals, et cetera. Polygram, who were the distribution arm of the company, at the time, was pretty much the biggest distribution oper-ation in Europe. So that's what [Q Prime] were looking for.'

The first Metallica release on Phonogram would be a four-track twelve-inch: *The $5.98 EP: Garage Days Re-Revisited* – the title a ref-erence to the subtitle of the B-side of the 'Creeping Death' single of three years before; an indicator that this was a collection of covers. It's long been assumed that this was conceived as a handy way of breaking Newsted into Metallica before embarking on a full-blown album. In fact, the record was made at the suggestion of Dave Thorne, who saw their forthcoming return appearance at that year's Don-ington Monsters of Rock festival as a perfect marketing opportunity for a new British release: 'I said, "Look, this is an amazing sales opportunity. I know you're not gonna have an album but we've got to put something out." They said okay, we'll go away and think about it.' Thorne's initial idea had been a straightforward single but Mensch told him, 'We don't do singles.' Thorne responded, 'Well, record something that will qualify for the singles chart but isn't a single. They came back and said, "We're gonna do *The $5.98 EP: Garage Days Re-Revisited*." Even now, Lars still credits me with this idea,

On the US Monsters of Rock tour, Tampa Stadium, Florida, May 1988 (*Ross Halfin*).

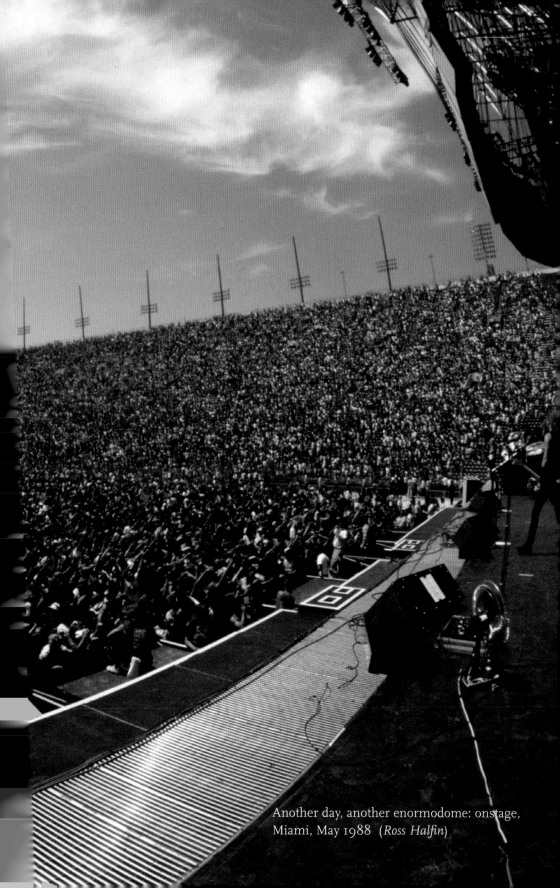

Another day, another enormodome: onstage,
Miami, May 1988 (*Ross Halfin*)

RIGHT: Lars, on the Black tour, 1991–93. BELOW: The 100 Club, London, Jason Newsted's first UK show, August 1987 (*both Ross Halfin*)

James backstage rubbing cream on to his badly burned arm, on the incident-filled Guns N' Roses tour, September 1992 (*Getty Images*)

The mid-nineties reinvention. ABOVE: Kirk arrives for the
MTV Awards, September 1996 (*PA*). BELOW: Lars and Kirk
deliberately infuriating James (*Getty Images*).

Fifteen years, just three co-songwriting credits: Jason Newsted giving vent
onstage to his anger and frustration (*Ross Halfin*)

which is very nice of him. But I hadn't conceptualised it.'

In fact, the idea – blasting out as-live versions of covers of underground metal and punk gems such as 'Helpless' by Diamond Head, 'The Small Hours' by fellow NWOBHM outfit Holocaust, 'Crash Course in Brain Surgery' by old-wave British metallists Budgie, and back-to-back versions of two songs by Cliff's beloved Misfits, 'Last Caress' and 'Green Hell' – was simple but brilliant. Rehearsed, as the title suggests, in the garage – although not at their former El Cerrito bolthole but across the street in Lars' newly soundproofed two-car garage at his very own house, bought with the extra money now coming in – then recorded in just six days at Conway studios in LA, 'about the same time it took to load in the gear on the last album', as James noted on the sleeve, the *Garage Days* EP was a riot from start to finish.

Opening with the sound of James humming while other voices in the background titter, before Lars' monstrous-sounding drums kick in and the whole thing takes off like a runaway train, just as the *Cliff 'Em All* video anticipated aspects of reality TV, so *Garage Days* massively predated the taste for lo-fi recordings of a decade later, emphasised by rule-breaking moments such as the fade-out of 'Helpless' fading back in again to the sound of guitar chords being wrenched from amps and Lars barking instructions from behind his kit. The speed and ferocity continue through the next track, Jason's bass erupting over the improvised intro and turning the ostensibly vintage rock anthem 'Crash Course in Brain Surgery' into a wild punk-metal powerhouse. The opening track on side two – 'The Small Hours' – is given an even more brutal treatment, lumbering towards you over the horizon like some mutant one-eyed alien monster from Kirk's growing collection of vintage sci-fi comics, smothered in nuclear dust clouds and the blood of puny humans. The real kiss-off, though, is the climax, two long-dead Misfits songs – 'Last Caress' and 'Green Hell' – bolted, Frankenstein-like, into one. Despite its defiantly wrongheaded lyrics ('I got something to say, I raped your mother today . . . '), 'Last Caress' was one of Metallica's catchiest tracks, its counter-intuitive sweetness wonderfully superseded by 'Green Hell', one of their fastest tracks since 'Whiplash', the whole medley lasting barely over three minutes; the joke compounded when the EP ends with an amusingly tuneless few seconds of the intro to Iron Maiden's 'Run to the Hills'. Ironically, the most Metallica-like track recorded at these sessions was actually left off the UK version of the EP, in order to qualify it for the singles chart – their commanding version of Killing Joke's 'The Wait', any traces of humour once more suspended as the band do the seemingly impossible and all but make the song their own.

For a band that would increasingly make superior production the foundation upon which their albums would stand or fall, the hastily recorded, 'not very produced' – as they wittily credited it on the sleeve – *Garage Days* EP arguably did more for Metallica's reputation at that precise juncture in their career than the most momentous album release might have. It made Metallica seem fun and accessible, qualities that had eluded them since their first album. And, yes, it was a good way of introducing Jason Newkid, as he's listed on the artfully 'makeshift' sleeve, to those fans waiting with folded arms to compare him to Cliff. It also gave Jason one of his first really good Metallica experiences, using his background as a carpenter and odd-job man to help Lars soundproof his new garage after the band decided they didn't feel comfortable working out of a plush Marin County rehearsal studio shared by Night Ranger and Starship. Jason brought in strips of carpeting to soundproof the walls, with the help of Lars' old pal from LA, John Kornarens (who still hadn't got his fifty bucks back). As Jason recalled, 'That was a fucking blast, man. You walked into the room, set up your amp the way you would live, put a microphone in front of it and you play the song. James was standing next to me . . . just doing his stuff. We recorded it there and then, mistakes and all. To me that's one of the best-sounding Metallica records because of its rawness.'

The plan, explains Thorne, was for Phonogram to use its clout to 'blast it straight into the charts. To make a massive statement about the band, and that's of course exactly what it did.' In fact, the EP went in at Number Twenty-Seven – good, not great, by contemporary chart

singles' standards but regarded as a significant success at Phonogram
as the record had been released in only one format: a twelve-inch vinyl
record. No CD, no cassette, no seven-inch formats. When Thorne had
played a snippet of 'Helpless' at the weekly strategy meeting, 'I kid
you not, within thirty seconds, the press girls and virtually everybody
else in the bloody room was going, "Oh, for god's sake turn that off!"'
When the record actually became a commercial success, 'That opened
up the floodgates at Phonogram for Metallica.' The EP also went gold
in America, but for half a million album sales, because it wasn't
accepted as a single configuration. Marketed there as a mini-album,
with the extra track, the cover of 'The Wait', now added, as it was for
Japan, the package was retitled *The $9.98 EP: Garage Days Re-
Revisited.* 'They had to do that,' explains Thorne, 'or it simply would
have sold that amount on import and Elektra [and CBS] would have
missed out.'

Equally impressive, from their new record company's standpoint,
was the band's willingness to help promote the record. They may not
have been the usual type of singles-orientated artists Phonogram was
used to dealing with but they more than made up for that by being
down-to-earth and ready to roll up their sleeves. For most major
artists, 'coming into the country doing promo meant a handful of
major interviews', says Thorne. 'Possibly a bit of TV and radio if it
was available. Then you might get other members of the band to do
some secondary interview type stuff. But Lars didn't just want to talk
to [the major music press], he wanted to talk to every bloody fanzine
you've ever heard of and a load that you haven't. Lars would come in
and spend four or five *days* in our office. He'd do literally sixty, seventy,
eighty fanzines. You couldn't get him off the phone.'

Thorne cites this readiness to always meet the media halfway as
one of the major contributing factors in Metallica's later popularity
with such temperamentally metal-hostile magazines as the *NME,
Time Out,* the *Village Voice, Rolling Stone,* and so on, up to the present
day and their current elevated status among the broadsheet newspapers. 'It was a combination of Lars' willingness to always go the
extra mile for the media,' says Thorn, 'and also something else. It all

comes down to the "c"-word: credibility. Every conversation I had with Peter Mensch, every meeting we had, every major decision we made, that was the word that was at the forefront: credibility. They would not do anything that would upset that applecart. They weren't gonna sell out because they were a band of the people. They came up through the tape-trading scene and that's where they wanted to stay. They didn't want to upset those people.'

Maybe so but Lars, they discovered, was also Dave and the rest of Phonogram's 'go-to guy' for both promotional issues and all relevant business decisions. 'I would talk to Mensch and he would then say to me, "Okay, now you've got to talk to Lars and persuade him."' Peter, he says, 'was obviously a guy who had a natural aversion to saying yes, especially to record labels. [So in the beginning] he got me to talk to Lars all the time. Lars was totally, *totally* immersed in the business side of things ... he was the guy who had to be persuaded. He would then go to the guy who was the *real* decision-maker in the band, and that was Hetfield – on the big things.'

Another added bonus in the label's attempts to garner maximum publicity for their first Metallica release was the band's decision to play – billed as 'Damage, Inc.' – an unannounced warm-up show for Donington at the 100 Club in Oxford Street, the legendary venue where The Clash and the Sex Pistols had performed in the late 1970s. When, near the end of the hour-long set, Jason's bass dropped out of the mix due to a technical glitch, word passed through the crowd that he'd passed out from the heat. The place was so unbearably hot and overcrowded it was impossible to verify this and when Jason's momentary 'collapse' was later misreported in *Kerrang!* it only added to the gathering list of grievances and personal slights against him that Jason was now mentally compiling. He even suspected the band of planting the story to their cronies on the mag as another wind-up. As Dave Thorne says, 'It was an insane night. My lasting memory was seeing Scott Ian being surfed around the whole crowd in front of the band ... a crazy night.'

Two days later the band walked onstage at Donington, where they were third on the bill below ex-Black Sabbath singer Ronnie James

Dio and headliners Bon Jovi. For thousands of Metallica fans, Donington was their first chance to see the new-look line-up. Conversely,
for Metallica it was important to prove they had barely changed at all;
that it was business as usual – not to diminish the loss of their
talismanic bassist, but to demonstrate that this was not some insur-
mountable obstacle. That there was still great substance to what they
did – and where they would be going next, no matter who now
occupied the side of the stage to James' right. The set began well
enough with three crowd-pleasing relics from the Cliff-shrouded past:
'Creeping Death', 'For Whom the Bell Tolls' and 'Fade to Black'. It
wasn't long, though, before they were dipping into the new EP in a
neat bit of cross-promotional euphoria and future foundation-laying,
injecting the huge element of fun the EP had winningly engendered,
even down to wringing out the woozy intro to 'Run to the Hills' at the
climax of the 'Last Caress'/'Green Hell' medley.

Then, just as they were building towards the climax of their set,
the audience's attention was snatched away by the arrival overhead of
the helicopter ferrying Bon Jovi to the backstage area. It seemed to
take forever to navigate its way over the crowd, buzzing loudly towards
the backstage area, where the ground was firmly 'cleared' by their
ground staff security so that Jon and his band could disembark
without having to engage with anyone else working there that day.
'Fucking asshole!' James raged when he came off stage. 'He deliberately tried to fuck up our set.' It hadn't been quite that bad – a
distraction, certainly, but one everyone bar possibly Hetfield got over
quickly – but James took it personally. Grabbing a marker pen he
scrawled the words 'Kill Bon Jovi' on his guitar. Jon Bon Jovi later told
me it had all been a misunderstanding; that he was appalled that
anyone would think he would deliberately try to ruin another band's
show, not least one appearing lower on the same bill as he. Jon made
it clear, however, that he still recalled Hetfield's comments on the
Donington stage two years before about 'spandex, make-up and oh
baby' songs and that there was no love lost between the two camps.

Metallica, self-styled dwellers of a permanent midnight world
where clean-cut early risers such as Bon Jovi were considered the

enemy, had been put in their place it seemed. What neither James Hetfield or Jon Bon Jovi – nor even Lars Ulrich, for all his secret dreams – could have foreseen was how drastically their positions would change over the next five years, and that it would be Metallica, bad boys dressed in black, who would ascend towards the heart of the sun, while Bon Jovi, once so untainted, would plunge like Icarus into the raging sea below, a reversal in fortunes so improbable that not even Peter Mensch could have considered it.

Or could he?

TEN
WILD CHICKS, FAST CARS
AND LOTS OF DRUGS

'**H**ey, man,' said Kirk, 'you can do something about that, you know?'
We were standing in the dressing room at the Newcastle City
Hall. Onstage, Glen Danzig, once of The Misfits, now fronting his new
self-named band, was doing the crowd a big favour by playing for them.

'About what?'

'Your hair. You're receding. Do something about it now, though, and
you can fix it.'

I stared at him. He had caught me off guard. My hair? We were talking
about my hair? I tried to play it cool, like who cares?

'Uh huh, and what's that?'

'Rogaine, man,' he smiled. 'You know it?'

I did actually. That is, I had heard of something similar: Regaine.

'Same thing, man,' he said. 'Minoxidil, right?'

My hairdresser had mentioned it to me the last time I'd had my hair
cut but I was so taken aback I'd pushed it to the back of mind. Now this.
Was my hair really doing that badly people were now just coming up to me
and mentioning it?

'No, man,' said Kirk, 'I just see it because I see it in me, too.'

I looked at his hair. Long, black, curly, kind of a high forehead but
otherwise ... what the fuck was he talking about? And to me?

'Seriously,' he said, 'you should try it. Before it's too late ...' He walked
off.

Later that night, over a beer and a spliff, I mentioned it to Big Mick the
sound guy. Mick and I often ended up together whenever I was with
Metallica. He couldn't get good black hash in the USA, and I could rarely

get good strong weed at home in London, not in the late Eighties. So we helped each other out. Somehow in Newcastle we'd both got what we were looking for. It was a day off the next day so Mick and the crew were holed up at the hotel with the band.

'What's this Kirk's going on about,' I said, 'Rogaine? Regaine? Do you know it?'

'Oh, Christ,' he said. 'It's Kirk's new thing. We're carrying fucking truck-loads of it on this tour. Between that and the fucking statue there's hardly any room for the equipment.'

Mick, with his thick, shoulder-length hair, wasn't the kind of guy who needed to trouble himself with the ins and outs of this one so he made a joke about it instead, in lieu of changing the subject to something – anything – else. Still, I was intrigued. The next time I saw Kirk, I asked him about it.

'Sure, man,' he said, 'you just rub it into your scalp like every day. You have to do it every day or it won't work. But it's cool. You should really try it,' he said again. 'Before it's too late . . .'

In the careers of the most successful rock artists, certain albums become such landmark releases they afford them a certain leeway with whatever they decide to do next. When that album comes near enough to the start of an artist's career, however, to constitute a significant breakthrough – commercially or artistically, or best of all both – if they are savvy, the logical next step is to make the follow-up along similar lines, thereby cementing their growing status among both their core constituency of fans, and keeping faith with the record company they depend on to work hard for them, plus promoters, agents, and their various media partners. Once that job is done, their fan base substantial and secure, they can then wrestle with the formula if they want to on subsequent releases. What they aren't advised to do is risk throwing the baby out with the bathwater by trying something completely different with their breakthrough follow-up.

This was the position Metallica found themselves in 1987 when it came to planning their fourth album: not just the follow-up to their breakthrough hit, *Master of Puppets*, but their first without Cliff Burton. The logical, safe option would have been to make a conscious sequel, in effect *Master II*; to both cash in on their now-established winning formula and prove that Burton's replacement by Jason Newsted had been achieved seamlessly. When, however, Lars Ulrich and James Hetfield came to sit down and talk about it one afternoon in October 1987, while winding through the *Riff Tapes* – the compilation of bits and pieces they routinely compiled between albums, little ideas that had emerged at soundcheck maybe, or odd musical movements Lars would hum and James would turn into chords on his guitar – they decided not to follow any of these rules and instead go for broke with something so completely different from what had come before as to be virtually unrecognisable from the Metallica template as established over their first three albums.

Or rather, Lars did. High on the million-selling success around the world of the *Garage Days* single EP and mini-album CD, and unduly taken with the rule-breaking sound of the debut album from a bunch of LA ne'er-do-wells called Guns N' Roses, he felt the time had come for Metallica to jettison the thrash lifeboat completely and go for a whole new approach. James, inured after years of putting up with Lars' non-stop talk of world domination, yet still lost and unsure how to proceed without Cliff's bullshit-o-meter to guide them, merely nodded his head. What did it mean anyway, all this talk of 'adding new elements to the sound' that Lars was so fond of expounding on? They would just put the songs together as usual and see what came up, right?

Certainly there was nothing new to their approach in that respect, the two working from home alone on a four-track, with Kirk invited down at a later stage to consider his guitar parts, and Jason not invited at all on the pretext that, with only four tracks to work with, there was no room for bass at that stage anyway. As a result, of the nine tracks eventually slated for the album – all essentially Hetfield/Ulrich compositions – just three would also bear Kirk's surname, just one Jason's, plus one Cliff's, a posthumous work melded from 'some bits and pieces' the bass player had left on tape, over which James intoned a four-line poem the bassist had also left behind entitled 'To Live is to Die'. In fact, the only big difference initially was the decision to record the album closer to home this time, in Los Angeles, a choice rooted, paradoxically, in a newfound conservatism – at least, away from the stage – and their sudden desire to be close to their various partners.

This was one aspect of their lives the young Metallica went out of their way to keep off-limits from the press, even the almost venally loquacious Lars, who became uncharacteristically tongue-tied the first time he introduced me to his English-born wife, Debbie. A fun, fair-haired, plain-talking girl from the Midlands, the two had met during the band's stay in London in 1984 and married early in 1987, during the brief hiatus when James was still nursing his broken wrist. It wasn't that Lars hid his wife from the press, it just happened to be one of the very few things he didn't talk at length about. Plus, ladies' man Lars didn't like to think of anyone cramping his style and while he clearly loved being around Debbie, the marriage was doomed to end just three years later. These, after all, were Lars' wild years and, with the band finally taking off, no time to be married to its principal party animal. As he later said, for a while they had considered naming their next album, *Wild Chicks, Fast Cars and Lots of Drugs*, such was the state of play in Metalliworld at the time. How could any homespun, working-class English girl hope to compete with that?

Kirk, too, had chosen just this moment to marry his pretty American girlfriend, Rebecca (Becky), the two tying the knot in December, just a few weeks before the band began work on the new album. From the outside, Kirk and Becky looked like the perfect couple, almost a mirror image of each other, with their long curly hair, elfin faces and large brown eyes. Becky was ditzy, airy-fairy, and fitted in neatly with Kirk's own public persona as the roach-sucking, comic-book-collecting, easygoing hippy minstrel. In fact, there was a new edge starting to emerge in the guitarist's character as he began living out his own rock star fantasies, sometimes involving Becky, sometimes not, and cocaine began to take preference over marijuana as his drug of choice. Their marriage, too, would end after just a few short years.

Jason, who had split from his longstanding girlfriend Lauren

Collins, a college student from Phoenix, shortly after joining Metallica, now became involved with a new girlfriend, Judy, who would become the first Mrs Newsted over the coming year, although they got divorced even quicker than Lars or Kirk, deciding they'd made a mistake almost immediately. The only one who didn't get married at this point was James, and he, ironically, was the one perhaps most deeply in love. Indeed, his girlfriend Kristen Martinez would later inspire one of Metallica's best-loved songs and one of the cornerstones of their far more widespread popularity in the 1990s, 'Nothing Else Matters'. That was the only time James even semi-acknowledged his affair with Kristen publicly, even going as far as to later claim not to have written the song about her at all, so deep was his hurt when they too broke up in the wake of Metallica's now rocketing success.

That, however, was in the future. There were no love songs planned for the fourth Metallica album. Instead, Lars was determined to place the emphasis on a new, harder edge, and he wanted to record quickly, unlike *MOP*, which even he agreed had taken too long. Besotted with the Guns N' Roses album, *Appetite for Destruction*, which contained so many swear words radio wouldn't play it, most of all he wanted to ensure Metallica didn't get left behind by what he called 'the new dicks on the block'. He later recalled listening to the first single from the *Appetite* album, 'It's So Easy', on a flight home to San Francisco and being unable to believe the unashamed misogyny of the line, 'Turn around bitch, I got a use for you', nor the pay-off at the end of the final verse when singer W. Axl Rose yells 'Why don't you just . . . fuck off!' 'It just blew my fuckin' head off,' Lars excitedly told James. 'It was the way Axl said it. It was so venomous. It was so fucking real and so fucking angry.' It was the start of an obsession with Axl and Guns N' Roses that would eventually see both bands touring together, although it would not be one shared with James.

When it became apparent that Flemming Rasmussen, their nominal choice to record with again, would not be available as quickly as they would have liked, Lars, secretly delighted, seized on the situation to put forward a more exciting alternative: Mike Clink, the Baltimore-born producer who'd overseen the recording of *Appetite for*

Destruction. Clink had begun his career as an engineer at New York's Record Plant studios, assisting producer Ron Nevison on hit albums by soft rock giants such as Jefferson Starship, Heart and, most notably, Survivor's huge 1982 hit single and album, *Eye of the Tiger.* Clink's main attributes, according to GN'R guitarist Slash, were 'incredible guitar sounds and a tremendous amount of patience'. Smart enough to realise the records he'd made before were essentially 'pop albums', he'd listened carefully when Slash had played him Aerosmith albums in preparation for the *Appetite* sessions. Interestingly, the album Axl had asked him to take special note of had been Metallica's *Ride the Lightning.*

With One on One studios in North Hollywood booked for the first three months of 1988, Lars asked Mensch to put a deal together that would bring in Clink as producer of the new album. Clink, a shrewd operator looking for a project that would extend his newfound reputation as the go-to guy for cutting-edge rock bands, was intrigued enough by the approach to accept at first time of asking. Nevertheless, on the surface it seemed an odd fit: Clink was known for capturing a looser, bluesy, as-live feel in the studio, while Metallica were known more for their almost icily precise sheet-metal riffs and machine-like rhythms. Somehow it would be Clink's job to marry the two. As he says now, 'They hired me because they enjoyed [and] really liked the Guns N' Roses records.' However, the message he got in his initial conversation with Q Prime, 'was that they do things the Metallica way. And I didn't really know what that was until I got into the middle of it.'

James was even less sure. No fan, he, of the GN'R record, as far as James could see, Clink wasn't anything special, just another of Lars' passing fancies. He watched patiently while they searched for a drum sound that seemed to match whatever requirements were going through both Lars' and Mike's heads, then lost patience when it came to his guitar sound. Although they managed to do what they always did at the start of an album and lay down a couple of rough-hewn covers in order to iron out any potential problems – in this case, Budgie's 'Breadfan' and Diamond Head's 'The Prince', tracks so rough they made the material on the *Garage Days* E P sound polished – instead of smoothing out their differences, it only highlighted how far apart their thinking still was, especially between Hetfield and Clink. 'I just flipped out,' said James, 'couldn't hang with it any more.'

Says Clink now, 'As much as I believe they wanted me to put my magic on the tracks, I think that they were used to doing things on their own and doing it their own way.' He adds, pointedly, 'I always felt that I was in the wings, waiting until Flemming got free or they could convince him to work on the record [because] at that moment in time it just wasn't working ... they bristled at the fact of someone trying to tell them what to do. And I think it was as much my fault as their fault. You know, I had just come off of the Guns N' Roses record and doing things my way, and having my say. And I kind of ran into a bit of a brick wall and it was difficult for me.' Clink also felt that 'the absence of Cliff was a little unsettling to them – in the back of their minds maybe they wanted something more familiar, because that was a big step without him'.

Whatever the real problem was, by the end of the third week of recording, Lars was on the phone to Flemming, virtually begging him to rearrange his schedule and fly out to rescue the sessions. 'Lars called me [and] said they were going nowhere and they were getting fed up with it and asked if I was available just in case,' says Rasmussen. 'I told him I had a lot of gigs booked and if he needed me there I should know pretty fast. I got called up the next day and he said come on over. Like, "When can you be here?"'

Arriving at One on One two weeks later, Rasmussen insisted the band start from scratch, keeping the rough cover versions, which could later be used as B-sides of singles, and just two of the drum tracks Clink had recorded with them, for the tracks 'Harvester of Sorrow' and 'The Shortest Straw'. Flemming thinks it didn't work with Clink because he 'probably expected them to be more of a *band*-band where everybody played at the same time and you kind of took it from there. And they were nowhere near that at that time. They were fucking around with guitar sound and had been so for like two or three weeks, and James was really unpleased,' he laughs. 'When

I spoke to Lars, he said, "We're not gonna do another *Master*. It's gonna be more in-your-face. It's gonna be as pumped and as upfront as possible."'

The end result was – as Lars had ordered – the hardest-sounding Metallica album yet, titled ... *And Justice for All*, after the final line from the Declaration of Independence, used here as shock-horror metaphor for the more general theme of anger at injustice that permeates every track. The trouble was that angry noise appeared to be all there was to most of it, to the point of deadening the emotions it was trying so hard to evoke; a roomful of mirrors in which all the reflections are hideously distorted. Mostly, the whole thing just sounded flat, the drums, busy but tinny, the guitars, revved-up but muted, the vocals almost uniformly shouted and aggressive. If this was Metallica becoming more in-your-face, the effect was to push all but the most avid, hear-no-evil fan away; as unlovely a creation as anything Dr Frankenstein had sewn and bolted together in his laboratory.

It was hard not to conclude that for the first time, Metallica was not playing by instinct but doing something it thought it should – that with Slayer's *Reign in Blood* having stolen the thrash crown they had so casually left lying around, and Guns N' Roses now threatening to beat them to the punch when it came to subverting more main-stream rock tastes, Metallica were no longer leaders doing what came naturally but playing mental catch-up. Looking outside themselves for pointers to the way forward rather than lighting the path for others to follow. That with only Lars' dreams and James' nightmares to guide them, Cliff's influence on Metallica would, from this moment on, be felt most powerfully by his absence. And that to begin with they were utterly lost. Writing about 'mental anguish' is 'what I like', James would boast: 'Physical pain is nothing compared to mental scarring – that shit sticks with you for ever. People dying in your life always makes you think.' Had Cliff's death become one of those things he'd thought about too much?

The first Metallica album clearly built for CD – with a total running time of over sixty-five minutes – the track sequencing still followed the same template as *Ride* and *Master*, beginning with a rallying-call opener, in this case 'Blackened'; lyrically a howl of rage against the destruction of the environment, musically very much in the mould of 'Battery', although less effective, and the only track on the album on which Newsted gets a co-credit. From there it was on to the self-consciously epic title track, one of the longest and most tedious songs the band would ever record. Built around a quirky Ulrich drum tattoo and the sound of marching guitars, with James railing against how 'Justice is lost / Justice is raped / Justice is gone ... ', at almost ten minutes long, 'Justice' digs its own grave and buries itself, eliciting a huge sigh of relief from the listener when it finally – finally – slams to a halt. It's not that it's such a bad Metallica track – it would have shone more brightly on *Ride*, perhaps, where the band was still establishing its credentials, and Hammett's guitars, for which he receives the first of his three co-writing credits, are exemplary. It's just that the whole endeavour is so earnest, bitter, unrelenting, that there is little of real excitement here, just the unhappy sound of one man and his pain. Similarly, the samey-sounding tribute-to-Cliff instrumental 'To Live is to Die' was a sincere gesture rendered almost meaningless by the fact that it's the longest track on an album choked with tracks that outstay their welcome.

The rest of the album – with one notable exception – continued along the same dark, tangled path. Again, it's not that tracks such as 'The Shortest Straw' or 'The Frayed Ends of Sanity' are outright bad – both typically brutish rockers that would have taken pride of place on *Ride*, perhaps – but after the sophisticated production and arrangements on *Master* and the warm, all-inclusive atmosphere of *Garage Days*, more was now expected of Metallica. Right at the moment they should have been delivering another sonic milestone, they had reverted to boorish type. What would have sounded scaldingly new four years before now sounded lumpen and off the pace.

Even the first single from the album, 'Harvester of Sorrow', was horribly plodding. 'Lyrically, this song is about someone who leads a very normal life, has a wife and three kids, and all of a sudden one day, he just snaps and starts killing the people around him,' Lars explained at the time. If only the music had sounded even half as interesting; the fact that it reached Number Twenty in the UK charts was probably down to the by-now-huge Metallica fan base that was ready to buy whatever the band did next, plus the variety of different formats Phonogram were now able to market the record in. Similarly, the next track fed to US radio, although not physically released as a single, 'Eye of the Beholder' – coming straight after the title track on the album, it sounded simply like more of the same, its saving grace on radio that its faded-in staccato rhythm was attention-grabbing enough to sustain the listener through the first couple of minutes before its droning repetitiveness finally zeroed you out. 'Do you see what I see?' James intones solemnly. 'Truth is an offence ... ', but clearly nobody had dared tell the band the truth about their new album.

The exception to all this – the sole gleaming diamond in the dirt – was the track 'One'; Metallica's most ambitious and successful musical experiment yet, and their most deeply affecting song. The macabre story of an infantryman who steps on a landmine and wakes to gradually discover he has lost everything – his arms and legs, his five senses – except his mind, which is now cast adrift, trapped in its own grim and impossible reality, 'One' was both nightmare writ large and musically transcendent journey. It was a thrash metal *Tommy* in miniature, depicting the protagonist's descent into living hell, wordlessly begging for death, capable of being seen both as existential metaphor for the human condition and the solipsism of the rock star life, its frantic climax also serving to relate a state of inarticulate teenage angst like no other rock song before or since.

Partially based on the 1939 Dalton Trumbo novel, *Johnny Got His Gun*, 'One' had started as a song James was thinking about based on the notion of 'just being a brain and nothing else' before Cliff Burnstein suggested he read Trumbo's book. The story of Joe Bonham, a good-looking, all-American boy encouraged to fight in World War I by his patriotic father, who urges him to 'be brave', when a German shell explodes near him, Bonham loses his legs, eyes, ears, mouth and nose. After coming to terms with his gruesome circumstances in hospital while surrounded by frankly horrified doctors and nurses, Bonham uses the only part of his physical being he is still able to control – his head – to tap out a message in Morse code: 'Please kill me.' 'James got a lot of input from that,' said Lars. So did Mensch and Burnstein when they heard the demo.

There was another important change to their strategy they'd decided on before going into the studio: unlike *Master of Puppets*, there would be at least one recognisable single and – even more significantly – video on the next album. Despite their public posturing, Dave Thorne says the question of singles had never been completely ruled out. 'When I'd quizzed Mensch about it in the past, he'd always said, "Well, if the right opportunity comes along, the band might consider it."' Thorne speculates that it was probably Elektra who 'they had a *strong* working relationship with' that probably convinced them to at least give it a go. In fact, both James and Lars had come round to the idea of a regular Metallica single and video since the unexpected success that year of *Garage Days* and, in particular, *Cliff 'Em All* – the first clear indication they'd had that they didn't need to make videos by anyone's rules but their own. Mensch and Burnstein, who already understood the huge sales value of having a single and attendant video on MTV, were merely biding their time, waiting for the right moment to broach the subject again with Lars and James.

That moment came with the realisation that 'One' might lend itself well to some sort of visual interpretation that would complement the music in an arresting, artistic way. They became even more excited by the idea when it emerged that Trumbo – a left-wing, pro-peace screenwriter hounded out of Hollywood during the McCarthy-era witch hunts of the 1950s – had actually directed a film version of the book, released in 1971 at the height of the Vietnam War. Might they be able to utilise scenes from it for a possible future video? Burnstein wondered. According to Rasmussen, they had actually bought the rights to the movie 'in order to use it in the video' before they had even begun recording with him: 'It was not much of a movie but they liked the look of it and thought it would look great in a video.' They also utilised some of the special effects on the original soundtrack, layering the sound of machine-gun fire and exploding landmines over the intro to the track.

As 'Stairway to Heaven' became for Led Zeppelin and 'Bohemian Rhapsody' for Queen, 'One' for Metallica represented the band at its musical apotheosis, containing all that was great and original about them in one incident-filled journey, from its quietly lush, heart-rendingly melodic guitar intro to its steadily building mid-section, up to its volcanic, lights-out climax; its lyrics coming straight to the terrifying point: 'Hold my breath as I wish for death . . . Now the world is gone / I'm just one . . .' This was not the standard rock stance of a Van Halen or Mötley Crüe, or even a Guns N' Roses. This was revelation, a song utterly removed from its time; its unforeseen side effect, to alter the circumstances surrounding Metallica for ever. You didn't have to be a Metallica fan to appreciate the artistry of 'One', any more than you have to be a Zeppelin fan to adore 'Stairway'. But if you were, it was a milestone moment; one the band would arguably never equal.

Tellingly, the only other track after 'One' that just about manages to transcend its laboured surrounds is the album's shortest, 'Dyer's Eve', its speedy razor-cut riff a moment of breathe-out relief after the tortuous slabs of prog-metal that precede it. The final track on the album, as climaxes go it's good but not in the same game as 'Damage, Inc.', its success a mark of how heavy-handed the rest of the album sounds next to it. It was also, interestingly, the first Hetfield lyric – 'Dear Mother / Dear Father / What is this hell you have put me through?' – in which he directly addresses some of the issues of his repressed childhood: 'It's basically about this kid who's been hidden from the real world by his parents the whole time he was growing up, and now that he's in the real world he can't cope with it and is contemplating suicide,' Lars explained. 'It's basically a letter from the kid to his parents, asking them why they didn't expose him to the real world . . .' It would not be the last self-portrait from the pen of James Hetfield.

With its flat, wooden sound, its increasingly hollow-sounding anger, its less-palatable-because-it's-more-real bitterness and, most of all, its horribly self-regarding posturing, instead of being the radically 'different' masterpiece Lars had envisaged, *Justice* was a sideways step at best, a miscalculation; at worst a disfiguringly weird statement they would all largely disown as time went by and better albums were made. Its only real saving grace was the extraordinary 'One' – and the fact that it united them in never again wanting to make an album so bleak in its outlook or dire in its musical palate. The days of Metallica the out-and-out heavy metal monster were now numbered.

The great irony was that the place where they seemingly aimed to be most innovatory was the area in which *Justice* sounds most unconvincing of all: the production. As Rasmussen says, 'The sound was totally dry ... thin and hard and loud.' In fact, the whole album seems curiously void of reverb, the special sauce used to make the most mediocre sound sparkle in a mix. Rasmussen doesn't disagree but maintains he delivered 'almost ninety-nine per cent' of the sound he was instructed to get: 'Everybody was really pleased with it once we'd finished and then about a month or so after, people were starting not to be so pleased. But over time it's probably the album that's influenced most metal bands *ever*.' Maybe so. Certainly David Ellefson of Megadeth wouldn't disagree: 'Because it was so progressive, it was complicated. In the early days we all prided ourselves on how fast we played. Then there came a point where we prided ourselves on how complicated we could be. Musical intellectual pride or some bullshit, you know?' He laughs. 'If there was just some bass in here this thing would be fuckin' heavy, you know? Really heavy ...'

As Ellefson suggests, the most glaring omission from the sound on ... *And Justice for All* was any evidence of Jason Newsted's bass; an unforgivable omission given that this was his first album with Metallica, and their first without Cliff Burton. Over the years there have been a variety of reasons given for this, from the accusation that Lars and James simply turned down the sound of Jason's bass in the mix as another part of his hazing; to the suggestion that technically they simply didn't leave enough room in there to hear Jason's bass between James' staccato rhythm guitar and Lars' booming bass drum.

'I was so in the dirt,' said Newsted, speaking more than ten years later. 'I was so disappointed when I heard the final mix. I basically blocked it out, like people do with shit. We were firing on all cylinders, and shit was happening. I was just rolling with it and going forward. What was I gonna do, say we gotta go remix it?' There were, he said, 'still weird feelings going on . . . the first time we'd been in the studio for a real Metallica album, and Cliff's not there'. Working alone with assistant engineer Toby Wright, he had used the same bass set-up as he would for a gig: 'There was no time taken about you place this microphone here, and this one sounds better than that . . . should you use a pick, should you use your fingers? Any of the things that I know now.' Recording three or four songs in a day, 'basically doubling James' guitar parts', he was in the studio alone for less than a week during the whole three-month period the rest of the band were working with Rasmussen. 'Usually nowadays I'd take a day per song. That's what I do on albums. But back then, I didn't even know anything about that shit. Just played it and that was that, right?'

Mike Clink says the lack of bass was an issue even when he was working with them: 'They weren't leaving enough room . . . sonically, to fit the bass in. But that was their concept and I think that if Cliff had been there it might have been a bit different. But with the new member, I felt he didn't have as much to say. I think he was just happy to be there, at that moment. I think Jason just said, "This is the way it is, let's roll with it."' He adds, 'It's also the sound of the guitar. It takes up a lot of room in the sonic spectrum. But ultimately that was the decision of the band and the mixer.' Rasmussen makes the same point about the mix. 'I know for a fact, since I recorded it, that there's *brilliant* bass-playing on that album.' Like Clink, however, Flemming was not responsible for the mix. That task fell to the production team of Mike Thompson and Steven Barbiero, whose previous credits included Whitney Houston, Madonna, the Rolling Stones, Prince, Cinderella, Tesla – and Guns N' Roses' *Appetite for Destruction*.

Mixing took place during May 1988, at Bearsville Studios in Woodstock, where James and Lars sat perched over Thompson and Barbiero's shoulders. Interviewed at the time by *Music & Sound Output* magazine, Lars' and James' comments certainly back up Clink's and Rasmussen's claims that they – and not the producers – were the real architects behind the sound on *Justice*. Asked how it differed from *Master*, Hetfield said: 'Drier.' He went on: 'Everything's way up front and there's not a lot of 'verb or echo. We really went out of our way to make sure that what we put on the tape was what we wanted, so the mixing procedure would be as easy as possible.' Both men complained that they didn't want it to be like *Ride the Lightning*, where 'Flemming was in a reverb daze'. More tellingly, asked what they had learned from the 'upfront and raw' sound of the *Garage Days* EP, Lars specifically mentioned 'that mix', with James elaborating: 'We learned that the bass is too loud.'

'And when is the bass too loud?' Lars chirped in.

'When you can hear it!' they answered together, laughing.

Joey Vera, who'd turned down the chance to do the job Jason eventually got but who was genuinely close to James and Lars – and Cliff – says Jason was 'more than capable' but that he'd heard 'James may have played the bass' on much of *Justice*. He also dismisses the idea that it was part of the ongoing hazing process: 'I'd be surprised if they did anything like that. It would be too malicious and too premeditated.' Instead, he believes it may have been 'this psychological way of them sort of hiding the fact that they were still recovering from what they went through [with Cliff's death] and that they weren't quite sure how to get out of it.' Also, 'They didn't want any attention going away from the fact that they were ploughing ahead ... and the way for them to do that, sonically, is to make the drums and the rhythm guitars the loudest thing you hear.' He concluded, 'When Cliff was gone they had to make it evident that, you know, the two of us is what you're gonna hear ... it was a way for them to sort of heal themselves. Like, you know, we need to be heard, this is how *we're* gonna be doing it. They didn't want to be distracted by who the new bass player was or how that role fit in sonically.'

Whatever the truth, by the time mixing had begun in Woodstock, Metallica was already back out on the road, on the US version of the Monsters of Rock festival: twenty-five dates at the biggest outdoor stadia in America, performing to upwards of 90,000 people a night; fourth on the bill below headliners Van Halen, the Scorpions and fellow Q Prime clients Dokken. I travelled with the band for the opening two dates of the tour in Florida, at the Miami Orangebowl and the Tampa Stadium. 'This has got to be the easiest trip we've ever done,' Lars laughingly told me. You could see what he meant. Although Metallica was on in the middle of the afternoon, they were the hot 'break-out' band of the tour and audiences were uniformly ecstatic. With just a forty-minute set to perform, the band also had an unusual amount of free time to fill. 'I've been drinking since I woke up this morning,' James announced with a belch before they went onstage in Tampa, at the start of the tour.

It wasn't just the drinking they were up to now. 'It was fucking great,' Lars would later boast to *Rolling Stone*. 'Girls knew we were part of the tour and wanted to fuck us, but at the same time we could blend in with the crowd . . . Like, "Who gives a shit? Let's have another rum and Coke and go back in the audience and see what's happening."' Which is exactly what they did in Tampa; photographer Ross Halfin and I walked to the very top tier of seats at the stadium with them, where they dropped their jeans and flashed the audience. The only one who wasn't regularly drunk was Jason, still exulting in his outsider status, nervously smoking weed alone back in his hotel room, or in the company of groupies too young to grasp his lowly status; still counting his blessings for finding himself in such a privileged, financially settled position, still wondering if Metallica would ever really feel like his band too.

There was now a small group of what they called their 'tough tarts' at every show; girls waiting naked in the showers; girls in bikinis they'd given passes to the night before whose names they could no longer remember; girlfriends of boy fans offered to the band almost ritualistically. 'I couldn't figure out why all of a sudden I was handsome,' said Kirk. 'No one had ever treated me like that before in my life.' Both Kirk and Lars were starting to use cocaine more regularly, too. Lars primarily, he said, because 'it gave me another couple of hours' drinking'; Kirk because it brought him out of his shell. And because he liked being out of his head; sitting there, stoned, gazing at horror movies, some on TV, some just playing out in front of him in real time in his hotel room.

The biggest drinker was still James, who would regularly polish off half a bottle of seventy-proof Jägermeister. He was also into the vodka, although his brand had improved: he now favoured Absolut. 'That whole tour was a big fog for me,' James later recalled. 'It was bad coming back to some of those towns later, because there were a lot of dads and moms and husbands and boyfriends looking for me. Not good. People were hating me and I didn't know why . . .'

It wasn't just irate husbands and boyfriends that James was falling foul of. Alcohol brought out the dark, mouthy Mr Hyde to his more usual monosyllabic Dr Jekyll. On a flying visit to London that summer, he had revealed to *Kerrang!* designer Krusher Joule just how black his drinking could make him: 'James and Lars had come to the office to discuss their next tour programme, which Geoff Barton was helping them with. Afterwards I took them for a friendly drink and we ended up at a pub round the corner from where I live in south London. By now of course we're all pretty pissed but we were having a laugh. Then one of my next-door neighbours showed up, a lovely woman, a little bit older and very straight, Mrs Normal. I remember turning round to introduce her and there was Lars standing with his cock out, just looking at her. Anyway, I told him to put it away, she was a taken woman, and we went back to drinking. Later, after the pub closed, we were walking back to my flat across this park and James started going on about "people coming to our country and taking our jobs". I said, "Hang on a minute, mate, you are descended from the people who came into that country and stole it . . . "'

This was not the kind of mission statement James was likely to take kindly to, especially not after an evening of hard drinking. 'All I remember next,' says Krusher, 'is we were going at each other. We literally just kind of ran at each other and hit. And I got him down! Face first, and put him in a headlock. You know, once you've got a headlock on it's a pretty fucking powerful wrestling hold. You just pull back and they're like, "Whoa! Stop!" Lars was standing there, pissing himself laughing. Then I realised that okay, I've got him down but once I let him go he's going to fucking kill me. So I was like, "Lars, help me here. We've got to negotiate. I'll let go of James if he promises he won't hit me and I promise I won't talk any more about the racist shit." So Lars talked to James, I let go of him, nothing else was said and we walked to the flat.'

'Things were starting to happen right then and things became available,' said James, looking back in 2009. 'Women, parties, you name it. We got sucked into that … It was fun.' He admitted that it wasn't funny, though, when he got so drunk he became violent: 'There'd be the happy stage. Then it would get ugly where the world is fucked and fuck you. I became … the clown, then the punk anarchist after that, wanting to smash everything and hurt people. I'd get into fights – sometimes with Lars. That's how resentments would get released, pushing and shoving, throwing things at him. He wants to be the centre of attention all the time and that bothers me because I'm the same way. He's out there charming people, and I'll be intimidating so people will respect me that way.'

Meanwhile, the band's reputation continued to grow with every appearance they made on the tour. When it became known that the Metallica T-shirt was selling more than any other bar the official event tee, even headliners Van Halen began to take notice, with singer Sammy Hagar making a big deal of coming over and spending 'face time' with them both nights I was there. Merchandising was increasingly where it was at for the rock business in the 1980s. Iron Maiden had become millionaires from profits on their merchandising long before their record sales; many American bands whose limited popularity outside the USA only allowed them to play a handful of shows in Europe or the UK could only afford to do so because of the phenomenal sales from their on-site merchandising operation. Gone were the days when the most money concert-goers could be expected to shell out for a show besides their ticket price was a tour programme. By 1988, the business of selling tour merchandise had become almost an exact science with the biggest artists selling over two hundred separate branded items at their shows. Giant merchandising companies such as Brockum in the USA and Bravado in the UK reckoned on selling between $25 and $50 per head, per show, organising their merchandising stands at concert venues so that the most expensive gear – tour jackets, programmes, posters and baseball caps – was situated by the doors, ready to grab the fans' attention as they entered. Smaller, much less expensive items – the two-dollar badges and wristbands, stick-on tattoos and denim patches – would be positioned closer to the door of the actual concert hall. 'The idea was you'd get the big ten- or twenty-dollar hit as they entered, all excited,' says one former merchandising vendor, 'then systematically take every last dollar they had so that by the time they were ready to find their seats, you got their last dollar or two. The idea was for them to leave without a penny in their pockets.' In Japan, where fans were already used to handing over their credit cards for in-concert 'merch', you could make ten times your usual profits. There, the promoters would arrange for the fans to buy their 'mementoes' on their way out of the venue, erecting barriers that snaked towards the exits past a long line of stalls selling every conceivable type of officially branded tat. 'In Japan, they figured on making $100 to $200 dollars per head, per concert-goer, sometimes more.'

Shrewd as ever, Lars and Mensch had taken note of how the most successful merchandising brands in rock built heavily on the element of collectability; how it was no longer enough to simply own a Tour '88 shirt; that the smartest bands produced a new shirt for each new situation they found themselves in. Here the undoubted 'kings of merch' in the 1980s were Iron Maiden, who had their own in-house artist and designer, Derek Riggs, producing both their record sleeves and their most collectable T-shirts and related tour merchandise; his most famous creation that of Eddie, the phantasmagorical monster who adorned every Maiden single and album – and consequently every significant piece of official Maiden merch. 'I liked the idea because it gave you great visual continuity,' Maiden manager Rod Smallwood would tell me, 'and it made the Maiden sleeves just stick out a bit more than the average sort of "could-be-anything" sort of sleeves most rock bands used then. And it became a very important part of Maiden's image, in that way.' Like Metallica, Iron Maiden did not do TV; could not be heard regularly on radio. 'But because Eddie struck such a chord with the Maiden fans, we didn't need to be. Wearing an Eddie T-shirt became like a statement: fuck radio, fuck TV, we're not into that crap, we're into Iron Maiden. And, of course, we've had a lot of fun with Eddie over the years, trying to find new and ever-more outrageous things for him to be and do. Sometimes the ideas come from Derek; usually, though, they either come from me or one of the band. But it can be anybody or anything that inspires us.'

A self-styled English eccentric and former art-school drop-out, Riggs produced thousands of images of Maiden's monstrous mascot in whatever setting the band's career took them: from the very Devil himself on 1983's *Number of the Beast* album, to mummified Egyptian god on the 1985 *Powerslave* sleeve, to laser-packing time-cop on 1986's *Somewhere in Time*. From there it was a short step to having Eddie become the defining image on all their merch; an idea that quickly developed into a goldmine for them. The possibilities were endless: Maiden plays Hawaii? Well, how about a picture of Eddie on a surf-board? Maiden does New York? How about Eddie as King Kong? The fact that Eddie had also transmogrified into part of Maiden's travelling stage show in the 1980s was also not lost on Metallica and Q Prime. With Metallica now planning for their first arena-headlining tour, Lars decided they would need their very own Derek Riggs; even their own Eddie, perhaps. The others did not disagree.

Metallica found their own Derek Riggs in one of James' skateboard pals: Pushead – real name: Brian Schroeder – who he had first met at a Venom concert in 1985. 'He'd seen something I'd done for The Misfits,' Pushead recalled for me, 'and he asked if I could get him a T-shirt of it. I said, sure, no problem. Then he wore it on the back of the *Master of Puppets* album, and that's when the whole Misfits cult thing took off.' When Pushead moved from LA to San Francisco they met up again through the skateboarding scene. Working from his one-bedroom apartment in San Francisco, surrounded by his collection of skulls (cow, monkey, alligator, human) the first thing Pushead did for the band was what became known as the 'Damage, Inc.' T-shirt: 'James wanted something like an animal type thing – like a wild beast … [But] it didn't work for me. So I went to a human skull and made the head a little bigger. James wanted fangs, so I drew them in, and he wanted the mallets, so I did that. Then they all came over and I showed it to them and they loved it.'

Next came the sleeve design for the *Cliff 'Em All* video: the four faces of the Burton-era line-up in suitably fearsome pose, arranged clockwise on a charcoal-grey background. As a fun piece it was just about acceptable. It was with his T-shirts, though, that Pushead's designs really came into their own. Next came the now highly collectible 'Crash Course in Brain Surgery' T-shirt: a gruesomely amusing, typically skull-based example of classic Pushead splat. Now, with the 1988–89 world tour about to begin, they asked him to step up production, beginning with an illustration for the inside sleeve of the *Justice* album cover: a hand, with the word 'f-e-a-r' tattooed onto its fingers, holding a hammer onto which their four – just about identifiable – faces are drawn. It was also a Pushead illustration that adorned the cover of the official 1988–89 Damaged Justice world tour programme, a play on the album's 'blind justice' sleeve: the Statue of Liberty as skeletal fiend, its scales wreathed in bandages, its sword lowered. They would also commission him to come up with sleeve designs for the two singles from the album: 'Harvester of Sorrow' and 'One'. Mainly, Pushead was to concentrate on designs for the numerous merch items that would feature throughout every leg of the tour.

Drawing a great deal of his inspiration at that time from better-known 1980s comic book artists such as Kevin O'Neil, famous for his Torquemada series in the same groundbreaking British weekly, *2000AD*, that gave the world Judge Dredd, Pushead was also indebted, he confessed, to psychedelic Sixties poster legend, Rick Griffin, although he bridled at any suggestion that his own lurid designs may have been similarly drug-induced. 'I've never taken drugs and drawn,' he frowningly told me. 'I've been straight since I was in high school. I don't even drink coffee.' Human skulls were what 'inspire me the most', he said. The only commission still missing from his portfolio, he noted somewhat sulkily, was for a full-bore Metallica album cover. 'I'd love to, obviously,' he said, 'But they haven't asked me yet.' It would be another fifteen years before they did, his outlandish pictures considered simply too cartoonish for the increasingly serious-minded way Metallica came to view their albums, until, finally, in 2003, they came up with an album – *St. Anger* – so clearly trauma-induced that a Pushead design was actually deemed a palatable corrective. In the meantime, so cool was Metallica's new Pushead-designed merch considered, that he quickly became the designer of choice for other huge rock names of the era such as Aerosmith and Mötley Crüe (his skulls-in-straightjacket T-shirt became the second most popular item of merchandise on the Crüe's wildly successful 1989 *Dr Feelgood* tour).

It was in New York at the end of June that Lars says he first realised how far the band had come since their previous American summer tour, with Ozzy, two years before. Hanging out after lunch with Cliff Burnstein, the manager had a treat in store for him. Suggesting they take a swing by the office of their booking agent, Marsha Vlasic at ICM, Lars was astounded when Marsha pulled out a tour schedule of dates provisionally booked for the band's own arena-headlining tour later that year. 'I look down at the first two weeks, and Indianapolis is there. Now, Indianapolis was always this joke between me and Cliff, about how in Indianapolis they just don't get it. That was the barometer. Lo and be-fucking-hold, we go to Indianapolis, and there are nine thousand people there. I remember thinking, "Wow, maybe all those people in Middle America *will* get it."'

There was a break in August, between the end of the Monsters of Rock tour and the start of Metallica's own headline world tour. Lars flew with his wife Debbie to London where they stayed at Peter Mensch's house, between brief visits to Debbie's parents' place in the Midlands. Lars also took the opportunity to do some hanging out backstage at that year's British Monsters of Rock show at Donington, headlined by his old favourites Iron Maiden. Also on the bill were his new favourites Guns N' Roses, who he would actually spend most of his time with, sharing a bottle of Jack Daniel's with Slash – whose trademark top hat Lars was famously pictured wearing at various drunk intervals – and swapping war stories with their notoriously troubled singer Axl, whose white leather jacket with the Guns N' Roses logo emblazoned across its back Lars was so taken with he later order a similar one for himself. (This was made to order by Brockum, the US merchandising company both bands shared, and the subject of much piss-taking from James and the others when it arrived.)

There was also one other band on the bill that Lars was more surreptitiously fascinated with: Megadeth. 'I always got the impression that Lars was always wanting to see what Dave [Mustaine] was up to, and was kind of inquisitive and always intrigued by what Dave did,' says 'Deth bassist David Ellefson now. 'It seemed like Lars especially wanted to retain a friendship and maybe competitively kind of always know what Dave was up to.' It was no surprise to either Ellefson or Mustaine then when Lars wandered over to their dressing room area backstage before they went on. High from his visit with Guns N' Roses, Lars was already too out of it to pick up on the bad vibes emanating from the band. As Ellefson explains, 'The whole group was just in dismay and disarray and dysfunction, because of [heroin] addiction.'

Both Ellefson and Mustaine had been junkies for over four years by then, during which time their 'disease', as Mustaine called it, had cost them a manager, girlfriends and several potentially great line-ups of Megadeth, whose career was, astonishingly, still then in its ascendency. 'I started off using,' Mustaine would tell me matter-of-factly, 'then it turned into abuse and then into full-blown addiction. It got like I couldn't see what was going on. I was powerless ... When Dave [Ellefson] and I first hooked up together, the extent of our getting high was just beer and pot. But we were hanging out with these jazz players, and jazz is synonymous with drugs. And they'd be saying, "Dude, all the greats do heroin! Charlie Parker, Miles Davis, blah blah blah". I was kind of fascinated by the thing of being a junkie too.'

At the time of the Donington '88 show, Mustaine told me, 'I was spending $500 a day ... on that stuff.' Having only just flown in for the show the day before, however, none of the band – with the possible exception of Mustaine – had been able to score. As a result, says Ellefson, they were all 'really, really strung out'. He just about managed to 'get through the show'. What made it worse, he says, is that they had reached that desperate stage as junkies where they were now lying to each other about who had smack and who didn't. For all Ellefson knew, Mustaine had some but wasn't telling him. Or maybe the whole band had somehow been able to get hold of something – and not told him, wanting to keep what little they had for themselves. Paranoia was rampant. 'Yeah, absolutely, because at that point the heroin thing is very dark, is very deceptive, it's very deep. It's just evil. All the dishonesty . . . everything is complete dysfunction, everything is bad.'

Seemingly oblivious to all this, Lars felt welcomed inside the Megadeth dressing room and settled down to 'chew the shit' with his old buddy Dave. Mustaine, in a surprisingly good mood for a junkie allegedly out of gear, even invited Lars up onstage to join them on the encore, which he duly did, singing along on backing vocals to 'Anarchy in the UK'. The crowd, grasping the significance of what was happening, dutifully cheered and played its part. Then the band and Lars staggered off back to the dressing room area, the Metallica drummer who had plotted his downfall with his arm around Dave Mustaine's neck. I was also there that day and recall registering only mild surprise at this unexpected turn of events. Lars liked to hang out, everyone knew that. And maybe big bad Dave had finally forgiven him. Maybe . . .

I was more perturbed when, wandering around the backstage area an hour or so later, I spotted what I imagined to be some drunken reveller face down in the dirt, barely moving. Concerned at his lifeless state, I went over to see if perhaps he was in need of some help, only to find, when I managed to turn him over, that it was Lars. He got to his feet very unsteadily, grinning, though, as only the seriously stoned do when they're feeling pleased with themselves. 'Hey, Mick,' he slurred, flinging his arms around my neck, 'how ya doing?' He started giggling. Wow, I thought, he must be really drunk. Then he pulled back and I noticed his eyes. They were utterly pinpricked, his face a mask of sweat.

'What have you done?' I asked, concerned.

'Been hanging out,' he giggled.

'Are you okay? Do you need help? Can you even stand?'

'I'm fine,' he drooled. He walked off, swaying as he went.

Fortunately, Lars' excesses were not confined specifically to drugs and alcohol. Still the same teenage nerd at heart that had misspent his youth collecting tapes and bootlegs when he should have been practising on the tennis court, Brian Tatler – delighted that Metallica had, yet again, decided to release a recording of an old Diamond Head song, 'The Prince', on the B-side of their forthcoming 'Harvester of Sorrow' single – recalls travelling down to London to hang out with Lars at his hotel, going to Shades to buy Metallica bootlegs (Lars already had over forty in his hotel room that he'd collected on tour). When Lars suggested they return to the Midlands together for Sunday lunch with Debbie's parents, Brian assumed he meant they take the train. 'Fuck that,' said Lars, and simply hailed a taxi. The bill, which Lars paid in cash: £180. Plus sizeable tip. 'He's always been incredibly generous like that,' says Tatler. That was the first time, though, he felt, that Lars had demonstrated any sign of rock star excess.

The fourth Metallica album, ... And Justice for All, was finally released on 5 September, just as Master of Puppets was officially certified platinum. Master had taken eighteen months to sell its first million copies in America; Justice would take just nine weeks, peaking at Number Six, their highest US chart position yet. Reviews were uniformly positive, with Kerrang! summing up the general view when it concluded that the album 'will finally put Metallica into the big leagues where they belong'. At record company level, however, behind closed doors there were serious concerns. Although the album would eventually match its American sales in Britain and Europe, it would take much longer to do so. Dave Thorne at Phonogram, who considered the production 'appalling ... particularly the lack of bass on it', spent the first few weeks of its release defending it to 'large numbers of opinionated people in the record company [who] were coming knocking on my door going, "This record sounds shit, what's the matter with it?"'

Nevertheless, the album went straight into the UK chart, reaching Number Four, an unqualified commercial success for an act that had never broken the Top Forty with an album before. The British and European legs of the Damaged Justice tour were also a sell-out, beginning in Budapest a week after the album's release. The tour reached Britain in October, where they sold out three nights at the Hammersmith Odeon. The big surprise of the tour was the band's new stage show, their first attempt at anything elaborate, featuring a twenty-foot replica of the album sleeve's blindfolded and bound Statue of Liberty – nicknamed Edna after Iron Maiden's Eddie – which collapsed melodramatically at the endless climax to ' . . . And Justice for All' each night, its head falling off as if guillotined. This was the era of the heavy metal pantomime as acceptable stage spectacle – led by Maiden's ubiquitous Eddie figure, now brought to life for the encores each night, and Dio's even sillier dragon (nicknamed Denzel), which singer Ronnie James Dio would 'do battle' with onstage – and in this context Edna's plummet to disgrace every night was almost dignified by comparison. Nevertheless, it could have its comic, Spinal Tap-esque moments, too, on the nights when the statue simply refused to collapse or just its head would roll off the stage into the audience, or half an arm would fall off, swaying gently before toppling onto the drum riser.

These were minor concerns, however; day-to-day cares easily overcome in the bar of the hotel every night. The band was already thinking ahead. Taking a wrong turn towards a dressing room one night in Newcastle, I found Lars and Mensch huddled together over a cassette player, scrolling back and forth through the seven-minute-plus 'One' looking for places where they might be able to edit it down to a length suitable for US radio to play. Seeing immediately that I had intruded on a sensitive moment – certainly for Lars, for whom the concept of editing album-length tracks into radio-friendly singles had always been antithetical to the Metallica philosophy – I accepted Mensch's suggestion to 'get the hell out' and closed the door behind me. In retrospect, though, it was exactly this sort of pragmatism that would soon separate Metallica from the likes of Iron Maiden and Motörhead; groups they had grown up worshipping at the altars of but were now poised to leave far behind – on every level. It was no longer enough for Lars Ulrich to be in 'the fastest, heaviest' band in America, he now had his sights set on a much larger glittering prize. Not just best, but biggest.

As Mensch later put it, Metallica were 'like the Grateful Dead of heavy metal. They can sell so much on their own, as they are. To take it further, it means edit a song for a single, do a video – all the usual stuff. And they realise that's the only way to expand the audience. It's not like the Sixties, when something really outside could make a mainstream impact.' Or as Lars commented: 'My whole view is that if taking the last guitar solo out could get the song out to more people who would hear, then buy the album, hear a fuller version and get turned on to Metallica music, then fine. "One" is nearly eight minutes long and has twenty-three guitar solos, so we could trim it a bit.'

Released in February 1989, in the middle of their first arena headline tour of America, what would really turn 'One' into Metallica's first really significant singles success, however, was not the radio-edit, although that played an important part; it was their agreeing finally to make a video to go with it. Another former hard-and-fast rule broken, it came with another plausible bit of Lars philosophy to explain it. 'If it had been crap, we wouldn't have put it out,' he said simply. 'That was the deal. But it worked so well, we thought, sure, why not?' Filmed in what looks like an underground bomb shelter – actually a disused warehouse in Long Beach – in December 1988, for a first video 'One' was a stunningly accomplished piece of work. Built around actual footage from the movie version of *Johnny Got His Gun*, starring Jason Robards, intercut with stark, strobe-lit shots of the band performing the song, the 'One' video would do for Metallica what none of their records or live performances, with or without Cliff, had yet been able to: both enhance their reputation as musical innovators and reposition the band centrally as mainstream rock stars.

It almost didn't happen, though, after the band was turned down by a succession of top-drawer video directors, before coming to an arrangement with Michael Salomon, best known previously for his work with Dolly Parton and Glen Campbell. The major issue for Salomon was finding the right balance between band performance and film footage. 'It's a complicated story and to do it with just one or two sound-bites here and there really wouldn't have made it,' he later reflected. In the end, Salomon decided to go with his gut instincts and simply make the best video he could, putting the band's vanity second, covering almost every solo with film footage, including snatches of dialogue occasionally obscuring the music. 'The musician side of them said, "That's not cool, we don't get to hear the music." I think they realised, though, that the story element was more import-ant.' This was an important lesson they would learn well. All their best future videos would relate back to the risks they took with 'One', all becoming mini-features in their own right, intercut with all sorts of images, of war, of prisoners, of nightmares, road trips, dreamscapes, white horses . . . eventually even girls.

Bill Pope shot the black-and-white performance footage at the same Long Beach warehouse where he had previously shot videos for Peter Gabriel and U2. Here, the band did put its foot down, insisting that the video showed them playing exactly the right notes, singing the right words, everything synched as though they were really playing, not just miming. 'We decided if it was not what we wanted we'd throw it in the garbage can,' said Lars. However, 'Pretty early on we felt we had something special in our hands. Whether it was great or shit, it meant something.'

The full, unedited video was nearly eight minutes long. Like the single, however, it was also made available to TV in edited form, minus the film footage, with a fade on the final couple of minutes of music. 'They never really objected,' said Salomon. 'They held off their judgement until they saw the final piece. By that point, three or four weeks later, they had gotten used to the idea.' Even then it was so at odds with prevailing trends in Eighties rock video, one MTV executive told Cliff Burnstein the only place 'One' would be seen was on the news. Undeterred, Q Prime applied its customary behind-the-scenes muscle and the full 'One' video was premiered on MTV on the night of 22 January 1989, on that week's edition of *Headbanger's Ball*. It instantly became the most requested video on MTV.

Smelling a hit, both Elektra and Phonogram prepared to issue the single in multiple formats, along with the specially edited versions for radio. By February, 'One' had become the first Metallica single to reach the US Top Forty, peaking at Number Thirty-Five; while in the UK it reached Number Thirteen. Dave Thorne, who became 'very involved' in the UK and European campaign for both the *Justice* album and, specifically, 'One', immediately grasped its potential for changing the whole perception of Metallica: 'I did some research and discovered that the book had been banned under the McCarthy era and was still unavailable in the UK or Europe. So I went to the publisher in America and we bought like five hundred copies then distributed them to the media so they could read the story and under-stand what the song or the video was all about. That had an enormous latent impact in getting people to realise that this was a band that wasn't just about noise and speed and headbanging. There was a deep, meaningful side to it.'

Under Thorne's aegis, Phonogram sent out the 'One' single with the book and a VHS cassette of the video as a press pack to shrewdly targeted music press people on *Sounds, NME, Melody Maker, Q* and numerous broadsheet newspaper critics, plus key figures at Radio 1, and all the commercial networks that aired weekly rock shows on their stations. 'It was a watershed moment. We definitely felt that.' 'One' single-handedly moved Metallica out of the same bracket in people's perceptions as Iron Maiden or Black Sabbath, and closer to that elevated realm of mainstream rock stars who actually had something to say: 'Metallica became the band that everybody revered because they just seemed to be able to take things to a level that the other [thrash] bands couldn't, and also do it in a way that was just so cool and understated really.'

'One' also achieved another landmark for Metallica when it attracted the attention of that year's Grammy academicians, the band becoming shortlisted for the newly created award: 'Best Hard Rock /

Metal Performance Vocal or Instrumental'. '"One" proved to us that things we thought of as evil aren't as evil as we thought,' said Lars, accommodatingly, 'as long as we do it our way.' The Grammys show took place at the Shrine Auditorium in LA on 22 February, where the band was invited to perform their much-discussed new song. It was a momentous occasion, the first time an unashamedly 'heavy metal' band had actually played live at the Grammys – even though it was the truncated, five-minute version of the song. Shrouded in shadows, colours muted so that they looked almost black and white, it was a stupendous performance from a band that Kirk later admitted was 'very nervous' playing for all the suits and ties. 'We were like diplomats or representatives for this genre of music.' There was a sense of outrage, however, when the band missed out on the award itself, that honour inexplicably going to Jethro Tull for their *Crest of a Knave* album – a decision so unexpected that none of Jethro Tull was there to accept it. Metallica put a brave face on it, like the whole thing was beneath them – they even suggested adding a sticker to the *Justice* album with the words: 'Grammy Award Losers'. But privately Lars was seething. 'Let's face it, they really fucked up,' he told me. 'Jethro Tull best heavy metal band? I mean, fucking come on!'

They didn't have time to stew on it, the US tour resuming just three days later. Along for the ride as support act was another up-and-coming Q Prime act, Queensrÿche, who had just released their own break-out album, *Operation: Mindcrime*. Although the two bands got on well as people – 'We drank a lot,' laughs singer Geoff Tate – musically, Queensrÿche saw themselves as occupying higher intellectual ground than the likes of Metallica, and while they were appreciative of the boost being offered such a high-profile tour would give them, having to win over Metallica's hardcore crowd each night was an exceptionally difficult proving ground. 'We were playing to a predominantly male audience,' says Tate, 'usually people of lower income, not a lot of education, heavy drinking, you know, heavy drug use ... go to the show and get violent and rage against society, kind of thing, you know? My world is not good and so I'm gonna take it out on the guy standing next to me, kind of person ... we met with a very violent resistance at first … every night it was like going out to battle. There were bottles flying and projectiles. I still have many scars from that tour. I think everybody in the band does, yeah.' He laughs again. 'You're talking about a bunch of idiots as an audience. I mean, really people that are uneducated. The way they react to anything new, of course, is with fear. That's a very typical human reaction but again as our forty-five-minute show progressed I think we won over a lot of people.'

There were other concerns, too; two occasions where young Metallica fans had committed suicide; in one instance, leaving a note requesting 'Fade to Black' be played at their funeral; in another, leaving a suicide note in which the lyrics to the same song were quoted. 'It's not something that brightens your day, but what can you do?' said Lars, pointing out that they had also received 'thousands of letters from kids telling us how that song gave them the will to live'. Then, on arriving for a show at the Memorial Coliseum in Corpus Christi, Texas, they awoke to a call from Mensch 'who said there's some shit going on – the local TV station is making a big deal because this kid apparently took some acid or other fucked-up drugs and went on a killing rampage, and the one thing that stuck in this witness's mind when he shot someone at point-blank range was that he was quoting one of our lyrics – "No Remorse".' Lars shook his head, disbelievingly. 'He got sentenced to death and there was this big yahoo when he stood up in the courtroom and quoted the lyrics again. But believe me,' he added nonchalantly, 'it's not something I have a day-to-day interest in.'

Having a 'day-to-day interest' in anything outside of the tour's own dizzying momentum was becoming impossible. After this leg of the US tour ended in April, it was off to New Zealand and Australia for the first time: the start of the biggest and most exhausting leg of the entire Damaged Justice tour, six months that would take them to Japan, then on to Hawaii, Brazil, Argentina, and back for another swing through North America. Support on most of these shows came from The Cult, another band with a substantial back catalogue now on the cusp of multi-platinum success, thanks to the elevated production work on their latest album, *Sonic Temple*, by producer of the moment, Bob Rock – a fact not lost on Lars Ulrich, in his never-ending quest to keep up with the rock Joneses.

I caught up with the band again during their May 1989 five-date tour of Japan, where I saw them play two shows at the Yoyogi Olympic Pool arena in Tokyo. They had been on the road for the best part of a year by that point but apart from James' stomach problems, which he appeared to be trying to alleviate by downing as much Sapporo beer and hot flasks of sake as he could, they seemed to be holding up well and in generally good humour. Money had come in and they no longer lived together as one, but they still went out together as a gang – when they were on the road, at least. All except for Jason, whose time in the shadows seemed not quite to be over yet, although the hazing had spread out more, aimed as often now at Lars or Kirk, but never at James – or not to his face, anyway.

Late at night they went to the Lexington Queen, a well-known hang-out for rock bands since the days of Led Zeppelin and Deep Purple, where it was said you could get a free drink just by mentioning guitarist Ritchie Blackmore's name. Strangely, the place seemed to be home also to several dozen beautiful young American models, dancing around in negligees, flown in apparently for regular work in Japanese TV ads and glossy magazines. There were also hundreds of young female Japanese fans who followed the band wherever it went, screaming out their names and begging for a chance to present them with the numerous gifts it is the Japanese custom to give. 'Kitten toothbrushes, Snoopy towels [and] pictures of yourself stumbling drunk into the hotel from the night before,' as James ungallantly put it. As Lars and I walked back to the Roppongi Hotel late one night, a gaggle of young female fans suddenly sprang out at us from where they'd been hidden in the bushes, crying and screaming, 'Rars! Rars!' One lucky girl got her wish and would not be returning to the bushes – not that night, at least.

At another, more private moment, I sat with the band having a meal, and listened as they talked about the new houses they had all recently purchased, or were in the process of procuring, on the solid advice of their accountants, ready for their return home as millionaires for the first time later that year. They were still new enough to wealth, though, to feign indifference, Lars protesting that he drove around in 'a piece-of-shit Honda'; James in a truck. Yet all I saw them in were limos and the private jet they travelled in while on tour in America – the same one previously used by Bon Jovi and before that Def Leppard. 'We put some money back into how we travel while we're on the road,' said Lars, 'because we're out there a long time and it just makes the whole thing easier.'

The more he went on, however, the more the others sniggered and made faces. 'How about that house you just bought?' teased Kirk. 'Where is it, like on a mountain?'

Lars looked at him, like shut the fuck up. It turned out the house he'd bought was situated so high on a hill that he was considering having an elevator built just so people could get to his front door.

'Do it,' I said. 'If you can afford it, why the hell not?'

'Yeah,' he said, 'you're right. I will . . .'

And he did.

ELEVEN
LONG BLACK LIMOUSINE

One on One studios, North Hollywood; late afternoon sliding slowly into evening; everybody's thoughts now turning to dinner.

Bob Rock and I sat together in a side leisure room chatting idly about a new vegetarian restaurant I'd discovered on Sunset called The Source. The sort of place where dudes wearing hemp shirts and knee-length shorts showed up with chicks in no shoes. Way too cool for school but the food made it all worth the while.

I was telling Bob about the grilled tofu, to die for, I said. He smacked his lips. Then James walked in and the atmosphere instantly changed, like the bad guy entering the saloon via the swinging doors, the piano player stopping mid-song, the guys at the poker table staring but pretending not to.

He didn't acknowledge us, just grabbed a seat and sat looking at the TV, the volume turned low.

'Red meat,' he said suddenly, in that deep slaughterhouse voice so familiar now from the records. 'White bread ...'

We got the message. Bob, already more used to this than me after months holed up in the studio with him, switched gear immediately.

'Nothing beats a good burger, though,' he said. 'You know, you can give the kids all the vegetables and good stuff in the world but if you really love 'em you just gotta take 'em out for a good burger once in a while.'

'Golden fuckin' arches,' growled James, still not looking at us but apparently tuned in.

'Yeah!' said Bob enthusiastically. 'They do a great deal at weekends now, too. Like a kids' burger and fries meal, with a Coke for like a buck and a half.'

'Fuckin' A,' said James, reaching for the remote. He began zapping through channels till he came to the news. Bush was on talking up his victory in the Gulf.

'I don't get it why he didn't just keep going till he reached Baghdad,' I said, just throwing it out, like one of the regular guys.

'Yeah,' said Bob. 'Like finish the job . . .'

'Nuke 'em till they glow,' said James.

Oh god, I thought. I can't keep up with this. I can't tell any more who's joking and who's not. Red meat, I thought. White bread . . . Jesus, where am I?

The summer of 1990 found Metallica at another crossroads. On paper, they were now one of the biggest, most fêted heavy metal bands in the world. Earlier that year they had won the Grammy they should have picked up a year before, this time for 'One'. They would also win a second Grammy in 1991 for their cover of Queen's 'Stone Cold Crazy', bashed-out as-live, *Garage Days*-style, for the double *Rubáiyát* album, a compilation of cover tracks to mark the fortieth anniversary of Elektra Records. 'Let's put it this way,' Lars told me at the time, 'if we release anything for the rest of the Nineties, every year we'll get a Grammy for it just because they fucked up that first year.' It was a prediction that turned out to be remarkably prescient. In terms of where Metallica went next, however, in reality their options had narrowed so dramatically in the wake of the one-dimensional *... And Justice for All* album that their choices were suddenly few. They could carry on the way they were going, make 'another Metallica album', sell another couple of million worldwide, and settle for being their generation's Iron Maiden, who had settled for being Judas Priest, who had settled for being Black Sabbath, who had settled for never being quite as important as Led Zeppelin, who were still not, in the Nineties, regarded as being remotely as interesting as Cream or even Jeff Beck, who, let's face it, were never going to be as highly regarded by history as Jimi Hendrix or The Who, both of whom lagged behind the Stones, The Beatles, Bob Dylan, and so on back into rock antiquity. Or Metallica could do what they had always insisted they would when the time came and do something utterly unexpected and fabulous. Rewrite the rulebook.

Easier said than done, of course, in an era when it was already felt that it had all been seen and heard before. There was, however, one area left that a band as defiantly uncommercial – on the surface, at least – as Metallica might aim for, which could not have been foreseen. To make the one record – the one outrageous move – they had sworn as kids they would fight to the death not to make. Yet the one, as men, they were now swiftly coming to realise their musical lives might depend on. That is, something so blatantly, unprepossessingly commercial no one – not even Lars Ulrich and James Hetfield – could have seen it coming.

First, though, like reluctant virgins on their wedding nights, the boys in the band would have to be wooed. Whatever else it was, *Justice* was a hit. Yet they would not be able to get away with making another album as ponderous and unfriendly to newcomers as that. Not if they wanted their career to continue on its upward trajectory. The question was: did they have the courage to try and take Metallica to the next level? Or had they, perhaps, already reached their highest plateau? How, in fact, did Lars and James see the story of Metallica panning out now that they had reached this point? The person who would put these questions to them was Cliff Burnstein.

Lars later recalled what he characterised as 'a very famous meeting in Toronto' in July 1990, at a festival where Metallica was appearing second on the bill to Aerosmith: 'Me, James and Cliff Burnstein sat down and Cliff said, "If we want to really go for it, we can take this to a lot more people. But that will mean we have to do certain things that on the surface seem like the same games other people play." But we were the ones playing that game, which makes it us, Metallica, just doing something else. And it was nothing to do with the music, it was the way we handled everything outside the music. The idea was to cram Metallica down everybody's fucking throat all over the fucking world.' Or as Kirk Hammett put it to me in 2005: 'We said, okay, we're gonna make an album, we're gonna put a lot of shorter songs on it, we're gonna get these fucking songs on the radio and we're just gonna indoctrinate the entire universe with Metallica. That was our goal and that's what we did! And it took everyone as a big surprise . . .'

It certainly did. What were these 'certain things' Burnstein spoke of, though; what 'games' would they need to play? Top of the list was finding a producer who could drag Metallica out of the heavy metal ghetto *Justice* had left them to rot in. Someone who understood the rock genre intimately enough to deliver an album that would retain the credibility the band had painstakingly built up over the years, but for whom the words 'hit single' were not some form of blasphemy. Someone, above all, with a proven record of mainstream success but who also had a detailed enough knowledge of what Metallica's music was at least supposed to be about. In the summer of 1990, there were very few names that sprang easily to mind able to fulfil such a remit. The biggest, most fashionable rock band in the world was then Guns N' Roses, whose *Appetite* album had now sold nearly ten million copies worldwide, and Metallica had already tried – and failed – working with their producer Mike Clink. The only other rock album in recent times that had emulated those numbers and made any sort of statement musically had been Def Leppard's *Hysteria*. But the producer of that album, Robert John 'Mutt' Lange, was a genius-perfectionist who used the studio like a blank canvas upon which he 'painted' his own highly evolved spectrum of sounds. A brilliant multi-instrumentalist in his own right, 'Mutt' was the kind of producer who insisted guitarists strike one string at a time, over and over again in order for him to build up the sound of the chords himself on computer; whose intricately layered vocals – lead and backing – comprised dozens of voices in harmony and counterpoint, interwoven and spun like silk; the sort of visionary technician who had long since abandoned the idea of using a 'live' drummer in the studio – years before it became the norm – so he could create more persuasive percussion sounds himself; a maverick conductor directing queer lightning. The idea of putting 'Mutt' together with Metallica was like asking a Formula One racing champion to pilot a chariot of horses, albeit highly trained thoroughbreds whose odds on winning were now seductively short, but animals nonetheless. Lange had also recently made it clear to Q Prime that he felt he had taken Def Leppard – until then, their best-selling, starriest clients – as far as he could and that he was now looking for something new, something more demanding from whatever project he next took on. Not remodelling Franken-stein's monster to look like Marilyn Monroe.

Q Prime did have one suggestion, though: a Canadian producer named Bob Rock, whose stock was riding high for the incredible jobs he had done on two of the biggest-selling rock albums in America of the past year: The Cult's *Sonic Temple* and Mötley Crüe's *Dr Feelgood*. James, true to his nature, was sceptical: 'No one fucks with our shit.' And months later, when I paid a visit to One on One studios to interview Lars about how the new album was coming along, he would tell me they had ended up working with Rock almost by accident. But the truth was Lars had needed little persuading, having become enthralled by the volcanic drum sounds on both Cult and Crüe albums.

'We'd never really liked the mixing on *Justice*, *Master* or *Lightning*,' he told me earnestly. 'So we were thinking, who can we get in to do the mixing? We felt it was time to make a record with a huge, big, fat, low end and the best-sounding record like that in the last couple of years – not songs, but sound – was the last Mötley Crüe album. So we told [Peter Mensch], "Call this guy and see if he wants to mix the record." He came back and said not only did Bob want to mix the record, but he saw us live when we played Vancouver, and really liked us and would like to produce the album. Of course, we said, "We're Metallica, no one tells us what to do!" But slowly, over the next few days, we thought maybe we should let our guard down and at least talk to the guy. Like, if the guy's name really is Rock, how bad can he be?'

This was disingenuous, to say the least. Lars had been as intrigued by the prospect of possibly bringing in Bob Rock as he had been previously with Mike Clink. Hanging out with The Cult on tour the previous summer, the *Sonic Temple* album had been a favourite on his Walkman, as had *Dr Feelgood*. He was also big rock star buddies now with both Crüe drummer Tommy Lee and The Cult's Matt

Sorum. He had been awestruck by what Rock had done for them in the studio. Plus, and most importantly, if Metallica was to go 'next-level', as Lars put it, with their next album it was clear they could no longer go it alone in the studio with Flemming Rasmussen. They just needed coaxing in the right direction. Shrewdly, Q Prime agreed to put Rasmussen on retainer for a month, in case things with Rock didn't work out, à la Clink, but from the moment Lars and James – alone – agreed to fly up to Vancouver and meet with Rock at his home, in the wake of their 'very famous meeting' with Burnstein just weeks before, the scene was set for Metallica to make what would be the most radical move of their career: go for broke with a big hit-making record. 'We told [Bob] that live we have this great vibe and that's what we wanted to do in the studio,' Lars said, 'It's really funny 'cos he turned around and said, "When I saw you guys live and then heard your record I thought that you hadn't come close to capturing what you do in a live situation." He basically said the same thing as we had and from then on we thought that maybe we shouldn't be so stubborn and maybe see where the fuck this would bring us.'

Where it brought them to was a place where James, who had once written 'Kill Bon Jovi' on his guitar, was now ready to spend months in the studio with one of the chief architects behind Bon Jovi's biggest hits; the place where Mötley Crüe, leaders of the selfsame scene Metallica had originally fled LA to escape, had made their biggest-selling album. What they hadn't bargained for was how hard Rock would make them work for their money.

Like all the best producers, Bob Rock was himself a more than able musician, adept on guitar, bass and keyboards. He had started out in his own band, The Payola$, who had a hit in Canada with the single, 'Eye of a Stranger'. The band later metamorphosed into Prism but it was his work as engineer with Prism producer Bruce Fairbairn at Little Mountain Sound studios in Vancouver that really made his name in the music business. Fairbairn's big break came through his work in the early 1980s on behalf of another, more successful Canadian band, Loverboy, who enjoyed a number of hits there and in North America with Bruce as producer and Bob as his engineer and point man. Working together and separately out of Little Mountain, they had created platinum-selling albums for second-division leaders such as Survivor, Loverboy and Black 'N Blue, before really hitting the big time in 1986 with Bon Jovi, whose *Slippery When Wet* album – and attendant hit singles 'You Give Love a Bad Name' and 'Livin' on a Prayer' – had single-handedly saved the band's till-then faltering career. (They had been on the verge of being dropped by their label – Phonogram, the same label Metallica was now signed to – when Fairbairn worked his magic, turning it into the biggest rock album of the year.)

Since then, Fairbairn had also helped rescue Aerosmith's career with the hit-laden albums *Permanent Vacation* (1987) and *Pump* (1989). By the summer of 1990, *Pump* had been on the charts for almost a year, had housed four chart singles, and was on its way to selling four million copies in the USA – exactly the kind of album, in short, that Metallica now set their sights on having. These achievements came at a price, though. As Aerosmith bassist Tom Hamilton later recalled, the positives of working with Fairbairn were that he was 'a very big, no-bullshit, in-focus, demanding producer who made sure the conditions were right to let the creativity happen. I mean, this guy had the ability to make us play better than even we thought we could play.' The price: 'A lot of it was painful because we gave up some control, big-time.'

When Rock ventured out as a producer in his own right – his first international success came with the debut Kingdom Come album in 1988 – he was determined to do things his way. Yet it was Fairbairn's uncompromising methods he employed to reach his goals. 'With Bruce, we kind of grew up together,' said Bob. 'Bruce's style of production is so different to mine, though. But the one thing I really got from him was about really concentrating on the performance end of it rather than a perfectionism kind of thing, which may sound bizarre coming from me but that's what I really try and concentrate on. I really try to facilitate musicians to be comfortable and really fill in the blanks when it comes to their needs, to get what they want accomplished.' Or as Mötley Crüe bassist and band leader Nikki Sixx later recalled of his time with Rock: 'Bob whipped us like galley slaves. His line was, "That just isn't your best." Nothing was good enough.' Rock would make guitarist Mick Mars spend weeks doubling a guitar part over and over again until it was synchronised to perfection. As for the lead vocals, some days singer Vince Neil 'would only get a single word on tape that Bob liked. Bob was critical, demanding and a stickler for punctuality.' He went on: 'No one had ever pushed us to the limits of our abilities before or kept demanding more than we thought we had to give until we discovered that we actually did have more to give.' He admitted 'the process was the antithesis of every punk principle I had held fast to as a teenager', but concluded, 'at the same time, I wanted an album I was finally proud of'.

Similarly, Metallica. Although they already had albums they were fiercely proud of, not least *Master of Puppets*, what they now craved – needed – was an album that opened their music up to the same audience that bought The Cult, Mötley, Guns N' Roses and, yup, even Bon Jovi. They wanted it all and Bob Rock was to be the one to help them get it, they decided. The only snag – on paper – was Rock's well-known reluctance to record anywhere but Little Mountain. However, as Lars told me, 'We really didn't want to do it in Vancouver – everyone comes to him. For a while I didn't think it was going to work out. Bob's got a big family and he wasn't that keen on coming to LA. Then when we played him the stuff I could see his eyes light up. We'd built a little eight-track studio in my house and made some rough demos; just me on drums and James.' The clincher was when they played him the roughs of an epic new track called 'Sad but True': 'It was like, boom! From there it was pretty much a done deal.'

Recording had begun the first week of October, 1990. By the time I caught up with Lars again at the start of 1991, he was obviously thrilled with the way it had been going. 'Looking back on our last four albums, they were great records. I'm not going to say anything bad about them. But we never thought that we'd done one where you think, there it is. That one album is it. You're never gonna be able to make a record like that but as close as you can get to that one album, this is fucking it,' he enthused. 'The new stuff that we've been writing is like a breath of fresh air. We're just really excited in a way that I don't think we've been excited before. Bob says he thinks it shows we've got a lot of soul . . . a lot of emotions that we don't let out easily, 'cos we're very guarded as people. He says that he could see through that right away. He says that one of his things on this album was to try and let us take down our guard and let out the shit that's in there.'

It was also, Lars confessed, 'us getting pretty bored with the direction of the last three albums. They were all different from each other, but they were all going in the same direction. You know, long songs, longer songs, even longer songs . . . It was time to take a sharp turn. The only way to do that would be to write one long song to fill the whole album or write songs that were shorter than we had done before. And that's what we did. I don't need to tell you again how I feel about being pigeonholed with the whole thrash metal thing. But the new shit's just got a whole new vibe and feel that I never knew Metallica were capable of.' The key was to begin by making sure the songs stayed focused. Consigned to the bin were numbers that lasted nine and ten minutes and went through several 'movements': 'I used to think it was cool, a sign of our fuck-you attitude to being commercial. Now I realise it was just basically because we couldn't play. It wasn't until we started with Bob that we really learned how to nail a riff or a rhythm or whatever. It's actually a lot harder to do but you don't know that until you finally try.'

Lars, in particular, would discover just hard that was when Bob insisted he simply wasn't up to the job and should take lessons in order to bring him up to speed. A room at the studio was set aside for Lars to spend several hours a day 'practising', upon which James pinned a handwritten sign: 'LARS' CLOSET'. Getting the drums 'right' would, in fact, set the project back several weeks. In the meantime, Bob worked with James on getting the best of the near two-dozen songs he had written with Lars – and occasionally Kirk (as with *Justice*, Newsted would achieve only one co-songwriting credit on the album) – into what the taskmaster producer considered recordable shape. Initially, this proved almost as arduous as coaxing a decent drum track out of Lars. For the first time in his life James, who had never been told his lyrics were not good enough, found himself rewriting verses, sharpening up choruses. In particular, Rock worked hard on getting it into the singer's head that it was easier – and better – to use one word where previously he'd been used to using several. Single words could be broken down into syllables that sufficed for entire lines in a song, as with the chorus of one of the potential singles, 'Enter Sandman', on which Hetfield's original lines were broken down into single words, using the syllables to stretch and tease the melody out of them. *En ... ter ... night ... / Ex ... it ... light ...*

James also came armed with something he never had before: an actual from-the-heart love song. Written while on the road and missing Kristen, the key line 'Never opened myself this way' summing up a musical moment unlike any one might have expected from Hetfield or Metallica, even as they strived for a hit. Suddenly, it seemed, Everyteen had turned into Everyman.

Speaking of it nearly twenty years later, James admitted that at first he 'didn't even want to play it for the guys. It was so heartfelt, so personal to me. I thought that Metallica could only be these songs about destroying things, headbanging, bleeding for the crowd ... I certainly did not think it was a Metallica song. When the guys heard it they were amazed at how much they, I guess, related to it. It turned out to be a pretty big song on that record [that] touched a lot of people.' It was also, he reflected in another interview around the same time, more than the usual confessional power ballad. It was 'about a con-nection with your higher power, lots of different things'. He recalled being invited to a Hell's Angels Clubhouse in New York where 'they showed me a film that they'd put together of one of the fallen brothers' and the soundtrack for the film was 'Nothing Else Matters': 'Wow. This means a lot more than me missing my chick, right? This is brotherhood. The army could use this song. It's pretty powerful.'

Powerful yes, but made even more so by Rock's last-minute add-ition of an orchestra, its score arranged by Michael Kamen. A pro-duction touch the band would never have considered themselves, their first reaction to it was negative. Listening back to it late one night, however, they suddenly saw the light. 'I used to call James Dr No,' Rock recalled. 'Whenever I was about to make a suggestion that seemed even a little off the wall, he'd say no before I'd even finished the first sentence.' It was the same when he also created a subtle bed of cellos for another sweepingly balladic track, 'The Unforgiven', underpinning the obvious Morricone influence with something even more impressive. Or the sitar-like guitar intro to 'Wherever I May Roam'; the bugling refrain from Leonard Bernstein's 'America' at the start of 'Don't Tread on Me'; the marching-band drums and bagpipe guitar at the start of 'The Struggle Within'. Even on the more obvious thrash-derived numbers such as 'Holier Than Thou', 'Through the Never' or 'The Struggle Within', Rock's influence meant the band now sauntered into view where previously they had simply battered at the door until it splintered; pedestrian thrash-templates transformed by the imaginative sum of the production into something greater than their otherwise predictable individual parts.

At other times, the producer simply insisted that they play together as a band live in the studio, as on the rhythm track to the monumental 'Sad but True'. Recalled Kirk: 'The energy coming off all of us playing was so intense and so locked into the groove, with so much attitude, that Bob Rock said, "We could take this track right here off the floor and put it straight on the album because all you guys played your asses off."' It was a musical adventurousness mirrored by Hetfield's new boldness with his lyrics. No longer did the words come from watching CNN, as they had for much of *Justice*. Now they came from somewhere much closer to home. In 'The God That Failed', he addressed specifically his mother's unnecessarily agonising death due to her devout, to the point of perversity, religious beliefs. 'Don't Tread on Me', a 'God Bless America' for the Nineties, seemed shocking coming so soon after the anti-war stance of their till-then most famous song 'One'. 'Of Wolf and Man', meanwhile, gloried in his love of the outdoorsman's life, fishing and shooting: 'I hunt / Therefore I am ...' Tellingly, the album's weakest track is its longest and the one which harks back most to the band's earlier days: 'My Friend of Misery', a mid-paced, blustering meditation on the ego-ravages of stardom.

Buried at the back of the album, this was the only track on which Jason Newsted was given a co-credit, and it was saved only by its Who-like mid-section where Hammett's guitar at least brings to it a certain poise. The bullying may have subsided now the band was off the road, but Jason's part in the creative process was still extremely limited. He hoped this would change as time passed and his role naturally grew. He hoped in vain.

In fact, all the playing on the album – including the vastly improved drums – excels on every level but Hammett's guitar, in particular, is exquisite throughout. Again, though, the biggest surprise comes from Hetfield, whose vocals take a quantum leap forward from the macho posturing of even his best *Master-* and *Justice-*era efforts, towards a more sensitive (his almost spoken-word outro on 'Nothing Else Matters'), even sweet (his high vocals on the chorus of 'The Unforgiven') quality unheard of before in his work. Even his guitar playing betrays a tinkling, newfound delicacy, as on the superb acoustic and electric playing on 'Nothing Else Matters', including the achingly searching guitar solo – so much so, indeed, that Hammett does not feature anywhere on the track.

The stand-out tracks, however, are its opening brace: 'Enter Sandman' and 'Sad but True'. The latter – a monolithic musical statement whose juddering rhythm had come suddenly while recording 'Stone Cold Crazy' for *Rubáiyát* – was destined for greatness from the moment an awestruck Rock, listening for the first time to the demo, told Lars and James he thought it could be 'a "Kashmir" for the Nineties'. The former, an even more crowning jewel and the must-have moment of all such classic albums, was another first for Metallica: an old-fashioned, born-lucky hit single. Based on the same little cartwheeling riff as other rock classics such as 'Smoke on the Water' and 'All Right Now', Kirk later recalled how he'd been listening to *Louder Than Love*, an early album by a then-unknown Seattle band called Soundgarden, 'trying to capture their attitude toward big, heavy riffs. It was two o'clock in the morning. I put it on tape and didn't think about it.' When he later played it to the others, however, Lars told him, 'That's really great. But repeat the first part four times.' It was that suggestion, said Kirk, 'that made it even more hooky'.

In the end, it took more than ten months to complete the album, would cost them than over $1 million, and sent them all, at various times, so crazy that nearly fifteen years later Rock would still describe it as 'the hardest album I ever made'. The band felt the same way. 'It was difficult with Bob,' said Lars. 'It was the hardest record to make with Bob because we didn't know each other and there was no trust yet. So we were very wary of each other.' They had pushed themselves so hard, 'we all started hating each other by the finish'. When I visited, halfway through, I noticed a boxer's punch-bag and gloves hanging up in one of the rooms. 'For fucking tension!' Lars guffawed when I pointed at it. 'You know that shit, you're trying to get something down and you can't get it down right and you just need to hurt something. Then you receive the bill for it next week. You can hurt that and not have to pay for it.' James, he added, had been using it a lot of late: 'But now that Jason has started doing his bass he uses it a lot, too.' It was, Rock concluded, 'a very tough album to record from the point of view of what they were trying to achieve and where they had come from and where I had come from. So it took a while to work out the way it was to be done.' More than just trying to make something accessible, this album was simply 'the first time you really felt that there was some real human emotion behind the music'.

Speaking with Lars at the studio while James sat on the other side of the glass, guitar cradled on his lap, working through the cyclical guitar part to 'The Unforgiven', it was clear they had been working towards a very specific agenda from day one. He talked of how, when the band had started out, his favourite drummers were technically gifted craftsmen such as Rush's Neil Peart and Deep Purple's Ian Paice: 'So for the next eight years I'm doing Ian Paice and Neil Peart things, proving to the world that I can play.' Now, after absorbing the lessons their new father-figure producer had instilled, Lars' two favourite drummers were Charlie Watts of the Rolling Stones and Phil Rudd of AC/DC – unflashy, solid as rock, foundation-builders. 'I used to think that stuff was easy but it's not, it's hard ... fucking hard.'

Another concession to the forthright commerciality of the new album was in its title – simply *Metallica*, eponymous titles being every major record label's preferred option: uncontroversial, uncomplicated and easy to remember. It was ironic then that the album would quickly become known not by that name but for the nickname given to it because of its forbidding, all-black sleeve – *The Black Album*. It was like the photo negative of The Beatles' *White Album* (itself actually titled simply *The Beatles*, but renamed by fans after its similarly featureless, all-white cover).

'It was one of our first days in the studio,' Lars explained, and he was browsing through a typically colourful heavy metal mag, noticing how the ads for various albums all looked the same. 'All these cartoon characters and all this steel and blood and guts. It was like, "Let's get as far away as possible from this."' As far away as they could get, they decided, was to have a completely bare, monochromatic sleeve, with no information whatsoever on the front, save the barely discernible image of a serpent coiled in one corner. (A symbol, perhaps, of the forbidden fruit they had now bitten into?) The colour they chose was inevitable. 'The fact is that we all like black as a colour.' Lars shrugged. 'Sure, there have been some people who've thought it was rather Spinal Tap, but if it came down to a choice between black and pink, you know what I mean? People can throw all this Tap shit at me all day, it just reflects off me. I don't give a shit.' Or, as James put it: 'Here it is, black sleeve, black logo, fuck you.'

Another, albeit more oblique, reference to the altered perspective of the new album, along with its more pronounced choruses and shorter tracks, were the bare minimum credits on the sleeve. Where in the past Metallica album sleeves had been crammed with credits and thank-yous – even occasional fuck-yous – the *Black* sleeve contained the lyrics to the songs, the names of the four band members and their instruments, and the barest production details.

Lars was sure, he said, that 'we're gonna get a lot of people saying we're selling out, but I've heard that shit from *Ride the Lightning* on. People were already going, "Boo! Sell-out!" even back then.' Just because the tracks were shorter 'doesn't mean they're any more accessible'. It was already clear, however, that increased accessibility was the whole point. The subject matter may have been as dark as ever – 'Sad but True', he said, was 'about how different personalities in your mind make you do different things and how some of those things clash and how they fight to have control over you', while 'The Unforgiven' was about 'how a lot of people go through their life without taking any initiative. A lot of people just follow in the footsteps of others. Their whole life is planned out for them, and there's certain people doing the planning and certain people doing the following' – but the music was now of many colours, all of them supremely eye-catching.

The best example of this was the track already designated the album's lead-off single: the enticingly named 'Enter Sandman'. 'That song has been on the fucking song titles list for the last six years,' Lars said in an attempt to waylay any suggestion it had been written specifically as a single for this album. 'I'd always looked at "Enter Sandman" and thought, what the fuck does that mean? Me being brought up in Denmark and not knowing about a lot of this shit, I didn't get it. Then James clued me in. Apparently the Sandman is like this children's villain – who comes and rubs sand in your eyes if you don't go to sleep at night. So it's a fable [which] James has just given a nice twist to.' He added: 'Six years ago I looked at "Enter Sandman" and thought, "Naw, let's write 'Metal Militia' . . . Metal all the way, you know?"' Not any more.

The most important thing now would be what their various record companies thought of the finished product. Elektra was ecstatic. This would be the kind of Metallica album the company could really get its teeth into – one with multiple hit singles, great production, broad-scale ideas; in short, something with what the business called 'legs'. Working off that giant buzz, Mensch scheduled meetings with various heads of department at Phonogram across Europe, beginning with Dave Thorne and the team in London.

'I don't think anybody can honestly say that when they listened to that album they thought, "This is going to be the biggest-selling metal album in the history of music,"' says Thorne now. But when Mensch first played them the album 'we were just gobsmacked because it was an absolute quantum leap on from anything that we'd ever heard anybody do, frankly, on the metal scene. And I remember him saying, in typical Mensch style, "Elektra got this fucking crazy idea, you know, going on about three singles, maybe four singles, I don't know what you guys think." Then he said, "I don't know which track you think should be the single." And I can remember saying, "*That's* the single, that track there – 'Enter Sandman'."'

Thorne was spot-on. Released in the UK ahead of the album, backed with a suitably phantasmagorical video (actually, a fairly ordinary, literal depiction of a 'sandman' haunting a sleeping child intercut with a band performance that made 'One' look like *Gone With the Wind*) and available in as many formats as Phonogram could devise – including regular seven-inch vinyl in black sleeve, with and without logo sticker; twelve-inch vinyl; three different CD versions; cassette-tape version; even box-sets, including limited-edition twelve-inch folder, plus the twelve-inch vinyl record and four 'exclusive' autographed Metallica photos, one of each member – 'Enter Sandman' reached Number Five, becoming along the way one of the best-selling singles of the year. The US release of 'Enter Sandman' was staged differently, timed to come after the album's initial sales burst, helping push it back up the charts as the single broke into the Top Twenty, reaching Number Sixteen, the video becoming a regular feature of daytime MTV for months to come.

Aware more than most of the power of word of mouth, the band also made sure their fans got a chance to judge the new album's merits ahead of release, holding special 'listening parties' in London, at the Hammersmith Odeon, and, most spectacularly, in New York at the 20,000-seater Madison Square Garden. Admission was free to Metallica fan club members and with the band also in attendance to introduce the album personally and sign autographs, both venues were packed. At the New York playback, James actually snuck into the audience during 'Nothing Else Matters' and was relieved to find 'They were really attentive … really listening to what it said.' In America it was also arranged for certain stores to open their doors at one minute past midnight on 12 August – the official release date of the album. Queues formed outside, in some cases, for up to eighteen hours before. A week later, *Metallica* – or the *Black Album* as it was already becoming known – debuted at Number One in both Britain and America. It also topped the charts in Canada, Australia, New Zealand, Germany, Switzerland and Norway.

The band was already out on tour in Europe when they got the news, at a hotel in Budapest, where they were appearing as 'special guests' – second on the bill – to AC/DC at that year's travelling Monsters of Rock festival. Lars said he read the fax from Q Prime and for a moment wasn't sure how to react. 'You think one day some fucker's gonna tell you, "You have a number one record in America" and the whole world will ejaculate. I stood there in my hotel room [and] it was, like, "Well, okay." It was just another fucking fax from the office.' At least, that's what he later told *Rolling Stone*. In truth, this was the moment he'd fantasised over since his days of chasing around after Diamond Head records and reading about the NWOBHM in *Sounds*. Complete validation for the years when he was a tennis loser; an LA reject, with a funny accent who never quite belonged anywhere.

Reviews were also more positive, and widespread, with the album subjected to the glowing critical spotlight not just in the metal press but across the board, as *Rolling Stone*, *NME*, *Time Out*, the *Village Voice*, the *LA Times*, the *New York Times* and others around the world lined up to sing its praises. This was the double-whammy Q Prime had banked on: commercial success on a scale previously thought beyond the reach of a 'genre' act such as Metallica, while still miraculously building on their critical profile. Suddenly, no one was using the words 'thrash metal' anywhere in Metallica articles. The subsequent *NME* cover story may have owed something, as Dave Thorne suggests, to 'the fact that Steve Sutherland was the editor and was married to the head of press at Phonogram, Kaz Mercer, who remains to this day Metallica's press officer'. But as he also points out, 'It was the right thing to do, obviously. Even the broadsheet newspapers were

[now] writing about the band. They genuinely were taking it to the masses, as they say.'

'I think also the reason we went next-level was because we knew we were on to something,' said Lars, 'that somehow when James and me had written these songs [we knew] there was a batch of songs that deserved that kind of level of work and that level of attention to details … that were worth fighting for.' It was also, he realised now, 'the element of the time, the element of the scene, the element of the temperature in music at the time'. That 'this was the beginning of the Nineties and all the pop stuff, the hair stuff, the whole LA thing was coming to an end. There was about to be a changing of the guard. There was a bunch of things brewing up in Seattle. There was a whole new kind of thing going on, and the whole music mainstream audience had been shifting very subtly further and further left over the course of the Eighties. All of a sudden all of the sixteen-year-old kids were ready to embrace different things. So you can't take out the sort of way the planets are aligning analogy. And the planets just aligned in '91, '92 when that record came out, it all just came together at the right time, with the right songs, the right producer, the right attitude and the right temperature on the music scene to create this absolute fucking monster that that record then became, for better or worse.'

It was, as Lars suggests, simply one of those once-in-a-lifetime albums: good for Metallica, who were now considered one of the most important bands of the coming decade. But beneficial also for the music scene in general, helping thrust open the door for alternative, underground rock to be accepted as a staple of American radio and TV, something then-unknown new names such as Nirvana, Pearl Jam and Soundgarden would take full advantage of before the year was out. The backdraught of this was that Metallica would no longer be considered cutting-edge. But that, Lars pointed out astutely, was because 'the mainstream has moved a lot closer to the new left edge than they were five years ago. To that bank clerk, Metallica's still the most fucking extreme thing he could get into.'

Not that it made them immune from criticism – writers who had been impressed by Hetfield's unflinching portrayal of the war victim in 'One' railed in the post-Gulf War atmosphere against the overt patriotism of the unapologetically flag-waving 'Don't Tread on Me'. But even here, the band had an answer: James, they pointed out, had written the song many months before the invasion of Kuwait, the flag he was flying not the Stars and Stripes but the one carried by the Culpeper Minutemen of Virginia during the revolutionary war, its coiled-snake banner – à la the *Black Album* sleeve – carrying the motto 'Don't Tread on Me'. (Indeed, a replica of the flag hung in One on One throughout the recording sessions.) 'America is a fucking good place,' James responded defiantly in *Rolling Stone*. 'I definitely think that. And that feeling came about from touring a lot. You find out what you like about certain places and you find out why you live in America, even with all the bad fucked-up shit. It's still the most happening place to hang out.'

Hetfield also, briefly, got into hot water over comments he made in the *NME*, characterising rap music as 'extra black', adding that it was 'all me, me, me, and my name in this song'. Again, he was unapologetic: 'Some of the stuff, like Body Count, our fans like because there's aggression there. I love that part of it. But the "Cop Killer" thing, kill whitey – I mean, what the fuck? I don't dig it.' It reminded him, he said, of 'the Slayer thing with Satan and tear-your-baby-up. Like going out and shooting cops. Hopefully, no one's going to go out and do either. People like it, it's fine. Whatever blows your skirt up, as my dad would say. It just don't blow mine up.'

Although second to AC/DC, everywhere Metallica went that summer they were the most talked about band on the Monsters bill. 'We've been very lucky with critical acclaim from a lot of fashionable magazines,' Lars acknowledged when we spoke. 'All these writers who would spew about Bruce Springsteen or Prince, usually. Metallica's kinda been lumped into that crowd in America.' Why them, though? Why not, say, Slayer? He took a deep breath as he tried to keep the condescension out of his voice. 'I think a lot of it has to do with our approach lyrically, and about wanting to confront issues that were more realistic and had more to do with things that were happening around us. I'm the first to line up for a Slayer record when it comes out, 'cos I think Slayer are the best at what they do. But lyrically, it's a whole different kettle of fish. We've always been very adamant about shying away from the metal clichés – one of them being the whole sexist, satanist crap. And as a consequence it seems all the trendsetting journalists have been throwing acclaim at Metallica right, left and centre . . .'

As Lars had predicted, there was, however, a significant shaking of heads among certain older Metallica fans. Accusations of sell-out were rife, justifiably so, from a certain old-school perspective. Even two decades on, it's a subject that polarises even their staunchest allies. The normally outspoken Robb Flynn, who had been such a big fan as a teenager, and whose band Machine Head was actually supporting Metallica on tour when we spoke in early 2009, managed to change the subject when I asked for his specific views on *Black*. As Joey Vera puts it, 'The *Black Album* was *never* in the cards . . . But they were very smart in what they did. And Lars probably had a lot to do with that, working with the management company. They made some really, really, really smart decisions, albeit maybe some of them questionable to some of the fans. But in the end they made very smart decisions all along the way.'

Others agreed. Says David Ellefson, 'The *Black Album*, sonically, is just one of the best-sounding records ever made in the history of multi-track recording.' Even Flemming Rasmussen, frozen out after carrying the can for the production nightmare of *Justice*, 'absolutely loved' the *Black Album*, he says: 'It sounded great, well produced, well played, I thought it was brilliant. They were doing a lot of the stuff I wanted them to do on *Justice*, in terms of sounds and all the things that simplified everything. They went from the really long songs to one song, one riff. And the fact that James suddenly had started taking an interest in singing pleased me very much. 'Cos this was like the first album where he actually sings, and where you can hear that he takes it seriously. I think it's a fabulous album.'

The big question was: what would Cliff have made of it? The feeling was that Burton, so long the uncompromising soul of the band, would have been frankly appalled by this turn of events. As Joey Vera says now, 'it's unimaginable' the band would have made such an album were Cliff still alive: 'I'm not saying they would have turned into King Crimson or anything, but you never know. It could have been this crazy who-knows-what, you know?'

Prophetically, however, in what proved to be his final interview, less than forty-eight hours before his death, Cliff told Jorgen Holmstedt of Sweden's *OK!* magazine that he thought Metallica would become more 'mellow and melodic' as time went by. 'We don't care about that right now,' he insisted, but was remarkably prescient about what might eventually happen, speculating that they would work with 'some big-name producer', something he said they had actually considered for *MOP*. 'If we get our wish,' he said, 'we'll probably record in Southern California, probably in Los Angeles.' He had not liked enduring 'the worst winter' of their months at Sweet Silence in Denmark, complaining that there had been 'no energy'. Next time, he said, 'it would be cool to do it somewhere where it's light and [there's] plenty of sun'. Cliff's musical tastes were certainly broad enough to encompass the 360-degree turn the *Black Album* had made. As Kirk told me, 'If we'd made another album with Cliff I think it would have been extremely melodic. Like, right before he died, I'll give you an example of what he was listening to ...' He listed Creedence Clearwater Revival, the Eagles, the Velvet Underground, R.E.M. and Kate Bush. 'Cliff was the most open-minded musically of us all.'

But even if Cliff Burton would have been comfortable with the shift in musical direction, how he would have responded to the other changes in the band remains open to speculation. What would their 'big brother' have made, for example, of them all living in LA during their near-year making the album, where they were all in their various ways now caught up in the rock star life, frequenting the Rainbow (the Hollywood watering hole where Led Zeppelin enjoyed some of their most notorious groupie-baiting nights) and hanging out with new friends such as the guys in Guns N' Roses and Skid Row? How would Cliff have reacted to the new era in the band where music was still important, but no longer the most important thing once they left the studio and earnest Bob behind each night and headed back to West Hollywood and the chicks and the coke and the booze and the twinkling neon ooze of Sunset Strip after dark, the high-five, hair-metal sound of KNAC blaring from the car radio?

Speaking to me almost twenty years later, Lars confessed, 'Whenever I think of the *Black Album* now, I think of spending a year in LA. I think of hanging out with Guns N' Roses, I think of hanging out with Skid Row, who were there making records at the same time. I think of going out to the studio in the Valley every day and fighting with Bob Rock about what was going on. I think of all the late nights and early mornings, probably the craziest year of my life in LA, living everything that you can imagine when you're twenty-six years old in LA and your dick is fucking six feet long.' It was, he added, 'great'. These were the days when Lars, James and Kirk (although still not Jason) would form an impromptu band one night with Axl Rose, Slash and Duff McKagan of Guns N' Roses, also roping in Skid Row singer Sebastian Bach, under the ha-ha name of Gack – insider slang for coke – to play a set at a birthday party for *RIP*, the most hellacious hair-metal magazine in America, at the Hollywood Palladium; the days when Lars and James would visit Slash at his pad for some 'outrageous partying'. In his autobiography, Slash recalls 'a girl James wanted to fuck and I let him take her into my bedroom. They were in there for a while and I had to get in there to get something, so I crept in quietly and saw James head-fucking her. He was standing on the bed, ramming her head against the wall, moaning in that thunderous voice of his, just slamming away, and bellowing, "That'll be fine! That'll be fine! Yes! That'll be fine!"'

The real fun, however, didn't begin until the band was back out on tour – although on the surface it appeared that there at least they were trying to move away from, as Lars put it, 'the metal clichés'. Just as they had worked to expunge the obvious 'tells' from their music and artwork, purged from their new stage show was the Iron Maiden-influenced paraphernalia of the Damaged Justice tour. Performing on an unadorned diamond-shaped stage, the emphasis was now on crowd interaction, with Kirk able to seemingly walk among the crowd while soloing and Lars on a movable drum-riser able to reach either side of the stage. Giant video screens were now mounted front and side, broadcasting close-ups of the band throughout, and the lightshow was much more subtle, blinding white light one moment, deep limpid shadow the next, casting James' face in a suitably eerie glow, à la the 'Enter Sandman' video. Even Jason now had more of a feature. Besides his never-quite-Cliff bass solo he got to perform a lead-vocal cameo on 'Seek and Destroy' – which also allowed James the space to roam free among the audience in the new show's most impressive innovation: the Snake Pit – an area set aside solely for the most fanatical fans situated right in the middle of the stage. Each night as Jason spat out the words to 'Seek . . . ', James would leap into the Snake Pit and get the kids to sing along, hugging them, yelling at them, making them part of the band in a way that no other groups did.

There was even room for a certain reflection, the show beginning each night with a twenty-minute video documentary depicting the band's history, dedicated specifically to Cliff Burton. Now firmly part of the Metallica mythology, the biggest cheer of the night would be for that moment when Cliff's image appeared: wayward hair, windmilling arm, permanently clad in cardigan and bell-bottoms the way Jesus would always be in white robes. A great moment for every-one, with the possible exception of Jason, who always paid lip-service to the Cliff Burton legend but must surely have grown sick of the constant reminder that he was only there through luck, and bad luck at that. The spell was only broken when James would turn to the crowd and admonish them, 'You all got the *Black Album*, right? Studied all your lyrics and shit? No fuck-ups now. Hey, any time this stuff gets too heavy for you ...' A moment's pause while the crowd jeered and James fixed a jester's crooked smile to his lips ... 'Tough shit!' There were occasional nods to the past – 'Creeping Death', 'For Whom the Bell Tolls', 'Master of Puppets', all played at such excoriating speed it was as though they wanted to get them out of the way as quickly as possible, ending each night with an extended, cataclysmic version of 'One' guaranteed to bring the house down, before an encore of 'Battery', delivered at even more pummelling speed. This was street rock as spectacle, the best money could buy, and that said everything about the new, all-singing, all-dancing, Nineties-version of Metallica that had eluded the original finger-pointing, chest-thumping, weirdly straight-laced Eighties version. Whatever was in the minds of Lars Ulrich and James Hetfield it was clear to the outsider that this was no longer about back-room, garage-roots authenticity but total devotion, all-out war, world domination. It was about being number fucking one, you fuckers . . .

Now firmly part of the establishment, in February 1992 Metallica picked up another Grammy, their third in a row, this time for 'Enter Sandman', which won the 'Best Metal Performance with Vocals' award. 'We gotta thank Jethro Tull for not putting out an album this year,' quipped Lars, all of the Shrine Auditorium yucking it up with him. Behind the laughter, though, was now steely-eyed intent. 'We worked so fucking hard on this album,' said James afterwards, 'so the fact that we won a Grammy for it this time actually meant something. All the other ones, I don't know what to do with 'em, really.' What about Lars, though – did it make him feel proud? I asked. 'Of course I like winning a Grammy!' he smiled, not the least bit sheepishly. 'I want a Grammy as much as the next guy; even *more* than the next guy.' He sat up straight in his chair. 'I'm just sitting here thinking nobody has asked me if I'm proud of it before. Come to think of it, I'm really fucking proud, I really am! I used to always think it didn't mean much, you know? But the truth is I guess it does . . .'

In April that year, Metallica confirmed its newly won place at rock's top table when the band appeared in London at the Concert for Life tribute show to the late Queen frontman Freddie Mercury, staged at Wembley Stadium. They performed three songs, all from the new mainstream-approved album: 'Enter Sandman', 'Sad but True' and 'Nothing Else Matters'. (All three songs were released as a special commemorative single the following week, with all proceeds from its sale donated to the Freddie Mercury AIDS fund.) Hetfield also sang 'Stone Cold Crazy' with the three surviving members of Queen, plus guitarist Tony Iommi of Black Sabbath.

Then in May, Lars and Slash co-hosted a special press conference at The Gaslight in Hollywood, where it was announced that Guns N' Roses and Metallica would co-headline a US tour together that summer. On paper it looked like a snug fit. The *Metallica* album had only just vacated the Number One spot when Guns N' Roses had issued their latest release – two double albums released simultaneously, titled *Use Your Illusion I* and *Use Your Illusion II*. The latter had swiftly followed *Metallica* to Number One while the former had also become hinged to the US Top Five. Eight months on, combined American sales of all three albums were now topping ten million. Guns N' Roses and Metallica on the same ticket together would be the largest, most lucrative concert draw of the year. It would also become one of the most incident-filled and controversial tours ever.

The brainchild, almost inevitably, of the Axl-besotted Lars, as former Guns N' Roses manager Alan Niven says now, 'As much as I loved Metallica – I would go just to see-hear "Seek and Destroy" and hope for "Orion" – I thought the idea of them touring with Guns N' Roses was absolutely absurd and a recipe for some kind of disaster. Who follows who for one thing? It's insane to forget it's better to be a hard act to follow than to follow a hard act.' Niven also 'found it most uncomfortable to be sitting in Duff's bathroom one night with Lars and co all gacked to the gills planning their onslaught on the world. "How am I gonna get around this one?" I wondered, and half thought to drop Lars off at the Hollywood Sheriff's station, in his blithering condition, ranting about the enormity of this sonic blitzkrieg, his arms waving expansively in the big windows of the Range Rover as I tried to quietly and unobtrusively slip down a traffic-less pre-dawn Sunset [Boulevard], instead of at his hotel, which I reluctantly did as the cold grey light of the day came up.' He adds wearily, 'God bless cocaine and the idiocies it induces ...'

In fact, the running order was the least of anybody's worries, with it agreed early on that Metallica, although billed as co-headliners and splitting the proceeds 50/50 with GN'R, would go on first, by simple dint of the fact that by this stage Axl Rose was keeping audiences waiting for up to three hours most nights of the tour. As Slash said, 'Metallica was not a band to pull that kind of shit at all, so they wisely opted to play first so as to avoid being pulled down by our bullshit.'

The twenty-five-date stadium tour began at the RFK Stadium, in Washington, in July. Axl was at the height of his megalomaniacal fame. To his usual on-tour retinue of chiropractor, masseuse, vocal coach, bodyguard, driver, personal assistant, PR, manager and gaggle of hangers-on masquerading as friends, he now added a psychotherapist, Suzzy London, and a professional psychic named Sharon Maynard, a short, middle-aged Asian woman nicknamed 'Yoda' by the rest of the band (after the mystic goblin in *Star Wars*) whose specialities included 'channelling' past lives, communicating with extraterrestrials and utilising the power of crystals. Sure enough, Metallica would go onstage each night bang on time – and Guns N' Roses wouldn't. Sometimes because Axl genuinely had throat problems; often times because he was still 'psyching himself up' back at the hotel. The energy might not be right, the vibes all muddled, or Yoda would simply advise him against it.

Ten days into the tour, at Giants Stadium in Rutherford, New Jersey, Axl was struck in the genitals by a cigarette lighter thrown from the audience. He hurled down the mike, tore off the white cowboy hat he was wearing and hobbled to the side-stage wings where he tried to catch his breath. A chant went up among the crowd: 'Axl! Axl! Axl!' Then the houselights came on and it became clear the show was over. The next three shows – in Boston, Columbia and Minneapolis – were all cancelled. The official explanation: 'severe damage to [Axl's] vocal chords'. The real reason: humiliation; fury; hubris? Only Axl really knew.

To begin with, Metallica took it all in their stride. They knew touring with GN'R would be 'a trip'. Besides, they were busy having their own, less public adventures. During the lull after New Jersey, James flew down to Mexico, 'had a few too many tequila poppers, got into a fight in some bar and had a bottle cracked over my head'. He was still carrying the scars when the tour resumed, on 8 August, at the Olympic Stadium in Montreal. At this point, a real, much more frightening accident occurred when, during 'Fade to Black', James badly injured his left arm after a mistimed pyrotechnic explosion, the twelve-foot flame leaving him with third-degree burns. Forced to abandon their set while James was rushed to the hospital, a frantic call was made to GN'R, still relaxing at their hotel, requesting that they start early that night to compensate for Metallica having to truncate their show. They all agreed, according to Slash, then had to wait for Axl, eventually going on three hours later than their own time slot, before leaving the stage early when the flame-tempered singer walked off after just nine songs, complaining that the onstage monitors weren't loud enough for him to hear his voice. Others whispered he was just pissed off at Metallica 'leaving him in the shit'. His parting message to the crowd: 'Thank you, your money will be refunded, we're outta here.' Righteously pissed off, having endured premature ends to both sets, more than 2,000 angry fans rioted as they left the venue, fighting with police, resulting in over a dozen injuries. As even Lars later wryly noted, 'That was the wrong night to have monitor problems.' Added James: 'I was so disappointed in [Axl] because he could have won so many people over by continuing the show.' Instead, 'There was a lot of unnecessary violence because of his attitude. He could have turned it into a great evening.' This time, seven shows had to be cancelled and rearranged. By then, Alan Niven had long-since departed – for talking back to 'the red-haired dictator', as he called Axl. But even his replacement, Doug Goldstein, had to admit the tour had become 'like people who go to watch the Indy 500. They don't go to watch the race. They go to see the crash.'

Backstage, there were even greater high jinks taking place. 'Axl was out to impress Metallica and everyone else,' recalled Slash, 'having backstage parties every single night.' Each day Axl would write large cheques to his step-siblings, Stuart and Amy, and instruct them to put together something 'special' for that evening's after-show entertainment. 'We'd spend a hundred thousand a night on parties,' recalled drummer Matt Sorum. One night would be 'Greek night – four greased-up, muscle-bound guys [carrying] in a roast pig'. Another night might be Sixties night, replete with lava lamps, psychedelic lightshows and slogans spray-painted everywhere: 'Acid is groovy'; 'Kill the pigs'. The only constant was the presence of a free bar, several pinball machines, pool tables, hot tubs and strippers dancing on tables. According to Roddy Bottum, keyboardist for Faith No More, who opened the show on a handful of dates, 'There were more strippers than road crew.'

For a while, Lars was in his element. Still doing large amounts of cocaine most days, sporting the replica of Axl's white leather jacket he'd had made, his was a regular face at these after-show parties. 'It was like, we're in Indianapolis,' he recalled, 'so there were Formula One cars everywhere, with all the girls dressed up in pit-crew uni-forms. It was decadence at the highest level I'd ever seen, a Caligula kind of outlandishness. There were orgies, sure. Was I involved? Yes. Well, I was in the same room – we'll leave it at that.' Ross Halfin recalls taking the band for a photo-shoot in Jacksonville, where Lars wore the white leather jacket 'and the band stood behind him making signs of the cross'. James, in particular, was getting seriously bugged. The GN'R tour 'was very extravagant, which was so un-me. The hot tubs backstage. I'd go back and drink their beer and shoot pool, that's what I'd do. By the time they'd come offstage I'd be gone so I didn't have to hang out with them.' For non-drug-taking James, Guns N' Roses 'were part of the enemy. Lars was out there in the white leather jacket and all that, posing up a storm. Lars is that way. He will be infatuated with certain people in his life and need to get into them. That's just part of him, I guess. He likes learning things from people who have that something. Axl had that.' As if to underline that fact, when the tour was over, Lars would not see Axl again for nearly fifteen years. 'Axl was two people,' said Lars, looking back later. 'You were truly left wondering what the fuck was going to happen next. When he was in a good mood, he was the sweetest guy, and when he forgot to take his medicine or decided to go off, he was kind of a freak. He was the last person I've ever seen, though, besides maybe Bill Clinton, that when he walked into a room every single person was drawn to him. That's a rare thing.'

Meanwhile, over a year on from its release, the *Black Album* was still selling hundreds and thousands of copies each week all over the world. Boosted by no less than five back-to-back hit singles – 'Enter Sandman' had been swiftly followed in the charts by 'The Unforgiven' (released in eight different formats in the UK alone), 'Nothing Else Matters' (also eight UK formats), 'Wherever I May Roam' (six formats) and, finally, at the end of 1992, 'Sad but True' (a further eight formats) – by the tour's end in the summer of 1993, the album had sold nearly seven million copies in the USA, and a further five million abroad. It had become one of those albums no self-respecting record collection did not include, eventually notching up more than fifteen million US sales, to date, and nearly twenty-five million worldwide, making it one of the biggest-selling popular music albums of all time, in any genre.

The final money-spinning leg of the world tour was dubbed the Nowhere Else to Roam tour, another large outdoor co-headlining stint, this time in Europe with Lenny Kravitz. Its crowning glory was Metallica's own headlining festival show back in England, in June, at the 55,000-capacity Milton Keynes Bowl. 'Obviously it's a great ego kind of thing to do it,' Lars had said over the phone prior to the band's arrival. 'But it's got to be right. I think Iron Maiden, when they did their first Monsters of Rock stadium tour probably did it better than anyone else; you've got to wait till the time is right. Now, all of a sudden this seems like the right thing for us to do.'

It certainly looked that way as I walked around the backstage area that afternoon. Lars was as friendly as ever, arriving at the festival site hours before he actually needed to, bounding around saying hello to friends old and new. The only difference, one couldn't help noticing, was the gaggle of MTV crew members who followed him everywhere, cameras and mikes lapping up every scrap of attention that came his way, including scenes of themselves filming ... themselves. The concert itself was flawless, with James now very much the star of the show, the archetypal metal frontman, intense, uncompromising, tall, thin, completely in control of the stage, a million miles and several lifetimes removed from the acne-ridden bundle of insecurities who had spent years trying to wriggle out of the frontman role. His bond with the audience now seemed unbreakable, complete, as though when he looked out at the thousands he saw a mirror image of himself looking back, fists raised. You could tell the audience, his people, felt they knew this man more intimately than they did their best friends. The hard-drinking, headbanging, woman-devouring, gun-toting, icon of good- (and bad-) time rock, of heavy fuckin' metal, as he called it, raging from the stage. And yet, for all that he projected and made them think this way, they didn't know the half of it – that even now James Hetfield was still only pretending, only doing what he thought he was obliged to do.

There were already signs of the change that was coming, but Metallica's fans had been too busy multiplying and worshipping to read into them. 'Having money, being part of all this freaks me out,' James had said in the band's first *Rolling Stone* cover story. 'I like being where most people can't find me, doing things by myself, or just being with good friends in the wilderness, camping or drinking or whatever. I get a lot of time to think about what this shit is really about and what makes you happy . . . Looking good, being seen in the right places, playing the fucking game. I get real sick of that shit. That has nothing to do with real life, with being alive.'

The truth of that, though, would only be revealed later. Much later, and only then when it was all but too late to do anything good – anything real – about it.

TWELVE
LOADED

It was a phone interview. Where once phone interviews had been the option of last resort, by the mid-1990s they were increasingly becoming the norm. The recession of the early Nineties had forced record companies to cut back on their budgets; overseas trips were not as common as they had been. More to the point, the advent of grunge had killed off so many of the old Eighties-style rock stars, magazines such as Kerrang! were also now starting to suffer, caught between dramatically reduced circulation and the fact that grunge stars like Nirvana and Pearl Jam simply didn't see themselves as Kerrang!-type bands. If you weren't from the NME or the Melody Maker you were ... well, somewhere much lower down the list.

Phone interviews it was then, unless it was a cover story or a similarly multi-page splurge. This was a glorified news story. That is, a feature-length, colour piece at the front of the mag but not yet a cover – that would come later when the band arrived to headline Donington. In the meantime, the record company drone explained, as Lars and the boys were still in America it was the phone or nothing. No biggie, I decided, it wasn't like I didn't know what he looked like ...

'Hey, Mick,' he drawled down the phone that night. 'Good to speak with you again, man, what's up?'

I explained the deal, like he didn't know already, and we got straight to it. I was spending the evening at home in my one-bedroom loft apartment in London. He had just gotten out of bed at his mansion in the plush Marin County part of northern San Francisco, where it was now early afternoon.

'Hey, I'm sorry we couldn't do this in person,' he said. 'It's just our schedules . . .'

'Not a problem,' I said. And it wasn't.

We chatted for twenty minutes, did our stuff, then said our goodbyes.

'Hey, good talking to you,' he said, 'let's have a beer or something when we next come over.'

'Absolutely. And if I don't see you before, see you at Donington!'

'Cool, man. Bye.'

I hung up. Nice guy, I thought. Despite . . . everything.

The next day I was chatting on the phone to someone who still worked closely with the band. I told him about talking with Lars the night before.

'Why did you interview him on the phone?' he said. 'Why not just wait and see him when he's here?'

'Because they need the story in time for the Donington announcement next week,' I explained.

'Yeah,' he said, 'but he's here tomorrow.'

'What do you mean?'

'He's here in London tomorrow.'

'Are you sure?'

'Yeah. He's coming in to buy some antiques. Wants to keep it quiet, though, doesn't want to get hassled by the usual . . . you know . . .'

We paused as what he was saying sunk in.

'I don't think he's staying for long, though,' he said, running to catch up. 'Probably only a couple of days or so . . .'

'And of course he'll be busy.'

'That's right.'

'Buying antiques . . .'

'Mmm . . . don't say I said so though.'

If the story of Metallica had ended with those final grand stadia shows in the summer of 1993, nobody could have complained. Over the past decade they had gone from LA outcasts – runts of the Sunset Strip litter, forced to try their luck elsewhere – to the very biggest, possibly even best, heavy metal band in the world. From the high-spirited but cringingly clichéd riffage of *Kill 'Em All* to the panoramic, calculated cool of the *Metallica* album, so mind-bogglingly popular they named it twice, where they went next, what they did from now on no longer mattered, not really. Certainly not to James Hetfield. As long as the band continued to make music, James didn't really care how many nights they now played in a row at Madison Square Garden or whether *Rolling Stone* put them on its cover again, they were Metallica and you weren't and that's all there was to it, fucker. Not even Jason Newsted felt able to complain. Or rather he did, but not about that. 'I never thought it was possible to have a Number One record with the kind of music we played,' he'd said, genuinely taken aback. But then Jason had never thought it was possible to do a lot of things until he'd joined Metallica.

The only person left who still demanded yet more was the boy for whom nothing was ever quite enough: Lars Ulrich. Indeed, if the first decade of Metallica's incident-filled career had been testament to his drive, his ambition and – not to be underestimated – his ability to accommodate the increasingly forceful personality of James Hetfield, even, for a short time, that of the mercurial Cliff Burton, the next ten years would say even more about Ulrich's fathomless desire to lift the whole enterprise still higher. Higher than anyone, perhaps not even Cliff Burnstein and Peter Mensch, would have been able to dream possible. Certainly further than Metallica's own fans could have imagined; so much so, the very concept of Metallica – all the old notions of what they stood for – would become stretched so thin that many older fans would follow them no further, disillusioned by what they saw as the band's ultimate sell-out. Not the making of an ultra-commercial album like *Black*, but, conversely, the conception of albums that, in their own hazardous way, ran against the grain more wilfully than anything they had managed in even their earliest, fiercest days. What James later called, with more than a hint of sarcasm: 'The great reinvention of Metallica.'

And so it was. Not just in the Metallica sound, either, but in the actual look of the band – most symbolically, their suddenly much-shortened hair. 'It's not like we all went out together for a group haircut,' said Lars, when I teased him about it in 2009. But in many ways that's exactly what they did do – or certainly appeared to have done, when the first publicity pictures of the 'reinvented' Metallica were published in the summer of 1996, in time for the release of their new album, *Load*, the much-anticipated, utterly unexpected follow-up to *Black*. There was also the equally sudden appearance of piercings, tattoos and – most shocking of all for hardcore metal fans – make-up. It was one thing seeing Kirk Hammett – always the most (comparatively) effeminate of the group – posing in mascara, showing off his new body tattoos and face piercings, including a labret (a small, silver spike) dangling below his lower lip, camping it up for all he was worth in order to alter the public perception of who the people in Metallica really were. Seeing Lars imitating him, though stopping short of the extravagant tattoos (Lars was game, not reckless), was also strangely digestible, knowing what lengths Lars would go to in order to keep Metallica in the public eye. Looking at James Hetfield, however, in his newly pompadoured hairdo and thick black eyeliner, sitting there in a white vest smoking a cigar, it seemed momentarily as though the world had gone mad. (The only one somewhat off the pace, as usual, was Jason, who had cut his hair short some months before and was actually in the process of growing it back when the first *Load* publicity pictures were taken.) There was pushing the envelope and then there was tearing it to pieces and tossing it in the air like confetti. Suddenly in 1996, Metallica – in the shape of Lars and his new closest ally in the band, Kirk – seemed perilously close to doing the latter. It was as though Lemmy had suddenly walked onstage in a long evening gown and tiara. Actually, it was more shocking than that. Lemmy would clearly have been joking. Metallica clearly were not. As one magazine editor within my earshot put it, when first perusing the *Load* promo shots, thereby summing up the reaction of a generation, 'What the fuck is this?'

The answer, in a word: survival. Just as Lars had been shrewd enough in 1990 to grasp that Metallica risked getting left behind if it didn't get with the programme and produce an album as commercially viable as less-credible-but-more-successful contemporaries such as The Cult and Mötley Crüe, so in the mid-1990s he saw the world had changed again and that if Metallica didn't change with it they might perish – just as almost all their contemporaries from the 1980s now had. The arrival of grunge and the ground-zero approach it engendered had seen to that.

In 1992, the *NME* had pronounced new boys Nirvana 'the Guns N' Roses it's okay to like'. It was a superbly telling phrase that Lars, although he initially railed against it, had quickly taken onboard, as first Nirvana, then Pearl Jam, Soundgarden, Alice In Chains and countless other, lesser lights that trailed in their blaze changed the face of rock so dramatically it became virtually unrecognisable to all but its newest followers. While on the surface albums such as Nirvana's *Nevermind* and Pearl Jam's *Ten* sat easily in the same collections as *Appetite for Destruction* and *Black*, beneath the surface it was clear something entirely different, something radical and new was now going on. This was rock but no longer with a capital 'R'. As if to emphasise its essential difference from what had immediately come before, most of the grunge bands had short hair and sported goatees, eschewed the costumed glamour of Guns N' Roses and Def Leppard *et al* in favour of genuinely battered old jeans and ill-fitting plaid shirts; the whole thrift-store look as down-tuned as their guitars. Most bizarrely, they all came not from New York or LA, or even London or San Francisco, but from a rainy north-western outpost named Seattle, famous previously for nothing much bar its micro-breweries and coffee bars and its thriving Boeing factory (soon to be overtaken as the number one local employer by the fast-emerging Microsoft industries). The kind of conferred exclusivity it was, literally, impossible to emulate, unless you too came from Seattle, which of course none of the Eighties' rock goliaths did. Paradoxically, however, hard rock and heavy metal in general, and Metallica in particular, had always been huge there, in the same way it had always been a core musical component of the similarly rainswept and industrially bleak English Midlands. Indeed, Kurt Cobain once described Nirvana's music as 'a cross between Black Sabbath and The Beatles' – exactly the kind of musical marriage, ironically, that Metallica might be said to be now aiming for.

There any similarities ended, though, with Metallica viewed from a grunge perspective as being very much in the older brother's camp. Impossible to compete with, the birth of grunge spelled the death of metal as they knew it till then, as overnight million-selling bands like Mötley Crüe and Poison, Bon Jovi and Def Leppard, Iron Maiden and Judas Priest, and, yes, Guns N' Roses and Metallica, looked seriously out of whack. In many ways, Metallica was fortunate its tour ended when it did in 1993, just as the grunge wave was peaking. After nearly three years on the road, a long break had always been on the cards. Now it would also serve as time away from a scene that was in such rapid transition it was like the precipice of a cliff crumbling beneath them.

As Lars said in 1996, on the eve of the release of *Load*, the album he prayed would spare Metallica from the same sorry fate that had claimed the careers of everyone from Iron Maiden to Ozzy Osbourne and Mötley Crüe, 'When we put out the *Black Album*, nobody knew who Kurt Cobain was. It's mind-boggling.' By then, though, grunge was all but over and Lars could afford to be kind. Speaking with him back in 1993, at the height of its influence, he was sounding distinctly threatened, angry even. 'I think the whole thing has more to do with an attitude than anything musical,' he told me tetchily. Pressed further, he admitted that 'Soundgarden made a great record and I think that Alice In Chains made a great record. But this whole thing about Seattle this, Seattle that ... I'm not really sold on the whole thing, you know? I wouldn't go out and wave any flags for it.'

What about Nirvana? I persisted. What did he make of them? His voice became cold. 'Erm ... what do I think about Nirvana?' he stalled, trying to think of the right thing to say, rather than show his real feelings. 'I don't mind Nirvana. They don't really do very much for me, but I don't mind them, you know, they have very nice, hummable pop metal anthems.' I laughed at that one and he went on, encouraged. 'Some of their attitude annoys me a little bit, though. Because they're so ... I dunno, they just seem really contrived to me, somehow.' It offended him in some way? 'No, just that whole attitude they have. "Oh, we don't wanna be a big band. We don't wanna sell a million records." If you don't want to sell any records, don't release any records, you know what I mean? They should just be glad there's a million motherfuckers that wanna listen to their stuff.' I had never heard him sound so old, so off the pace. He sounded like Dee Snider seeing Metallica onstage for the first time all those years before, then turning to Jonny Z and asking: 'What is *that*, Jonny?'

Eventually, though, Lars would come to terms with the whole thing, once it had been tamed in his mind. Meanwhile, others had also tried to keep up. Judas Priest singer Rob Halford, whose homosexuality had been no secret in the business but largely been kept from the fans for the past twenty years, chose this moment not only to leave Priest for a solo career, but also to publicly come out, live on MTV, where he appeared in his new Nineties guise of make-up, black fingernail polish and a flurry of black feather-boas. None of this inflamed the interest of the grunge generation, who merely tittered. Iron Maiden singer Bruce Dickinson also read the runes and left the band for a solo career, recording two self-consciously 'different' albums, neither of which was a hit, and soon found himself back playing clubs – neither fish nor fowl in the new post-grunge era. Others, such as Mötley Crüe and Poison, merely grunged-up their acts, shedding important members and losing countless fans. Others still, like Maiden and Priest, simply carried on as they always had, King Canute stoically commanding the tide to turn even as their careers were being washed away, bringing in new, copycat singers and merely delaying the inevitable. (All would later revert to previous, more conspicuously successful forms in order to forge new careers in the coming classic rock era, but that was still some years away and could not have been anticipated back in the grunge-is-all killing fields of the mid-1990s.)

The only survivors were those few Eighties stars who had always exhibited as much brains as brawn, and even they had to work out their strategies carefully in order to successfully pull it off. Smart cookies such as Bon Jovi and Def Leppard, both of whom conspicuously amended their public image, cutting their hair, ditching the metaphorical shoulder pads, even sprouting semi-convincing facial hair, temporarily ditching the big rock anthems for less showy but more easy-on-the-ear power ballads, hoping no one would notice the incredible lengths they were prepared to go to in order to keep their careers alive. Things were moving fast again now, though, and even they were sent scurrying back to the drawing board as grunge was suddenly holed beneath the waterline by the grim suicide, in April 1994, of Kurt Cobain, putting a shotgun in his mouth after pulling a syringe from his arm. Within months the emphasis had switched in the UK to something called Britpop – indie bands with suddenly loud guitars and nicely contrived bad attitudes that made the grunge stars seem over-earnest, musically flatulent and – biggest crime of all – badly dressed. Bands such as Blur, Oasis, Pulp and the usual gaggle of slipstream followers were the new music-mag messiahs whose artful mien reached back to a time before hard rock and heavy metal, to the pre-dawn days of The Beatles, The Kinks, The Who and the Small Faces. In the summer of 1995, in fact, Lars had become so infatuated with Oasis – to Britpop, what Metallica had been to thrash – he actually began following them around on tour, the unashamed superfan again, hanging out with twenty-three-year-old Liam Gallagher and sharing a gram or two with his older but not necessarily wiser brother Noel.

As he later told *Mojo*, 'I'm the one who will go and find out what goes on in Oasis-land or Guns N' Roses-land or Alice In Chains-land. I'm so curious to see how other bands do things. It's fun to sit down with Liam Gallagher and talk complete and utter nonsense about music.' Had Liam ever heard of Metallica, though? Did he even know who the motormouth with the funny name and weirdly mangled accent was? Or why he kept turning up at gigs on their US tour that year? It didn't matter, not to Lars. Just as he had done with Diamond Head all those years before, he really was there as a fan, to look and to listen and maybe learn. Just as with Diamond Head, he probably didn't even get round to mentioning he actually played the drums, sometimes, you know, a bit.

If the music was changing around them, so was the business. In 1994, Metallica filed suit in a San Francisco court against Elektra, seeking to be released from their deal. Their original contract had been for a fourteen per cent royalty rate, for seven albums. They had never renegotiated, not even after they first hit Top Ten pay dirt with *Justice*, as would have been the norm for most groups in that position, looking instead to put together a new, partnership-based deal when the current one ended. In 1993, they were alarmed to discover, however, that none of the various video, DVD and box-set compilations they had released counted as one of the nominal seven albums stipulated by their original Elektra contract – not even the *Garage Days Re-Revisited* mini-album. They considered this particularly unfair as the original drafts of their contract were still based on the conventions of the 1970s when artists routinely released two albums a year, and video, DVD and boxed sets did not exist.

As a result when they came to renegotiate their deal in the wake of the huge success of the *Black Album*, they did so from the ground up, putting together a new joint venture/partnership agreement with Elektra president Bob Krasnow, in April 1994. The new contracts were still being drawn up when they were then cancelled in the wake of Elektra's takeover by the Time Warner Music Group that summer. TWG chief Bob Morgado appointed Doug Morris, president of Atlantic, as the new president and head of Warner Music US (which included Elektra, Atlantic and Warner). Subsequently, Krasnow resigned at Elektra, as did Warner's chief, Mo Ostin. Lars wasn't underselling the situation when he described them as 'the two most music-oriented company bosses ... We've had a great thing going for ten years but it's a very different situation, a different set of rules than a few years ago.'

Metallica's lawsuit demanded that they be released from what remained of their original Elektra contract so they could sign with another label 'free and clear of any interference from or obligation to Elektra'. In response, a Time Warner statement claimed the suit was 'without merit. The contract is a valid and binding document and Elektra will vigorously enforce its rights to the fullest extent of the law.' The result was a declaration of war by the band. It wasn't just about the money, Lars insisted: 'We were more interested in the long-term outlook.' They had deliberately not renegotiated in the wake of their success on the basis that 'Bob [Krasnow] would make it up to us later.' More specifically, they wanted more control over back catalogue and a larger share of bottom-line profits. 'There would be a greater gain in the long run only if we made good records people were buying,' Lars told the *Washington Post*. 'The beauty of the partnership is it's down to us.'

Morgado, however, 'preferred a more traditional risk/reward structure where the label takes a risk by paying substantial advances', explained Metallica attorney Jody Graham, 'which are then recoupable by artists' royalties. Then they get the rewards for risking that money.' Unusually, however, Metallica had never been in an unrecouped situation, so there was no basis for Elektra constructing a deal based on 'risk'. The success of the band had effectively eliminated any element of risk for years to come. As Lars astutely pointed out, 'We're a record company's dream because we don't require radio promotion or marketing. We don't go out and make million-dollar videos. We tour until we fall on our faces and that buzz generates word of mouth. We're as low maintenance a group as you can get.' He may have been overstating the case somewhat – the expensive videos and promotion were very much becoming the norm even for Metallica – but the principle still held. Moreover, according to Metallica's legal argument, in recent years it had accounted for up to twenty per cent of Elektra's domestic billings, generating more than $200 million in revenues in the USA alone. The fly in the ointment, and the straw that Elektra clung to, was that the band had officially still only recorded four of the seven albums it had originally contracted for. The counter-argument: that aside from the albums, Metallica had also released the *Garage Days* EP – regarded as a Top Thirty mini-album in the USA – and a special deluxe edition box-set in 1993 titled *Live Shit: Binge & Purge*, containing three live CDs and two live concert videos, which retailed in the USA for $100 (where it sold over 300,000 copies) and in the UK for £75. There had also been the release of two platinum long-form videos with *Cliff 'Em All* and *A Year and a Half in the Life of Metallica* (detailing the recording of the *Black Album*), 'despite having no contractual obligation to do so'.

By December, Lars was in New York, where depositions for the looming court case were now in process, sitting in the same room as Robert Morgado, 'him nervously smiling over at me. It was quite funny being in a room with twelve lawyers. And me sitting there after sleeping three hours, still drunk from the night before, with my shades on, not having showered in a week.' Eventually, a new agreement was reached when Burnstein and Mensch accompanied Lars to a meeting with Doug Morris and his advisers. 'We said, "All the people who can fix this are in this room. We don't need to deal with lawyers, with the food chain. Let's talk this through."' Two hours later they 'came to an agreement that everybody felt comfortable with'. Lars stuck his hand out, Morris shook it, 'and there was the deal'. Metallica hadn't walked away with an unequivocal victory. They would still need to deliver three more albums, but under much improved financial terms and conditions, in regard to how they chose to deliver material for those albums, the impact of which would be felt over the next five years.

The other members of Metallica, meanwhile, were undergoing their own re-education – literally, in the case of Kirk, who actually enrolled for a semester at the City College of San Francisco, where he took classes in film, jazz and Asian studies (the latter reflecting his mother's Filipino heritage) and came away with straight 'A's. Now divorced from Rebecca, who got a sports car and a significant financial settlement, and living back in the heart of the city – modelling his home as a Gothic retreat full of long, candlelit corridors, the walls covered in rare Hollywood posters for the original *Frankenstein* and *Dracula* movies, its vast ceilings hand-decorated in paintings of moon-bathed night scenes full of forked lightning and thunderclouds – Kirk was suddenly part of a younger, more boho crowd. This was something that became a huge influence on his metamorphosis into the make-up-wearing, pierced and tattooed character we would meet for the first time on *Load*. Musically, he had also moved on, although, unlike Lars, not into the emotional quicksand of grunge or self-referential peacocking of Britpop, but towards more left-field musical innovators such as Nine Inch Nails, Aphex Twin and The Prodigy, groups who positioned themselves as musical emissaries of the near-future, subverting their guitars with the greater intelligence of computers. He was also greatly impressed by outré image-mongers like Marilyn Manson and Perry Farrell, with their portrayal of a neo-Gothic, quasi-religious image that owed something to piercings and make-up and even more to the twisted ideals of self-immolation.

'You can only be what the public thinks you are for so long before it becomes boring,' Kirk said in 1996. Since the phenomenal success of *Black*, he had 'begun to feel quite objectified'. Going to college helped reconnect him with reality, albeit a more select version of it: 'When I met people, they'd go, "Wow, I always thought you were this big mean person. But you're really very nice – and kinda short." A lot of people get fixated on what they need [Metallica] to be – appearance-wise, how we should sound.' None of this frankly interested either Kirk or, he was pleased (though not entirely surprised) to discover, Lars. It would become this mutual desire to multiply the range of Metallica's inspirations and thereby increase its influence, both musically and otherwise, along with their mutual fondness still for experimenting with drugs, as ecstasy now joined cocaine and (in Kirk's case) marijuana as recreational drugs of choice, that would draw the drummer and guitarist closer together in the mid-Nineties. Both divorced, having rejected the straight life, and more intent than ever on 'seeing what's out there', as Lars put it, their newfound bond also had the side effect of making James feel more isolated from the group's central purpose than he ever had been, putting him at a certain remove and continually on his guard – the two allowing themselves to be photographed kissing each other, knowing the uptight Hetfield would find such images infuriating – as the two sought to challenge his leadership again and again over the coming years. 'I know he's homophobic. Let there be no question about that,' Lars would later claim in *Playboy*. True to form, James took exception to the pictures of Lars and Kirk kissing – which circulated briefly in 1996 – but understood the motivation. 'Totally,' he said in 2009. 'I'm the driving force behind their homosexual adventures. I think drugs had something to do with it too,' James laughed. 'I hope!' Kirk would later disingenuously characterise this period as 'playing referee' between Lars and James, but the fact is he was never closer to Lars – or further away from James – than now.

If these misadventures were meant to make a point to Hetfield, it was one that was lost on rock fans who remained largely unchanged in their own views. Either they were already okay with their own sexuality and that of others, or they were the type of young dolts to write 'Lars is gay' posts on veracious Metallica chat-rooms, the remnants of which still crop up today across the internet whenever anyone has anything derisive to say about the band. Lars, though, was merely role-playing. Determined as ever to keep Metallica relevant, turned on by the newfound freedom his wilful abandonment of the band's old image had allowed him, behind closed doors he still preferred the straight, conservative life of the millionaire businessman. His new hilltop home in Marin County came replete with indoor racquetball court, home movie theatre, rec-room with pool table, CD jukebox and a patio view of San Francisco that was like a map splayed out before you, all guarded at its electronic gates by a matching pair of cannons. Away from home Lars liked to go scuba-diving. He was also about to get married again. After Deborah there had been a significant affair with Linda Walker, a former leading light at Q Prime who'd left her marriage and given up her job to live with him. But the fall-out from the success of *Black* had taken its toll there, too, and Linda had eventually moved out. Now Lars began an affair with Skylar Satenstein, an emergency doctor and former girlfriend of actor Matt Damon, who had been the inspiration for the 'Skylar' character in his breakthrough hit movie, *Good Will Hunting*. Lars and Skylar would eventually marry in 1997, later having two sons: Myles, born in 1998, and Layne, in 2001.

Lars now had the money and wherewithal to begin a serious art collection: a passion, like music, inherited from his father. As he told me in 2009, 'For many years it became really the only area where I felt I could express myself creatively outside of Metallica. And that it was a place where I was on my own. When you spend as much time in a gang like Metallica, once in a while you need to just do stuff on your own. And you need to feel that you have an identity that's you and who you are and not you as part of something else.' He laughed self-consciously. Talking about being the biggest metal stars in the world, that was kids' stuff. But talking about his art collection ... 'For many, many years that was the place where I really needed solitude and some sort of creative sanctuary. That's where I would go.' He liked to collect 'schools' of art: abstract expressionism; the COBRA movement; art brut. And prized individual works by modern painters such as Jean-Michel Basquiat, the black American former graffiti artist who produced neo-expressionist classics in the 1980s before his death of a heroin overdose at just twenty-seven; Jean Dubuffet, the French painter-sculptor who pioneered the concept of 'low art' before his death in 1985; and Willem de Kooning, the Dutch-American abstract expressionist who had been one of the original 'action' paint-ers. Lars also had 'the best collection of Asger Jorn [Danish painter, sculptor] on this planet'.

James Hetfield, meanwhile, was involved in less cerebral pursuits but more challenging emotional issues. In common with both Lars and Kirk, his longstanding relationship – with Kristen, subject of 'Nothing Else Matters' – had not been able to survive the ravages of the three-year *Black* tour. His way of dealing with it was not to seek out new pleasures, or more esoteric forms of self-expression, but to re-immerse himself in some of the old ways. When he wasn't drinking beer, watching the Oakland Raiders, he was working in his garage, customising cars and motorcycles. After his '74 Chevy Nova there had been his all-terrain four-wheel-drive Blaze, which he nicknamed The Beast. He was also building himself an impressive collection of vintage guitars, with special emphasis on those from 1963, the year of his birth. Going out, he liked to stay hidden, either choosing country and western bars or restaurants where he knew he wouldn't be hassled. He rarely went to rock gigs and when he did, he would become so ill at ease he would have to get seriously drunk to face it.

Mainly, when he wasn't working, Hetfield liked to go hunting. Like Lars, he'd bought a big spread in Marin County. Unlike Lars, he'd turned his into what the drummer only half-jokingly characterised as 'the biggest hunting lodge in the universe, with dead deer coming out of every wall and rifles hanging everywhere'. Hanging out at a friend's place outside San Francisco where it was 'tough to get to without a four-wheel drive', James could 'just sit there on the porch, drinking, playing music'. Now a member of the National Rifle Association, he kept a growing collection of guns, was a good shot, and saw himself as an environmentalist, belonging to Ducks Unlimited, an organisation dedicated to the preservation of US wetlands. His dream, he told *Rolling Stone*, was to own his own ranch 'somewhere out in the middle of nowhere'. He loved nature, he said, being out in the wilderness. 'There is not much more of it left. It makes me hate people. Animals, they don't lie to each other. There is an innocence within them. And they're getting fucked.'

The most significant event in his life in this period, though, was meeting up again with his father, Virgil, who he had not spoken to for over ten years; an unforeseen occurrence that would have long-lasting repercussions for him, as both a son and father in his own right. An intimidating presence, Hetfield knew his own outwardly taciturn personality stemmed from the strained relationship he'd had with his father. 'A lot of it had to do with me proving manhood to myself. A lot of the things that I felt my dad didn't teach me, like working on cars, hunting, survivalism. Things like that. I really felt that I had to go and learn those things and prove to myself that I'm okay, that I can do it. My dad was like that.'

This, then, was to be a one-step-at-a-time reconciliation, not a total embrace. 'There's still a lot of unanswered questions,' he said at the time. 'You could hate someone like that for ever.' At least, though, they were able to spend time together again, 'hunting, things like that'. Father and son also shared a love of country music. When a college radio station invited James on to appear side by side with country star Waylon Jennings – 'to get the two outlaws together of certain different styles of music' – they suggested James might like to conduct a mini-interview with Jennings. 'I guess Dad helped me out with a few of the questions,' he later recalled. 'It's funny 'cos my dad wanted me to get a CD signed for him and then Waylon brought some Metallica stuff to get signed for his son. So it was completely cool.'

After so many years apart, James confessed: 'I saw a lot of myself in him.' Not that they discussed the past in any detail still, 'because there's no doubt that we'd argue about things'. He didn't want to 'stir the water up'. The past, he'd decided, 'just fucks things up – always'. These would be issues between father and son that would remain unresolved, and that Hetfield would later be forced to return to – after his father's death. Already seriously ill at the time of their brief reconciliation, Virgil Hetfield died on 29 February 1996, after a two-year battle with cancer. James was with him at the end and got the chance to say goodbye. Like his mother, his father had stuck to his terrifyingly rigid Christian Science principles. Although he still found himself struggling with the concept, James looked on his father's way of dealing with his illness – eschewing regular forms of medicine in favour of rising at dawn each day, doing his daily lesson – with a much greater degree of admiration this time. 'He stuck with it to the very end. And that, I think, helped him keep his strength – his knowledge that he did it his way.' They had spent hours discussing not just his family's religion but faith in general, 'and I let him know there were no bad feelings ... I had sorted out a lot of my anger in his departure, his never being around.'

Four days after Virgil died, James Hetfield flew to New York to finish off the recording of *Load*. 'I kind of went back to when Cliff died,' he told *Rolling Stone*. 'We got back to work and got some of the feelings out through the music.' Not in the angry sound of apocalyptic songs such as 'Dyer's Eve' from *Justice* or 'The God That Failed' on *Black*, but in the more resigned melancholy of dramatic tracks like the brutally frank 'Until it Sleeps', with its haunting 'So hold me, until it sleeps ...' refrain. The achingly sad, country-tinged 'Mama Said', with its wincingly honest reflections: 'Apron strings around my neck / The mark that still remains ...' Most bleakly, 'The Outlaw Torn', where the targets are blurred between mother, father and son, but utterly specific in the desolation left behind: 'And if my face becomes sincere / Beware ...'

If the *Black Album* had been the first Metallica record to contain truly personal, adult insights into the scarred emotional landscape of its principal lyric-writer, the songs on *Load* would take the whole game forward several more steps. Hetfield would insist later that the lyrics were meant to be 'kept vague' to allow others their own interpretations but it was clear from tracks such as 'Poor Twisted Me' ('I drown without a sea'), 'Thorn Within' ('So point your fingers ... right at me'), 'Bleeding Me' ('I am the beast that feeds the beast') and others, that James was addressing his true feelings to only one 'other': himself. There were songs that appeared to be directed at the outside world with the old familiar pathos – 'Cure' (drug addiction as metaphor for moral 'sickness'); 'Ronnie' (based on the real-life shootings in Washington, in 1995, by schoolboy Ron Brown) – but essentially this was a one-way trip to the dark centre of the Hetfield psyche. As such, 'King Nothing', ostensibly about the kind of king-size egos he had sneered at on the Guns N' Roses tour, became in reality a song about the so-called anti-star James now saw in his own dressing room mirror. Similarly, 'Hero of the Day', not really about 'them' but 'us', and 'Wasting My Hate' – 'I think I'll keep it for myself'. This was Hetfield not being vague but disturbingly open and, for the first time, sounding utterly unsure, almost pleading for help.

Musically, there were now even greater revelations taking place – an area where James suddenly had far less to say than the newly 'reinvented' Ulrich and Hammett. Ironically, in fact, James suddenly had more in common, musically, with Jason, now living with a new, post-*Black* girlfriend in a quiet East Bay suburb, playing basketball with the neighbourhood kids: 'I come home from a tour, I've got a box-load of shirts for them.' By default, both James and Jason had become the metal purists of the band. Neither had felt particularly moved or threatened by the grunge years. Neither even knew of Britpop. And neither would be over-impressed by the musical – and/or sartorial – expositions of latter-day MTV sinners such as Marilyn Manson or The Prodigy, although Jason was more open to at least learning about these phenomenon, becoming most fascinated by the advent of funk-metal evangelists such as the Red Hot Chili

Peppers and Faith No More, with particular reverence for the flamboyant bass playing of Chili Pepper co-founder Michael 'Flea' Balzary.

All of this had almost no bearing whatsoever when it came time to record the *Load* album. More influential than ever, Kirk would share credits with James and Lars on seven of the album's fourteen tracks. But Jason didn't even get one co-credit this time, so firmly was he excluded from the process. This was particularly galling as he had 'submitted more material than ever before for a Metallica record'. They had tried out some of his ideas, he admitted, but 'James writes this shit that is just so good, it's hard to compete with it'. Hiding his real feelings, he would only say, 'I feel more satisfied putting my bass parts on James' cool writing than I would getting five of my songs on the record.' In truth, however, it was eating Jason up and he began working on a variety of extra-curricular projects, recorded in his home studio. Even that avenue of expression was closed to him, though, when Hetfield decreed he should not be allowed to release any of this music, lest it weaken Metallica's own fan base. This situation turned 'pretty ugly for a while', according to Lars, when a demo Jason had made with friends under the band name IR8 was played on a local San Francisco radio station. 'I was fucking pissed,' snapped James. 'I always thought that when one guy jams with somebody else, that will fuck with Metallica. The fist is no longer four fingers. It's not as strong. But he was strangled. He wants his music to be heard.'

Even working on *Load*, Jason could fall foul of James' temper: 'There were times on this record when I'd walk into the control room while he was doing his bass thing. He'd be doing some Flea funk part, and I'd count to one hundred before exploding.' James would laugh it off later, start to see Jason's side of things. 'Why did we get him in the band if we didn't like him?' But that was one question never answered quite adequately enough. According to Jason at the time, 'I said, "You guys are always getting to be out there doing your thing. And I always want to back you up. But somehow, somewhere, I gotta let my shit out."' Or as he put it wearily eight years later: 'James has the last word on everything.' The day of reckoning, though, was coming.

They had started out with thirty tracks, demos recorded over the last couple of months of 1994, in Lars' basement studio, The Dungeon, then begun the serious work with Bob Rock at The Plant studios, in Sausalito, in March 1995, where they would continue off and on for most of the next year, with a break for the summer festival season. By the start of 1996 the band was in New York, working out of three studios at once: Right Track, in Manhattan, where they were finishing up recording overdubs in one room while mixing proceeded in another; and Quad Recording, across the street, where additional mixing took place. In the end they would have nearly all thirty tracks fully recorded: in effect, enough material for at least two, possibly three albums, although nobody outside of the band knew quite why yet.

In their determination to save Metallica from post-grunge obsolescence, Ulrich and Hammett had combined to create what, in retrospect, was Metallica's boldest, if not always their most likeable, move yet. It wasn't that they had left thrash far behind; it was as if they had tried to shrug off the very sound of Metallica itself; a self-conscious reconfiguration that had begun with the haircuts and tattoos, the make-up and piercings, and now found its apotheosis in the kind of bluesy, far-out rock 'n' roll that liked to shimmy and shake where once it had preferred to shatter and explode. 'When someone says "Metallica", they think heavy metal, thunder and lightning, long hair, drunk kids,' explained Kirk. 'But times have changed and the kind of person who listens to metal doesn't necessarily look like that. And why should we? Why should we conform to some stereotype that's been set way before we ever came into the picture?' There were a couple of long tracks – 'Bleeding Me', over eight minutes, and 'The Outlaw Torn', over nine – but these were exceptions. The rule of thumb was now to keep things tight, rhythmic, or 'greasy' as Lars and Kirk liked to describe it in the studio – a move that Bob Rock was more than happy to facilitate. It was, he said, 'a chance for them to kind of look at what they had done and to try some different things', although, 'when you're as big as Metallica you do that out in the open and you may not get everything right'.

As if to try and compensate for the continued emphasis on shorter, catchier songs, *Load* was actually Metallica's longest album yet, with a total running time of 78:59. To ram the point home, initial pressings even had stickers that boasted its extra-long playing time – another odd throwback to the days when Lars would sit there timing each track in order to make sure they were long enough. Then, embarrassingly, the final track 'The Outlaw Torn' had to be shortened by a minute to fit.

Mostly, they got it right. 'Ain't My Bitch' (a Mötley Crüe-style title for a song not about 'chicks' but someone with no concern for anyone's problems but his own, replete with Kirk on slide guitar, another first for a Metallica album), which opens, is as roaring and anthemic as anything from their immediate past. Everything else, though, is so shiny-new at first it's hard to see past the dazzle – what James would later call 'the U2 version of Metallica'. In fact, for many Metallica fans, then as now, *Load* was the beginning of the end. It wasn't just the music. It was what it stood for. For a band for whom one of the foundation stones of its reputation had been its apparent disregard for current trends, the new sound of *Load* was outrageous, beyond the pale. Even the album sleeve seemed designed to get up as many noses as possible. Where once there had been lyric sheets, now in the booklet that came with the CD – designed by Def Leppard favourite Andie Airfix – there was a postmodern clutter of snatches of lyrics, Rorschachian inkblots and a dishevelled spread of pictures that would have fitted perfectly in the pages of a fashion mag.

Most controversially, the front sleeve was built around a detail from a picture titled *Semen and Blood III* – an abstract, fiery-coloured, cauldron-splash set against a mottled black background not a million wavy lines away from the kind of languid psychedelia of a gig poster from the 1960s – by New York artist Andres Serrano. Originally created, in 1990, by Serrano mingling his own semen with bovine blood and placing the messy results between sheets of Plexiglas, it was Kirk who first suggested the image as the album cover after coming across it in a photo-book of Serrano's work, *Body and Soul*, which he'd bought during a visit to San Francisco's Museum of

Modern Art. 'When I first saw the picture, I thought it looked like hot-rod flames, because I have a hot-rod-flame tattoo,' he recalled, blandly. It didn't hurt either that Serrano's art was well known for courting controversy. His 1987 image *Piss Christ*, a cloudy amber rendition of a crucifix submerged in Serrano's urine, had attracted predictable opprobrium from the Church, with the Revd Donald E. Wildmon launching a public campaign against it. Republican senators Jesse Helms and Alfonse D'Amato also denounced Serrano from the Senate floor, the latter tearing a photo of *Piss Christ* in two, while Helms publicly branded Serrano 'a jerk'.

A Brooklyn-born New Yorker of Hispanic-African ancestry, the then forty-five-year-old Serrano was a former drug addict who had first made an impact on contemporary art circles in the mid-1980s, becoming a regular target – somewhat in the mould of the late Robert Mapplethorpe – for right-wing Reagonites in their attempts to stymie federal funding of the arts. Ironically, the Catholic Church was less concerned. In 1991, he was allowed access to nuns and friars in Europe for a series of typically outlandish portraits, also included in *Body and Soul*, along with 'artful' close-ups of corpses in morgues laid out on tables. When Kirk showed Lars *Semen and Blood III* he 'jumped on it the second I saw it'. James and Jason, typically, were less impressed. So much so, Newsted walked out of the room every time the subject came up at band meetings and later refused to comment on it in public. 'I think he cares too much about what the fans think,' shrugged Hammett. 'Whereas I care what the fans think, but I'm not going to let that dictate or censor what I do.' Hetfield made his feelings crystal-clear. 'I was worried about not being able to get the music into the K-Marts of the world,' he admitted at the time, in a weird reverse-echo of why they had renamed their first album *Kill 'Em All*.

Speaking in 2009 to writer Ben Mitchell, James admitted he was uncomfortable with the whole motivation behind the music and image of the *Load* era: 'Lars and Kirk drove on those records. The whole, "We need to reinvent ourselves" topic was up. Image is not an evil thing for me, but if the image is not you then it doesn't make much sense. I think they were really after a U2 kind of vibe, Bono doing his alter ego. I couldn't get into it ... The whole cover thing, it went against what I was feeling.' He was also resentful, he said, about 'being left out of the bond that they had through their drug use – Lars and Kirk were very into abstract art, pretending they were gay, I think they knew it bugged me. It was a statement around all that. I love art, but not for the sake of shocking others. I just went along with the make-up and all of this crazy, stupid shit that they felt they needed to do.' It was the first time, he confessed, when musically, rather than the bold new statement Lars and Kirk made it out to be, the band felt unsure of its footing: 'A lot of the fans got turned off quite a bit by the music but mostly, I think, by the image.'

For Lars Ulrich, however, the logic was obvious. If Metallica could no longer be expected to fulfil the role of outsiders – that job having been taken by the grunge generation – then the least they should do is try to ensure they arose to that pantheon of bands that existed somewhere way beyond the conventions of rock fashion. 'Now you got U2 and R.E.M. – and Metallica,' he said in 1996. 'In America, these borders just don't exist any more. After Cobain came along, everything became so blurred. Nowadays, bands are just bands: some are harder, some are softer, but heavy metal and pop and this and that ... it's all just one big fuckin' soup.'

In the end a compromise was reached over the Serrano painting, in that only a detail from it was used on the finished cover while the title *Semen and Blood III* does not appear anywhere in the credits. Speaking from his New York home now, Serrano says: 'Initially, when I met Kirk and Lars at the Paula Cooper Gallery [in New York], I don't think they were looking for anything controversial. They just saw something that was strong, appealed to them, and it was abstract and yet also substantial or tangible in a real sense at the same time ... I don't think it was a novelty.' Although he wasn't familiar with their music, 'I knew their name and reputation,' he says, and was delighted by the approach. 'I've always wanted for my work to appeal to those outside the art world.' Kirk, he revealed, had also bought the original. Later, there would also be 'a great T-shirt of *Load*, which I still have. I'd wear it down the street and people would give me the thumbs-up.'

Along with the reinvention came a palpable feeling of upgrading. There was a new Metallica logo, too: smoothing off the sharp edges of the original, simplifying and modernising its appearance, transforming it from obviously 'metal' to clearly 'alternative'; Ross Halfin, king of the heavy metal photographers, was now supplanted by Anton Corbijn, U2 iconographer and Depeche Mode make-over artist, while the video for 'Until it Sleeps', the first single, says more perhaps about the 'reinvented' Metallica than the music even on *Load*. Directed by Samuel Bayer, who had previously worked with Nirvana and Smashing Pumpkins, the video was shot in LA over forty-eight hours in early May and premiered on MTV less than three weeks later. Referencing Hieronymus Bosch, represented by such figures as the human-eating monster from *The Garden of Earthly Delights*, the fall of Adam and Eve from *Haywain*, and Christ in the Crucifige Eum (Crucify Him) scene from *Ecce Homo*, most rock fans would simply have got the obvious Marilyn Manson influence – Lars, with his shirt open, showing off his newly pierced nipples, Kirk's face streaked with lurid make-up, all the band with nice new haircuts, whatever the song was actually about subsumed beneath the greater message: aren't we weird and interesting, look we have make-up and neo-biblical imagery too, we aren't just Iron Maiden or even Megadeth and Slayer, truly. The result was an even bigger hit than 'Enter Sandman' had been. Metallica's first – and only – Top Ten single in the USA, and its second Top Five hit in the UK, 'Until it Sleeps' went to Number One in Australia, Sweden and Finland, and became a massive hit in Canada, Norway, Germany, Austria, Switzerland, Holland and New Zealand. Interestingly, the one big record-buying market that proved resistant to Metallica's new *point-de-jour* make-over was France. Despite two of their singles from the *Black Album* reaching the Top Ten there, 'Until it Sleeps' was a resounding flop, as were all the subsequent singles from *Load*.

The videos for the 'Hero of the Day' and 'Mama Said' singles were less garish and more impressive, directed by Anton Corbijn. The latter was wonderfully understated, depicting a cowboy-hatted James sitting alone in the back seat of a car while playing the song on an acoustic guitar, winding down some lost metaphorical highway, the other three band members only glimpsed in passing, peeking at him through the windows. At the end the view pulls back to reveal the set-up, James in a back seat prop inside a studio. He then walks over to a white horse, takes its bridle and walks off-screen, not so much into the sunset as back to the dressing room. 'Hero', meanwhile, centred on a drugged-up kid staring at TV, unfurling on every channel a *Load*-related theme, including a Western movie titled *Load*, starring James and Jason; a boxing match with James as cornerman and Kirk and Jason as the fighters; a drink called *Load* being advertised by Lars and James in matching suits; a game show called *Hero of the Day*, hosted by a smirking Kirk and Jason, with Lars and James as contestants; and Kirk as news anchorman. It ends, finally, with the kid passing out and dreaming of tiny robot creatures, rendered in stop-motion, crawling from his ear. He comes to, abruptly and throws up in the toilet.

This was genuinely good, entertaining stuff, elevating the band's status critically and reinforcing its position in the business as serious players. Nevertheless, album sales overall were down, not just in France but across the world, despite *Load* going to Number One in both the USA, UK and nine other countries. It's fairly normal practice, of course, for a huge-selling album to be followed by a less spectacular but still impressive sales pattern. But *Load* sold less than half the numbers of *Black*. Depending on which way you looked at it – or whether, perhaps, you were Lars or James – either the shift in gear had achieved the desired effect and kept the band at Number One, or had significantly reduced its audience.

The reviews, which seemed to congratulate Metallica on merely surviving more than making good music, were uniformly excellent. *Rolling Stone* claimed the album boasted 'a wholly magnetizing groove that bridges old-school biker rock and the doomier side of post-grunge Nineties rock'. In the UK, *Q* gave *Load* four stars and said, 'These boys set up their tents in the darkest place of all, in the naked horror of their own heads', but added, apparently straight-faced, 'they've never needed the props'. Except those supplied by

Anton Corbijn and their various make-up artists and costumiers, presumably. The *New York Times* gave a more balanced, accurate summation when it wrote: 'On *Load*, Metallica has altered its music, learning new skills. Hetfield has committed himself to melodies, carrying tunes where he used to bark, and he no longer sounds sheepish when he sings quietly.'

Just as it had been with *Black*, in the real world the most asked question from long-term fans was what Cliff Burton – on the tenth anniversary of his death – would have thought about it. 'I know one thing,' says Gary Holt. 'They would have never got Cliff to cut *his* hair off.' He laughs. 'I'll go to my grave believing that. And I don't think Cliff would have been too fond of band photos smoking cigars and drinking martinis with short hair and suits on. That just wasn't him, you know?' John Bush, who left Armored Saint in 1993 to join Anthrax, as part of their own post-grunge reinvention with the *White Noise* album, sees it from the opposite perspective: 'If as an artist you're not taking any chances, you're a pussy – that's what I think. So I don't have a problem with *Load*. What was worse, in my eyes, was that it seemed a little bit forced, in the sense of their image. It was trying to stay away from the whole "metal" term, and I think it was a little bit exaggerated. But there were still some great songs ... I don't think they have any reason to have any embarrassment for it, by any means.' As David Ellefson points out, it was the bands that didn't try and meet the new reality at least halfway that experienced the real problems. He recalls how when Megadeth released their *Youthanasia* album in 1994, 'We were trying to submit videos to MTV and they just said no. We were like, what? Why not? "No, we're not playing that now. We're playing Nirvana, Pearl Jam and Alice In Chains ... " And Metallica eked through. They were the only band of the so-called Big Four that squeaked through.'

Looking back in 2009, I asked James what he thinks Cliff's reaction would have been to the wholesale changes ushered in by *Load*. 'Well, I certainly would have thought there would have been some resistance, for sure. I probably would have had an ally in all of the stuff that you're mentioning. I think the *Black Album* was a great album and I appreciate the fact that we did have the balls to do that and have Bob to work with us. It had to be, it really did. You know, when I go back and I listen to *Justice*, it couldn't have stayed on that path.' But with *Load*, 'I would certainly think that I would have had an ally that was very against it all – the reinvention or the U2 version of Metallica ... There's some great, great songs on there but my opinion is that all of the imagery and stuff like that was not necessary. And the amount of songs that were written was ... it diluted the potency of the poison of Metallica. And I think Cliff would have agreed with that.' With the benefit of hindsight, even Kirk agreed. 'I think [Cliff] would have embraced the direction we were going in, because he was always into very, very melodic music. [But] as far as the image is concerned, he would have fucking spat all over it and fucking swore. He would have just said like, "You guys are fucking crazy!" and probably, "I'm out of here." Or: "Don't do it."'

Back in 1996, however, the revolution continued apace. The *Load* world tour began with the band headlining that summer's Lollapalooza extravaganza. A travelling annual festival show instigated by Jane's Addiction frontman Perry Farrell in 1991 and presented as the totemic pinnacle of the Alternative Music Nation, the announcement that Metallica would be gate-crashing the party that year came as yet another controversial move in the band's self-reinvention, and at first appeared to win over almost no one. Hardcore Metalliheads viewed it as another example of the band's sell-out to the grunge generation; Lollapalooza freaks saw it as a hijacking by the very music and culture it had been specifically designed to reject. (Ozzy Osbourne had already been turned down as a potential headliner that year, initialising the birth in October of the first Ozzfest shows: Lollapalooza-style festivals aimed more specifically at metal fans.) The previous year, Metallica had followed their Donington Monsters of Rock show with festival appearances in Europe alongside Sugar and Sonic Youth; there had also been a bill-sharing show with Courtney Love's band Hole in the Arctic Circle village of Tuktoyaktuk, Canada. None of this had generated undue comment, one way or the other. Lollapalooza was different, though, sparking months of debate, led

373

by Farrell himself, then negotiating the sale of his share in the enterprise, who branded it no less than a betrayal of his original anti-establishment vision. With Soundgarden, the Ramones, Rancid and Screaming Trees booked to appear below Metallica on the main stage, it was hardly that. Nevertheless, with Kirk Hammett – who had been to every Lollapalooza and even played at a couple, guesting with Ministry and Primus – the only member of the band with any first-hand knowledge of what the event meant to the world at large, there was something intrinsically contrived about their haste to be shoehorned onto the bill now. 'The part I like most is we're hated again,' said James defiantly. 'I kind of miss that. People like us too much now.' Careful not to push the boundaries between 'old' and 'new' Metallica too far, though, despite one of their guests in a revolving slot on the tour being Waylon Jennings, who James admitted had been an inspiration for 'Mama Said', the band would never dare to play 'Mama' live.

But perhaps their most radical move was the announcement the following summer that they would be releasing a sequel to *Load* – smugly titled *Reload* and comprising those tracks that remained from the original *Load* sessions. The idea of recording two albums' worth of material and releasing the second CD halfway through a lengthy world tour a year later was one Axl Rose had told Lars about back in 1990 – had been the plan, in fact, before record company compromise meant that Guns N' Roses eventually released their two *Illusion* albums on the same day. Lars had always kept the idea in the back of his mind, though. The fact that it also helped service the new deal with Elektra, in terms of delivering another album quickly, could not have hurt either.

If only the album itself hadn't been such a let-down. From its bland, uneventful cover – another Andres Serrano painting, this time titled *Piss and Blood* – another red-tinged amber landscape, with only one central swirl this time, resembling, perhaps, a woman's vagina, to its copycat inner booklet – more Rorschach inkblots and snatches of lyrics in lots of daintily distressed fonts – to its similarly copycat music, *Reload* looked and sounded exactly like what it was: leftovers

Clean and serene. James Hetfield, post-rehab, 2003 (*Corbis*)

Lars testifies before the US Senate Judiciary Committee in his battle against Napster, joined by (centre) Roger McGuinn of The Byrds and (far right) Hank Berry, CEO of Napster, July 2000 (*Getty Images*)

The new black. Left to right: Lars, James, Kirk and Rob Trujillo, April 2003 (*Getty Images*)

Still the same comic-book reading guy: Kirk Hammett, 2010 (*Getty Images*)

James Hetfield 'reaches out' onstage at the SECC in Glasgow, March 2009 (*Getty Images*)

The self-styled 'Samurai Whisky Warlord' Rob Trujillo onstage at
Madison Square Garden, New York, November 2009 (*Getty Images*)

Rick Rubin, 2010
(*Getty Images*)

Lars, accompanied by current partner Connie Nielsen, arrives at a Hollywood film premiere, May 2010 (*Getty Images*)

Bob Rock, 2010 (*Getty Images*)

James Hetfield, 2009: 'I'm not gonna start writing about picking flowers now' (*Ross Halfin*)

from the main course. Beautifully played, beautifully produced by Bob Rock, beautifully photographed by Corbijn and designed by Airfix, but as remarkable as a faded piece of fax paper.

There were highlights but they were few: the ferociously catchy opening track, 'Fuel', would have sounded at home on any previous Metallica album, its lyric a wonderfully concise metaphor for those who drive their lives like their cars: too fast. 'The Memory Remains', released as the first single, was another fine moment, on the surface an old-fashioned riff-heavy metal song, about the perils of stardom, only let down in its overcompensating desire to snazzy things up by featuring Marianne Faithfull in a completely perfunctory rasping cameo, da-da-da-ing to no discernible effect, other than the principal aim of making the band seem cool, even Hetfield getting sucked into the postmodern mire with his throwaway line: 'ashes to ashes, dust to dust, fade to black ... '. The band would perform the song with Faithful on both *Top of the Pops* and *Saturday Night Live*, the latter helping push the single into the US Top Forty – their last appearance there for twelve years. The single of 'Memory' also contained the full 10:48 version of 'The Outlaw Torn', retitled 'The Outlaw Torn (Unencumbered by Manufacturing Restrictions Version)' along with an explanation on the single's back cover of why the 'cool-ass jam at the end of "Outlaw" got chopped' from *Load*. Still wanting to have their cake and eat it, the 'M' from the original Metallica logo was now used to make a shuriken-like symbol known as the 'Ninja Star', which became an alternative logo on this and other future releases and merchandising items.

Less interesting but still somehow a cut above the rest of the album is 'The Unforgiven II', which comes with the same *Few Dollars More* intro as the original but then gives way to a plodding riff, although Hammett's guitar almost saves it, the whole echoing the original melody and its restrained vocal, but ultimately collapsing under its inability to come up with something new and genuinely different. The only other half-decent track is 'Low Man's Lyric', which at over seven minutes is far too long for this funereal-paced dirge, but does at least start out more interesting, the hurdy-gurdy (by Bernado

Bigalli) and violin (by David Miles) adding a relief texture, with lyrics which appear to find James begging forgiveness for what sounds suspiciously like the infidelity of the long-distance rock star. It was like a bizarre sea shanty in which the captain begs not to go down with the ship.

Elsewhere, however, it was truly turgid fare such as 'Devil's Dance', a poor attempt at stoner rock – then the coming thing – with lots of brilliantly played but pointless guitar; 'Better Than You', which sounds like it could have come from an inferior Nine Inch Nails or possibly Marilyn Manson session. 'Can't stop the train from rolling,' James intones solemnly, like a sleepwalker. When the single version won the 1998 Grammy for 'Best Metal Performance' it was a toss-up between who was most sick: the group who recorded it to prove there was more to them than just metal, or the genuine metal fans who wouldn't have been seen dead listening to it. Then there was the generic rock of the interchangeable 'Slither' and 'Bad Seed', the dreadfully titled, musically uneventful 'Carp Diem Baby', and, worst of all, the even more dreadfully titled 'Where the Wild Things Are', stolen from the children's book but, unlike 'Enter Sandman', with nothing whatsoever added to it, musically or lyrically, to make you feel they'd enlarged or reconfigured the story, rather than just swiping the title 'cos it sounded 'cool'. This last, also, tellingly, was the only track on *Load* or *Reload* where Jason gets a co-credit. Then just when you think it can't possibly get any worse, there is 'Prince Charming'. How low on inspiration, one wonders, did they have to be to come up with this melange of triteisms and factory-fodder riffs? 'Attitude' was another bottom-of-the-barrel title, presumably about James' hunting fetish, but sounded more like Ratt in their heyday. 'Whatever happened to sweat?' James bellows. Whatever happened to riveting riffs and impassioned lyrics? Then finally 'Fixxxer', a monumentally awful title for a monumentally irritating song which goes on for an incredible eight minutes, convinced that it's some sort of 'Voodoo Chile' for the pierced-labia generation. Perhaps it is.

Released onto an all-too-suspecting world on 18 November 1997, *Reload* did as it was supposed to and went straight to Number One in

America, but only got as high as Number Four in the UK. It also did less well in Japan but just about managed to equal the success of *Load* elsewhere, in terms of chart positions. Overall, however, it barely sold half of what *Load* had done, which had sold less than half of what *Black* had done. Speaking in 2003, Bob Rock said he thought 'people really recognise that era for their haircuts more than anything and you know it's just like anybody, you want your bands to stay the way you love them and the way you want to hear them. It's like I had the same thing when Led Zeppelin did *Led Zeppelin III*, it was mostly acoustic and I hated it; now it's one of my favourites. People want bands to represent something and they want them to stay there. But I think history will show that those are really great albums and especially in the lyric department.'

While Rock was right about the extent to which more experimental albums, while not necessarily selling as well, are key components in extending the lifespan of a group's career, it doesn't alter the fact that musically *Reload* represents the nadir of Metallica's recorded career. As grand experiments go, had they stopped at *Load*, history would now applaud them. As it stands, *Reload* stained that achievement considerably. Although they may not have realised it yet, Metallica – now the most famous, all-conquering heavy metal band in history, whatever clothes they wore – was about to enter the bleakest period of its career. A time of albums full of covers and rehashed old stuff; even an album of classical music versions of their greatest hits. A period when Lars would reveal himself to be a business-savvy, number-crunching brand-protector who would risk alienating his fans – to the point of actually prosecuting them, if needs be. When James' demons would finally come home to roost to the extent he would need to rethink his role in life – and whether that included room for a group like Metallica. When Kirk would retreat back into the shadows, happy once again to settle for being the musical lynchpin between James and Lars, if only James and Lars would agree on anything at all; and in which Jason would finally tire of being the Newkid and do something about it, the only thing, in fact, he could: leave.

All of it, to a lesser or greater degree, was perfectly understandable, yet all of it was in danger of pulling the group apart as never before. Indeed, it would be another six years before Metallica was able to write and record a wholly new album and by then it was almost too late to save them.

THIRTEEN
MONSTRUM

From the first time I saw him – in London, at the 100 Club in 1987, the place so hot and crowded the sweat peeled from your face like old skin – to the last – turning up like a ghost in Some Kind of Monster, soft, sensitive eyes still full of anger, still trying to make the others see what only he could have seen – it seemed Jason was never entirely happy. He was just one those guys, big long face, taking everything so seriously, taking it all on his unhappily jutting chin. Not the kind of guy you'd ever see just cracking up laughing, not even after a doobie. One of those guys who meant well, who you just didn't wanna be around for long, knowing you'd always fall short of his excruciatingly high expectations, like some never-grown character left behind from The Catcher in the Rye.

It wasn't just being in Metallica and what it had done to him; it seemed to be something that had been there long before that. An itch you couldn't quite scratch. That was the feeling I got anyway whenever I saw him – either up-close, frowning about something, or entirely impersonal, far away on some stage that always looked just that little bit too big for him.

That first time at the 100 Club you couldn't really tell anything, except that it wasn't Cliff up there any more. Occasionally there would be a break in the human tide and you got a glimpse, a quick Polaroid flared around the edges … James, hunched over the mike, his right arm blurring away at the battered face of his Flying V … Lars at the back, furiously pumping arms and legs, a drowning man trying somehow to climb from the sea … Kirk in brief silhouette, his shadow, as always, appearing to flit in and out of sync with the rest … And the other one, the new kid, the only time you really noticed him was when he collapsed

*from the heat and the roadies rushed to try and revive him. Later –
many months later – when we finally met, at the restaurant at the hotel
in Miami, he'd snarled when he heard my name and denied anything
of the kind had ever happened, and, who knows, maybe I did get it
wrong, me and all the other people yelling and pointing. I had never
experienced the 100 Club like that before. Not even during the punk
years, at the club's worst, had I witnessed scenes like that. The way the
rest of the band shushed him down, though – laughed over the top of
his protestations, like saying they didn't care whether it had happened
or not, just don't blow our good scene – made me feel for him. Just
another one of those accidental things that only mattered to him, the
new kid, they seemed to be saying, the sense that things like that were
happening to him all the time, that my inaccurate review had been just
one more pin in his voodoo doll.*

*Then, years later, watching him in the movie, seeing the hurt in his face
still so raw like he was on the verge of tears – angry, self-righteous tears –
talking defensively about how his music was 'my children', in that way
people who don't have kids tend to do, I felt sorry for him all over again, in
the way one does when one sees an animal in pain, the lack of a common
language making the offer of comfort impossible, wanting to offer your
hand but afraid it might get bitten.*

*Fourteen years, six albums and just three miserable co-write credits
later, the impossible shadow of Cliff Burton looming ever larger with
every year that passes, if joining Metallica was still the best thing that
ever happened to Jason Newsted, then leaving them finally in order to
regain control, some vestige of self-respect, was at least the second-best
thing that ever happened to him. Truthfully, I only met him a few times,
spoke to him even less often, and barely knew him at all, just read the
signals he was constantly sending out, loud and clear, the same as
everybody else. And now he was gone I wouldn't miss him at all. Nobody
would. Not like they still did Cliff. And that was the real nub of the
problem right there. Nothing Jason Newsted did or does or will one day
do can ever compare to all the things Cliff Burton didn't live long enough
to do or not do . . .*

*

For Metallica, the years between *Reload* in 1997 and their next full-bore album, *St. Anger*, in 2003, were a wasteland. There were records and tours aplenty, endless news items and high-profile events, but essentially, when you got right down to it, there wasn't anything great or new to say, few positive vibrations, very little upward trajectory. Just a long time staring down the barrel of a gun, as if daring the worst to happen; for someone to come along, as indeed they duly did, and point out that the emperor's new clothes were, in fact, made of nothing more substantial than hot air. Having won over the music business by proving they weren't such freaks after all, that they could happily coexist within the mainstream, retain credibility and still make hundreds of millions of dollars for everyone involved – shedding the thrash stigmata before beating the grunge hordes at their own game – the one enemy Metallica could not finally overcome, it seemed, was itself. No longer young, never remotely pretty, bloated by fame and success and full, suddenly, of the kind of hubris that had destroyed the original rock giants at whose feet they had once worshipped, Metallica now appeared more dead than alive, existing off past glories, one of the all-time greats, but of increasingly less relevance to those who would own the new century about to dawn.

In November 1998, exactly a year after *Reload*, had come the double CD, *Garage Inc.*, its first disc comprising eleven newly recorded cover versions, its second disc a sixteen-track compilation of the original *Garage Days Revisited* EP/mini-album, plus all the covers recorded for their various singles' B-sides over the years. With the new tracks recorded in the same spirit as the old – laid down as-live in the studio, warts and all (or as many as producer Bob Rock could, in all conscience, allow) – both CDs absolutely crackled with energy, providing a fine counterpoint to the airlessly manicured sound of *Load* and *Reload*, as though Metallica had rediscovered its inner animal. Yet there was a heavy air of contrivance hovering over the package like a bad smell. Released, in part, to combat bootleg sales of albums containing such relatively rare material, *Garage Inc.* was also an attempt to claw back some of the credibility with the metal community Metallica had sacrificed in its mid-1990s 'reinvention', while at the same time retaining the extra dimension of the band's image Lars and Kirk had worked so hard to stimulate. So while the original Metallica logo returns to the front cover, the band shot – once again by Anton Corbijn – has them posing as grease monkeys outside their 'garage', with Lars, who doesn't smoke, holding a cigarette, and Kirk still trying to look cool in eyeliner and sculpted tash, brandishing a stogie and a bottle of beer, odd accoutrements for a working mechanic. The accompanying booklet is once again designed by Andie Airfix and retains the same fashionably distressed look and feel as the *Load* and *Reload* designs, although its design places one foot deliberately in the past by reproducing the original artworks for the *Garage Days* and 'Creeping Death' twelve-inch vinyl sleeves, along with a series of chronologically arranged pictures and memorabilia from the archives going all the way back to the Mustaine era.

The choice of material on Disc One also reflects the desire to keep faith with the past while retaining their newly *à la mode* edge. Among the inevitable Diamond Head cover ('It's Electric') and nod to the 1980s hardcore metal scene (a medley of Mercyful Fate songs), the whole thing is book-ended by covers of *two* songs by early Eighties Brit-punks Discharge ('Free Speech for the Dumb' and 'The More I See'). There are also no less than five covers of signature tunes from 1970s bands that either directly influenced Metallica ('Sabbra Cadabra' by Black Sabbath; 'Astronomy' by Blue Öyster Cult; 'Whiskey in the Jar' by Thin Lizzy) or had had some impact since ('Turn the Page' by Bob Seeger, heard for the first time on his car radio as Lars was driving across the Golden Gate Bridge en route to his mansion in Marin County). There are also two indirect acknowledgements of the influence Cliff Burton had on the band in 'Tuesday's Gone' by Lynyrd Skynyrd and 'Die, Die My Darling' by The Misfits. And, finally, one overt example of aligning themselves with the present generation of invulnerably credible rock goliaths in a commanding version of 'Loverman', from the 1994 Nick Cave and the Bad Seeds album, *Let Love In*.

Released in time for the Christmas gift-buying market, *Garage Inc.* satisfied the needs of a market geared to greatest hits packages, without the album actually being labelled as one, while at the same time both extending and consolidating the cross-promotional demographic of the now vastly disparate Metallica fan base. Fun but not too frivolous, lightweight but loaded with historical import, it was a credible stopgap to keep the band working out on the road while fulfilling its obligations to Elektra, Phonogram and Sony. Something for everybody, in fact – except perhaps the serious Metallica fans still waiting for the real follow-up to *Load*. As the *NME* noted in its review, Metallica may have grown up 'on a diet of spandex, studs and the long-lamented New Wave of British Heavy Metal ... speeding all that up and thrashing it around to the nth intense degree', but on *Garage Inc.* 'they come unstuck when they try to be trad, as with their sludge-boogie-plus-indulgence reading of Black Sabbath's "Sabbra Cadabra", or pub rock chug through "Whiskey in the Jar". Meanwhile Blue Öyster Cult and Bob Seger covers, not to mention a sing-along Lynyrd Skynyrd power ballad, suggest middle-age spread affects the most terminally adolescent minds in the end.'

The result was yet another Number One hit in the USA, but a decidedly less successful release everywhere else, not least in the UK, where it scraped to Number Twenty-Nine – Metallica's lowest chart position for a new album since *Master of Puppets* nearly thirteen years before. There were also three singles issued from *Garage Inc.* – 'Turn the Page', 'Whiskey in the Jar' and 'Die, Die My Darling'. None of them even made the US Top 100, while only 'Whiskey' made the lower reaches of the UK Top Thirty. Even so, their version of a song that had been a Top Ten hit in Britain, in 1973, was derided for Hetfield's misinterpretation of '*Wake for my daddio*' as '*Whack for my daddio*', due to Lizzy singer Phil Lynott's Irish accent, thus rendering a key line of the chorus insensible. He was forgiven, though, if for no reason other than nobody really takes these cobbled-together packages terribly seriously. So it was – and remains – with *Garage Inc.*

It was, however, a *tour de force* compared to what came next: another double CD, released just twelve months later, this time of a live orchestral performance, punningly titled *S&M* [Symphony and Metallica]. An ambitious collaborative project with celebrated classical composer Michael Kamen and the San Francisco Symphony Orchestra, recorded over two nights at the Berkeley Community Theater in April 1999, it presented a selection of Metallica songs rearranged for group and orchestra. This had been done before, of course, notably by Lars' beloved Deep Purple, whose 1969 performance with the Royal Philharmonic Orchestra at London's Albert Hall resulted in the *Concerto for Group and Orchestra* album. Since then, the idea that rock – that most grandiose and self-regarding of all pop idioms – might be wrought even larger by the addition of an eighty-piece symphony orchestra and conductor had been explored in several ways by various different artists; from the neo-classical stylings of progressive rock colossi such as Rick Wakeman, whose 1974 album *Journey to the Centre of the Earth* combined band, symphony orchestra and choir, to Emerson, Lake & Palmer, who performed regularly in America in the late 1970s with a full orchestra, and Roger Waters performing Pink Floyd's *The Wall* in Berlin in 1990 with an East German symphony orchestra; via the less serious guitars-meets-cellos of the Electric Light Orchestra (ELO) and the post-punk modernism of Malcolm McLaren and his 1984, proto-techno version of 'Madam Butterfly'. Even the Scorpions had recorded an album with the Berlin Philharmonic, *Moment of Glory*, which followed just months, in fact, after Metallica's.

Hardly a new idea then, Kamen, a fifty-year-old American orchestral composer, conductor and arranger mainly of film scores, had also worked previously with Pink Floyd, Queen, Eric Clapton, David Bowie and several other high-profile rock artists. It was in the wake of his original introduction to Metallica in 1991 by Bob Rock, who'd invited him to write an orchestral arrangement for 'Nothing Else Matters', that Kamen first suggested 'some sort of collaboration' on a grander scale. Eight years later he got his wish. According to Kamen, the idea was 'to create a dialogue between two worlds that celebrate the power of music'. Aside from the financial motivation, which was significant – the chance to record another five-million-selling album out of essentially two nights' work, along with the attendant redirection of buyers once again towards the band's back catalogue – it was never really clear what Metallica actually hoped to demonstrate with the collaboration.

Kamen studied Metallica's music for six months – the equivalent, he reckoned, of completing three movie soundtracks – scoring arrangements for twenty-one of their songs, including two new Hetfield/Ulrich compositions, 'No Leaf Clover' and 'Human'. There had been an initial rehearsal with the SFSO's principal players, followed by two lengthy rehearsals with both band and full orchestra, for which harpist Douglas Rioth arrived on a motorcycle, his tattooed arms clutching some Metallica CDs he would ask them to sign. 'There's also [some] snotty old bastards giving you the evil eye, like, "Fuck, you guys are cavemen. Your music sucks,"' complained James. 'But there were others that understood what we were trying to do; they could see that we fucking mean this shit, man. We have a passion in our music and our music is our life. They just grew up learning it different. They studied theory and we studied *UFO Live*.' The show itself was also filmed, and later released on DVD. To promote the album and DVD, Metallica also performed single concerts with orchestras in Berlin and New York. Questioned after the Berlin show, however, James laughed it off. When they were first presented with the idea, he said, 'We thought, "Fuck, that's got failure written all over it. It's like fucking in church. Let's do it!"' Playing down the whole thing still further, he added: 'It would be fun to take [the orchestra] on tour and watch them fall into the debauchery hole and completely turn into rock ruins. Taking them on the road and watching one beer turn into five beers and all of a sudden they're in jail, divorced and hooked on heroin and smashing their cellos onstage.'

Presented in yet another Airfix-designed package, replete with by-now-obligatory Corbijn photos, the whole was decidedly underwhelming once the novelty had worn off. As always there were highlights – the grand rendering of the instrumental 'The Call of Ktulu' (misremembered on the new CD booklet as 'The Call of the Ktulu') is breathtaking, as is the reworked Morricone opening, 'The Ecstasy of Gold'. The two new songs – 'No Leaf Clover' and 'Human' – are also impressive, both more genuinely experimental than anything from the *Load/Reload* period; the latter a swaggering, emotional trial by fire with band and orchestra meshing to spectacular effect; the former a sweeping, atmospheric piece that somehow allows oboe and keyboards to sit snugly alongside the explosive guitars, drums and treated vocals. The remaining seventeen tracks, however, merely highlight what an odd, difficult fit the two highly emotive forms of music make. 'One' sounds neutered; 'Enter Sandman' simply a mess. Even something like 'Nothing Else Matters' – Kamen's original entry point into the band's music – sounds lacklustre, perfunctory. Others, such as 'Hero of the Day', work better but only because the orchestra tends to stay more in the background. Ultimately, what may well have been a unique live experience becomes, on record and DVD, little more than a home movie: fascinating, no doubt, for those who were there, but something that doesn't stand up to repeated listening/viewing for the rest of us. It couldn't even be argued this time that Metallica had shrewdly judged the market; this was a package seemingly designed to please no one: not hardcore metal fans nor the nu-generation of Limp Bizkit and Slipknot fans then rising to challenge their superiority, just as the grunge stars had done nearly a decade before.

Reviews were upbeat if somewhat lukewarm. In Britain, *Q* was avuncular, describing it as 'another just about forgivable flirtation with Spinal Tap-esque lunacy'. *Rolling Stone* claimed the album 'creates the most crowded, ceiling-rattling basement rec room in rock ... The effect is ... one of timelessness.' Later, however, it changed its mind, describing *S&M* as Metallica's 'very worst disc ... just as useless as every other album on which a rock band plays their hits with an orchestra'. Nevertheless, it reached Number One in America, although it did not even gain entry into the Top Thirty in Britain. 'No Leaf Clover' was also issued as an obligatory single – the only one from the album – but that was not a hit even in America. As *Metal Hammer* editor Alexander Milas says now, 'If you go back to *Justice* or *Ride* there's this fury and passion that just didn't exist any more. All of a sudden Metallica didn't seem to be aware of who they were as a band ... they appeared every bit as rich and divorced from the common man as they possibly could.' He adds, 'Even though some of the music is actually quality, I really like "No Leaf Clover", for example, this was a down and dirty thrash metal band that had become part of the elite.'

If as recording artists Metallica were now beginning to take on the appearance of jaded old gods, as concert masters they were still considered a top-drawer ticket, as monolithic and unmissable as the pyramids. So what if they would never make another album as good as *Master* or as popular as *Black*, who cared if they had lost the plot artistically, they still kicked ass live, right, dude? What they then did next, however, almost wrecked their reputation completely.

In early 2000, it was discovered that a demo of a thunderous new Metallica track – a kind of mini-me 'Enter Sandman' called 'I Disappear' – earmarked for the soundtrack of the forthcoming *Mission: Impossible II* movie was receiving radio play in the USA. Outraged, they ordered an investigation; the source of the leaked track was traced back to a new, pioneering 'peer-to-peer' internet service named Napster. Conceived from a computer programme written by a nineteen-year-old college freshman named Shawn Fanning, which allowed users to trade music files without paying a tariff – essentially, providing free music – further investigation revealed that the site had attracted an estimated thirty-eight million users in its first eighteen months. They also discovered that the entire Metallica back catalogue was freely available via the site. At this point the whole band, but Lars in particular, decided something had to be done, instructing Q Prime to look into the legal position. The result was a lawsuit filed at the District Court, in California, in April 2000, alleging that Napster violated three areas of US law: copyright infringement, unlawful use of a digital audio interface device, and the Racketeer Influenced and Corrupt Organisation Act. Suits were also simultaneously filed against Indiana University, Yale University and the University of Southern California, for contributing to copyright infringement by allowing their students the technology to use Napster. Metallica's lawyer, Howard King, said: 'We don't know how realistic it will be, but we will see what we will find out when we go through the Napster files to see if we can find the people who have downloaded them and if we can then we will go after them.' He added: 'Our goal is to put

Napster out of business in total and bury them.' In an official statement, Lars justified the action, saying it was 'sickening to know that
our art is being traded like a commodity rather than the art that it
is. From a business standpoint, this is about piracy – a.k.a. taking
something that doesn't belong to you; and that is morally and legally
wrong. The trading of such information – whether it's music, videos,
photos, or whatever – is, in effect, trafficking in stolen goods.'

Less well publicised was the fact that Napster was already being
sued by the Recording Industry Association of America (RIAA). A
rock band threatening to sue its own fans, though – that was news.
Hiring an online consulting firm, NetPD, to monitor the Napster
service for a weekend, a list of 317,377 internet users who it was
claimed had illegally traded Metallica MP3s was then personally hand-
delivered by an indignant Lars to Napster's San Mateo headquarters:
thirteen boxes of over 60,000 pages of legal paperwork. At Metallica's
request, the users were banned from the site. A sophomore student
at IU, Chad Paulson, and founder of the website Students Against
University Censorship, was quoted as saying: 'I can't believe [Metal-
lica] have to or would sue their fans. I am sure that nobody anticipated
this. I think it is a big hypocrisy on their part, because Metallica allows
fans to record their live concerts and freely distribute their recordings
like Dave Matthews and Phish.' Within days, however, both Yale
and Indiana had blocked Napster use on campus. As a result, both
universities were dropped from the Metallica lawsuit. USC also later
followed suit.

The battle over the legitimacy of the site raged on, and in July
pictures of Lars arriving in his limo to testify before the US Senate
Judiciary Committee made the TV news across America. Eventually
Federal Judge Marilyn Hall Patel would order Napster to place a filter
on its own site within seventy-two hours or be shut down immediately.
A settlement was also eventually reached between Metallica and
Napster when the German media conglomerate Bertelsmann BMG
looked into buying the rights to Napster for $94 million, with the site
blocking users from file-sharing tracks by any artists that objected to
the process. Presented publicly as a win/win situation for both sides,

Metallica's lawsuit effectively closed down Napster in its original form. Less than two years later the company would file for Chapter II bankruptcy protection. By September 2002, when another judge blocked its sale to Bertelsmann under US bankruptcy law, Napster was obliged to liquidate its assets. These days Napster exists as an online provider of legal downloads for subscription fees to members. The real loser in the war with Napster was arguably Metallica, such was the permanent scar it left on the band's public face. Metallica may have had all the legal rights in the Napster case but publicly it was the website that would occupy the moral high ground, becoming Robin Hood to the band's nasty Sheriff of Nottingham. This was not just in the minds of the fans who had been using the site, but also in the majority of the music press in Britain and America, even with other artists, who publicly came out in favour of Napster. Fred Durst of nu-metal stars Limp Bizkit said pointedly, 'The only people worried about [Napster] are really worried about their bank accounts.' He then agreed for Limp Bizkit to participate in a free nationwide US tour to generate support for Napster. In a letter to the *New York Times*, rapper Chuck D said: 'Unlike many of my fellow artists, I support the sharing of music files on the internet. I believe artists should welcome Napster. We should think of it as a new kind of radio-promotional tool.'

This last point was one shared by many fans who claimed they only used the file-sharing service to 'preview' tracks of albums they would then buy online or in-store. Critics, meanwhile, pointed out the hypocrisy of a band such as Metallica, who first came to prominence via the cassette-tape-trading scene of the pre-internet early 1980s, now complaining about their fans trading in the modern equivalent. Whatever one's view of how readily copyrighted material should be made available over the internet, this last accusation was disingenuous at best. Making a cassette-tape recording of a record then mailing it out to a friend, who may then make a second- and third-generation recording of that tape is a laborious process, the quality of the recording diminishing slightly each time a copy is made. To suggest it might significantly reduce an artist's ability to sell original copies of their recordings is spurious. The difference with Napster was that one fan putting one track online could result in millions of perfectly recorded copies being downloaded in a single day. The threat to an artist's livelihood is obvious. As Scott Stapp, lead singer of Creed, said at the time, 'My music is my home. Napster is sneaking in the back door and robbing me blind.' Rap godfather Dr Dre also came out in support of the band, demanding an additional 230,142 Napster users be similarly banned from downloading his music. After being made a 'disingenuous' out-of-court settlement, Dre filed a lawsuit against Napster on the same grounds as Metallica.

Taken aback by the furore, Lars – usually so shrewd a judge of fan opinion – had completely misread the situation. From his and Q Prime's point of view, the Napster lawsuit was just another day at the office. Three years earlier they had threatened Amazon.com with a lawsuit for selling an unauthorised album of rarities – the action that had partly prompted the release of *Garage Inc.* – and had gone after online retailers N2K, distributors of the Dutch East India Trading Co., and independent British label Outlaw Records over the sale of a bootleg live album. In January 1999, they had also filed a lawsuit in a federal court in LA against Victoria's Secret, the women's lingerie catalogue, seeking injunctive relief and damages when it was discovered they had used the name Metallica on lipsticks without authorisation. They also sued Pierre Cardin over the marketing of a Metallica tuxedo. There was no P R backlash then and both companies eventually settled out of court. Just weeks after Lars' Napster court appearance, the band was suing the centuries-old fragrance manufacturer Guerlain for trademark infringement over their new perfume named Metallica, a vanilla-based scent then on sale for the headbanging price of $175 for an 8oz bottle. They also sent a 'cease and desist' letter to department stores including Neiman Marcus and Bergdorf Goodman for daring to stock the perfume, claiming 'dilution, unfair competition, false designation of origin and injuring the heavy metal band's reputation', revealed Jill Pietrini, the lawyer acting for the band. When the response they received was 'not quite acceptable', they launched a suit seeking punitive damages, requesting the court to order Neiman Marcus to destroy the perfume.

The problem with the Napster suit was that this time the band appeared to be penalising its own fans. As such, the Napster case beamed the media spotlight on Metallica more searingly than ever before. Suddenly, both fans and media were turning against them; the internet a hive of invective against the band. On the Metallica Usenet group, there was a lengthy, ongoing thread entitled 'Kirk and Lars are gay', while a hilarious spoof Metallica ad from an outfit calling itself Camp Chaso (the brainchild of producer, director, writer and now political columnist Bob Cesca) became one of the most popular items on the net. It depicted a cartoon Lars as a tiny greed-obsessed motormouth, with James pictured as his gargantuan, mono-brain-celled ogre, yelling slogans such as 'Money good! Napster bad!' The pair of them were apparently wading in a mountainous pile of sacks with dollar signs on them as the mini-Lars yells about how rich the band are; railing against the 'dickless cocksuckers who try to steal our music with their motherfucking Napster' and how the band's lawyers will 'hunt you down like the table-scrap pilfering grab-asses you are'.

As Alexander Milas says, it all left Metallica looking like 'the anti-christ. It had soured the entire universe on Lars Ulrich, who had pretty much successfully identified himself as the biggest dick in the galaxy.' Milas recalls seeing Metallica at the RFK stadium in Washington on their Summer Sanitarium tour of the USA that year: 'Right in the middle of Metallica's set they actually stopped playing and a video came up on the big screen. It's like Lars Ulrich drumming and he's got a Pepsi right next to him and someone off-screen takes the Pepsi away and he stops playing drums, and goes: "Hang on a minute, that's not cool, they took my Pepsi. You know what else is not cool? Taking people's music and . . . blah blah blah." I'm not even joking! I mean, I'm paraphrasing, because by then I was shouting and so were fifty thousand other people. I've spent like a hundred bucks, which is an absolute fortune when you're that age, to listen to Lars preach to me about not stealing the records when I owned everything and the singles already. It was just completely disgusting. It actually turned me off from them. In retrospect, you can completely see their point but at the time they were the wrong persons to be the spearhead of that awareness campaign.'

The zeal with which Lars was pursuing the Napster situation was becoming out of proportion to other previous legal actions. Suddenly there appeared to be a very personal dimension. This only worsened as criticism against Metallica began to build in the media. At the 2000 MTV Video Music Awards Lars famously scored another own goal when he appeared in an anti-Napster video skit with the show's host, Marlon Wayans. Wayans played a college student downloading 'I Disappear' in his dorm when Lars suddenly appears, demanding an explanation. When Wayans' character explains he's not stealing, only 'sharing', Lars proceeds to demonstrate the error of his ways by first drinking his Pepsi, then getting the Metallica road crew to empty his room of all his stuff, slapping Napster stickers on everything first. The video caused a certain amount of mirth from the industry guests in the room. But Lars' appearance onstage later that evening was greeted by much more voluble booing from the public-admittance section of the audience. Despite looking decidedly uncomfortable, Lars later claimed he was 'unaware of it' until he got offstage. When Shawn Fanning appeared to respond by presenting an award while wearing a Metallica shirt, announcing pointedly, 'I borrowed this shirt from a friend. Maybe, if I like it, I'll buy one of my own,' he received unreserved cheers. Again, Lars later brushed it off, claiming 'the whole thing was planned', and that the organisers had originally asked him to co-present the award with Fanning but that 'Napster's lawyers pulled him out of it' at the last minute, concerned Lars would use the occasion to worsen the situation with their client. Talking to *Playboy* just a few weeks later, however, Lars made a point of saying he thought 'It was the worst awards show, hands down, that I've ever been to' and that he had left early to have dinner with friends.

Portrayed as the greed-driven villains of the piece, even James – who'd taken a back seat while his wife, Francesca, gave birth to their second child, a son, Castor, in May 2000 – admitted he had 'cringed at certain interviews: "Oh, dude, don't say that."' Lars, however, while also shuddering at some of the unexpected positions his hard-line stance put him in, ultimately remained unrepentant: 'If you'd stop being a Metallica fan because I won't give you my music for free, then fuck you.' It seemed the feeling was mutual, however, and to this day the Napster debacle has hung like a shadow over everything Metallica has tried to do, their various attempts to make amends – including the cringe-making vision of Lars taking part in an internet interview explaining why file-sharing was actually good for fans, particularly in places such as Saudi Arabia where downloading tracks was the only way they had of accessing music they could not buy on CD. 'I think it's great,' he said. 'Obviously it's the way to share this stuff and I think it's awesome. I think that we were somewhat flabbergasted at some early internet things that were going on a few years ago but we're at peace with that.'

Far less public but even more immediately damaging was the long-predicted meltdown of Jason Newsted, whose official departure from Metallica was announced in January 2001. Ostensibly the split had come about because James wouldn't let Jason release an album by his side-project band Echobrain. In reality, the split had been coming almost since the day Jason had joined. 'During the last couple of tours he was totally withdrawing from everything,' James told *Classic Rock* in 2003: 'Going into his own little world, wearing headphones all the time, never communicating, and we certainly weren't kings of communication, either. We were just four guys who would shut up, play and let the beast roll on.' More to the point, as Lars recalled the last time we spoke in 2009, Jason was 'intense, very serious ... he joined as a new member, obviously, and I think sort of stayed a new member, pretty much for all the fourteen years that he was in the band'.

At the time, though, Lars was too distracted with his own problems. Now separated from Skylar and their two-year-old son, Myles, he was living temporarily in a hotel suite in New York while mixing the debut album by Systematic, *Somewhere in Between*, for the Elektra-backed boutique label TMC (The Music Company) he had recently formed with record exec Tim Duffy. (The label would later run aground amidst personal animosity between the two co-founders.) Lars couldn't have cared less just then what Jason was up to. Kirk, meanwhile, thought the Echobrain album was 'great' and was happy for him to release it. Jason had been quick to point out how many other artists' records James had appeared on – including vocals for the track 'Hell Isn't Good' on the *South Park: Bigger, Longer and Uncut* movie soundtrack; cameos on two Corrosion of Conformity albums; and playing guitar on a Primus album track. But James wasn't 'out trying to sell them', he replied, and compared Jason's working on a side-project to 'cheating on your wife'. Reflecting on the situation two years later, Lars felt free enough to admit the reason for James' hard-line stance was down to 'control issues'. He said, 'James has his vision of the perfect family, and it's almost kind of mafia style. You're part of the family and if you step outside of the family you're betraying the family, and you'll get ostracised. And that is at the heart of a lot of the stuff that we've tried to work through in the last couple of years.'

There had reportedly been a nine-and-a-half-hour band meeting at the RitzCarlton Hotel in San Francisco, which had followed an equally intense get-together a week earlier. Newsted was given the choice: forget Echobrain and stay with Metallica, or release the Echobrain record – and forget Metallica. Jason resigned the same day. His official statement referred to 'private and personal reasons, and the physical damage I have done to myself over the years while playing the music that I love'. Behind the scenes, however, he admitted he had felt 'almost stifled'. What hurt most was that Jason had always looked up to James, in much the same way as James had once looked up to Cliff. '[James] taught me determination and perseverance,' Newsted would recall. 'People have tried to burn him and break him, but he'll always jump right back up. And kick your ass. No matter what differences we've had . . . I'll always regard him as one of the best musicians ever.'

James, too, would come to look back on the whole episode with regret as the years passed. Speaking in 2003 with the newfound clarity that sobriety had brought him, he admitted it was his own 'fears of abandonment and control issues' that lay behind the way Jason's desire to record his own music had been mismanaged: 'It makes sense that I would ... try to grip harder to keep the family together, that no one would leave, for fear that they might find something better somewhere else, when initially all [Jason] had to do was go jam with some other band and find out that, you know, Metallica is home. You don't know what home is until you leave, and he'd maybe have become more grateful to be in Metallica. That's certainly one ending to that story.' He was honest enough to admit, though, that Echobrain 'wasn't the only reason that he left. A lot of other things combined and caused him to escape into a future of his own elsewhere, and search for happiness, and we're all hoping that he finds it.'

In the meantime, Metallica had a new album waiting to be delivered. With Jason out and the will to find an immediate replacement simply not there, Bob Rock offered to play bass on the album and the others gratefully accepted. More badly scarred from the huge dent the Napster fracas had left in their reputation than they were ready yet to admit and still reeling from the psychic wounds Jason's unhappy departure had reopened, for the first time the band was entirely unsure as to which direction their music should take. Rock and metal had undergone a huge renaissance in public taste since the last time Metallica had entered a recording studio seriously in 1995. Nu-metal, as evinced by rap-rock crossover stars such as Limp Bizkit and Linkin Park, had replaced them at the cutting edge, but there was no way they were going to convince James Hetfield to try competing as a rapper, while the classic rock market – although undergoing its own resurgence in the shape of zillion-selling reunion tours by the original line-ups of Kiss, Black Sabbath, AC/DC, Iron Maiden and others – was not yet seen as a comfortable fit for the band.

Pragmatism was now the order of the day and, unable to suggest anything more concrete, they were happy to take Bob Rock's lead in proposing a more collaborative approach, going into the studio empty-handed and literally seeing what happened, an idea previously considered anathema to the controlling Hetfield and Ulrich. Taking a six-month lease on an old army barracks just outside San Francisco called the Presidio, at Rock's suggestion the sessions would take on a far more 'free-thinking' aspect than on previous Metallica albums, with lyrics for once being worked on by everyone – quite literally, as they all sat together in a room and took turns writing down lines, Rock included. 'We've really kind of changed our process in the way we're approaching this [album],' said Rock. 'We loaded in a lot of my equipment from my studio [and] we recorded there for two months, and we put down about eighteen kind of song ideas. It's definitely a different approach. The whole thing [has] a very live feel ... almost like a garage-type band atmosphere, only with great recording equipment to capture at the moment of conception so to speak.' He predicted, 'What this album is going to be like is ... what they are as people, what they're thinking and where they're at.' It would certainly become that, though not remotely in the way Bob or indeed the band had originally conceived.

There would be another, entirely unexpected ingredient this time: the addition to the day-to-day team of a $40,000-a-month 'performance-enhancement coach': Dr Phil Towle. A former sports psychologist who had worked, most famously, with the Tennessee Titans' defensive lineman Kevin Carter and the legendary NFL coach Dick Vermeil, Towle's first foray into the music business had been with Rage Against the Machine guitarist Tom Morello. Hired by Q Prime to try to bring the remaining members of Metallica – and Bob Rock – back to some sort of emotional tempo that would permit them to work well again in the studio, despite their recent setbacks, Towle not only instigated intensive two-hour daily sessions, he stayed around for the rest of the day and night, becoming increasingly more involved in the actual making of the album.

In their attempt to reinvigorate their music, post-thrash, post-grunge, post-reinvention, post-orchestras, post-fame and fortune and, clearly in subtext, post-Napster and post-Jason – and now group-therapy – the band would create a new form of Metallica music whose most immediate feature would be a complete dearth of guitar solos and an unlikely, cut-and-pasted drum sound; a genuinely distressed, fiercely antagonistic package, reflected in song titles such as 'Frantic', 'St. Anger', 'Some Kind of Monster' and 'Shoot Me Again'. How happy the rest of the world would be with the end results, however, would prove to be a matter of the utmost debate, more so even than on *Load* and *Reload*. But that discussion was still some considerable way off when, after just three months of working like this at the Presidio, James arrived one morning with unexpected news. He was checking himself into rehab, effective immediately, and all other plans would have to be put on hold – indefinitely.

'When we started playing music after Jason leaving,' James said later, 'the music was not all it could have been. We started to write and then as we were going deeper into ourselves, and exploring why it was that Jason left – what it meant to us, and all of that – it started stirring up a lot of emotions and a lot of stuff about how we could better ourselves as individuals. So I made the decision to go into rehab.' Jason's departure may have been the spark that finally lit the fuse but the reality was that Hetfield had been questioning his own mental and emotional state since the days when he would plan his week around whatever days he was going to have a hangover on. He'd first given up drinking back in 1994, when – in recovery terms – he 'white-knuckled it' for almost a year, not drinking alcohol but not feeling any happier with his choice. He was soon back drinking again throughout the years of the *Load* and *Reload* world tours.

Since the death of his father and then his marriage in August 1997 to Francesca Tomasi – a former Metallica crew member – he had been swinging back and forth between on-the-wagon sobriety and on-the-road hell-raising, even after the birth of their children Cali (in June 1998) and Castor. Happy to play the gentle giant family man at home, away from home – not just on tour but on his frequent, all-male hunting trips – James was still the same short-tempered human grizzly he'd always been. When, during a short vacation during those initial months working on the new Metallica album, he found himself away for his son Castor's first birthday – hunting bear and drinking double-strength vodka on the Kamchatka peninsula in Siberia, a four-hour helicopter ride from the nearest small town – he finally began to crack. When Francesca then confronted him, threatening to leave with the children if he didn't do something about his monstrously selfish behaviour, 'That was the end for me,' he confessed.

The upshot was an eleven-month programme of rehab – 'a nice little cocoon', he called it. Not so nice to begin with, though, during those earliest, most painful days of recovery: 'I realised how much my life was fucked up. How many secrets I had, how incongruent my life was, and disclosing all this shit to my wife. Shit that happened on the road ... Women, drink, whatever it is.' Making a clean breast of things had a knock-on effect with the rest of the band, too: 'Like I'm this whistleblower and then all of a sudden: "Er, wow, isn't it terrible, honey, that he did that?"' Yet, as far as James could see, looking back almost ten years later, 'it was the saving part of Metallica, there's no doubt. It had to come to an end a certain way.' Tormented by the thought of losing both his wife and his band, he decided: 'I've got to get it together or they're both going to go away and then what?'

It also had an immediate effect on another, more tangential project that would now blossom into one of the most fascinating of the band's career. A month before arriving at the Presidio, they had agreed to allow New York-based film-makers Joe Berlinger and Bruce Sinofsky to make a documentary about the recording of the album. Best known previously for their collaborative 1992 debut, *Brother's Keeper* (an acclaimed examination of the murder trial of Delbert Ward) and, four years later, *Paradise Lost: The Child Murders at Robin Hills*, Berlinger was also known, less flatteringly, for his solo fictional debut, *Book of Shadows*, the critically derided follow-up to *The Blair Witch Project* – such a disaster that Berlinger went into hiding for a period. Now back working on documentaries with Sinofsky again, their first major project would be the Metallica documentary.

Their initial ambitions for the film were modest: this would essentially be a promotional tool, just as the 1991 documentary video *A Year and a Half in the Life of Metallica* had been for the *Black Album*. The deal was that Metallica would pay for the cost of producing the film but Berlinger and Sinofsky would be allowed unprecedented access. The two film-makers had dealt with the band previously on the soundtrack for *Paradise Lost*, a film 'about heavy metal on trial as much as the kids accused in the film', according to Berlinger. Since then there had been vague discussions about making a Metallica documentary movie, but 'they'd always have the excuse, "We're not ready to pull the curtain back"', recalled Sinofsky. 'As it turned out, the time that we were invited in, in March of 2001, they were at their most vulnerable, they were at their all-time low, at a time that you would expect that nobody would allow a camera crew – especially a crew like us who make very in-depth films. But they invited us in, gave us complete access; never told us, "We have a meeting now, so you can't come in." Every door was open, nothing was ever locked. We were never asked to leave. They treated us, in terms of access, better than any other project that we've been involved in.'

When they continued filming throughout the fall-out from James' decision to lay down tools and seek psychiatric help, the film now transmogrified into something else entirely: a close-up study of people in crisis. Named *Some Kind of Monster* after one of the new tracks, the most surprising thing about this documentary full of shocks was that Metallica allowed it to be made at all. But then this was the new era of reality TV. Hetfield was still ensconced in his prolonged rehab programme when the first episodes of a groundbreaking new TV series called *The Osbournes* began airing in the USA – a phenomenon that had not escaped the Ulrich radar any more than it had anyone else's in 2002. As the main driver behind the film project, Lars' instincts to push Metallica towards the latest trends proved to be inspired this time, even though he could not have imagined how differently the film would eventually turn out. When it was premiered at the Sundance Film Festival in February 2004, film critics were so impressed that they put it forward for 'Official Selection'. Some music critics predictably compared it to the spoof 1980s 'rockumentary' *This is Spinal Tap*. But that was to miss the point entirely. Not only were there few laughs in *Some Kind of Monster*, the insights it offered of a major band unravelling before one's very eyes struck a chord far beyond the rock and metal – or even alternative – audience. As such, it also achieved for Metallica something that the new album it showed them desperately struggling to make would not manage to do: rehabilitate their reputation, restoring them from out-of-touch,

Napster-crushing millionaire spoilsports back to somewhere closer to the truth-preserving musical vigilantes they had been perceived as previously.

Not that they knew this at the time it was being filmed, as practically every scene from the movie makes clear. Indeed, rather than look like they were about to return as triumphant conquerors, for most of its 160 minutes *Some Kind of Monster* portrays Metallica as being hopelessly at sea. Beginning, literally, with their equipment being loaded into the Presidio, and ending over two and a half years later with the band's first tour since Jason Newsted's departure, via the Napster-baiting debacle, the arrival of Dr Towle, James' sudden retreat into painstakingly lengthy rehab, the appointment of a new bassist, and many other things neither Berlinger or Sinofsky could possibly have predicted, we get a real sense of how close Metallica was to imploding throughout the months and eventually years the album and movie were being made. From those first few weeks in the studio, with James constantly 'in a shit mood' and at loggerheads in particular with Lars, to the excruciating eleven months he was away – when the others had no idea where he was, or if he was ever coming back, 'I'm preparing for the worst,' says Lars – the cameras keep rolling, defying rule number one of showbiz: never show the strings and wires.

'Lars, Bob Rock and I had continued getting together for meetings just to keep the faith,' recalled Kirk in 2003, 'keep the momentum going and just keep in touch, because everything was falling apart around us and we felt that if we held strong and held it together at least we had each other. It was a pretty cold realisation that we hadn't heard from James for X amount of time and I had to think of a back-up plan. I'm the kind of person who always needs back-up plans or, as my therapist says, exits, escape routes. So I sat down and thought about it long and hard and thought, "Do I have enough things in my life to fill the void if Metallica is gone?" And I discovered that I did. I also asked myself if I would carry on in music, and there was no question; it's what I do. But was I ready for the big drop? And it would have been a drop; right back down to the ground, it would virtually have been like starting over for me. [But] after realising that I could, it gave me enough confidence to wait things out rather than just panic about the situation that was going on with the band.'

James, too, was conscious the band might be on the brink of collapse without him. 'I think each one of us went through that possibility in our own minds, and what that meant to us, and that was a healthy thing,' he reflected, 'to identify that each one of us as people is more important than Metallica the thing, the machine and the creative force. I certainly went through that in rehab; I completely stripped everything about me to the bone and rebuilt myself as an individual. Growing up in Metallica was all I knew, and I didn't realise how much I was using and manipulating with it. But yeah, after Jason left and I went into rehab the other guys certainly spun the wheels in their heads wondering how to control their futures when it wasn't up to them, it wasn't up to any of us really, but coming to that realisation was important. It made us stronger as individuals and it gave us real perspective on how much we mean to each other and how much we'd taken each other for granted.'

Kirk recalled how when James finally sent them a message, four months after leaving for rehab, 'saying that he still needed some more time to sort things out and he had no idea how long that would be', the band really did think it was over: 'It was a long time coming. After we hadn't heard from him for six weeks or so, Lars and I were driving each other loony speculating on what he was doing and why we hadn't heard from him and what was going on in his head. In the meantime, friends would come up to us and say: "I ran into James at the mall. Damn, he looks good." And we're like: "What is this? Friends of the band are seeing James and we're left in this holding pattern." That continued through the whole of September and October until the third week of November. My wife had a surprise [birthday] party for me and I saw this guy standing in the corner, casting a familiar shadow, and it was James. I was so glad to fucking see him, and I could instantly see from looking into his eyes that there was a new clarity there; a new awareness and a new sensitivity that I didn't detect before. It was totally amazing, we were able to exchange a few words, and I was able to make sure for myself that he was okay and functioning on a somewhat sane level. But he told me, "You know, it's still going to be some time." So we actually didn't start hooking up until March [2002] and only then did we start having meetings and reconnecting with each other. But that was the adjustment period that we had to go through to adjust to the new James Hetfield, and it was just as much of an adjustment for him to us.'

For James, his first time back with the band, was 'very scary. Any of the firsts in sobriety are scary, just leaving rehab was scary. Going through some absolutely cathartic experiences [and] then coming out into the world was scary. You were in a nice little cocoon of safety there, so you can tear down and rebuild. But, oh boy, coming out was scary. "What should I do? What should I not do? Where should I go? Uh, I don't want to go in here, because something might trigger me into this and that." You know, the fear of just living, it was with me for a little while. So coming right back into the band, it just didn't work. And it was hard to explain to them how it wasn't time yet. I needed time to adjust to the world and I couldn't just come and plug in because every time we plugged in and started playing together it was like a security blanket, the world went away and everything was fine. It was a safety zone and I didn't want to forget about all the other stuff that had to happen; like me explaining to them what I need; how it's different for me and how the dynamic has changed, and how we're not going to be going on two-year tours any more. My family is important to me and I can't let my children grow up without me and all the other priorities, how they lined up in my life. And it's become contagious, you know, that stuff spread within the band and we all started taking a look at ourselves and becoming a lot more respectful of each other and our needs.' He had felt like a stranger suddenly, he said: 'Totally, I had to reintroduce myself to those guys and they didn't know what to think ... To them, to my wife, to everybody.' Even, he said, 'to myself: "Is this me talking? Man, I'm not even thinking about what I'm saying and all this shit's coming out, you know, and it feels right and it feels okay." And yes, especially to my wife, you know: "I know you, you're very manipulative," and addicts are pretty manipulative, and, "Ah, this is just an act," and after two years, it's a way of life now. But yeah, there was a whole dynamic change that had to happen within the group. And certain things had to shift … One person changes and everyone else around them, all relationships, friends, everything changed.'

One of the new conditions James requested was that he only work in the studio between midday and 4 p.m. each day – something the others acceded to, only to run out of patience when he then insisted they not work on the album either beyond those hours, prompting a scene in the movie where Lars – eaten up by James' suggestion that no one even *discuss* the music in his absence – paces the room and tells him, 'I realise now that I barely knew you before,' followed by a shot of James taking off on his motorcycle to attend his infant daughter Marcella's ballet lesson.

Other remarkable scenes from the movie include a cringingly painful meeting between Lars and Dave Mustaine that takes place while James is still in rehab. In this, the eternally wronged guitarist talks about how he still wishes the band had 'woken me and said, "Dave, you need to get counselling,"' rather than simply hand him a Greyhound ticket that cold morning in New Jersey in 1982. There are some equally telling scenes with Jason, in which he damns their recruitment of Towle as 'really fucking lame', and in which Lars, Kirk and Bob attend an Echobrain gig in San Francisco, only to discover Jason has already 'left the building' when they go backstage afterwards to wish him well. Then there is the now white-whiskered Cliff Burnstein sneaking a glance at his watch while listening to a playback of the album; Lars' Gandalf-like father, Torben, suggesting they 'delete' a gloomy instrumental piece they had planned to open the album with; some evocative stock clips from the band's past, notably one of a much younger James lifting a beer to toast some vast, outdoor festival audience, telling them how drunk he is; a clearly frustrated Kirk arguing – in vain – for at least one guitar solo on the new album. Up to a fitful climax in which the new album – almost too aptly titled *St. Anger* – is finally released to devastatingly bad reviews (not shown in the film) but still tops the US charts. There is a more genuine sense of epiphany, however, when, near the end, the band is shown shooting a video at San Quentin prison, with James shakily but touchingly assuming the mantle of the late Johnny Cash.

There are also giddy glimpses into the newly chilled Kirk Hammett sporting a cowboy hat on his now-long-again hair as he gazes out at the ranch he has purchased, or explaining how he recently took up surfing, an activity completely at odds with his previous image as someone who only came out after dark; the auction of most of Lars' art collection at Christie's in New York. 'Can we get some more cocktails here?' he asks, woozily, as the auction total passes the $40 million mark. Just as eye-watering are the scenes of Lars testifying before a senate committee, claiming that Napster had 'hijacked our music' as, outside, fans destroy their Metallica CDs; or Bob Rock trying to coax some music out of the fractured ambience that ensues after James finally returned to work, not just producing and playing bass, but throwing in lyrical ideas and doing his best to remain tight-lipped during their numerous therapy-induced squabbles.

Best – and worst – of all are the often toe-curling scenes with Dr Towle. Seen one moment sticking up signs in the studio with the words 'Zone It' on them, or suggesting the band enter a 'meditative state' when jamming together, some might find it easy to dismiss him as offering little they couldn't have found just as easily in a self-help book. It's through their sessions with Towle, however, that they finally address the fact that they never properly dealt with the death of Cliff Burton, and that they allowed that unexpressed grief to turn them against Jason first and then against themselves. As Towle told *Classic Rock*, 'There was healing that needed to be done with Cliff Burton in using psycho-drama role-playing. We didn't do it, but it was done in James' rehab process. The band never said goodbye or grieved appropriately ... They just ploughed on like they've always done, sweeping things under the rug ... So much of what they've learned is that past undone and unfinished [business] contaminates the present.'

One of the less harrowing sequences in the movie shows them auditioning bass players. Early on, they vow the new guy will not suffer the same fate as Jason. Consequently, the people they try out come from high-profile bands in their own right, including Pepper

Keenan from Corrosion of Conformity, Scott Reeder from Kyuss, Chris Wyse from The Cult, Twiggy Ramirez from A Perfect Circle, Eric Avery from Jane's Addiction, and Danny Lohner from Nine Inch Nails. Each has something different to offer. But as Lars astutely points out, 'If Cliff Burton showed up today maybe he wouldn't be the guy, either.' Eventually, though, the guy they do decide on, Rob Trujillo, has the most in common with Cliff musically – with his fulsome finger-picking style – and personally, in his laid-back, almost stoic ability to deal with anything the others might throw at him.

Born in Santa Monica, California, on 23 October 1964, Roberto Agustín Miguel Santiago Samuel Trujillo Veracruz had learned bass at fifteen. Growing up listening to the snapping rhythms of James Brown and Parliament but playing Black Sabbath and Van Halen songs at backyard parties, he was studying jazz at college when he dropped out to join Metallica's contemporaries, Suicidal Tendencies, whose punk-metal crossover became absorbed into the proto-thrash scene (and who supported Metallica on tour in 1993). More recently Trujillo had been in Ozzy Osbourne's backing band, appearing along the way on albums by funk-metallists Infectious Grooves, a solo album by Alice In Chains guitarist Jerry Cantrell, and other one-off projects. Then thirty-eight and married with two children, a bulky, surfer dude rarely seen out of calf-length shorts and cut-off tee, unlike the men of Metallica he had never contemplated cutting his waist-length hair. But then Rob Trujillo was not a man lacking in knowledge of his own self-worth. He was vacationing in Tahiti when he got the call. 'Well, come on over to the studio, we'll hang out,' he recalled being told by Kirk. With 'zero time to learn songs' he began by playing 'Battery', which he already 'kind of knew', followed by 'Sad but True', 'Whiplash' and 'For Whom the Bell Tolls': 'They don't tell you a film crew is going to be there, and they're making a documentary – until twenty minutes before – "You're okay with that, right?" It's funny. Prior to that, I was always trying to hide from the cameras Ozzy had following him around for his TV show. This was obviously going to be different.'

The mixture of competing emotions on his face when they make him the offer is evident in the film, placing his head in his hands and groaning, 'I don't know what to say,' when they inform him he will receive 'an advance' of $1 million just for joining. 'There's this whole mystique about what they're like, you know, the evil Metallica. I didn't see that. Actually, at first, not seeing that evil Metallica kind of made me uncomfortable.' Rob Trujillo joining 'had a pretty calming effect on the band', observes Alexander Milas. 'He wasn't just a lapdog. He had this incredible pedigree. Rob wasn't going to be overawed or overwhelmed by Metallica. And he brought so much. He described himself as like "a Samurai whisky warlord", which I think pretty much sums up his stage presence. He's just so fun to watch. An electrifying bass player – how many of those can you name?'

When, towards the end of *Some Kind of Monster*, James learns of Towle's plans to relocate his family to San Francisco then accompany the band out on tour, he becomes concerned that the good doctor 'thinks he's in the band'. Trying to discuss this with him provides one of the most awkward moments in a stupendously awkward film, the therapist clearly squirming at any suggestion that he might have finally outstayed his welcome, and in so doing appearing more con-flicted and needy even than Jason. He talks of having 'visions' as a 'performance coach' and making sure the new bass player is 'right'.

Looking back on the movie five years later, Lars told me, 'They started filming us in the studio and all of a sudden fucking hell broke loose, and then it turned into something else. And so I'm proud of the fact that we let it become what it became, and I'm proud of the fact that we didn't stand in the way of it. It sort of turned into its own thing, and Joe and Bruce felt that they were witnessing something special with their cameras and they asked us to trust them and kind of go on this ride with them because they felt there was something truly unique happening. And we trusted Joe and Bruce enough to let them kind of do their thing. In some way there was something quite liberating about that. Because once you free yourself to that point, then you stop being self-conscious ... very quickly it stopped being us and them and became all of us together.'

Had it actually aided the process they were going through?

'I do think that in some way one could argue that the cameras, certainly with some of the more therapy stuff that we were doing when we were really trying to come clean with each other, I think the presence of the cameras helped us not in any way filter or censor ourselves ... there was a vulnerability and a nakedness there that was probably complemented by the presence of the cameras – in those moments when we were sitting in front of each other and saying pretty much what we were really thinking and feeling.' He laughed, still conscious of just how 'naked' they had allowed themselves to be.

The other thing we get to see close-up in the movie, of course, is the tortuous conception of the most controversial, certainly the hardest to listen to, of all Metallica's albums. In among the anger and frustrations, the perceived betrayals and emotional backdraughts, the songs on *St. Anger* reflect Lars' personal travails with Napster, the loss of Jason, the ghost of Cliff, and the people they had become in Metallica, conflicted, overstretched, insanely rich, and now, suddenly, immensely self-doubting. Musically, the results are far from pretty. Not only are there no guitar solos, but the drums sound machine-like, like an anvil being pummelled. And there are no quieter moments, no ballads, no instrumentals, no place to escape the fearful maelstrom of crazed guitars, rubber-band bass and utterly pained vocals. Taken piece by piece, tracks such as 'Dirty Window', 'Invisible Kid' and 'Shoot Me Again' were some of the fiercest, most convincingly honest, if musically disjointed moments the band had laid down since the sonically disfigured but brutally forthright *Justice* fifteen years before; certainly more original and heartfelt than the lacklustre 'I Disappear', which directly preceded it. Taken as a whole, however, which is clearly how *St. Anger* is meant to work, it is a bitter pill to swallow. 'I'm madly in anger at you!' Hetfield wails on the title track; 'My lifestyle determines my deathstyle', he earnestly exhorts on 'Frantic'. When the final track, 'All in My Hands' ends with him repeatedly screaming, 'Kill, kill, kill, kill!', the silence at the end leaves you staring into yourself.

Conceived by committee, not even the band liked all of it. According to Kirk, only four songs got all four votes (including Bob's) to be on the record. Rock's anti-production hardly helps, the various sections of each song shuffled and reshuffled before being cut-and-pasted together on a computer screen. Later, Kirk would complain that he had recorded over a hundred guitar parts in the course of the album, but had no idea where each had been used, or why most hadn't. Rob Trujillo, he added, was not the only one who had to learn the songs from scratch before they could play them live. David Bowie and Brian Eno may have done similar things with their music in the past, U2 and Radiohead also. But this was musical experimentation on a level previously unknown in hard rock.

As if to somehow sugar the pill, when *St. Anger* was released in June 2003, it came in a bewilderingly naff Pushead-designed sleeve – a comic book image of a bunched fist with a rope knotted around the wrist. This only served to further confuse critics already hostile to its self-conscious attempts at radicalism. Reviews were almost uniformly sour. *Rolling Stone* called it 'a mea culpa to long-time devotees as the now Newsted-less trio crafted a complex riff marathon once more, this time accompanied by cathartic lyrics from a newly sober, therapy-suffused Hetfield. But production oddities – such as a drum sound that makes Lars Ulrich sound like a two-year-old banging pots and pans with a spoon – are jarring. And poor Kirk Hammett, the band's soloist and a man who has weathered the squabbles of the two figureheads for twenty years, is rewarded with no solos. Now there's something to be angry about.' For most first-time listeners, says Alexander Milas, '*St. Anger* was an absolute mess'.

Metallica's marketing director told Kirk the album was 'a fucking commercial disaster'. Relatively speaking, he was right. Although it reached Number One in America and another dozen countries, and Number Three in the UK, overall *St. Anger* sold approximately half of what *S&M* had done and remains probably their most unpopular album, more so even than the obsequious *Reload*. 'It still annoys me to this day,' says writer and long-time Metallica chronicler Joel McIver, 'because the band regard it as a symbol of rebellion and a catalyst for change when in reality it's just a collection of dull riffs and puerile lyrics.' For the first time since *Master of Puppets*, however, Metallica weren't out primarily to make an album that pleased fans or critics, but to please themselves; an album that spoke to them on the deepest level, come what may. In this regard, it could be argued, they succeeded completely; that *St. Anger* should be viewed in the same historical light as equally personal, often misunderstood, even loathed albums as Neil Young's *Tonight's the Night*, Bowie's *Low*, John Lennon's *Plastic Ono Band*; as feral as the demented *Funhouse* by The Stooges; as self-pitying as its other blood cousin, *In Utero* by Nirvana; as off-putting as Lou Reed's *Berlin*. Albums that reflected the huge personal crises the artists had gone – or were still going – through but which everybody else originally found impossible to listen to without wincing, or simply taking them off, infuriated that they didn't fulfil their remit and entertain in the conventional manner.

'It's [about the] deep-seated anger that's deep within our personalities,' said Kirk. 'We've been exploring our inner personalities and discovering that there's a lot of fucking residual anger there that came from our childhoods and it's something that fame, money and celebrity is not an antidote for.' On *Kill 'Em All*, he said, 'we were very angry young men and now we're very angry middle-aged men. What happened in our childhoods is part of our mental foundation, and tapping into it in a positive way is something we've found out how to do in the last two years, and that is the sound of *St. Anger*.'

Would purging their anger affect their creativity now, though?

'I can see how someone could get caught up in that fear of running out of creative juice,' allowed James. 'But I truly don't believe that. Music was a great gift for me and I discovered that somewhat early, but I don't need alcohol, I don't need anger, I don't need serenity, I don't need any of those things to be creative.' All he needed now, he said, was 'life – I've been trying to dump everything else: sex, drugs, rock 'n' roll; chocolate's a real struggle these days – or work. You know, in rehab I saw it all, people taking certain behaviours to extremes to where it becomes an addiction; compulsive activity that just started to ruin their lives. So anything can really be taken to that extreme, but I'm comfortable with the unknown right now, and trusting of it, so life is filling that hole. Life on life's terms is okay for me.'

The reason the album sounds so fragmented, James told me, was because that's 'exactly where we were at that point. For me, *St. Anger* kind of stands alone. It's more of a statement than an album to me. It's more of the soundtrack to the movie, in a way. Here's what's going on in our lives and documenting it, you know? But in that fragmentation it brought us together. So it was a very necessary piece of the puzzle to get us where we are today.'

Even *Some Kind of Monster* – now regarded as a high-tide mark in the band's career – attracted mixed reviews when it was first released. In the *Observer Music Monthly*, Charles Shaar Murray called it 'primo car-crash stuff, replete with moments of the Higher Bathos'. The *Village Voice*, once art-encrusted champions of the band, described it as 'a two-and-a-half-hour puff piece about how "important" Metallica are and, worse, how much "integrity" they have'. Over the years, however, this often cringe-inducing movie has proved to be a more inviting entry point into the Metallica story for people new to the band than any of their albums. Like all great art, its appeal has proved universal: you don't have to know Metallica or like heavy metal to relate to what's going on there, or to be shocked and amazed by it.

'It's funny,' says David Ellefson, 'cos you watch *Some Kind of Monster* and people are talking about, "Oh and then they had a therapist." I'm like, gimme a fucking break! [In Megadeth] we had, like, *four* therapists!' He laughs. 'I'm like, fucking been there, done that, lived that movie. In fact, that's the one thing we *beat* Metallica to. We fucking beat 'em with group therapy!' Says Alexander Milas, 'I remember when I first watched it, getting really emotional. Metallica by that point had become such a pinata, for me as a journalist but also as a fan, it was always that thing of: oh, it was all better before the *Black Album*, that's where it ended – with Cliff. All of a sudden they were revealed to be human beings with flaws and emotions. And I actually began to like Lars Ulrich again. It resurrected my love of Metallica, as a band of the present and not just as a relic of the Eighties. At the same time, I was pretty shocked that they did it. It was almost like they were committing an act of supreme penance toward their fans.'

For James Hetfield it was about far more than that, though. Before the events shown in the movie, 'Things weren't working for me; it affected family life, it affected band life, it affected everything that went on around us.' It wasn't merely a case of now he was out of rehab things could go 'back to normal'. From this point on, there was no 'normal'. Life in and out of Metallica would be 'a work in progress'. He loved being in Metallica but he was no longer the titty-squeezing, vodka-guzzling twenty-something dude with the long straggly hair and beer-stained Misfits T-shirt. He had allowed the real James Hetfield – whoever that was – to disappear. Now he wanted him back: 'Not just within the band or on tour, but at home. You'd try to escape that feeling but no matter where you went you were identified as that guy in Metallica, and as corny as it sounds, you take that on. You kind of submit to it, and you're signing autographs when you're trying to eat dinner with your kids, or having photos taken when you're on vacation. But you don't have to do that. Any human would say, "Can you leave me alone for a second?" And in all of that attention, how lonely I was and how lost I was, and in a lot of denial about it. Of course, it happened for a reason and there's some good things that I take from my past, but I've found a new love for life as me instead of the guy in Metallica.'

It was just a shame that it took Jason leaving to set the ball in motion. 'I think that if Jason had just stuck it out for two or three more days rather than coming to that one meeting and saying, "I'm out of here, no questions asked," things would have been a lot different in the band,' said Kirk. 'It's been a huge learning experience and something that Jason set in motion for all of us. He was the sacrificial lamb for our spiritual and mental growth as well as our creative growth, and it just sucks. It's medieval.'

FOURTEEN
THE NEW BLACK

It was years later, another lifetime, more than one, and we were both bullshitting, going through the motions the way old pros do, making with the nice. He was on form – when wasn't he? – and so was I. An article, not for Kerrang! any more but for The Times; not about the new album any more, heavy though it certainly was, but about the recession, and how rock had become big again because of it. It was November 2008 and the world's banks were on the verge of collapse but Metallica was back doing better than ever. Could the two things somehow be linked? Neither of us believed it for a second of course but that's what the paper had asked for and as we both stood to make something out of it – good promo for him, nice profile for me – we played along. Eminent figures in our fields, talking bollocks and being paid in kind for it as the rest of the world went to hell in an out-of-order ATM machine.

The thing that really struck me afterwards was how surprised I had been, just for a moment, to realise how much he'd forgotten about me . . . about us. Assuming there had ever really been an 'us'.

'Hey,' he'd said at the start, pleasantly mangled accent still intact, although more Americanised by the years, as you'd expect, 'who'd have thought that time in Miami, shit-faced, the next time we spoke we would have six kids between us?'

He was talking about that night on the Monsters of Rock tour in 1988, sprawled in his hotel room listening to those dreadful early mixes of the turgid Justice album. We had spoken many times since then, seen each other in different places – Tokyo, Los Angeles, London, rapped on the phone, had dinner with friends – and I was momentarily affronted that all

412

that came to his mind was that one distant, drug-encrusted night.

Then I thought about where he had been in the interim, the two-year tours, the $15 million mansions, the second ex-wife and lovers I'd never known, the private art collection so precious and vast it had to be kept hidden in an air-conditioned vault somewhere in the Californian desert, before being sold off, or 'passed on' as he now put it – one of those air-conditioned phrases the very rich use to describe something the rest of us struggle to get our heads around. The cocktails with Courtney Love, the tennis matches with John McEnroe, the court cases and life coaches and zillion-dollar merch deals; the endlessly ringing cell phone. The shit that just always happens, wherever you are and whoever you might be, but most especially it must always seem if you are Lars Ulrich, big-brain inventor of the heaviest metal band of them all.

'Yeah,' I said, 'who'd have thought . . .'

The real rehabilitation of Metallica began out on the road. The Madly in Anger with the World tour began officially on 30 April 2003, when they gave their first public performance with Rob Trujillo in the band during a video shoot for the 'St. Anger' single at San Quentin prison. A remarkable piece of work – not least the moving little speech James gives the menacing-looking inmates before filming starts, unseen in the final video cut but shown in *Some Kind of Monster* – it was still hard not to view it as terribly contrived; all part of the PR campaign to prove they had gotten over their icky make-up and men-kissing phase and gone back to their hard-as-fuck roots. Except, of course, the men in Metallica were never really hard in the first place: Ulrich was a middle-class kid who had identified the main chance and gone for it, wholly and unashamedly; Hetfield the living embodiment of the Wizard of Oz, a small, rapidly beating heart hiding behind a big scary screen, frantically tugging at levers and praying no one would ever glimpse the real him; Hammett the eternal softie who'd managed to keep his head down without entirely losing it, even if it had meant keeping himself nicely toasted for most of it. The only one who exuded any real-life menace was Trujillo, and even he had hardly been born on the mean streets; he just looked like he had. As Alexander Milas puts it, 'I'm sorry but, you know, there's just like no credibility in your band doing anything like that [prison video]. How can you believe in a metal band that moisturises? It just can't happen.'

Nevertheless, it takes balls to come out, as James did, and tell the assembled mass of bald and tattooed musclemen, 'Anger is an emotion I've struggled with pretty much all my life.' They were at least trying to re-establish their musical identity, and taken at face value the 'St. Anger' video is the most hard-hitting thing Metallica had done since 'One' nearly fifteen years before. A week later they were the latest subject of MTV's *Icons* tribute show, where contemporary metal acts that had once stood across the great Napster divide, such as Korn and Limp Bizkit, showed up to pay their respects. It was another significant plank laid in the public re-entry programme they were now embarked on. Metallica also played live, their first live public performance with Rob, and their first since James' return from rehab. 'We're looking forward to spreading this new lust for life we have,' he told *Rolling Stone*, doing his best to sound confident. 'There's a new strength in Metallica that's never been there before. There are still fearful parts, too. But I'm pretty well set up. And I'm really proud of the new music. I think we did something where the pedal does not let up.'

They knew the real test, however, would come once they returned to the road proper. James, in particular, was anxious, terrified that he might relapse, undoing two years' worth of work he'd already undergone. Just as with the studio, there would have to be new work rules agreed; the most important concerning the behaviour of those around the singer, rather than Hetfield himself. Namely, the others could drink, could do what they liked, but they would need to be polite about it and preferably out of James' backstage orbit. 'Me, Kirk and Trujillo can still throw down, believe me,' Lars was quick to reassure. 'There's no issues. James has been an angel with that. He doesn't preach, or police, or get up in everybody else's shit.' Being sober on the road 'felt great but scary at the same time', said James. He wondered 'how many hours have been wasted sitting in a bar somewhere talking to people you'll never see again?' Instead, he tried seeing it all as 'you would have done if it was your first tour', going sightseeing and finding out about the various places around the world he now found himself in, rather than just treating it all as one amorphous drunken blur as he might have done in the past.

To ease themselves in, Metallica undertook a four-night run of shows to fan club members at San Francisco's Fillmore Theater (formerly the Fillmore West). By June they were back in Europe, headlining festivals, their first there for five years. Despite James' earlier demands about 'no more two-year tours' the Madly in Anger world tour ran for nineteen months, selling out venues right through to its final date in San Jose, California, on 29 November 2004. Extra breaks were built in along the way, to allow James, and them all, time back home with their families. But in every other respect, to the outside world it looked like business as usual. In Paris they played three shows in three different clubs in one day.

The rotten album reviews were largely overhauled in the public mind by the reception *Some Kind of Monster* received after it previewed at the Sundance festival in February 2004. 'We hear a lot from our peers in other bands about how much they've seen this movie and how many things ring true for so many [of them],' Lars told me. 'It was better received in the film industry than it was in the music industry [and] in the music industry it was better received by the peers than the punters. I think a lot of punters felt that it was like, whoa, maybe this is just a little too much [information]. I think some punters were a little miffed. But the peer group and all the cats in all the other bands were very complimentary and could certainly relate to most of it.'

The same month as Sundance, Metallica won yet another Grammy for Best Metal Performance, this time for the 'St. Anger' single. That summer they also completed the second of their US Summer Sanitarium stadium tours, with Linkin Park and Limp Bizkit applying the hip seal of approval as guest supports on the bill. Rob Trujillo took it all in his giant, crablike strides. 'I ignored the media and even the fans,' he said. 'I just told myself, "I'm going to be Robert [and] give one hundred per cent as me." ' Easier said than done, he later admitted.

'It was intense. I had to learn the catalogue of music, twenty-two years of music. And I had to learn the *St. Anger* album.' He also had to learn how to deal with the complicated relationships, strung like an aged web across the stage, between the three main members. 'You gotta know how to balance each person,' he said diplomatically, 'because they're so different.'

In 2005, they took a year off, the first time they'd done that voluntarily since 1994, the outbreak of peace only interrupted in November when they agreed to appear as special guests to the Rolling Stones – the only group left Metallica was happy to play second banana to – at two massive shows at the AT&T Park football stadium in San Francisco. For a band that counted so heavily on unity and togetherness, on keeping the whole stronger than its sum parts, the three members who had played on every Metallica album also spoke of their need to express their individuality; to seek solitude when the touring was finally over, or the last track finally recorded. At heart, they were all still loners, even if they were all, in their own ways, now making strenuous attempts to integrate family lives into that oneness.

James had fully settled back into his new home life with Francesca and their third child, 'my little angel', Marcella. For the first time he had been there for the birth, cutting the umbilical cord: 'my daughter pretty much glued us back together'. He no longer went hunting, either: 'Nowadays it doesn't feel necessary, killing things just to kill them.' His den was still stocked with the mounted heads of animals he'd hunted, including a boar, an antelope and a 1,600-pound buffalo that took four rifle shots to finally put down. But for kicks, James now preferred to go 'one hundred and fifty miles an hour in my car'. Certain that both he and Metallica were stronger for having survived their ups and downs, he said: 'I've gone through life trying to avoid struggles, either drink them away or hide from them, but being able to face them and take them on and knowing that you are going to grow after you have walked through the fire and be okay, all of these things that we have been talking about – Napster, Jason, rehab – have made us stronger as people and as a band. We've gravitated towards each other and realised the gratitude we have for being alive and in Metallica.'

Lars, meanwhile, was now living with the Danish actress Connie Nielsen, who he'd first met during a break from the Madly in Anger tour at the end of 2003. They would later have a son together, Bryce Thadeus Ulrich-Nielsen, born in San Francisco on 21 May 2007, to go with their other children, Myles and Layne, from Lars' marriage to Skylar, and Sebastian, from a previous relationship of Connie's. Thanks to a combination of Metallica, Napster and *Some Kind of Monster*, Lars was now such a household name in America that he even appeared in a special celebrity edition of *Who Wants to Be a Millionaire*, on which he raised $32,000 for the Haight Ashbury Free Clinic (providing primary care for patients with substance abuse and mental health issues). After selling off most of his art collection, Lars was back to collecting again. As he said, 'It's one area where I can go and be myself. It's not about being the drummer in a rock band. I'm accepted for who I am in the art circles. I love going into artist spaces and galleries and auction houses.' It was, he said, 'my place of sanctuary'. Speaking to me from his backstage hidey-hole in Glasgow in 2009, he explained the kind of thing he was into nowadays: 'Most of the artists that I buy are painters. I'm a little more of a painter guy than a sculpture guy. A lot of contemporary art these days is more about the idea than about the execution. And I'm a little bit more about the execution than the idea. I'm interested in those moments between a painter and a canvas, more so than how clever some idea can be . . . Pollack, De Kooning, Rauschenberg, Jasper Johns, Rothko, you know, Gorky. And then some European guys like [the painter and sculptor Jean] Dubuffet. But mostly painters . . .' He had even begun some canvases of his own, although 'not enough to warrant talking about. Trust me! Paul Stanley and Ronnie Wood shouldn't worry!' he laughed.

Kirk Hammett was also enjoying his version of domesticity, living in the Pacific Heights section of San Francisco, in his haute Gothic mansion full of dark oak interiors and opulent crucifixes and stuffed two-headed sheep, with his Hawaiian wife Lani and their son, Angel

Ray Keala, born in September 2006, as well as their dogs Darla and Hoku, and various cats. (They would have a second son, Vincenzo Kainalu, born in June 2008.) They had met at the height of the *Load* era and while they also spent time at their ranch, horse riding, or hitting the beach to surf, Kirk was still essentially the same incense-burning, indoors guy he'd always been. He, too, had become a collector, although his art centred as always on old Hollywood movie memorabilia. He still enjoyed reading comic books, old and new. 'I'm still very much into all that stuff, yeah,' he told me in 2009. 'I don't think I'll ever grow out of it, you know? I still fucking read comic books, I still watch horror movies, I still buy toys. I'm still that guy; I just have more of it now.' The original 1931 *Frankenstein* movie was still his 'all-time favourite. It's a tie between *Frankenstein* and *Bride of Frankenstein.*' His favourite book was 'probably the *Tibetan Book of Living and Dying*'. He was into yoga, he said, and reading 'Buddhist philosophy. Buddhist teachings resonate heavy with me.' A believer in karmic law, he was vegetarian; his favourite drink no longer beer, but champagne. 'Classy, yeah,' he chuckled. And of course he rarely passed a day without picking up his guitar.

Musically, what really sealed the deal in terms of Metallica's public rehabilitation was their decision to turn their summer 2006 festival appearances into a twentieth-anniversary celebration of *Master of Puppets*, performing the album for the first time in its entirety, track by track. They were getting in on the classic rock market somewhat belatedly but now they'd got there they were making the most of it, as always. Speaking with Kirk at the time, he described *MOP* as 'my favourite Metallica album. I really felt we gelled as a band and we gelled as people, and that's what *Master of Puppets* became. And that only ended because we lost a dear friend and we had to pick up the pieces and start again.' Looking back now, he said, he felt that *Master* and *Black* were still the band's best albums: 'We had this vision. For *Master* we just wanted to make the heaviest, most consistent album we could; with the *Black Album* it was more about spreading the Metallica gospel – and still being heavy at the same time.' It was the making of *MOP* that still stood out most in his memory, though, because 'it was just an amazing time for us. We were putting all the right notes in all the right places. But we didn't set out to make something that would stand the test of time twenty years from now. That wasn't on our radar at all. We just wanted to make the best possible album we could make at the time. We really just set our sights to that and buckled down. And we always felt that if we did indeed give it all we had and it didn't pan out the way we wanted to, at least we could say we tried our best. That was our attitude. Frankly, I'm amazed it still sounds so fresh. I put it on the other day, just to give it a listen ahead of talking to you, and my thought was: if you released *MOP* today it would be right up there with all the newest releases – you know, sound-wise, quality-wise, recording-wise, concept-wise – it's still relevant today. Even the lyrical content, the things James was writing about back then, it's still relevant today. The music, the sounds, the attitude, the approach, it's all still relevant today 'cos people are still using those techniques today that we kind of forged. We were aware of how much people expected from us. We were a different band, we were an extreme band and we were aware of the fact that we had a very unique sound, and we were just very bent on expanding upon that sound. And it all just went right for us . . .'

Entitled the Escape from the Studio o6 tour (where they had been working on ideas for their next album), they first performed the album all the way through at the giant Rock am Ring festival in Germany on 3 June. Including the first-ever complete performances of 'Orion' (in the past, only highlights of the middle section had been performed as part of either Jason's bass solo or impromptu instrumental passages within other numbers). As well as *MOP* in its entirety, it was notable that only one number – 'Fuel' – from the *Load/Reload* era was included and none at all from *St. Anger*. The usual three numbers from *Black* – 'Enter Sandman', 'Nothing Else Matters' and 'Sad but True' – formed the backbone of the encores and the usual three from *Ride the Lightning* ('Creeping Death', 'For Whom the Bell Tolls' and 'Fade to Black') were all played at the start of the show. Plus, just 'One' from *Justice*, and only 'Seek and Destroy' from *Kill 'Em All*, Kirk playing his Boris Karloff guitar; James with extra-long goatee; Lars, hair thinning but stamina still high; Rob gurning through 'Orion' while channelling the spirit of Cliff. It was an amazing spectacle that would be repeated later that same month at the Donington festival in England – now rebranded as the Download festival – and again over the remaining dates in Ireland, Estonia, Italy and, in August (after another break), for two shows in Japan and a final climactic performance at the Olympic Main Stadium in Seoul, South Korea on 15 August.

Meanwhile, behind closed doors, plans were already being laid for an even more surprising, if typically shrewd, return to their roots with their next album. Halfway through recording *St. Anger*, Phil Towle had told them: 'All this work you're doing right now is not for this record, it's for the next one.' And so it proved. Reading the runes as wisely as ever, the band had gone out on a limb and decided not to include Bob Rock in the new project. Coincidentally – or perhaps not – there had been an online petition that included the virtual signatures of more than 20,000 fans calling for Metallica to jettison Rock as producer. His crime: too much influence on the band's music. Or, more accurately, scapegoated for all the years of tinkering with the formula; metaphorically blamed for the shortened hair, make-up and unsettling scenes of self-doubt and therapy-speak in *Monster*. It was as if he had never been fully forgiven for being the guy who came in and transformed Metallica from a thrash metal caterpillar into a squillion-selling mainstream rock butterfly with the *Black Album*. Now he never would be. Someone, it seemed, had to take the rap for *Load* and *St. Anger*. Rock affected a public nonchalance at odds with his real feelings, saying only that the petition was hurtful for his children. 'Sometimes, even with a great coach, a team keeps losing,' he said, as if in apology. 'You have to get new blood in there.'

The band agreed and in February 2006 it was announced that the next Metallica album would be produced by Rick Rubin. Metal fans cheered. Rubin was the man who had signed Slayer and produced *Reign in Blood*, still regarded as the greatest thrash metal album of all. But while Rubin's grass-roots credentials were impeccable, the real reason he was chosen had as much to do with his more recent and much more widespread reputation as the producer *de jour* who had single-handedly rebuilt the career of Johnny Cash, saving it from the ignominy it had fallen into, with his series of *American Recordings* albums that utterly transformed his fortunes, artistically and commercially, in the 1990s, to the point where Cash was bigger than ever at the time of his death in 2003. That Rubin had just done an almost identical job on Neil Diamond with his remarkable 2005 comeback album *12 Songs* – rescuing a once-great songwriter from the creative purgatory of Las Vegas residencies and media scorn – was not overlooked, either. Nor, more to the point, that at the same time Rubin had been helping Cash reignite his career he had done a similar job for AC/DC, insisting that the original line-up be reinstated before shepherding them through their best album for decades in *Ballbreaker*, in 1995.

A large man generally dressed in billowing shirts and khaki camouflage trousers, with his enormous scraggily beard, trademark wrap-around shades and chubby features, Rubin resembled a hippy-ish Orson Welles, and certainly there is something of the musical auteur about him. Rubin liked to go barefoot to meetings, espoused a Zen philosophy of vegetarianism and karmic law, fingering a string of lapis lazuli Buddhist prayer beads as he talked, closing his eyes and rocking silently back and forth as he listened intently to music, before pronouncing gnomic judgement. His voice surprisingly soft and always reassuring, many of the artists he worked with called him The Guru.

As an overweight Jewish boy growing up in Lido Beach, on New York's Long Island, music had been a passion for as long as Rubin could remember. Interestingly, considering the career he was to have, he loved The Beatles but 'never really liked the Stones'. Whatever the musical medium – from heavy metal to country, from hip hop to pure pop, all of which he has put his hands to at some point – it was always the strength of the songs that mattered most, he said. Hence his inspired suggestion to Cash, then in his mid-sixties, to cover rock songs such as 'Hurt' by Nine Inch Nails, 'Personal Jesus' by Depeche Mode and 'Rusty Cage' by Soundgarden. (He also suggested Cash try Robert Palmer's 'Addicted to Love', but that proved to be one postmodern experiment too many for the sexagenarian.) 'I have no training, no technical skill,' Rubin insisted, although he could play guitar and plainly knew his way around a recording studio, 'it's only this ability to listen and try to coach the artist to be the best they can from the perspective of a fan.'

Along the way Rubin had produced crucial career-defining albums for the Beastie Boys (*Licensed to Ill*), LL Cool J (*I Need a Beat*), The Cult (*Electric*), the Red Hot Chili Peppers (*Blood Sugar Sex Magik*) and many others. Yet despite his background, melding rock with rap – as well as his groundbreaking work with the Beastie Boys and LL Cool J, Rubin had also produced 'Walk This Way', the first major rock-rap crossover hit, for Run-DMC and Aerosmith in 1985 – Rubin's first love had always been rock and heavy metal. Working with Metallica would be a unique opportunity to bring all his considerable talents to the table.

'He's all about the big picture,' said Lars of the earliest sessions with Rubin. 'He doesn't analyse things like drum tempos or tell James to play something in F sharp. He's more about the feel: is everyone playing together? Rick's a vibe guy.' Or, as Rubin put it: 'The right sound reaches its hand out and finds its way. So much of what I do is just being present and listening for that right sound.' Quick to praise, he was also swift to pass judgement. 'There's not a lot of grey with him,' said Lars. 'He really speaks his mind. Either something's great or something sucks.'

Rick had known Lars, James and Kirk for years, but they had never worked with him before and came new to his methods. 'Imagine you're not Metallica,' Rubin had told them early on. 'You don't have any hits to play, and you have to come up with material to play in a battle of the bands. What do you sound like?' This was the sort of statement, James decided, that gave the project instant 'focus'. According to Lars, 'Rick said he wanted to make the definitive Metallica record.' For Rubin – a true metal fan who'd once turned down the opportunity of working with Ozzy Osbourne, he told me, 'because I'm only really interested in making a classic Black Sabbath album that tries to recapture that golden era' – that was code for making the sort of Metallica album that had only previously been thought possible during the Cliff Burton era. Or as Lars put it: 'Every time there was a fork in the road, we said, "In 1985, we would have done this."' Rob Trujillo, from his more typically down-to-earth perspective, had simply remarked on the fact that Rubin insisted they stand up in the studio while playing 'and rock out, like we would live'.

The end product, as promised, harked back explicitly to the band's 1980s albums – now, a generation on, considered classics of the genre – even down to the new album's pre-CD choice of just ten tracks. All but one was over six minutes long – another clear sign of the album's focus – and all were credited equally to all four members, something that had decidedly *not* happened back in the Eighties. Any hope that this might really be some sort of return to the golden era of Metallica is quickly extinguished, however, with the opening brace of tracks, 'That Was Just Your Life' and 'The End of the Line'. Both over seven minutes long; both, on first listening at least, plucked wholesale from the top deck of the *Ride the Lightning* chocolate box; both all but forgotten minutes after they have juddered to their predictably explosive climaxes – like most of the album, in fact. This is not to say that tracks such as 'Broken, Beat & Scarred' (over six minutes) or 'The Day That Never Comes' (almost eight) aren't solid, full-on Metallica recordings: the latter is redolent of some sort of built-in-the-laboratory *Load*-meets-*Justice* hybrid that starts off relatively quietly then takes off halfway through into an all-out Iron Maiden-style freak-out; the former is like a more conventional, if much better mixed, outtake from *Justice*, down to its pillaging of the guitar solo from 'One'. It's just that there is little that lingers in the memory in the same way 'Creeping Death' or 'Leper Messiah' did the first times you heard them.

The dreadfully titled 'All Nightmare Long', another near-eight-minute old-school thrash epic shot through the prism of Rubin's 21st-century production values and the best track on the album, finds James downstroking his guitar with genuine ferocity as Kirk seems to make up for all the solos he never got to play on *St. Anger* by jam-packing them in here. The formidably bouncy 'Cyanide' which follows (over six minutes) sounds like something from *Master* via the best of *Load*, if that's possible, and it dawns that for the first time since the 1980s Metallica are allowing the songs to go where they will, not completely into the big 'movements' of yore, but certainly abandoning the commercial template that had served them so well with Bob Rock. None of the tracks fade out, either, but simply vanish into flames. The other stand-out moment is 'The Unforgiven III', a moving piano soliloquy, with strings and horns, extemporising over the atmospheric intro of the original, before moving into a song nearly eight minutes long, like 'Nothing Else Matters' meets 'Orion'; the only self-consciously slow track on an album determined to complete the circle, rather than break the mould, including the most enormous guitar-fest three-quarters of the way through; a real love-it-or-hate-it moment, and better for it. After that, however, the album rather plunges, beginning with 'The Judas Kiss', eight more minutes recalling the band that recorded 'Sad but True' *and* 'Disposable Heroes', with more-frantic-by-the-moment soloing from Kirk, which, rather than galvanise the listener, has the opposite effect of making them wonder if this doesn't smack too much of box-ticking; painstakingly putting Humpty Dumpty back together again only to find his oval arse where his pointy head had once been, and vice versa.

This feeling reaches its apotheosis on the album's most bloatedly self-referential – and, frankly, embarrassing – moment in the near-ten-minute instrumental 'Suicide & Redemption', clearly intended as a big 'Call of Ktulu' moment that, against the odds, might just have succeeded if it didn't go on (and on). The only track to fade out, it's a safe bet most general listeners will have exercised the skip option on their CD players/laptops/iPods long before then. This underlines the chief failings of the album: the completely tokenistic feel it all has; the very 1980s signage it gives everything. Ending with the shortest track at just over five minutes, 'My Apocalypse' is yet another track entirely given over, it seems, to somehow recreating the golden era of the band; redolent of the title track of *Master of Puppets*, its riff straight from 'Battery'. The question inevitably occurs: who is all this meant to please? Those fans too young to have experienced the real thing first time around? The producer whose modus operandi centres on recapturing the spirit of those heydays? Or perhaps a band that has now so thoroughly lost its way, musically, it simply wishes to wipe the slate clean and go back to what it perceives as simpler, more heartfelt times? Or more cynically, to simply tap into the classic rock market in the same way AC/DC, Iron Maiden and Kiss now do, reinforcing the nostalgia for a not-always-shared past grown way out of proportion to its original meaning? As if everything after *Black* had not really happened and, like Bobby Ewing, the band had simply stepped out of the shower to begin again where they had left off before everything went, you know, all fuzzy and freaked-out and fucked-up?

That certainly seemed to be the message they were sending out when James characterised the new songs as 'like old Metallica ... but with more meaning now', or when they had begun performing the title track to ... *And Justice for All* again in their latter shows. Kirk, meanwhile, had begun referring openly to the new album as feeling 'like the band's sixth album' rather than what would be their ninth – i.e. the follow-up to *Black*, rather than *St. Anger*. This from one of the main instigators of Metallica's mid-1990s musical rethink.

These were not reasons, on their own, to damn the new Metallica album, however. If most of the lyrics seemed to concern death, that was fine, too. As J.R.R. Tolkien once put it, 'the best human stories are always about one thing: the inevitability of death'. What ultimately disappointed were not the songs – solid enough attempts to at least do what they had once been best at, delivering thrash metal anthems for the headbanging crowd – and certainly not Rubin's production, which, despite his reputation for valuing atmosphere over technical perfection, was super-tight and glossy. It was the sense of a band bringing a well-defined, carefully thought-out product to market; something that could be forgiven when, in the case of *Black* – their first major attempt to do so – it had resulted in such great work as 'Enter Sandman' and 'Sad but True'; or, paradoxically, in the case of *Load,* where the determination to subvert their own image clearly took such precedence over the actual songs. But here, on an album that purported to refute such notions in favour of a return to old-fashioned principles of musicianship and honest artistic endeavour – of, as Jason Newsted, of all people, put it, '[working] for eight hours a day in a rehearsal room like brothers should' – it hits entirely the wrong note.

From the ponderous sound of the heartbeat that opens the album (as if the broken body of Metallica was coming slowly back to life on the operating table, like the moment in Kirk's beloved *Frankenstein* when the good doctor cries: 'It's alive! It's alive!'), to its truly cringe-inducing front cover image of a coffin – a motif that, excruciatingly, would feature throughout the two-year world tour they would embark on to promote the album – to surely the worst title of any Metallica album ever, *Death Magnetic*, an oblique reference to how so many rock stars have died young, as if magnets for death, this is Metallica-by-numbers; thrash-made-easy; the classic sound of a golden-era band delivering its goods with knobs on but few, if any, surprises for those of us whose memories are now longer than our hair. Even the pedantic sleevenotes seem hopelessly ill thought out, like a grown-up's idea of a child's drawing, the lyrics to the tracks partly disabled by the coffin-shaped cut-out that runs through every page and made even harder to decode through being scattered in random order, beginning with the last track first (perhaps not so randomly after all then). Naturally, there are the usual Anton Corbijn band shots, but even they – studied poses of each member standing in shades and leather jacket against a grainy black-and-white wall – could have been taken by Anton Anyone.

None of this stopped *Death Magnetic* becoming the most colossal success when it was released worldwide on 12 September 2008, going straight to Number One in thirty-two countries, including both Britain and America – the first time that had happened since *Load* twelve years before – thereby proving that metal fans would take even substandard prime-time-era Metallica over postmodern, Napster-baiting, therapist-consulting Metallica any day of the headbanging week. The album had shifted more than 490,000 copies in its first three days in the USA, making Metallica the only band in US chart history to have five albums debut at Number One (breaking their previous tie with The

Beatles, U2 and the Dave Matthews Band). Reviews were also highly complimentary. The *New York Times* praised the album for 'compositions that are nasty and complex', while *Time* magazine claimed that 'songs fly by with the force of the world's angriest amusement-park ride, and when they set you down, often after seven or eight dizzying but tuneful minutes, giddiness is the only appropriate response'. The grass-roots reaction was the same, with the *Kerrang!* review proclaiming that 'Metallica once again sound like one of the most exciting bands in the world' making 'a mockery of the modern [metal] competition'.

The key to this success, Lars told me some months later, during the band's second round of arena-headlining dates in the UK, 'was timing'. *Death Magnetic* was 'a reconciliation with the past'. He had wondered if it was possible for the band to return with such fervour to its thrash roots. 'But I knew that if it was gonna happen, the only way it could happen would be organically. It was not something that could be forced: "Now we have to sit down and make another of these records that has one foot in what we did in the Eighties."' It had been made possible by 'the combination of Rick Rubin; the combination of the twentieth anniversary of *Master of Puppets* and how we [re]familiarised ourselves with that record, started playing it again, became comfortable with it; the Rob Trujillo element; again the planets aligning ... All of a sudden it was just like there we were in the thick of it again, and it felt good and it felt right and it felt real – through a little bit of prodding from Rick Rubin and some pep talks about how we didn't need to sort of deny that side of us and blah, blah, blah.'

It was as much about Bob Rock *not* being there, as Rick Rubin being there, James had told me earlier that same day: 'I think Bob had gotten comfortable. We had gotten too comfortable with each other, especially going through all of the emotional draining of *St. Anger*. We learned so much about each other, we were too close, I think. It was good to move on and I think Rick Rubin is the exact opposite of Bob Rock. The fact that we were able to sit down and write ourselves, somewhat pre-production ourselves, do things for ourselves without Rick Rubin babysitting or sitting over our shoulder the whole time, that was where we were able to try our wings out again and fly as a band, after all these near-death experiences of the *Monster* movie and *St. Anger*. So it was the right thing at the right time. Not to talk bad about Bob whatsoever, because he's taken us places that we never would have gone before. We've learned so much from him.' But this, suddenly, was different. It had to be.

Old friends had their own views. Flemming Rasmussen describes *Death Magnetic* as 'a good step in the right direction', but adds: 'I think they should have called me. You know, if they want to do an album like that, why don't they fucking just call me?' He added: 'It doesn't sound nowhere as good as *Ride* or *Master*, for sure, no.' Could he ever really see himself working with them again, though? 'I've got no idea. I hope so.' Xavier Russell offers a similarly cautious response: 'I think it's a lot better than their recent albums. It is a sort of return. Some of it's even a bit earlier than *Master of Puppets*.' The trouble, says X, is that 'You hear it through and think that's quite good. Then after it's finished you think: can I remember any of the songs?' Geoff Barton says, 'I hate the production. If they're attempting to reactivate the spirit of 1986 they've done quite a good job. But I don't think it's all there, to be honest.' He adds: 'The strange thing is to see the band going almost full circle and becoming nostalgic about those days.' When Geoff interviewed James about the album, '[he] was very, very nostalgic about the thrash days. *Metal Hammer* had just produced a thrash special and he had a copy of it and he was looking at it and there were almost like tears in his eyes.'

The success of *Death Magnetic* was about more than just the strength or otherwise of the songs, of course. It was about simple old-fashioned marketing and promotion – it's no good having the Second Coming if no one is there to see it – delivered in a thoroughly modern way. Months before the album was shipped out to stores, a new website, www.missionmetallica.com, was launched, in anticipation of both internet piracies – now, almost a decade on from Napster, a part of everyday life – and to maximise interest in owning a 'hard copy' (i.e. record or CD) of the forthcoming album. Initially offering visitors to the site behind-the-scenes insights into the recording, including contact with producer Rubin, it also promised a veritable treasure trove of exclusive content, such as fly-on-the-wall video footage, audio clips of works-in-progress and archival photos from their time in the studio. The 350-plus minutes of footage would eventually reach nearly ten million people across 161 countries. There was also an exclusive for the fan club – or, Mission Metallica members, as they were now dubbed – with the album being streamed a day before its official worldwide release, thus building a priceless word-of-mouth buzz among the internet community. Mission Metallica members also got first dibs on buying tickets for the forthcoming tour. On top of this, fans could interact directly with the band, who invited them to post clips of themselves performing Metallica songs on YouTube, which Lars viewed personally before posting his own video to offer his thanks. The clip had received more than 1.2 million hits by the time the album was released a week later. For a band that had actively positioned itself at the start of the decade against the growing influence of the internet, Metallica was now one of the bands positively leading the way with how to utilise the available technology. Whatever mistakes Lars had made, you couldn't say he didn't learn from them. Fast.

Meanwhile, back on terra firma, Metallica also set a new record for the most radio stations in history to sign up for an 'exclusive' broadcast, entitled *The World Premiere of Death Magnetic*. The programme, promoted by *FMQB* (the trade magazine for the US radio industry), was hosted by Dave Grohl and Taylor Hawkins of the Foo Fighters, and featured the four Metallica members being interviewed. It was aired on more than 175 stations across the USA and Canada. Just for good measure, the first single from the album, 'The Day That Never Comes' was also issued and immediately topped both the Mainstream and Active Rock Charts, while seven more tracks from *Death Magnetic* simultaneously charted across three US radio formats – Alternative, Active Rock, and Rock – an almost unheard-of feat for any artist. There were similar blanket promotional efforts made in Europe and the UK. Britain's Radio 1 turned 12 September into Metallica Day and devoted its entire twenty-four-hour output to the band and its new album, climaxing with the live broadcast of a special cut-price fan-club-members-only show at London's O2 Arena. A similar event was held in Berlin.

Metallica didn't quite get things all their own way, though. As ever, the internet was there to confound and connive. On 2 September, ten days before its official release date, a French record store knowingly jumped the gun and began selling copies of the album. Within hours, online versions of it were flying onto file-sharing networks around the world. This time, however, Metallica had anticipated the move and were ready with their response. 'By 2008 standards, that's a victory,' a determinedly chilled Lars told *US Today*. 'If you'd told me six months ago that our record wouldn't leak until ten days out, I would have signed up for that. We made a great record, and people seem to be getting off on it way more than anyone expected.' The internet community still had one more trick up its virtual sleeve, however. Two days before the official release date, a site called MetalSucks.net posted a link to a Russian website with a domain that offered the album in edited format. Cheekily dubbed *Death Magnetic: Better, Shorter, Cut*, the edited online album had cut each track by an average of two to three minutes, as if in imitation of a review by prominent Pitchfork online commentator Cosmo Lee, who'd declared the album redeemable only by cutting the exorbitantly lengthy tracks drastically.

Ultimately, however, Metallica now owned the internet in ways it would not have been considered possible in the bad old days of battling Napster. Six months after *Death Magnetic* came the release of *Guitar Hero: Metallica*. An Activision computer game for which the band had taken time out from promoting the album prior to release in order to film the various motion-capture scenes, *GH:M* featured twenty-eight of Metallica's best-known numbers, plus twenty-one tracks from Metallica-endorsed artists, from obvious old-school choices such as Motörhead, Diamond Head and Judas Priest, to cool metal newbies like The Sword and Mastodon. Viewed from a certain angle, this was the shrewdest piece of business Metallica had done since inviting Bob Rock to help them become a commercial hit nearly twenty years before. *Guitar Hero*, a devilishly simple but infinitely clever computer game that distilled the essence of playing a musical instrument down to the push of a button, had already proved to be a revenue stream so great that it was being talked of as one of the innovative new ways the net might actually help rebuild the record business it was then currently almost single-handedly dismantling; even a possible entry point for a new generation of guitar-worshipping kids to get into rock in the first place.

Devised by a computer hardware company called RedOctane – partly responsible for an older arcade game named *Guitar Freaks*, a big hit in Japan, and now looking to produce a home-gaming version – the original *Guitar Player* game was made for around $1m. The inaugural edition had a metal-style logo on the box and a hand-held controller shaped like a Gibson SG – signature guitar of choice for AC/DC's Angus Young and Black Sabbath's Tony Iommi – and had been an immediate hit, winning awards and glowingly reviewed as 'probably the greatest rhythm game ever invented'. Realising that the 'magic source' – gaming-industry-speak for the extra ingredient that made the product unique and must-have-now-able – was the guitar-shaped peripheral, the forty-seven playable songs the original featured was expanded to sixty-four for *Guitar Hero II*, the fifth-biggest-selling game when it was released in 2006. Now available for both PlayStation 2 and X-Box 360 platforms, the latter version came with a Gibson Explorer-shaped controller. The key this time, however, was the addition of real-life rock stars such as AC/DC and Aerosmith, Van Halen and Guns N' Roses. 'We'd hit the sweet spot,' said developer John Tam. '[The bands] understood that we're not going to embarrass their music, we're going to actually pay homage to their music and get it to the point where people are going to understand their music in a totally different way than they've ever experienced it before.'

The franchise was now worth hundreds of millions of dollars; rivals were starting to spring up, most notably the MTV Networks developed *Rock Band* game. It wasn't, however, until Activision bought RedOctane for $100m, specifically to acquire *Guitar Hero*, that the game took off outside devoted gaming circles: the extra edge that would power *Guitar Hero III* being the arrival of an instantly recognisable real-life rock star to front the franchise: Lars' old pal Slash of Guns N' Roses (and latterly, his offshoot group Velvet Revolver). Until then, although it featured real songs by real bands, the game had relied on a series of sound-alike avatars with faux rock-star names such as Axel Steel and Izzy Sparks. Slash was the first major real-life star to agree to have himself motion-captured and that image transferred directly into the game. 'I'm not a real video game guy,' Slash admitted to *Classic Rock* writer Jon Hotten. 'When I signed on to do it, it was only the nerdy kid in me that made me say yes. Everything else about me said, no don't do it.'

With Slash's instantly recognisable avatar now front and centre, suddenly the game became an item of interest way beyond its natural demographic of gamers. Released in October 2007, it now featured seventy-three songs, and was available across not just PlayStation and Xbox platforms but also Wii, PC and Mac. It made $100 million in just its first week. A month later it was officially the year's biggest-selling computer game. Activision could hardly keep up with the Christmas demand. Six months later, it had sold more than eight million copies. By the time the next version of the game was ready to go in March 2009 – with Metallica replacing Slash as the fron-tispiece – the existing version had exceeded one billion dollars in sales revenue and was said to be the second-biggest-selling computer game of any kind since 1995.

For Slash, who had received a generous but fixed fee and no royalties, the impact this had was about much more than money; already one of the most famous guitarists in the world, Slash's image now extended far beyond the existing rock-buying audience. 'I have a specific story that will sort of shine a big bright light on that fact,' he explained. 'A friend of mine who's a producer, he's got, I guess, a six-year-old little boy. I went over to their house, and I'd never met his little boy. I went over there, and the kid lost his mind. "You're the guy from *Guitar Hero*." He couldn't get over it. A bit later on that night, he came over to me and went, "Hey, do you play real guitar too?"' He laughed. 'It's definitely changed the way we look at selling records, because as the record business goes into decline, the gaming business has been selling a lot of music. That's been an interesting development, for sure. If you're in a band, the luckiest thing you can have is a guy from Activision or from the *Rock Band* people come along and say, we'd like to chronicle your career. There is a lot of money in it.'

Something Metallica – who had already contributed images and songs to *Rock Band* – had taken serious note of by the time they stepped up to the plate to take part in their own billion-dollar version of *Guitar Player*. Lars, smartly, played down the whole thing, brought it back to the level of simply entertaining the folks. 'Our kids love playing *Guitar Hero* and *Rock Band*,' he told *Rolling Stone*. 'It's awesome. There's something really positive coming out of video games. It's so cool to sit there and have your kids talk to you about Deep Purple and Black Sabbath and Soundgarden.'

As ever, though, the real business of Metallica took place out on the road. The World Magnetic tour would actually find the band out on the road for the best part of the next three years, but the schedule was now built specifically to combat the stresses and strains that would otherwise be placed on the four husband-and-fathers who now populated the band. 'We do two weeks on and two weeks off,' Lars told me, the band flying home to California wherever they were in the world, literally going straight from the stage of the final show into a limo and onto a private jet. Nice work if you could get it, the 2009 year-end issue of US trade bible *Billboard* reported that the World Magnetic tour had earned a total ticket-sale gross (so far) of $76,613,910. The same issue calculated that between 2000 and 2009 Metallica had earned a total ticket-sale gross of $227,568,718. Astonishing figures, but giving only a fraction of the true financial picture, once profits from record and merchandising sales had also been factored in, possibly doubling or even trebling that final figure.

The show itself was initially built around the new *Death Magnetic* album, as would be expected, but would go through various changes as each new phase of the tour unfolded. The Metallica live show has always been a purist experience, the band all dressed in uniform black whatever phase of their twisting career they happened to be going through. So it had been with the first phase of the World Magnetic tour: a show staged in the round and built around a faintly ludicrous circle of coffins, concealing the lighting rig, but with the emphasis firmly on what can fairly be termed all-round family entertainment. As I watched from one of the high-price boxes at London's O2, I marvelled at the diversity of the 20,000-strong crowd. Below, surrounding the stage, were the sorts of rabid, devil-horn-saluting fans one might have encountered in their true heyday twenty years before. To my right and left were other boxes full of young female fans, the kind normally only found at a Robbie Williams show, dancing as though listening to Michael Jackson, making sexy such previously thought impregnable musical edifices as 'One' and 'Sad but True'. Thanking those Metallica fans each night who had 'stayed loyal', James added for those kids present too young to have seen the band play before, 'You got some cool parents.' It was a comment he would make a habit of somehow working into those shows, tossing guitar picks out to the crowd whenever he spotted anyone young enough to warrant one. He still strode the stage like a lone gunman, spitting copiously and growling into the mike, but James Hetfield the proud husband and father was no longer buried so far below the surface you couldn't see him. Indeed, he was now all but impossible to avoid.

Robert Trujillo, his bass slung low between his bare knees, stalked the four corners of the stage as though on patrol, carrying a machine-gun through a jungle swamp. Lars and Kirk did as they always had done, the latter hunched over his guitar, the first signs of middle age, perhaps, creeping up on his steadfastly laid-back demeanour, trotting around the stage perimeter with just a little more care; the former still leaning over his kit, standing and gesticulating wildly to the audience as he always had, making it clear should anyone still be in any doubt that he had never been just the drummer, but a frontman in his own right. Most amazing for this ancient survivor from their now golden past was the sight of the band remaining on stage long after the houselights had gone up, as silver inflated balls emblazoned with the Metallica logo rained on the audience and the four band members walked around, casually chatting to their fans, kicking the balls their way and throwing out guitar picks, leaning over to touch hands. Mainly just walking around and talking to them; a welcoming echo of the days when they stood at the backstage doors of the tiniest shit-holes and waited for the dozen or so most curious fans to come and tell them where they'd gone wrong that night. It went on and on, ten minutes, twenty minutes ... Never having seen any artist do such a thing – particularly not when playing in the round, when getting away from the stage at the end is usually a matter of concealed exits and absolutely no returns – I found it all quite moving.

A few weeks later, on 4 April, Metallica was inducted into the Rock and Roll Hall of Fame. 'It's still somewhat surreal,' said James, emanating pride and well-being, before adding: 'The other part of it will be us kicking in the door a little bit. We've got a lot of other friends that we'd like to bring in to the Rock and Roll Hall of Fame. There's a lot of heavy music that belongs in there.' Other artists being inducted that year included rap pioneers Run-DMC, virtuoso guitarist Jeff Beck, soul singer Bobby Womack and R&B vocal group Little Anthony and the Imperials. Headlining, though, would be Metallica, who flew in straight from two shows in Paris. To help them celebrate, the band also personally invited several hundred family members, friends and associates who had had some influence over their career, purchasing six tables for the event – held in the Public Hall Auditorium, a historic venue where The Beatles had performed in 1964 – at a cost of upward of $50,000 each. 'They are the gold standard for contemporary metal,' said Hall of Fame curator Howard Kramer. 'Despite their fame, they've never made an effort to cash in. People believe in them. That's why they're still there.'

Among so many familiar faces from their past, all flown in at the band's expense – including Ron McGovney, Jason Newsted, Bobby Schneider, Jonny and Marsha Z, Martin Hooker and Gem Howard, Xavier Russell and Ross Halfin, Michael Alago and Flemming Rasmussen, Bob Rock and Rick Rubin, Dave Thorne and Anton Corbijn, Torben Ulrich and Ray Burton, to name just a few – there was one notable exception: Dave Mustaine. Dave had been invited but had declined once he'd been informed he wouldn't actually be inducted himself. As he sardonically told Dave Ling of *Classic Rock*: 'Lars Ulrich called me up and offered the chance to come and not be inducted – to sit in the audience. "It's only for people who've been on the records," is what I was told. That would have been awkward.' He added: 'I'm no longer struggling with past demons – that game has ended. But you know what? If God wants me in the Hall of Fame, I will be there.'

A pity, as it might have offered the band a chance to include one of their earliest classics in the short set they performed live that night. As it was, both Jason and Rob played bass during 'Master of Puppets' and 'Enter Sandman', while Cliff Burton's father, Ray, accepted the honour on his son's behalf. Unlike Mustaine, Jason Newsted had learned enough to make his own peace with the band. As he'd put it earlier, 'We're business partners for the rest of our lives.' He had been 'depressed for about six weeks' after he left the band, then he'd toured with his band Echobrain, spent some time playing with Canadian thrash iconoclasts Voivod, even, bizarrely, filled Rob's shoes for a while by joining Ozzy Osbourne's backing band. Mainly, Jason said, he had 'enjoyed life. No one can tell me what *not* to do any more.'

Just before the event, I had asked Lars a final word on the subject of Jason. He said: 'It sometimes got a little difficult because there were times where there [were] personality issues within the band. Where his dedication – and I mean this in a positive sense – to perfection and the pursuit of everything being next-level, sometimes clashed a little bit with the rest of us because it's still rock 'n' roll, at the end of the day. And sometimes it felt like it got dangerously close to something more in the direction of athletics or something akin to troop movements, or military position-level strategies and stuff. Once in a while you just wanna go, "Fuck! We're in a rock 'n' roll band!" although a fairly hard and heavy one.' He added: 'I wanted to be in music because I wanted to be away from living these incredibly structured lives and have a little bit of a fly-by-the-seat-of-your-pants energy to it also. Do you know what I mean? So I think that sometimes it got a little too next-level serious, and sometimes there were some personality clashes. But I got nothing bad to say. Jason was an incredibly loyal and dedicated member, and always gave his all.'

The final plank in the new foundation as classic rock untouchables came in the summer of 2010 and a return to Britain and Europe for the Big Four tour. That is, eleven outdoor festival shows headlined by Metallica but also featuring on the bill Slayer, Megadeth and Anthrax – climaxing with a massive show to over 100,000 people at Knebworth, the 500-year-old stately home that has staged some of the most historic rock festivals of the past forty years. Following in the footsteps of such giants as Pink Floyd and Led Zeppelin, Metallica had already headlined their own show there in the summer of 2009. Now, in August 2010, they would do so again with the Big Four, as part of that year's travelling Sonisphere weekend, another guaranteed 100,000-plus sell-out.

Metallica, Slayer, Megadeth and Anthrax had never played on the same bill before, despite their shared histories. As a result this would become the most anticipated live event in the European rock calendar that year. The tour kicked off with a sold-out show to 55,000 people on 16 June at Bemowo Airport in Warsaw. Over the next few weeks they would repeat the experience in Holland, Germany, Spain, Sweden, Switzerland, the Czech Republic, Bulgaria (where the show was simultaneously broadcast in HD to various cinemas around the continent), Romania, Turkey and England. The most anticipated tour of the summer, the question was how the four bands would get on. As well as the well-aimed barbs sent their way by Dave Mustaine, Metallica had also endured taunts from Slayer over the years. Guitarist Kerry King had called them 'fragile old men' after seeing *Some Kind of Monster*. 'Oh, listen,' joked Lars, 'the reason we did that movie was to piss Kerry King off. Being the source of his amusement, that's great!' But then it was easy to set aside differences when there was so much at stake. Where once Lars would feel ultra-competitive in the company of Slayer and Megadeth, in particular, calling up to get the merch figures each night on their joint Clash of the Titans tour in 1991 (which had also featured Anthrax), he now professed to merely 'feeling supportive' to Metallica's fellow travellers. 'I don't feel the need to prove how big my dick is any more,' he told me.

At the opening show in Warsaw, the massive airfield seemed to be all horizons and sky, apart from the stage itself, which stuck out like a giant monolith, surrounded by people. The backstage area comprised a few tents stuck together with buses parked behind them. Only a few people walked around, including the bands. Golf carts zipped off to the stage every now and then, taking the musicians the 200 yards or so to the rear of the stage. There was very little to keep the handful of British journalists present entertained, just the occasional bored security goon and bus driver, but no managers, certainly no groupies or other obvious revellers. Lars was hanging out with some people; Rob, too. Tom Araya stepped off the Slayer tour bus in his bedroom slippers. Dave Mustaine wandered around with his grown-up son. It was all quite weird and deserted, the emphasis on keeping things low-key. The only rock 'n' roll element was a stall giving away free local vodka, staffed by big-boobed models in air-hostess uniforms – a nice touch laid on by the local promoter, presumably.

Onstage, Anthrax did exactly the same show they played when they reunited in 2005 – mostly *Among the Living*-era material ('Anti-Social', 'Got the Time') and a smidge of Black Sabbath's 'Heaven and Hell' in passing tribute to the recently departed vocalist Ronnie James Dio. Megadeth were on fire. The recent return of bassist David Ellefson to the fold after a five-year exile seemed to have revitalised them. The set was a run-through of *Rust in Peace* – in preparation for a twentieth-anniversary version of the album about to be released – and some greatest hits. Lots of 'we love you's from Mustaine. Slayer did their 2010 show, which is to say no headbanging from Araya as his neck was still out of whack following an injury, but still a powerful set. As Joel McIver, who was also there, says, 'Metallica really did reign supreme, with a much longer set – the others had between forty minutes and an hour – plus pyro, a bigger production and of course the fact that it was night-time helped.'

But then, Big Four or not, this was only ever going to be about one band. As Ellefson says now, 'Every time a new Metallica record would come out, [Megadeth guitarist] Marty Friedman would go, "Well, one more time, that's why they are the kings." You know, they talk about the Big Four. Quite honestly, there was a Big One, and that was Metallica. They were *miles* and *miles* ahead of all of us – they're the U2 of heavy metal. They kind of transcended everything. They are true royalty. As far as the rest of us, there's a Big One and then quite a ways behind them there's the other three of us.'

The question is: where do Metallica go from here? Well, that depends, as ever for a band with antennae as long and sensitive as this, on the zeitgeist. No longer the musical adventurers they first became famous as, they have spent the vast majority of their career successfully co-opting whatever the prevailing musical trends are into their own unique story, their real genius not for having invented the last great truly influential musical genre in rock, but for having so stealthily and successfully ridden the waves that have ebbed and flowed like a torrent these past near-thirty years. The Big Four festival tour has been another shrewd move and a resounding sales success, with the tour now set to resume across the USA in the summer of 2011, and permutations thereof slated to follow in subsequent years, modelled along the lines of Ozzfest or Lollapalooza. Peter Mensch also let slip in a 2010 interview that the band would be undertaking, as he told *Classic Rock*, 'a Metallica tour that will blow your mind. They will only play in ten cities but it will be a huge undertaking.' He likened it to 'Metallica's equivalent' of Pink Floyd's famously theatrical early Eighties live show for *The Wall*. Furious at his slip, the Q Prime manager has refused to say any more but it's believed the show will feature huge back projections and that, musically, it will look back on the band's entire career with special guest appearances from some likely – and not so likely – guests, and that the cities will include London, New York, San Francisco, Paris, Berlin, Sydney and Tokyo.

What is more certain is that right now, with the record industry on its knees and new ways of delivering music constantly being investigated, there is no compelling reason for them to release a new album, although with the numbers for *Death Magnetic* so over-whelming – more than five million worldwide sales and still counting, as I write in the late summer of 2010 – they will presumably do so, maybe even another self-styled sequel of sorts. All we can be really sure of is that the platforms on which their music will be delivered will be various and absolutely up to the minute. As another champion of theirs, former *Kerrang!* and *Metal Hammer* editor – now Universal Records executive – Dante Bonutto says, 'I think they'll give people a choice of how they want to buy their music. And I think they'll create formats that will reward fan loyalty. I think the vinyl thing will stay important to Metallica, the box-sets, the whole area of collectability. And bundling all these formats together will probably be an important part of what they do now as well. 'Cos why not? Choice right across the board will be the thing to do.'

Only seven artists have sold more albums in America than Metallica. Three of them – The Beatles, Led Zeppelin and Pink Floyd – are officially defunct. Of the others – the Eagles, Aerosmith, the Rolling Stones and Van Halen – while they still tour and record sporadically, all can now be considered nostalgia acts, great to see, but no longer considered in the vanguard when it comes to making new music. Until recently Metallica was the sole exception. Not just touring and recording but still considered vital, even important. For how long that will continue, however, only time will tell. At this stage, it hardly matters. Their appeal will remain undimmed. Will there ever be another band like Metallica, or is that world gone for ever now? 'That's a very, very good question,' says Bonutto, 'and I think as time goes on the answer to that is looking increasingly like a no, and that the real rock monsters, of which Metallica are a latter example, just aren't being replaced.' Because of that, Metallica 'are becoming increasingly valuable as festival headliners, and album makers, because there's people that want to buy it and there's a lot of them. And that's increasingly rare in the music industry. The industry's now working against bands like Metallica existing and creating what they've done over that long a period of time. So this may well be the thing that's not going to be replaced, which makes them like an endangered species and hence incredibly special.'

And what, one wonders not for the first or probably the last time, would Cliff Burton have made of his band's travails in the wake of his unexpected leave-taking? Received fan wisdom has it, of course, that Cliff would have been outraged by some of the changes Metallica has been through; that he was a musical fundamentalist who would have kept the band artistically pure and that there would have been many more albums as wonderfully unique to the band's original vision as *Master of Puppets* and *Ride the Lightning*. That is to overlook the fact that Cliff's own musical tastes were always so much broader than the heavy metal – let alone the even narrower thrash – spectrum allowed. That he was a lover of Lynyrd Skynyrd and R.E.M., Kate Bush and the Velvet Underground. That he worshipped at the vocally harmonic temple of Simon & Garfunkel and was still a devoted student of the most godlike musical genius of them all, Bach. Cliff was no fool, either, and had been thrilled to pieces when the band finally began to make money, immensely proud of that success and as hungry and determined to sustain it as the rest of them. Ultimately, we will never know what Cliff Burton would have made of the way their worlds changed after the *Black* album. It might just as easily be argued that he would have been the first to embrace the massive changes they made, encouraging them to even greater feats of musical cross-pollination. Metal bands aren't supposed to evolve: AC/DC, Black Sabbath and Iron Maiden sound basically the same now as they did on their earliest (still best) recordings. One gets the feeling Cliff would have railed against that idea even more strongly than Lars and Kirk, and to a lesser but no less significant extent James did. All we can be sure of is that, as James told me the last time we spoke, 'he had such a character to himself, and it was a very strong personality, he did creep into all of us eventually. And he's missed greatly from this guy sitting here.'

And if Metallica never again quite matched the peerless beauty of the work they did while Cliff was still around, they have other, equally great achievements with which to assure themselves. Back in 1988, a twenty-five-year-old Jason Newsted – still smarting from the bum behaviour dished his way but better placed than anybody to see how the band really worked when the doors to the dressing room were closed shut – told *Rolling Stone*: 'Metallica is going to be one of the bands you look back on in the year 2008 that people will still listen to the way I still listen to Zeppelin and Sabbath albums.' The stats certainly back up that prediction. Sales of Metallica's albums currently stand at a little over 100 million copies worldwide (sixty-five million in North America alone), earning them gold and platinum certifications in more than forty countries. The *Black Album* earned the prestigious RIAA Diamond Award (for sales of ten million copies in the USA) and sold more than twice that overall. There have been numerous awards: nine Grammys and dozens of other prestigious awards.

More importantly, just like Zeppelin, Metallica have skated on thin ice with practically every album they've made, risking alienating die-hard fans by attempting something new and interesting, even when it nearly killed them. 'I know, I know,' said Lars, 'and, listen, hey, that will forever be part of our legacy.' Putting out another one a bit like the last one has never been their way, I said. 'That to me would have just killed this band because that was not who we were as people. And if the band is an extension of who you are as a person, then it wouldn't have been right. It just would not have been right.'

As Dante Bonutto says, 'Any band that's gonna have a long career – and that's the hardest thing in this business ever to achieve – your career has to be a journey, it can't be a plateau. You have to have the ups and downs. If you have those moments you've got somewhere to come back from, something to react against. It's very important to create those dynamics in a career and Metallica succeeded in doing that. Lars always had the vision that Metallica could be as big as Led Zeppelin or whoever. He also had an encyclopaedic knowledge of the history of rock, knew what went wrong with groups and what went right with them. With Metallica you could argue that what originally was their weakness – being so extreme – ultimately became their strength. So they were always the cool band that was heavier than anyone else and were coming from left-field. And of course, what's left-field today is now the mainstream of tomorrow. But if you start in the middle you've got nowhere to go. You have to start at the perimeter, and they were right on the edge with their first album.'

So is Metallica set fair now for the next few years? I asked James the last time we spoke. Will you be thinking along the same lines for the next album, doing it the same way, with Rick again? 'We don't know. We don't know what the future holds, and that's the beauty of the artist's part of being in a band. What we're playing right now, the stuff from *Death Magnetic*, what we're playing onstage, it fits right in with the stuff that we love doing. And it feels right. It's really, really easy to bash your last record. It's almost a cliché. I'm not bashing *St. Anger* at all. It was exactly what it needed to be. It was perfect. But playing those songs live right now don't fit into the set so much. Not that they won't later. But the direction we're on right now with *Death Magnetic*, it feels really good. And I like the potency of this record. I like the way we've gone back to the *Lightning, Puppets*, where you've got a less amount of songs but they're all really good. We're all really into playing every single one of them live. They fit right in. It's effortless.'

For Kirk Hammett, 'It was absolutely important that we went through all this bullshit that we had to go through, because when it spit us out at the end, we were better people; better, wiser, and more aware of just how fragile the Metallica thing really is – fragile as hell. We have a saying that we used to kick around HQ: you're never more than thirty seconds away from total and utter complete chaos and disaster. I mean, in thirty seconds everything could fall into shit. So it's taught us to learn how to appreciate all that we have so much more than how we used to just take it for granted. It's a great place to be and we went through the meat grinder but we're still together we're not just a fucking quivering piece of hamburger in the corner.'

The last time I spoke to Lars Ulrich I asked him how his relationship with James had changed over the years. 'A lot of the basic elements are still the same,' he insisted. 'Instead of it having changed, it's expanded. And that's obviously a kind of a different thing. The one thing that me and James do share is a love for music – a love for hard music and an unparalleled love and passion for all things Metallica. It's been twenty-eight years now and obviously the glue that holds us together is Metallica. The other thing that's happened in the last ten years or so is that we have another element to our relationship, which is the whole thing with the children. We have kids. I have three kids, he has three kids. They're all sort of the same age, they all hang out together. So obviously being parents of similar age kids has brought a whole other dimension to our relationship. And nowadays we sit around and talk a lot about other things than music, you know, our lives out in the suburbs of San Francisco, about, you know, carpooling and soccer games and fucking lunchboxes and homework and all this stuff. You know, obviously we have very different personalities, but in some way I think we've realised over the years our different personalities really complement each other and really are sort of necessary for both of us to have in order for both of us to feel complete, in order for both of us to feel like we have something to offer. [We have had] ups and downs. But when I look back on it, it's never derailed to the point of not functioning. Both me and him, we're pretty responsible. We answer phone calls and we show up more or less on time, when we're supposed to. We hold up our end of it, and the great thing about it is that we realise that what we have between us is greater than the individual parts. And that, I think, has always been kind of the unwritten, underlying message of Metallica, and the relationship. We do love each other and we cherish each other, and we've had problems maybe explaining that or vocalising that in the past. But, you know, as we get older and we have more and more cool moments, I think we also share a similar journey in that we spent a lot of our young years really worrying mostly about two things, about getting drunk and getting laid. We were sort of oblivious to most other things. Then as you turn the corner of forty and all of a sudden you start sitting there, opening your eyes and realising how awesome a lot of these things are around us.'

'It did start as music and it still is very important,' said James, when I asked him the same question. 'I mean, obviously we have different musical tastes and that's fine.' It struck him, though, while he had been listening to a radio interview with Kirk recently in which 'he was talking about how him and Lars are so close. They have the same political views, the same social interests, and things like that. And I just started thinking about it. Like, you know what, Lars and I don't share any of that. We're pretty much the opposite at everything – except when we play music together. Like, hey, I hear it going here. Yeah, me too! You know, whenever we'll take a break, we'll go away for six months from each other and come back together and start talking about where our lives have taken us, and "Oh, I've been listening to this and discovered this." "Wow, me too!" So it's kind of ... parallels, in one way. And then complete opposites in the other. I think that is the beauty of it. That has helped us battle through a lot of things together but given the extreme differences there's lots of different viewpoints you can learn and take from.'

How would this newfound mutual understanding impact on his own creativity as a songwriter, I couldn't help wondering. 'Cos that's the big one, isn't it? You get happy and suddenly you stop writing ...

He laughed. 'I think every person who goes through something like what I've gone through very much worries about that: "Well, that's where my creativity has come from." [But] the creativity, it will come from where it has to come from. It is the spark within that is the catalyst. Anything can be digested and be spat out, Metallica-like. When I'm happy, I'm writing the heaviest riff possible. When I'm feeling in a good place I pick up the guitar and I'll write the fattest riff ever. So it's quite the opposite, I must say. Being happy is not over-rated. But also, there will always be anger issues with me, no matter what. I have the tools to deal with them now. I can see past the moment into the next moment and not take things so personally. The forties have been the best so far for me, and it's amazing how much better it could be from here. I don't know if there is, but there always seems to be another cool piece of the puzzle revealed.' He paused, then added: 'I'm not gonna start writing about picking flowers now. I'm just not ...'

NOTES AND SOURCES

The foundations of this book, in terms of quotes and the facts of the story so far as I have gleaned them, are based on my own original investigations, beginning with the various interviews and conversations over the years I have enjoyed with Lars Ulrich, James Hetfield, Kirk Hammett, Cliff Burton, Ron McGovney and Jason Newsted, and many others, some of whom for private reasons do not wish to be named.

Those who agreed to be interviewed specifically for this book include Ron McGovney, Brian Slagel, Bob Nalbandian, Patrick Scott, Ron Quintana, Brian Tatler, Lemmy, Joey Vera, John Bush, Gary Holt, Jonny Z, Marsha Z, David Ellefson, William Hale, Jess Cox, Michael Alago, Martin Hooker, Gem Howard, Flemming Rasmussen, Geoff Tate, Bobby Schneider, Steve 'Krusher' Joule, Dave Thorne, Mike Clink, Alan Niven, Andres Serrano, Joel McIver, Alexander Milas, Xavier Russell, Geoff Barton, Malcolm Dome, Dante Bonutto and a handful of others who prefer not to be named.

Other voices that have provided me with invaluable information and insights over the years, through magazine and newspaper interviews but also from personal anecdotes or even chance remarks, include Jim Martin, Slash, Joe Satriani, Scott Ian, Dave Mustaine, Ozzy Osbourne, Big Mick Hughes, John Marshall, Peter Mensch, Cliff Burnstein, Ross Halfin, Brian 'Pushead' Schroeder, Rod Smallwood, Bob Rock, Fish, Huey Lewis, Dennis Stratton, Dave Murray, Robb Flynn, and again others who would prefer not to be mentioned here. I am indebted to all of them for their honesty and generosity of spirit. I have also spent a great deal of time over the years compiling as much background material as possible from as much published – and, in a few cases, unpublished – material as there is available, including books, magazine and newspaper articles, fanzines, websites, TV and radio shows, DVDs, demo tapes, bootleg CDs and any other form of media that contained useful information, the most important of which I have listed here.

However, extra special mention should also go to a handful of books and articles that proved especially helpful, in terms of adding to my own insights and investigations. First and foremost to the series of excellent books and articles by renowned Metallica and thrash historian Joel McIver, whose books, *To Live is to Die: The Life and Death of Metallica's Cliff Burton* (Jawbone, 2009); *Justice for All: The Truth About Metallica* (Omnibus Press, 2003); and *The 100 Greatest Metal Guitarists* (Jawbone, 2008) were especially helpful. Also, Bob Nalbandian, for allowing me access to his excellent Shockwaves internet archive; Harald Oimoen, for allowing me to quote from his heart-rending 1987 interview with Jan and Ray Burton; and Ben Mitchell, whose superb 2009 *Classic Rock* interview with James Hetfield he has kindly allowed me to quote from. Similarly, Ian Fortnam's earlier, equally insightful 2003 interviews with James, Lars and Kirk for the same estimable magazine; Joe Matera for the splendid offer of his 2003 Bob Rock interview, quoted here; Rob Tannenbaum, whose excellent April 2001 *Playboy* interviews with Lars, James, Kirk and Jason were utterly groundbreaking; and the always first-class David Fricke in *Rolling Stone* (still the best). Also, Paul Stenning, whose book *Metallica: All That Matters* (Plexus, 2009) shone interesting new light on the band's earliest years; Brian Tatler's fascinating memoir, *Am I Evil* (www.diamond-head.net, 2010); Chris Crocker's *Metallica: The Frayed Ends of Metal* (St Martin's Press, 1993); Stephen Davis' *Walk This Way: The Autobiography of Aerosmith* (Virgin Books, 1999); *The Dirt: Mötley Crüe – Confessions of the World's Most Notorious Rock Band* (Harper Collins, 2001); and *Slash: The Autobiography* (HarperCollins, 2007).

There were many others, too, all of which I have endeavoured to list below, and all of which deserve praise and acknowledgement in the roles they played in helping shape the direction of this book and to which I extend my thanks and would urge readers to seek out. Most of these articles I purchased either when they were first published or via a back-catalogue resource. Many, however, I now discover are available via the internet. If you can get hold of the originals, though, I would recommend it for there is nothing quite like holding – feeling and smelling – the real, now-yellowing thing. Again, my utmost thanks to one and all.

MAGAZINES AND NEWSPAPERS

Dave Mustaine interview, Bob Nalbandian, *The Headbanger*, January 1984
DM interview, *Metal Forces*, 1984
Kerry King interview, Sylvie Simmons, *Kerrang!*, April 1985
Cliff Burton interview, Harald O, February 1986
Lars Ulrich and James Hetfield interviews, Steffan Chirazi, *Sounds*, 15 February 1986
James Hetfield, *Thrasher*, 1986
LU interview, Sylvie Simmons, *Creem*, October 1986
LU interview, Paul Elliot, *Sounds*, February 1987
LU interview, Dele Fadele, *NME*, 21 March 1987
JH, Scott Ian interviews, Simon Witter, *i-D*, April 1987
LU and JH interview, Richard Gehr, *Music & Sound Output*, September 1988
LU, JH, Jason Newsted and Peter Mensch interviews, *Rolling Stone*, January 1989
LU interview, *Kerrang!*, February 1989
JH article, *Mega Metal Kerrang!* No.15, summer 1989
LU interview, Christine Natanael, *Metal Mania*, January 1990
LU and JH interviews, Mat Snow, *Q*, September 1991
LU, JH and Bob Rock interviews, *Rolling Stone*, November 1991
JH interview, David Fricke, *Rolling Stone*, April 1993
LU and legal team interviews, *Washington Post*, October 1994
LU interview, David Fricke, *Rolling Stone*, May 1995
LU, JH, Kirk Hammett and JN interviews, *Rolling Stone*, June 1996
LU interview, *Kerrang!*, September 1996
JH interview, *Washington Post*, April 1997
DM interview, Joel McIver, *Record Collector*, 1999
Michael Kamen interview, *Star Tribune*, 7 January 2000
JH interview, Ian Fortnam, *Front*, February 2000
Chad Paulson interview, Melissa Arnold, *University Wire*, 14 April 2000

LU, Howard King, Scott Stapp, Dr Dre interviews, Andrew Martel, *University Wire*, 24 April 2000

Jill Pietrini interview, Jojo Moyes, *Independent*, 16 December 2000

LU, JH, KH, JN interviews, *Playboy*, April 2001

JH interview, *Rolling Stone*, June 2003

LU interview, *Rolling Stone*, July 2003

LU, JH, KH interviews, Ian Fortnam, *Classic Rock*, August 2003

Dr Phil Towle interview, Martin Carlsson, *Classic Rock*, August, 2003

LU article, *Classic Rock* Status Quo Special, 9 November 2003

BR interview, Joe Matera, 2003

LU, KH, CB, JN interviews, *Kerrang!* Special, 2004

LU interview, *Rolling Stone*, August 2004

Rob Trujillo interview, Gemma Tarlach, *Knight Ridder / Tribune News Service*, August 2004

Rick Rubin interview, Lynn Hirschberg, *New York Times*, September 2007

LU interview, *Metal Hammer*, October 2007

LU interview, *Rolling Stone*, April 2008

LU, JH and KH interviews, *Rolling Stone*, June 2008

RT interview, *Rolling Stone*, October 2008

LU, JH and KH interviews, *Mojo*, December 2008

LU interview, *Stereo Warning*, 2008

JH interview, Ben Mitchell, *Classic Rock*, July 2009

Slash and John Tam interviews, Jon Hotten, *Classic Rock* Slash Special, 2010

TV, RADIO AND FILM

LU interview, KUSF Radio, June 1983

Jeff Hanneman, *Arena*, BBC, 1988

JH, KM, John Marshall, Mick Hughes, *Behind the Music*, MTV, 1998

Ron Quintana, Harald Oimoen, *The True Story: Metallica, DARK SOULS*, circa mid-1990s

LU, KH, JN, PT, Cliff Burnstein, DM, Torben Ulrich interviews, *Some Kind of Monster*, 2004

JH interview, *The Culture Show*, BBC, 2005

INTERNET SOURCES

Ron McGovney interview, http://demos.metpage.org/, 1996

Lloyd Grant interview, http://demos.metpage.org/, January 1997
   www.metallica.com

DM interview, Fredrik Hjelm, Shockwaves, 2001

DM interview, Dave Navarro's *Spread TV*, 10 April 2008,
   www.ManiaTV.com

DM interview, Bob Nalbandian, Shockwaves, 2004

Cronos interview, Richard Karsmakers, www.Fortunecity.com, 1996

FURTHER ONLINE SOURCES

www.MetalSludge.com

www.rollingstone.com

www.Wikipedia.com

www.Forgottenjournal.com

www.blabbermouth.com

www.GlobalNet.com

Uk.movies.ign.com (for the Berlinger and Sinofsky interviews, 12 July 2004,
   by Spence D.)

www.MTV.com

www.MetalSucks.net

AP Online

Torben Ulrich interview, Leigh Weathersby, www.amazon.com, January
   2005

Cronos interview, Malcolm Dome, originally broadcast on
   www.totalrock.com, September 2009

INDEX